About the Author

Marina Martin owns The Type-A Way, a business efficiency consulting firm that focuses on process automation and efficiency improvements across organizations. In addition to consulting services, The Type-A Way also offers a web-based task management system for Type-As called TaskTackler (www.tasktackler.com). Marina can usually be found at a Seattle coffee shop sipping an Americano, at marina@thetypeaway.com, and at www.thetypeaway.com.

Dedication

This book is for Tom

A chance for me to create

More than I consume

We miss you.

Author's Acknowledgments

Endless thanks to my acquisitions editor Mike Lewis and my editor Tracy Brown Hamilton for being wildly patient with me as we made it to the finish line with this manuscript. I appreciate you both more than I can say.

Thanks also to the following for their contributions to this book: Frederick Buchman, Conrad Carlberg, Stephen R. Covey, Neil DeCarlo, Peter Economy, Nick Graham, Craig Gygi, Charles Hannabarger, Mark Layton, Bob Nelson, Erica J. Olsen, Natalie J. Sayer, John A. Tracy, Tage C. Tracy, Michael Wallace, Larry Webber, and Bruce Williams.

My deepest appreciation for my clients, who have taught me so much over the last decade and without whom I could never have written this book.

Thank you to my little ones — Abby, Lucy, Mark, Eli, Bradleigh, Alan, and Halleck — for not minding that Auntie Marina sometimes had to work on her book instead of getting to play. I promise to make that time up to each of you.

Special thanks to Uptown Espresso in Belltown for being my "third place." The vast majority of this book was penned at your tables.

Publisher's Acknowledgments

We're proud of this book; please send us your comments at http://dummies.custhelp.com. For other comments, please contact our Customer Care Department within the U.S. at 877-762-2974, outside the U.S. at 317-572-3993, or fax 317-572-4002.

Some of the people who helped bring this book to market include the following:

Acquisitions, Editorial, and Media Development

Project Editor: Tracy Brown Hamilton

Acquisitions Editor: Michael Lewis

Copy Editor: Nancy Reinhardt

Assistant Editor: David Lutton

Editorial Program Coordinator: Joe Niesen

Technical Editor: Alina Geike

Editorial Manager: Carmen Krikorian

Editorial Assistant: Alexa Koschier

Art Coordinator: Alicia B. South

Cover Photos: © -Oxford- / iStockphoto.com

Cartoons: Rich Tennant (www.the5thwave.com)

Composition Services

Project Coordinator: Katie Crocker

Layout and Graphics: Jennifer Creasey, Joyce Haughey, Andrea Hornberger, Laura Westhuis

Proofreaders: John Greenough, Glenn McMullen,

Indexer: Riverside Indexes, Inc.

Publishing and Editorial for Consumer Dummies

    Kathleen Nebenhaus, Vice President and Executive Publisher

    Kristin Ferguson-Wagstaffe, Product Development Director

    Ensley Eikenburg, Associate Publisher, Travel

    Kelly Regan, Editorial Director, Travel

Publishing for Technology Dummies

    Andy Cummings, Vice President and Publisher

Composition Services

    Debbie Stailey, Director of Composition Services

Contents at a Glance

Table of Contents

Introduction

· ·

*W*elcome to *Business Efficiency For Dummies*!

Inefficiency affects organizations of every type and size. Even in the most positive economic climate, companies benefit from decreasing defects and avoiding waste. When times are tougher, enhancing efficiency can often mean the difference between keeping the doors open and having the bank seize the building. Perhaps the biggest benefit to be found is in the more common situation between those two scenarios: dedicated business owners who have been running races against the clock for *years* trying to eek out just one more round of payroll.

True business efficiency is much more than a mathematical equation from which you eliminate every possible penny and second. The idea that the road to greater business efficiency is littered with pink slips and punch cards is actually quite harmful. As you see throughout this book, efficient changes are those that positively improve a company's metrics in ways that don't degrade its mission or its values.

An efficient business is a more pleasant, more productive, and downright *happier* workplace for everyone. It's a place where clear communication empowers employees with knowledge and reduces the chances for mistakes. It's a place where smart process automation assigns the tedious tasks to machines and the human tasks to the humans. And it's a place where employers harness the best their employees have to offer by giving their teams the flexibility and autonomy to balance their work lives with the rest of their life.

It's my hope that this book helps shine a more positive light on the term "efficiency" by helping you, as business owners and executives, improve two key skills: thinking more creatively when it comes to addressing quality-enhancing and cost-cutting measures, and developing a deeper understanding of how a change in one area of a business almost invariably has a ripple effect upon all the others. If you can master these two concepts, then you can make your business better for your investors, your employees, your customers, and your bottom line.

About This Book

There's no shortage of books on business productivity, Six Sigma, and change management, but there's no book on the market quite like this one. By reading *Business Efficiency For Dummies*, you can expect to discover

- ✔ The very best parts of popular methodologies like Balanced Scorecard Strategy, Six Sigma, Lean, and Agile.
- ✔ How true business efficiency is a complex web of factors, and not just a simple comparison of dollars in and dollars out.
- ✔ The exact steps for getting from where your organization is today to a much more efficient version of itself.

(Not So) Foolish Assumptions

Because you picked up this book, I assume a few things about you:

- ✔ You're affiliated with an organization, whether that's a nonprofit foundation or a for-profit corporation. (Although there are some personal efficiency tips in this book, it's primarily organization-focused.)
- ✔ You're in a position to create positive change in your organization. (This usually means you're the business owner or in upper management, but it's not required!)
- ✔ You want to create higher-quality products and services with less effort and at a lower cost.
- ✔ You're seeking greater efficiencies in your organization.
- ✔ You want results, and you won't settle for a lengthy white paper or simply closing up shop.

How This Book Is Organized

This book is broken down into five separate parts. The first part is a high-level overview of business efficiency and the process for becoming more efficient, which I cover more thoroughly in Part II. Parts III and IV apply this process to specific sectors of your business, such as change management, communications, and event management. Finally, the book closes with some brief top ten lists to jump-start your efficiency brainstorming.

Part I: Business Efficiency Basics

If you're not sure quite what business efficiency means, or what sorts of returns it can have for your organization, read this part. This part also includes a detailed overview of popular efficiency-enhancing methodologies such as Six Sigma, Lean, and Balanced Scorecard Strategy. I make regular references to these systems throughout the book, so getting up to speed on the basics here will make later chapters clearer.

Part II: Making Strides toward Efficiency

So you're sold on the idea of being more efficient, but you're not entirely sure where to start. Or perhaps you have a specific inefficiency in mind that you'd like to tackle, but the path from here to efficiency is somewhat murky. That's where Part II comes in. I go through every step of the general process, from measuring where you are now, to brainstorming and recognizing inefficiencies in every corner of your organization, to understanding how making a change in one corner can have huge effects on another corner. This part is your efficiency toolkit: When you know the way, you have the resources to attack almost any problem.

Part III: Increasing Operational Efficiency

Some efficiency improvements cover the entire organization, or at least entire sectors. This part follows the roadmap of Part II down the path toward change that affects the business as a whole. To start, I get your creative juices flowing on process automation opportunities in multiple areas, complete with step-by-step instructions for many of the highest-yield improvements I've come across. This part also covers improving the efficiency of your finances, as well as your customer service, human resources, sales departments, and policies. Finally, there's a special chapter on manufacturing efficiency for companies in this field.

Part IV: Increasing Employee Efficiency

In addition to enhancing efficiency company-wide, giant gains can be made in improving the workflows on a more granular, employee level. This part starts with the mother of all efficiency-enhancement projects: effective *change* management. Efficient employees are empowered and knowledgeable, and they are also excellent communicators, two topics covered in this part.

There's also a special chapter (my personal favorite) on enhancing personal efficiency — something every single employee can benefit from. This part moves on to increasing the efficiency of meetings, closing with a chapter that ensures that you and your whole team have the tools to generate and execute efficient project plans in your everyday work lives.

Part V: The Part of Tens

These brief Top Ten lists can jump-start your problem-solving creative juices. The first identifies areas where just about any business can improve, and is a great place to start if you don't already have a specific issue in mind. Then, I cover efficiency best practices that you can (and should) read again and again as a quick reminder of the right (and wrong) ways to go about this process. Finally, the top ten hidden hurdles to overcome in pursuit of efficiency is meant to temper tendencies to take efficiency to the extreme; there *is* such a thing as too much of a good thing.

Icons Used in This Book

Business Efficiency For Dummies uses the following four icons to indicate supplementary information:

This Tip icon indicates a suggestion, tool, or best practice that complements the surrounding material.

Pay attention to this icon, as it indicates a potential efficiency trap you may fall into or an important consideration to keep in mind when making a decision. I'm not one to issue warnings lightly, so take heed.

Because technology is usually core to business efficiency enhancements, and it would be *in*efficient to stick this icon five times on every page, I do use it occasionally to point out particularly geeky details.

The notes along this icon are mental refreshers and high-level bullet points. In the future, you can return to the book and just skim the Remember icons to bring the key points back to the forefront.

Where to Go from Here

Don't worry that you need to read this book cover to cover. If you simply can't wait to get started, read Chapters 1, 8, and 20 for some projects you can tackle right away.

If you're feeling overwhelmed by inefficiencies in your business, or if you don't know where to begin, focus on Part II. This part guides you through the efficiency-enhancing process on a higher level, helping you to identify existing issues and map out a plan to address them. You can use this process again and again to make your business more and more efficient.

After you've gone through this process once or twice, you can refer back to Part I as a roadmap for future projects.

If you have (or want) a specific project in mind, turn to the relevant chapter in Parts III or IV. Each of these chapters follows the steps outlined in Part II to tackle a particular issue, such as improving customer service or sales efficiency.

If you get stuck or have questions, I'd love to hear. You can reach me at marina@thetypeaway.com or via my website at www.thetypeaway.com. Subscribe to my business efficiency blog for regular updates and answers to questions I receive from readers.

Part I

Business Efficiency Basics

The 5th Wave   By Rich Tennant

"I sense you're in a hurry, so I'll be brief."

In this part . . .

*B*efore you get too deep into increasing your organization's efficiency, it helps to figure out what efficiency really means. If *Lean* sounds like a goal to reach at the gym or you think a *Balanced Scorecard* has something to do with baseball, this part will get you up to speed on the major efficiency-enhancing methodologies so you can talk *5S* and *Six Sigma* like a pro (and know which approaches make the most sense for your company).

This part also covers the high-level process of addressing inefficiencies, which I hope you will turn to again and again when you need a quick refresher or guidance.

Chapter 1

Business Efficiency 101

*L*ots of people talk about running an efficient business, but just what does that mean, exactly? In this chapter, I share my definition of business efficiency and how that definition applies to your particular organization.

For as long as people have been doing business, they've been uncovering ways to do business more efficiently. Producing a higher-quality result in less time and at a lower expense is one of the key tenets of business competition. Some of these strategies have been codified into formal methodologies such as Six Sigma, Lean, Kaizen, and Total Quality Management.

In this chapter, I give you the lowdown on the basics of (and differences between) some of the most common methodologies. I'll be drawing upon some of the best practices from each throughout the book, so knowing the gist of how each one works will help you narrow down which may make the most sense for your situation.

Of course, if you're reading this book, you're probably itching for a way to improve your business efficiency *today*. Don't worry. I cover some changes you can implement relatively quickly to get you started before you embark on a larger-scale efficiency project.

Understanding Business Efficiency

If we're going to talk about increasing your efficiency, it helps to get on the same page regarding what efficiency actually looks like.

In essence, business efficiency means making the choices and adopting the tools and processes that generate the *best* results at the *least* cost. By cost, I'm not referring to just dollars and cents, but also impacts on all other resources, including time and employee happiness. Too often, people focus on the financial aspects of efficiency while ignoring or underestimating the effects on other areas. Trust me, you do not want to run or work at a business that focuses on cost savings above all else.

I like to consider efficiency through the lens of a *Pareto Improvement*, named after Vilfredo Pareto. When you make a Pareto Improvement, you improve the situation of one person without negatively impacting anyone else. Giving John a higher salary without reducing anyone else's salary *or* sacrificing someone else's raise is a Pareto Improvement. If, however, you only had enough money to give either John or Mary a raise — so John's raise comes at Mary's expense — it is *not* a Pareto Improvement.

More broadly, business efficiency is the application of Pareto Improvements in a way that considers not just individuals but also sectors of the business. A change is efficient if it increases customer service satisfaction *without* negatively impacting the IT or Finance departments.

 This is in opposition to the idea of a zero-sum game, wherein there is a finite resource and adding some to Person A by definition means taking some away from Person B. Some people view world safety as a zero-sum game — when the United States gains four nuclear missiles, it is four missiles safer, and every other country is relatively less safe.

 The terms *efficiency* and *effectiveness* are often used interchangeably, but they do not mean the same thing. A terribly inefficient process can still be quite effective. Effectiveness is how often a process gets to its stated end result. Walking and running are two effective ways to get to the store, but running may be more efficient given the circumstances.

Understanding that Efficiency is different for everyone

In light of the definition I just gave, it's important to understand that there is no mathematical equation for efficiency that applies universally. Your organization's specific goals, values, experiences, and resources all color whether a given choice is efficient or not.

For example, if you run an organic dairy farm, it would never be efficient to give your cows daily antibiotics en masse. This would make your milk non-organic, and effectively lower your output to zero no matter how much actual milk was produced. If you are a non-organic dairy farm, however, then antibiotics may make perfect sense to lower your healthcare costs and bovine fatality rates.

Additionally, resource costs are relative. Adopting the very latest technology is usually *not* the most efficient option for a low-tech business when it doesn't have the employee skills to use it correctly or the in-house technical support to maintain it.

Similarly, making one change that saves 30 minutes per employee per month may not make that much of a difference in a four-person firm, but would free up the equivalent of multiple additional employees if a 1,000-person firm made the same decision.

Sharing knowledge with others

Efficiency enhancements rarely happen in a vacuum. Even enhancements that seem straightforward, such as reviewing a bank statement and realizing you are paying "too much" on equipment maintenance, rely on outside factors. There is no set correct amount to pay for equipment maintenance — what matters is what everyone *else* is paying for it, and how your business and its needs fall on that scale.

There are always improvements to be had, new skills to learn, and new efficiency-enhancing technologies entering the market. I've been thinking about efficiency nonstop for over a decade and I still learn new things every day.

The business world is generally a secretive one. There is much concern about competitors gaining access to your customer base, stealing your best employees, or digging the secret sauce recipe out of the garbage can. (I have actually, literally seen that happen.) But when it comes to efficiency improvements, there's much to gain from sharing. In fact, if Motorola hadn't shared its internal process for improving quality and cutting costs, Six Sigma would never exist. Same with Toyota and Total Quality Management.

So the next time you're at a Chamber of Commerce meeting or an industry trade show, don't be shy about talking efficiency shop. Not only can sharing tips help build strong bonds with vendors and potential clients, but you'll likely be surprised at the value of the ideas you hear in return.

Looking at Efficiency-Enhancing Methodologies

We cover a number of established business improvement processes like Six Sigma, Lean, and Total Quality Management throughout the book. Here's the crib sheet on the major ones to get you up to speed.

Six Sigma: Mathematical efficiency

Originally codified at Motorola in the 1980s, Six Sigma is a business improvement process that relies on quantified performance measurements and a strong managerial team and buy-in. The term *Six Sigma* is often used interchangeably with a *Six Sigma performance* (3.4 or fewer defects per million opportunities) or a *Six Sigma improvement* (efficiency gains of 70 percent or greater).

Six Sigma in a nutshell

The key differentiations of the Six Sigma approach include:

- ✔ **Setting a mathematical focus:** If you cannot measure it numerically, it's not a Six Sigma project.

- ✔ **Saving, not avoiding, costs:** Six Sigma calculations don't account for avoiding costs in the future, only for lowering existing costs.

- ✔ **Having big ambitions:** A "Six Sigma improvement" is an improvement of at least 70 percent. Six Sigma is not designed for small gains here and there.

- ✔ **Focusing on quality:** At its base, Six Sigma is focused on the ruthless elimination of defects and variation throughout a production process and in a final result.

- ✔ **Bringing everyone on board:** More than other methodologies, Six Sigma has many clearly defined roles for employees across an organization, ranging from Yellow, Green, and Black Belts to Champions, functional representatives, and deployment leaders.

- ✔ **Believing in determinism:** Six Sigma relies on the belief that your organization is responsible for its own defects, which is great — because then your organization is fully capable of remedying them!

The Six Sigma formula

The basis of Six Sigma is the following formula:

$$y = f(x) + \varepsilon$$

In this equation, *y* is your end result (such as the finished product you sell). The *x* refers to your original inputs, which you transform or otherwise manipulate to turn into the finished product. (You may have more than one *x* in your process.) The function *f()* *is* the transformational process. Finally, the ε refers to the errors throughout the process. Six Sigma is all about eliminating or minimizing the ε.

Six Sigma is best for organizations that are fully committed to improvement, manufacturing companies, Type-A personalities, large companies, and organizations that communicate well.

Agile: Rapid movement from within

Originally developed to address the pitfalls of traditional project management when applied to software development projects, Agile is now an approach you can adopt for projects in most any industry. Instead of putting the majority of effort into one long-range plan, Agile operates on a succession of tiny "sprints" with significant measuring and re-evaluation between (and during) each sprint.

Agile in a nutshell

The key differentiations of Agile Project Management include:

- **Short delivery times:** The faster, the better! Milestones are rarely more than a few weeks out.

- **Focusing on customer needs:** The desires of the customer take front and center in determining the order of projects, product releases, new features, and related decisions.

- **Customer involvement:** Instead of just involving customers at the start and end of a project, Agile teams communicate with them throughout the entire creation process.

- **Minimal documentation:** If the document does not directly enable the creation of results, an Agile environment usually foregoes it.

The Agile manifesto

The Agile movement actually has its own manifesto, which is as follows:

> We are uncovering better ways of developing software by doing it and helping others do it. Through this work we have come to value:
>
> **Individuals and interactions** over processes and tools
> **Working software** over comprehensive documentation
> **Customer collaboration** over contract negotiation
> **Responding to change** over following a plan
>
> That is, while there is value in the items on the right, we value the items on the left more.

Even though the manifesto specifically references software development, there's no reason you cannot replace the term with your own industry or product.

Agile is best for technology companies, smaller teams, companies that are (or can become) comfortable with a rapid pace, and companies with products that constantly change, as opposed to a relatively standard product line that is constantly reproduced.

Lean: Seeking to do more with less

Born at Toyota, Lean is what it sounds like — a lighter, leaner way to achieve results. A Lean process is ruthless about getting rid of not just errors, but also steps, processes, and people that don't ultimately add value to your end product or service. Less structured and mathematical than Six Sigma, but with a similar focus on customer needs and reducing defects, Lean is all about getting as close as possible to a waste-free process that results in maximum customer value.

Lean in a Nutshell

The key differentiations of Lean include the following:

- **Focus on the customer:** Lean is almost religious about listening to the voice of the customer, or VOC. If a step doesn't add value to the end product from the customer's point of view, Lean strips it out.

- **Weeding out waste:** There are seven types of waste, or *muda*, in Lean, and much attention is paid to eliminating them.

- **Just-in-time attitude:** In Lean, it's a waste to produce anything in anticipation of customers' desires. Instead, you produce only when you have orders in hand.

- **Visual representations:** As opposed to the mathematical approach of Six Sigma, Lean uses value-stream maps to visually draw out processes. While a right-brained, list-oriented person can construct a value-stream map with basic text, it's also possible to draw *beautiful* value-stream maps if they help to communicate better.

The seven wastes of Lean

There are seven kinds of waste that Lean focuses on eliminating. They are defined in Chapter 4.

Lean is best for incremental improvements, organizations that focus on their people and culture, companies that want a less mathematical and more flexible approach than Six Sigma.

There's also a blended methodology known as Lean Six Sigma, though it is not necessarily a perfect marriage of the two processes. In fact, many professionals argue that by trying to use both simultaneously, you lose the best of both. I believe that this is true if you are using a strict Six Sigma or Lean approach, but if you are like many organizations and only using a portion of one or the other, then it can be beneficial to see what the other has to offer. For example, you can strive for a breakthrough Six Sigma improvement by eliminating waste Lean-style.

Balanced Scorecard: Four key areas

While methodologies like Six Sigma and Agile may have mutually exclusive viewpoints on the right way to manage a project, Balanced Scorecard plays nicely with most other systems. It was developed to move the trend of focusing on financial measurements into a more holistic system of metrics across four equally weighted quadrants.

Balanced Scorecard in a nutshell

The key differentiations of Balanced Scorecard strategy include:

- **Focus on knowledge growth:** Few organizations measure, let alone give balanced weight to, internal knowledge and growth — but Balanced Scorecard brings these metrics front and center.

- **Multi-level viewpoints:** Scorecards look at the same data on three levels: long-term, short-term (3–5 years), and immediate (today) to keep your eye simultaneously on the big picture and the here and now.

- **Compatibility with other methodologies:** You can use scorecards to measure progress towards goals when using any (or no) formal efficiency-enhancing methodology.

The four scorecard quadrants

A balanced scorecord includes measurements across four key areas:

- **Financial:** Revenue, net profits, expenses, payroll, and other routine monetary metrics.

- **Knowledge and Growth:** How are your employees growing in their skills and knowledge? This question is carefully considered and answered by a knowledge scorecard.

- **Productivity:** In effect, how efficient is your internal organization? This scorecard measures productivity in hard numbers.

- **Customers:** Not just how many customers you have, but retention rates, satisfaction numbers, and other customer-focused figures.

Balanced Scorecard is best for every organization that measures itself and companies primarily composed of knowledge workers.

Kaizen: Incremental improvement

Kaizen is not a one-time planned process but rather an *approach* to work that places the focus on greater efficiency. A Kaizen workplace puts people first — in pursuit of eliminating waste (à la Lean), it focuses on eliminating the hardest and least-pleasant work from a production process. In practice, Kaizen is a series of constant, small improvements.

Kaizen in a nutshell

The key differentiations of Kaizen include the following:

- **Putting employees first:** A Kaizen improvement would never add difficulty or unpleasantness to an employee's workload. Employees are highly involved in the improvement process.

- **Constant process:** While it's possible to have Kaizen projects, it exists mostly as a way of life in which waste is constantly identified and eliminated as it surfaces.

- **Individual responsibility:** Kaizen expects that if a particular employee encounters waste, she will address it. It doesn't wait for a top-down approach or a suggestion box.

Kaizen events

A *Kaizen event* is a group activity, lasting between a day and multiple days, in which a team identifies and implements a significant improvement in a process. Commonly a Kaizen event is kicked off with a *Waste walk*. A Waste walk is almost a game in which the most amount of waste is eliminated in the least amount of time. A team gets together and runs through a process over the course of a few hours or a day, trying to identify every possible waste: waiting, communication lags, product defects, and so on. Each waste is remedied where possible and then the process run through again, until either time runs out or all identified wastes are removed. This activity is also often referred to as "picking the low hanging fruit."

Get people that don't know the process involved in the Waste walk, as they come in with open minds and are more likely to ask critical questions.

Kaizen is best for Lean organizations, small teams, and organizations that give employees some degree of autonomy and responsibility.

5S: The Japanese path to efficiency

Unlike the other methodologies that can be applied to a variety of scenarios within an organization, 5S is only concerned with your physical workspace. The drive behind 5S is the belief that a clean, well-laid-out office contributes to increasing employee well-being, reducing defects and saving time.

5S in a nutshell

The key differentiations of 5S include the following:

- **Focus on physical space:** 5S is about making your actual office more efficient. In 5S, even the placement of a plant can be relevant (and improved upon).

- **Freeing up space:** It's a success by 5S standards if you reclaim 100 square feet previously lost to excess inventory or even garbage cans. "Cleared space" is a key metric.

- **Communications board:** Almost like a scrapbook for cleanliness, 5S relies on bulletin boards with employee photographs, floor plans, and before/after photos. Teams can actually have fun with this board, which encourages ongoing participation.

The 5S's

Originally based on five Japanese words beginning with "s" (when translated into English, anyway), equivalent English "s" words have since been massaged into the process. These are defined in detail in Chapter 13.

5S is best for manufacturing plants, large offices, and neat freaks.

Total Quality Management

Total Quality Management (TQM) actually preceded Lean, and much of its focus on waste-reduction, continuous improvement, and the elimination of defects has since been rolled into Lean. However, TQM by itself can provide significant efficiency gains even if you don't adopt a fully Lean approach. As the name implies, TQM is, well, *totally* focused on quality.

The key differentiations of Total Quality Management include:

- ✒ **Obsession with quality:** In a TQM environment, everyone talks about quality, thinks about quality, and measures quality at every turn.

- ✒ **Employee empowerment:** Under TQM, if an employee notices something that's causing defects, he has the power to remedy it directly. No need to assemble a team or write a project plan first (although for more systemic problems, a more extensive solution may be necessary).

- ✒ **Small improvements add up:** Often improvements made in the spirit of TQM are small — not Six Sigma improvements of 70 percent or greater. However, in the aggregate, these gains can really add up.

Total Quality Management is best for businesses that produce products that must meet high quality standards; not for organizations that currently produce low-quality or highly variable-quality results.

Considering Other Ways to Be More Efficient

This whole book is about ways to make yourself and your organization more efficient — but I understand that most people want to dive right in and start making changes. The following sections suggest a few places to start:

Buying time with Time management

Time is often an organization's most precious resource, because lost time can never be restored and the amount of time any given person is available — no matter how much caffeine she may consume — is quite finite. The following ideas can help shave *hours* off not only your own work day, but also the days of all employees, leaving more time free for more important, more meaningful work:

- ✒ **Keyboard shortcuts:** Mastering keyboard shortcuts for the computer programs and websites you use often can save minutes on every single computing task you perform. (It also reduces your risk of repetitive-motion injuries by reducing mouse/trackpad use.) For example, I can open, label, and archive an e-mail in Gmail by hitting just four keys in succession.

  You can also use keyboard shortcuts to insert standard blocks of text, ranging from an e-mail signature to a sales pitch, or even to launch particular Web pages or software programs. Check out ActiveWords for Windows (`www.activewords.com`) or TextExpander for Mac (`www.textexpander.com`) for more.

✔ **Macros:** If you ever use Microsoft Office for repeat tasks, such as mass find/replace in a supplier spreadsheet or performing certain calculations, you can usually write a macro to record the process *once* and then apply it to the entire document. This saves time *and* boredom (because the most boring tasks are often best suited for a macro). Macros can even be used to guide end users through filling out a form in a particular manner.

✔ **Scheduling apps:** Trading five e-mails back and forth to decide on a meeting time is a pet peeve of mine. It is a huge time suck. You can skirt around this dance entirely by using a scheduling service like TimeBridge (`www.time-bridge.com`) or, for a group, Doodle (`www.doodle.com`) to show others when you're available and let them book appointments directly.

Getting human resources involved

Functional departments like human resources are often left out of efficiency-enhancing discussions and brainstorming, because they seem like a static resource as opposed to an internal team made up of human beings who can make errors or use inefficient processes. However, there's usually as much room for improvement in human resources as there is in other areas of the organization.

One place HR can improve efficiency is by avoiding firing poor employees by not hiring them in the first place. No one likes to fire an employee, even if that person is truly lousy at what she does and makes everyone else in the office miserable. (Well, okay, I don't mind firing those folks.) Much has been written on ways to fire kindly, diplomatically, and/or without putting yourself at risk legally. What people discuss less is how to *avoid hiring in the first place.*

Almost as if they're on auto-pilot, most human resources departments post new job offerings and begin the process of filling a position as soon as that position's previous occupant departs. This is *not* efficient, as an employee's departure is the ideal time to reevaluate that role from a number of perspectives.

Do we even need this role? Can we reduce this full-time role to part-time or switch to a contractor or outside vendor? Do we need someone with a slightly (or drastically) different skillset? What if the replacement had less experience (and a commensurately lower salary)?

Managing more efficiently

Efficient management means every task is executed on time, the first time, and with no duplication. Getting a team to this point requires clear communication tools and a dedication to giving your team members the resources they need to perform their best.

Set up clear communication tools

Managers have varying degrees of comfort with not knowing what their reports are doing at any given moment. Some are more trusting (or simply less concerned) and can go weeks without even an informal update. Others try to assuage their own discomfort by calling four meetings a day, paying surprise desk-side visits, and reminding everyone of upcoming deadlines like a broken record.

Micromanaging is the very height of inefficiency. It wastes your time, it wastes the employees' time, and it erodes trust. I feel very strongly that micromanaging creates a sense of resentment on the part of employees to the point that they are far less motivated to complete work on time, to par, or at all.

You can gain a great deal of transparency into team members' progress without being a constant source of interruption by implementing the right communication tools. Namely, a granular task management tool that everyone updates and has access to can help you see exactly which tasks remain open and which have been tackled.

Protect your team members

One often-overlooked role of a manager is to shield her team members from outside influences that can interfere with or prohibit their productivity. An efficient manager is a guard protecting her team's resources, one of which is *time*. No employee should be expected to drop what he's doing and handle tasks assigned to him randomly by outside employees or upper management (unless this *is* his role in the company, such as an IT support rep). The feeling that your time is constantly at risk of being co-opted by unknown forces can make it impossible to concentrate on bigger tasks at hand.

You can, and should, also protect your employees from unnecessary meetings. (More on this in Chapter 18.) Where possible, it's also more efficient to corral meetings into particular days or parts of the day (such as the morning) so team members have blocks of time long enough to complete their actual assignments.

Give clear assignments

It sounds obvious enough, but I've almost never seen it done consistently. A well-oiled team needs to know exactly what to do, when to do it by, and what to do immediately after finishing. Getting in the habit of communicating and delegating tasks clearly is probably *the best* skill of an efficient manager.

Finding technological resources

Aside from the technology tools mentioned in the other sections, there are some overarching resources that most any business can benefit from exploring, including:

- ✔ **A content management system (CMS):** Gone are the days when you need to pay a Web developer an hour's wage to swap out a sentence on your company website or bold some text. Most websites now integrate a CMS to some degree, which allows users with no HTML or programming experience to edit written content on the website just as they would in a word processor. Popular CMS platforms include WordPress (www.wordpress.com), Drupal (www.drupal.com), and Joomla (www.joomla.com).

- ✔ **A customer relationship manager (CRM):** Originally little more than fancy address books, today's CRMs are powerhouses of efficiency. You can use them to send and track e-mail marketing campaigns, print mailing labels, track customer support cases, send product warranty reminders, sync with your order fulfillment department, and much more. I've even helped psychiatrists customize their CRMs to track patient medication schedules, getting alerts when high-risk patients didn't refill by a particular date.

  Top CRM platforms include Salesforce.com (www.salesforce.com), SugarCRM (www.sugarcrm.com), and BatchBook (www.batchblue.com).

- ✔ **A central file server:** E-mailing multiple versions of a document around to employees gets complicate and inefficient really fast. Instead, use a central file storage repository to make it easy for anyone to find the document they're looking for and to handle version control for often-revised files.

  Aside from running your own server in the office, which usually requires on-site IT resources, check out Google Drive (www.google.com/drive) or Dropbox (www.dropbox.com).

Discovering why money matters

So many people (and organizations) sign up for recurring services and then forget about them — never noticing the small credit card charges here and there — that most vendors actually *bank* on a revenue stream from inactive customers.

Root out unnecessary costs with the 5 Whys

If you want to start increasing efficiency at your company, take a look at your bank statement. (If you're at a large organization, an expense sheet for your department may be a more manageable start.) Go through each line item and follow the "5 Whys" exercise. At the first expense, ask "Why?" Then ask "Why?" in response to that answer, and so on, until you have asked "Why?" five times. It can feel silly at first, especially for expenses that may seem perfectly obvious (like property tax), but you'd be surprised by the cost-savings ideas that this simple act can generate. At the very least, I can guarantee you'll find some expenses that you don't need to be paying *at all* or that you haven't comparison-shopped in a long time.

Ask for savings

Finding a more affordable rate for supplies, utilities, or even credit card interest rates doesn't have to be a large project. Often, all you have to do is call and ask! I'm not suggesting calling up your main supplier and threatening to jump ship for his competitor if he can't give you a better rate. Just ask: How can I lower my costs? There may be a number of savings avenues you didn't even think to explore, such as a discount for electronic billing or automated payments, volume discounts, or the opportunity to switch to an equivalent (for your needs) but more affordable item.

Chapter 2

Unfolding Your Efficiency Roadmap

*M*any different factors are at work that reduce your business's current efficiency, but there are a number of steps you can take toward *increasing* efficiency. Skipping steps or going about them in the wrong manner usually means failing to meet your optimum efficiency potential.

In this chapter, I give you a broad overview of the process you need to follow to weed out and permanently eliminate inefficiencies in your organization. I go into greater depth for each of the five steps in the next section, but it's helpful to know where you're headed and how each step flows into the next.

How would you track down inefficiencies in Six Sigma versus Kaizen? What tools are available for researching the far-reaching implications of a potential solution *before* you implement it? I whet your appetite with some examples before you dive into the real action in Part II.

This chapter serves as a shortcut of sorts for your efficiency journey, especially by the time you complete the full process at least once. In the future, you can return here to quickly remind yourself of what step comes next and *why* it's important, then look to the relevant later sections (or other *For Dummies* books) for more detailed guidance.

Understanding the Steps to Efficiency

Tackling inefficiencies in your organization encompasses five steps:

1. Measuring where you are now (and subsequently, where you are along the way)

2. Sussing out opportunities for improvement and potential ways to realize that improvement

3. Considering the immediate and far-reaching consequences of potential solutions

4. Setting goals

5. Executing a clearly defined project to achieve those goals

Measuring Where You Are Now

You can't improve anything if you don't know where you stand currently. Without a starting point, you have no official idea whether the changes you implement in hopes of *increasing* efficiency actually help or take you ten steps back.

Knowing how to accurately and objectively measure your organization according to certain metrics is an invaluable skill.

Even if improving efficiency isn't a top priority for you right now, I bet you care a lot about certain other measurements, such as revenue, profit, and the number of orders you're receiving.

Certain measurements can be straightforward: How many dollars entered our bank account this month? How many exited it? How many employees do we have? How much did we spend on payroll this month? What is our average electric bill for the last 12 months?

Sometimes, straightforward measurements reveal inefficiencies right off the bat. A number may simply "feel" wrong to you, and additional research will show it's way too high. However, a bit more math is usually needed to get to the deeper roots of an organization's inefficiencies. That's where the various efficiency-enhancing methodologies like Six Sigma and Lean can come in and really shed light on what's happening.

Using the Six Sigma calculations

Six Sigma takes the idea of *quality* to a whole new level. A process that operates at Six Sigma has 3.4 defects (or fewer) per million opportunities. (An opportunity is a point at which a defect might enter the system. For example, when Marge hands a product to Steve on the assembly line, there's a chance she may drop and damage it — that's one *opportunity* for error.)

Six Sigma is far and away the most mathematically driven method for reducing waste and errors in your organization. In fact, *Six Sigma For Dummies* has entire chapters on calculating averages, standard deviations, and other mathematical equations. Measuring your business from a Six Sigma perspective requires time, dedication, and company-wide participation, and it's definitely not for everyone.

However, there's a certain magic to seeing your company from a purely mathematical perspective. For one, it can transform a desperate situation into one that you can turn around. All you have to do is reduce ε in the equation $y = f(x) + \varepsilon$. That's certainly easier to digest than a stack of overdue bills on your desk.

 Interested in Six Sigma but concerned your math skills aren't quite up to par? Pick up *Business Math For Dummies*, which helps you refresh your memory on fractions and long division and slowly works you up into more complex equations. Soon you'll be calculating Sigma in your sleep!

Measuring with a Balanced Scorecard

Too often, an organization begins a measurement process — deciding what to measure, gathering recent data points, digging up historical details, compiling them in spreadsheets, and performing various analyses — but then does not follow through on *continuing* to measure itself. This not only sets the stage for having to start all over at square one two years down the line, but also causes participants to quickly lose steam when they see that the work they put into measuring never leads to any results.

Whether you're 100 percent committed to Six Sigma or you're content to just measure a few simple data points, you can use a Balanced Scorecard. This scorecard traverses three levels — the long-term, medium-term, and day-to-day — across four areas: productivity, knowledge growth and transfer, customers, and finances.

For much more on constructing your own balanced scorecards, explore Chapter 3 and/or pick up a copy of *Balanced Scorecard Strategy For Dummies*.

Going forward with measuring

The process of measuring at the start of a project is the same exact process you'll go through to measure during, at the close of, and after a project. (Although it's certainly easier to take subsequent measurements once you get all your ducks in a row at the start!)

Knowing this, you should always be mindful of ways to make it easier to take measurements in the future. For example, you can:

✔ Set up automatic data exports from your software system so you don't have to manually chase down data.

✔ Request monthly summary reports from your vendors.

✔ Have accounting enter certain expenses in a separate spreadsheet that you can quickly analyze as needed.

✔ Create an Excel template to automatically analyze and compare your latest data points.

Discover pivot tables! Available in major spreadsheet programs such as Microsoft Excel and Google Spreadsheets, a pivot table can perform fast, detailed analysis on large data sets. Once you set up a pivot table the way you want it, it will continue to operate and update as you add to or modify the data behind it. For example, a pivot table of monthly sales totals will grow dynamically as you add new months' figures.

Identifying Inefficiencies

Once you've taken measurements across your organization, you can use them like a road map to your inefficiencies. Working backward from each measurement, ask (or research) what contributes to that figure. Customer satisfaction scores, IT expenses, employee benefits, hours spent in meetings — every figure is worth investigating and reassessing.

Measurements aren't the only way to arrive at the issues your company needs to address. A single brainstorming session with employees can provide a treasure trove of potential projects to take on. Reviewing customer complaints, talking to vendors, or simply looking over the receptionist's shoulders can also reveal inefficiencies to tackle. Chapter 4 walks you through more ways to find out where your organization can use improvement, and Parts III and IV dive into specific areas such as customer service and internal communications.

The Pareto Principle, named after the Italian engineer Vilfredo Pareto who developed the field of microeconomics, is the "law" that 80 percent of negative results are due to 20 percent of the inefficiencies. Identifying the inefficiencies that are making the biggest impact can lead to fast and tremendous improvements in efficiency across your organization.

Finding *solutions* to the problems you recognize is a similar process. While measurements usually don't lead you to both a problem and its solution simultaneously, all the other tactics — namely brainstorming and researching what potential solutions exist outside the organization's realm of knowledge — can lead you there. Finding and selecting the right solution to an identified inefficiency is the start of a new project.

Projects versus Six Sigma projects

Six Sigma doesn't work for — and for that matter, doesn't officially *accept* — just any inefficiency as a project. For starters, Six Sigma wants big, flashy gains. If you're not going to save 70 percent of costs or reduce over 70 percent of defects, it's not a Six Sigma improvement. (This doesn't mean it's not still worth doing. It just means it's not a Six Sigma project.)

In Six Sigma, a project:

- ✔ Has a financial impact to EBIT (Earnings Before Income Tax) or NPBIT (Net Profit Before Income Tax) or a significant strategic value
- ✔ Produces results that significantly exceed the amount of effort required to obtain the improvement
- ✔ Solves a problem that is not easily or quickly solvable using traditional methods
- ✔ Improves performance by greater than 70 percent over existing performance levels

When a particular problem is selected to become a potential Six Sigma project, it goes through a critical metamorphosis — first from a practical business problem into a statistical problem, then into a statistical solution, and, finally, into a practical solution. When you state your problem in statistical language, you ensure that you will use data, and only data, to solve it. Statistics force you to abandon gut feelings, intuition, and best guesses as ways to address your problems.

Two Lean ways to find inefficiencies

Lean provides a less-mathematical map to your inefficiencies, in fact, it *literally* provides a map in the form of a value-stream map.

To construct your own map to efficiency, start in the upper-left corner with an initial input, such as steel rods, an HTTP request, or a customer order. Trace that input along the entire path it takes to become your final output, whether that be pistons, a PDF file, or a box of books. At each step, dig deep to find inefficiencies in the transformation process that input goes through.

To take it a step further, you should question the mere *existence* of each step. The "5 Whys" exercise — asking "why" five times in succession — works great here for really understanding why each step is necessary (if it even is).

One of the key takeaways is the idea of seven types of waste, known as *muda*. Reviewing a value-stream map seven times, each time from the perspective of identifying and eliminating a particular type of waste, is one highly effective way to uncover new inefficiencies. The seven wastes — a.k.a. TIM WOOD — are (unnecessary) transport, inventory (*any* inventory goes against the Lean way), (unnecessary) motion (such as reaching across yourself to grab a part), waiting, overproduction, overprocessing, and defects.

Kaizen workshops

To really draw out inefficiencies in a particular process, you can hold a Kaizen event. During this event, which may last just a few hours or extend for a number of days, all participants walk through a given process step-by-step at the place the process happens — often in slow motion. At every point, the process is analyzed for both waste and potential improvements. Scenes are reenacted with small changes to see their impact on the later parts of the operation. Although Kaizen events are time-consuming — no normal work is planned or expected during workshop time — they can also be far more revealing and productive than merely hypothetical reenactments.

Taking it all in before trying to fix it

In the beginning phases, you want to capture as many inefficiencies as you (or your team members) can recognize, and correspondingly capture every possible solution that comes up. As with all good brainstorming exercises, you can't start vetting solutions and narrowing down options until you're relatively sure your current list of options is complete.

In Chapter 4, I get more in-depth about ways to store all this information for later, when you need to go back to the drawing board to take a different approach to remedying an issue, or when you're riding the waves of an initial success and need a new challenge to tackle.

Considering the Impact of Potential Solutions

It's easy to assume you know which solution to use to address a given inefficiency problem, but you know what they say about assuming. Most people I work with are aware they have to consider the immediate impacts of a change — time to implement, cost, and so on — but completely overlook some of the more far-reaching effects on other aspects of the business, such as human resources or IT, or even on the organization's goals and values. A responsible efficiency-enhancing project considers a solution's potential impact on every corner of the company *before* starting to implement it.

Correlation is not causation! In other words, just because your sales team placed more phone calls in March does not necessarily mean that the jump in sales in March is a direct result of those additional phone calls. Perhaps your product was featured on a top blog, or all the customers who ordered last March during a special promotion are now reordering, or the market changed in your favor. Understanding and internalizing this concept is important when it comes to vetting solutions. March sales may have been up and it may seem perfectly reasonable to hire additional sales staff to make even more phone calls in April. But if the phone calls weren't causing the bump in sales, then you'll find yourself facing a significant payroll increase without a corresponding increase in profits.

Looking at a problem from all sides

When you're selecting between potential solutions, it's often external forces that provide the most clarity regarding the best fit for your organization. Failing to consider a new project from a full 360 degrees introduces unnecessarily high levels of risk. Areas to consider include finances, human resources, legal issues, impact on quality, customer service, customer and employee sentiment, technology hurdles, time, the organization's goals, available skills and resources, the longevity of the solution, downtime required, and what will happen if the solution fails when implemented.

You can't effectively vet solutions in a vacuum or on your own. Actively solicit feedback from management and everyday consultants on the ground. Ultimately, you'll want to assemble a team of functional representatives from every department of the company who can provide feedback from their particular area of expertise.

Don't let your team devolve into a panel that rejects every suggested project. It's not up to them whether the project comes to exist, only to share their concerns for the project team to further investigate or plan ahead for.

Keeping an ear to the ground

Having an open dialogue with your entire company reaps many benefits. You never know who, based on outside experience, internal knowledge, or just plain luck, will first identify a core inefficiency or suggest the best remedy for that inefficiency. Further, after you're in the swing of implementing projects, it's the people who are actually implementing the change who are best qualified to report back on issues and even additional improvements.

You can never predict every possible impact that executing a given project may have on your organization. (If you can, there's a 1-800 psychic hot line career in your future!) This makes feedback channels all the more important, so you can hear initial rumblings of a problem before they become serious issues.

Setting Clear Efficiency Goals

After you have an idea of the issues you want to address, you have to state what sort of improvement you're seeking. Not only does a goal provide context for determining an action plan — the steps to save $1,000 are often far different from the steps to save $100,000 — but it's also the *only* way you can know when you finish a project and whether that project was a success.

Although the process for reaching goals may vary, every efficiency-enhancing methodology from Lean to Six Sigma incorporates the same focus on setting goals that are easily understood across the organization.

Defining clear goals

The best goal is one that an objective outsider can immediately understand and, more importantly, evaluate. Even if she has no background in the subject matter, this stranger should be able to clearly say whether the goal was met after hearing the goal and reviewing the associated data points.

Vague or warm and fuzzy ideals, like "create a fun work environment" are good mission statements or company guidelines, but make for lousy goals because there's no associated objective measure. If you want to measure fun in the workplace, you'd have to come up with your own metric system (Moh's Scale of Fun, perhaps?) with data points you *can* measure, such as employee satisfaction scores on a survey, the number of social events held in a month, the number of attendees at optional social events (assuming that attendance at an optional event indicates employees are enjoying themselves), or pieces of flare.

 As you set your goals, make sure you're consulting functional representatives who can speak to the feasibility of your objectives. For example, you wouldn't want to set a goal to make the company website load in half the time without talking to someone knowledgeable from IT. You can and should also explore external resources for vetting your goal's feasibility — perhaps internal IT support isn't aware of certain speed-enhancing technologies that a consultant specializing in website enhancements can share.

Understanding the types of goals

Goals are multidimensional, and a variety of goals ensures that you are keeping an eye on the big picture *and* that a single point of failure does not necessarily stop you from succeeding in multiple other arenas. Your team may set goals relating to finances, sentiment (employee or customer — or even vendor!), product or service quality, speed of production or response times, employee or customer retention, knowledge gain and transfer, safety, or any other metric relevant to your organization.

Choosing the best next project

You need to set goals *before* selecting specific projects, because a project is largely defined by what it's supposed to accomplish. You may also need multiple projects to achieve a set of goals, or often multiple projects to achieve one single goal. There's no one-size-fits-all way to choose which project to tackle first. Strategies include picking those that save the most money, are easiest or fastest to complete, solve an obnoxious problem that aggravates employees, or are the hardest to accomplish (with the idea that getting the hard stuff out of the way can provide serious onward momentum for all subsequent work).

You don't need to tackle every goal all at once. Project selection doubles as a goal prioritizing process. Goals that won't be addressed this time around get tabled until you have the resources to take on additional projects.

Executing Your New Efficiency Plan

Execution is usually where people *start* a project, but this is rarely the most efficient strategy. If it works, it's more likely that you were lucky rather than that you are just too good for project plans. You need to follow the five steps, but you also need to compose a comprehensive execution plan, before you go about implementing changes.

I know it can feel like a chore — especially in the beginning, when mastering a change process is a project in itself — but the risks that planning offsets, coupled with the additional gains you can (and will!) benefit from, are real. And I promise that once you've been through the process a few times, not only will it become second nature, but you'll have a cadre of former execution plans to build upon, replete with rich historical data about pitfalls to avoid or strategies that worked particularly well in your organization.

The steps I outline in Chapter 7 for executing your efficiency-enhancing project plan follow the basic standards of project management, which you can read more about in *Project Management For Dummies*. Individual methodologies like Six Sigma and Lean have their own specific approaches to this process, which can (and do!) take up entire books unto themselves. You can read more about the differences between their project management styles in Chapter 19. Broadly, the components of an efficiency-enhancing plan include:

✔ **Background information:** An efficient execution plan doubles as a mechanism for getting new team members and interested outsiders quickly up to speed on the issues at hand. Include a problem statement outlining the inefficiencies you're seeking to address, your ideal outcome, and any recognized risks or constraints on your ability to reach these objectives (such as a very small budget, only two hours a week to work on your goals, or a lack of adequate internal expertise).

✔ **Clear tasks and responsibilities:** If I had to pick one component that's most important, it would be a clear list of tasks and deliverables. You're not expected to have the knowledge to write every step yourself, but it is a project owner's responsibility to track down that information in order to truly scope a project. "Build an app" is not a step — it's a wildly general statement that can take three hours or three years. Every necessary role also needs to be defined, so that you can then assign people to these roles.

✔ **Resource planning:** How many dollars and hours is this project expected to use? How does that fit into the available resources of the organization? I frequently see people give time and financial estimates, but I almost never see them consider those figures in light of every other active project. Your project may "only" require five hours a week from accounting, but if there is just one person in accounting and 16 active projects, then something has to give.

✔ **Planning for the project itself:** A successful project requires clear and regular communication among players and externally to the project audience. This calls for check-in schedules and policies (Does the technical writer check in once a day or once a month? With whom?), setting a schedule, assembling an audience list, and assigning real humans to the earlier-defined project roles. Also, what happens if the project exceeds budget, takes too long, loses key players, and/or fails to meet its objective? Plan ahead. Having an efficient project *process* in place makes it infinitely easier to roll with the inevitable punches.

With Agile Project Management (APM), your execution plan is a series of small sprints instead of one long comprehensive plan. APM works best in environments of frequent change, like software development (where Agile was first developed) or the development of a new product line, where new features and obstacles are constantly introduced and need to be managed.

Part II
Making Strides Toward Efficiency

The 5th Wave   By Rich Tennant

"But rather than me just sitting here talking,
why don't we watch this video of me sitting
here talking?"

In this part . . .

No matter what your inefficiencies, there's a general process you can follow to stamp them out (and even track them down). While you may have some obvious problems you know you want to fix, I'm willing to bet your organization also has some systemic inefficiencies that you have yet to dig up. Recognizing that no book can cover every possible issue in-depth, this part serves as your guide for tracking down, evaluating, prioritizing, and addressing inefficiencies. You should be able to follow this roadmap no matter what the nature of your business is or how efficient you are currently.

Chapter 3

You Are Here: Measuring Where You Stand

In This Chapter

▶ Understanding the value of measuring your business

▶ Knowing what to measure and why

▶ Choosing your measurement method

▶ Collecting and storing measurement data

I can't overstate the importance of measuring your business in ways beyond mere dollars in and dollars out. In fact, Harvard Business School's Robert Kaplan and David Norton developed the Balanced Scorecard methodology specifically to address this hyperfocus on financial measures and to bring light to other equally important metrics such as customers, growth, and productivity. Financial efficiency is a key part to running an efficient business — productivity becomes a moot point when your doors are closed — but it's by no means the only part. Taken too far, you can save every possible cent and still find yourself with a sub-par product sold by a defeated sales team to a dwindling customer base.

The goal of measuring is to get the most information before you start making any decisions about what changes to make, who should be making them, or how to go about making them. While your business may have some low-hanging fruit that you can improve upon right away, chances are that a thorough survey of the current situation will reveal deeper and even unexpected avenues to pursue. Focus on collecting accurate, broad data first and don't worry about making any decisions with it quite yet. (That's what the next chapters are for!)

In this chapter, I get into the right measuring mindset, review a number of questions you want to answer during the measuring process, and give you the lowdown on how to measure with the big boys like Six Sigma and Lean.

Why You Bother Measuring

If you're in debt, sending collectors to voicemail and tossing bills into the back of a bottom drawer may temporarily make you feel in control, but it does nothing to actually help you improve the situation. Barring a lucky lottery ticket, the only way to dig out is to open those envelopes, tally up the amounts due, and start making payments.

The same is true when it comes to business efficiency. You can love the idea of being more efficient and follow the suggestions in every other chapter, but if you don't know where your business is at today, you won't know where you actually stand. Perhaps your product quality is nearly perfect already, and your focus may be better placed on something like customer service or building overhead. On the other hand, maybe you're actually behind the eight ball in an area that you assumed was running at peak efficiency, and some new technology or a more experienced manager can be a game changer. If you don't measure now, all your improvement efforts are basically shots in the dark.

If you decide to charge full-speed ahead down the path to greater business efficiency, I can guarantee that obstacles and frustrations along the way may tempt you to give up. Improvement takes commitment and hard work. A single scathing complaint letter can make you feel like every customer is about to abandon ship, or an increased supplier fee may dredge up nightmares about not being able to make payroll. Really knowing the big picture — that customer satisfaction is up 290 percent or that overall costs dropped $2 million last year — can motivate you and your team to stay the course.

What to Measure and Why

So you're sold on the idea that you need to measure, but measure what, exactly? I've got some ideas, many drawn from other books in the *For Dummies* series, about what questions to start asking in order to start to understand your efficiency starting point.

Measuring dollars in, dollars out, and dollars lost

Increasing income while decreasing expenses is what people usually think of when they hear "efficiency," although it's never quite that simple. When you're measuring financial milestones, always keep in mind the non-obvious and long-term costs such as employee time and warranty-related expenses. Ask yourself these questions:

- ✔ How much are you spending in employee salaries? How does this break down across department, skill level, and seniority?

- ✔ How much are you paying in taxes? How much, in terms of time and expense, are you paying to prepare your taxes?

- ✔ How much does it cost to hire one new employee, from marketing the open position to completing training?

- ✔ What is your monthly infrastructure overhead? Include mortgage interest, property taxes, utilities, and landscaping for each building, and gas/maintenance for company cars.

- ✔ How much do you spend on shipping? Include direct mail costs, envelopes, and shipping materials in addition to employee time spent preparing and delivering packages.

- ✔ How much does it cost to produce one unit? This one's tricky, and most businesses can never get a 100 percent accurate figure, but try your best. Start with the resources needed to earn one sale and go on through manufacturing, delivering, and supporting that sale.

- ✔ What's your revenue per customer? How about per customer referral? What's the average single order amount compared to the average lifetime order amount?

- ✔ What percent of revenue comes from each sales leg of your business? For example, is the majority of your profit in selling a product, accessories, or support?

- ✔ How much does it cost to resolve a customer complaint?

- ✔ What are your sales per employee? Per department? Per product line?

- ✔ How do your prices compare to those of your competitors?

Finding out how people feel about you

Sentiment analysis is one of the trickiest metrics to measure, but it has far-reaching implications. If your customers aren't happy, that's usually a sign of room for improvement. That improvement may take the form of higher product quality, faster customer response times, quicker shipping, lower prices, or better marketing — or some combination of all of those.

Sentiment goes beyond customers. How do your employees feel about the company? About your HR policies? About how much time they spend in meetings? Happy employees who are proud of the company they work for and who feel respected and taken care of by their employer will consistently give you better service, productivity, and communication. But on the other hand, if you discover your employees feel like they can do no wrong and that they're guaranteed to get their next paycheck no matter how much they slack off, that can reveal an entirely separate issue. Think about these questions:

✔ What's your employee retention rate? If employees are constantly aban-doning ship, you're spending time and money hiring and training a constant stream of people — expenses that you can save if you can stop the employment leakage.

✔ What are your employees' biggest grievances with their jobs?

✔ How much of a voice do your employees feel they have in company decisions? How much autonomous decision-making authority do your employees have?

✔ What percentage of customers is completely satisfied at the close of a support request? How about at the conclusion of an order? How would they rate your pro-activeness in terms of providing them with important information up front, so they don't have to chase you for it?

✔ What's your repeat order rate among customers?

✔ How many customer service complaints are resolved the first time?

Figuring out how fast you're moving

Time is an often overlooked resource, but in many ways, it's the most valuable one. Even if you had the money to pay every employee to work 100 hours a week, you won't generally be able to convince them to give those hours to you. You can't return hours and you can't order more — so measuring how you're currently spending your time is an important safeguard against potential time wasters. Find the answers to the following questions:

✔ How many hours does each employee spend at work each week?

✔ How many breaks do employees take? How do they spend this break time? Are legally mandated breaks being honored?

✔ How many hours each week are employees engaged in non-work-related activities at work (such as surfing Facebook)?

✔ How long, in minutes, does it take for a customer support ticket to be resolved satisfactorily?

✔ How long is the average sales call? Support call?

✔ How long does it take to convert a customer from first point of contact to a first sale?

✔ How many hours does each employee spend in meetings each week?

✔ How long does it take to receive approval for a $50 expense? A $500 one? A $15,000 one?

✔ How long is your cycle time? *Cycle time* is how long it takes your product to move through the entire assembly process.

✔ How long is your *lead time*? That is, the time between receiving an order to the delivery of that same order.

✔ What's your *Takt Time*? This is the minimum rate at which you must operate in order to keep up with customer orders.

For a more thorough list of time wasters and measurement techniques, check out *Time Management For Dummies*.

Measuring time is rarely black and white, especially when it comes to measuring how humans spend their time. A ten-second customer support call is probably *not* efficient, and sometimes a couple of minutes of chitchat is what it takes to create a personal connection between a customer and your company. While important to track, you need to look at other metrics before acting on time measurements alone.

Doing a competitive analysis

Measuring how you stack up against the competition and within the marketplace can unearth potential inefficiencies in every aspect of your business. For example, if your competitors are able to sell the same product at a much lower price, is that because their product is of shoddier quality or because they've got some technological assets that significantly lower costs?

Strategic Planning Kit For Dummies suggests measuring the following:

✔ How big is your market in terms of number of customers, units sold, or dollar volume?

✔ What are the overall trends and developments in your industry? How many of these are you incorporating?

✔ What is the rate of market growth or shrinkage over time? Are there any differences in market growth by time of year?

✔ How big are your competitors? What companies have what portions of the market?

✔ What products or services do your competitors offer? How do they differ from yours?

✔ How does competitors' pricing compare with yours?

✔ What marketing strategies and tactics does the competition use and to what degree of success?

✔ What are the key factors for success in the market you're trying to serve? Are there any specific media outlets for reaching this market directly? What percentage of these markets are you utilizing?

✔ How do customers perceive the problem your product or service is intended to solve? How serious do they believe the problem to be? What benefits would be most important to them?

✔ How do customers solve the problem today?

✔ What costs do customers incur now to solve the problem?

How You Measure

Measuring may seem black and white — how many dollars entered our bank account last year? How many vacation days did the tier-two sales team take in May? — but it's actually quite nuanced. It's rare to have a single data point upon which you can improve efficiency. A real *butterfly effect* is at play when it comes to the impact one change can have on the efficiency of many other aspects of your business. The right measuring method has everything to do with your how efficient your business can become in the future.

Six Sigma measurement: Total precision

Six Sigma is the ultimate means of calculating precise efficiency measurements. In fact, the term *Six Sigma* is (among other things) a mathematical description for a process (usually in manufacturing) with 3.4 or fewer defects per million units produced. Some businesses can never reach this standard, although it's always a worthy goal when aiming for quality improvements. Six Sigma has evolved into an entire process for ferreting out and eliminating production defects, but at its base, it's a series of accuracy measurements.

While the methodology is called Six Sigma, different sigma levels exist — for example, 233 defects per million is five sigma. If you want a strong measure of product or process quality, measuring it in terms of Six Sigma is a challenging but worthwhile place to start.

Six Sigma measurements, listed here, can easily complement other measuring systems. For example, a Balanced Scorecard (covered later in this chapter) may contain spots to keep track of sigma measures alongside other metrics.

✔ **Keeping your eye on the target:** Six Sigma keeps your targets in check with CTXs, short for "critical to *X*," where *X* is the category of the target. For example, a CTQ would be a Critical To Quality goal. You set the range of acceptable figures, and continual measurement makes it readily apparent when you're about to veer off course. A single product can have a tremendous number of CTXs — a new car has over 10,000 separate CTQ targets.

The efficiency butterfly effect

Acting on inaccurate or incomplete information can have a negative ripple effect across your entire organization. Say you total last year's expenses by department, purely by adding up receipts. The IT Department spent $200,000 less than any other department last year, so you don't feel the need to pull the IT director aside for a hard chat about reining in expenses. Other department heads, fed up with a two-week average response time to tech support requests, resent this perceived "special treatment" and are a little less motivated to do their best. A more thorough investigation would have unearthed not just this hidden resentment, but also shown that adding another programmer at

$150,000 per year could have meant new software customizations that would save at least 7 hours a week per person across the entire company in data-entry time.

There's no one right way to measure in every circumstance. Multiple methodologies exist to address specific measurement questions, such as customer service satisfaction or product quality. The difference is greater than just choosing between mathematical equations — there's also a rich body of advice on the right questions to ask, the best tools for gathering specific data points, and best practices for making sure your measurements really reflect the big picture.

- ✔ **Focus on perfection:** Six Sigma, originally developed at Motorola, became famous for the quality gains and cost savings the process brought about. Six Sigma measurements are as precise as possible and designed to work best on a large scale to reduce errors.

- ✔ **Hearing the voice of the customer:** Most of your targets ultimately relate back to the needs of your customers. At their most basic, your customers have a need for your product to work as promised. They also have expectations about delivery time and technical support. Six Sigma reminds you to listen to, and measure, your customers' insights.

- ✔ **The breakthrough equation:** The equation below is the heart of Six Sigma, where y is your goal result, x is the input (or inputs) required to get there, and f is the process by which you transform the input into the result. E represents errors in the process, and the goal of Six Sigma is to reduce this figure to as close to zero as possible.

$$y = f(x) + E$$

For a more thorough review of Six Sigma measurements, pick up a copy of *Six Sigma For Dummies*.

Balanced Scorecard: Measuring finances, customers, growth, and productivity

The Balanced Scorecard approach to measuring gives equal weight to customer, productivity, growth, and financial measures. You develop scorecards in each of these four areas that most closely reflect your company's needs and goals, and constantly strive to improve those scores. Creating scorecards is an excellent exercise for any company, and keeps you continually focused on measuring.

Choose your lens

One advantage of scorecards is the focus on measuring your organization from different levels, or lenses. If you want to measure efficiency from a broad, top-down level, you'll use a strategic-level lens that looks at overall statistics like customer retention rates and profit-and-loss ratios. On the other hand, an operational scorecard would look at the state of your organization in more minute detail, such as calculating lead times or customer service response times. If you're just starting out, you may want to begin with a more narrowly focused scorecard and then plan to expand to a strategic-level outlook when your lower-level scorecards show improvement.

Balanced Scorecards should cascade, which means you can view the same metrics across different sections of your company. This helps you speak the same language and make accurate comparisons between and across departments.

 If you start measuring too broadly too soon, you'll miss out on the clues that a more-focused scorecard can provide. For example, a company-wide income and expense analysis doesn't show that the marketing department outspends all others two-to-one, which may call for further investigation into its financial health.

The four legs

The four areas to keep scorecards on are:

- **Customers:** If your customers aren't happy, you're not going to be in business for long. The Balanced Scorecard approach encourages you to interact with your customers to understand (and measure) their wants and needs. The customer scorecard also keeps an eye on metrics that directly impact customers, like delivery speed and product quality.

- **Internal business processes:** Internal business processes are an often-overlooked aspect of a business, even though they play an integral role in your company's ability to succeed. Efficient inner workings allow your team to respond to changes in the market faster, keep your employees around longer, and help your teams out-think the competition, in addition to saving money by avoiding defective projects or extra inventory. One key benefit of the Balanced Scorecard approach is giving equal weight to these measures alongside the more obvious financial and customer legs.

✔ **Finances:** Successful financial measurements have as much to do with a strong vocabulary as they do with a reliable calculator. For example, you'll want to define what numbers are "above the line," like sales, and which ones are "below the line," such as taxes. Without these definitions, your financial scorecard numbers can vary wildly from day to day even if your financial bottom line doesn't fundamentally change. Under the Balanced Scorecard approach, your measures should be simple and clear — advanced metrics don't need to be on your scorecard.

A financial scorecard contains three parts: a financial objective, financial measurements, and example targets. In the initial measuring stage, you don't have to set specific financial goals, but should rather think of the measurements you'd need to make in light of certain categories of objectives. For example, if your objective is to increase your stock price, you'd want to keep a close eye on gross profit, net profit, and growth rates.

✔ **Learning and growth:** Even if your organization is at the top of the market and the peak of efficiency, it still has to grow and adapt to the times in order to stay relevant — and afloat. Proactively encouraging employee education, innovation, and research and development is a key part of steering your company in the future instead of simply finding yourself drifting along. That's why Balanced Scorecard places such importance on the growth of organizational knowledge. Metrics on a learning and growth scorecard include the speed at which information travels within your company, the percentage of time employees spend on innovative endeavors, and average training times.

For a complete explanation of the Balanced Scorecard process, head over to *Balanced Scorecard Strategy For Dummies.*

Lean measurement: Examining costs beyond labor

While every efficiency-enhancing methodology focuses on customer value, it's Lean that really drives this point home. From a Lean perspective, everything starts and ends with the customer. A Lean culture uses data to empower employees to make decisions that enhance customer value, the Holy Grail metric. If you have customers, you can benefit from measuring your business in a Lean way.

Creating a value stream map

Lean reminds us that measurements aren't limited to rows of mathematical equations. A value stream map is a simple diagram of every step involved in the material and information flows needed to bring a product from order to delivery, starting on the left with procurement of raw materials and moving on to the right when customers take possession of their product or service. Intermediate data points are listed throughout the middle of the map. These maps are great for right-brained executives, who work better with visuals instead of raw data points and serve as a way to raise consciousness of opportunities for improvement.

You'll want to start with a *current state map* for your process, which follows a product's path from order to delivery to determine the current condition. After having identified your improvements to the current process, a *future state map* is constructed to achieve a higher level of performance. Your future state map becomes your current state map, and the process can be improved on again.

These maps should specify factors like cost, time, defect level, and manpower in detail at each point. The outcome of a future state map is always the customer's ideal product in terms of quality, price, and delivery time.

Measuring the seven wastes

Lean focuses on measuring and eliminating seven key types of waste:

- **Transport:** Whether you sell refrigerators or do management consulting, you want your deliverable to pass through as few hands and across the shortest distance possible.

  While transport traditionally refers to how far a physical product moves across a warehouse (or across warehouses), you can also measure in terms of number of hand-offs. For example, after your sales team closes a deal, perhaps a consulting agreement has to be e-mailed to an attorney, who sends it to an office manager to FedEx it to the client, who faxes it back to the receptionist, who e-mails the assigned consultant. On your process map, you would mark each "transport" and then look for ways to shorten the journey.

- **Unnecessary inventory:** A corollary to the waste of overproduction, unnecessary inventory refers to keeping more raw materials on hand than you need to produce on Takt Time.

- **Unnecessary motion:** In an ideal Lean manufacturing plant, each employee would take the absolute minimum number of steps and move their arms the absolute minimum number of times to create the customer's ideal, defect-free end product.

  Measure motion by observing employees at each step in the process map. Depending on the step, motion may mean physical steps taken, the number of times someone reaches for a tool, the number of clicks at the computer, or the number of characters typed into a terminal.

  Track excess inventory at each step in your process maps. Are there points at which excess materials or partially created goods wait to be used? What costs are you incurring in terms of storage space and labor to organize and store this excess inventory?

✔ **Waiting:** From a Lean perspective, all waiting is, by definition, waste. If your employees have downtime during work hours, this is waste. Similarly, any time your customers have to wait for delivery beyond the most efficient production time is waste.

Count waiting times at each step of the process map, making sure to consider lead times that begin with supplier procurement. Many process maps start at the point at which you receive raw materials, when you really have to begin counting at the point of ordering those materials to understand the total life-cycle time for a given product. After you've measured the time spent at each step, you can work at reducing those times where possible.

✔ **Overproduction:** In a Lean company, you operate as close to Takt Time as possible — in other words, you operate on a schedule that produces enough products to satisfy client demand, and no more. Extra finished goods require additional storage space, risk degradation or damage over time, require time and labor to store and retrieve, and present a risk if customer demand changes and no one purchases the excess.

Measure overproduction toward the end of your process maps. Are you storing excess finished inventory at the end? How much, and for how long?

✔ **Overprocessing:** Remember that Lean is all about the customer, and the goal of your future process map is to show the most efficient way to give your customers their ideal end product. In Lean, every process step that doesn't contribute to the customer's ideal end product — no matter how efficient this step may be — is waste.

After you have a complete process map, you can go through each step one by one to investigate its impact, if any, on the end product. Every step falls into one of three categories: value-adding (adds value to the customer or end-product), non-value-adding (adds zero value to the customer or end-product), and necessary but non-value-adding (adds no value to the customer or end-product, but must be done to keep the process going).

✔ **Defects/rework:** Every defect in your entire production process is waste. Defects are much more specific than a sub-par end product. Ordering the wrong amount of a raw material, equipment malfunction, and even a single bent nail are all defects. The three types of defects are: defects in the end product, service defects (for example, customer service issues), and internal scrap (defects caught before the end product makes it to the customer).

Your aim is to do it right the first time. In order to count defects, you usually need to start by identifying each potential place for error. Counting defects only after the fact means you may miss some defects you never thought to account for in the first place. Shadowing employees at each point in the production process and encouraging their input into the process map will better highlight more minute steps, and you can then track defect rates for each particular input. Six Sigma measurements work well for tracking defects in a Lean process.

Find out more about Lean, including example value stream maps, in *Lean For Dummies*.

5S: Tracking the five necessary attributes

5S began as a Japanese system for tracking and encouraging a clean, well-organized workspace. The 5S's stand for Sort, Simplify, Sweep, Standardize, and Sustain. Tracking how often your office garbage cans overflow may seem insignificant relative to measuring profits or defective parts, but it matters more than you may realize.

Think back to the last time you had to deliver a speech or other presentation. Would you have preferred to deliver it (a) two days after your last shower, in your pajamas, on a noisy street corner or (b) freshly showered in a pressed suit in a bright, clean conference room? Your words may be the same in either scenario, but the status of your environment absolutely affects your delivery and results.

This is where 5S tracking come in. 5S helps you look at your current office in terms of cleanliness, organization, and efficient use of space, ranging from the distance between employees and their tools to the layout of the manufacturing plant floor. You can also easily introduce 5S to your office environment.

The 5S Status Board and Lean tools

When using Lean tools and 5S, you post and update measurements on a status board — usually one per department. Measurements include the following:

- **Before-and-after shots:** Photograph your current space, from multiple angles and in every corner. This is your stating point. Remember those puzzles that ask you to find the seven differences between two similar images? After your first round of 5S, there should be measurable visual improvements in all your before-and-after shots.

- **Spaghetti diagrams:** So called because the outcome often looks like a plate of spaghetti. Draw a floor plan, to scale, of every work area. Mark key stations such as the supply workbench, the receptionist's desk, and garbage cans. You will use this floor plan over and over to measure distance traveled for various tasks. Many business owners are *shocked* to discover how much the placement of seemingly innocuous equipment like a soda machine can have on employee productivity.

- **Returns:** If you deal with physical inventory, excess or reshuffled product is considered clutter under 5S. Track how often pieces move — particularly if they ever move backward in your supply chain — and how much physical space this excess occupies. As you improve, you will track square footage that you free up in addition to the dollars and labor saved in lowered transit rates and the removal of unnecessary production.

Information is also inventory. How much space is being taken up by data you don't need? How many files are saved in triplicate (or beyond) across company computers instead of in a centralized location?

✔ **Timing:** When you're overhauling a floor plan or database schema, a staggered approach rarely works. You need to set aggressive deadlines to move departments through their organizational improvements quickly. Post these schedules so you can track adherence.

Before-and-after tracking is crucial to your success. If you don't measure, you don't know how much you have improved in terms of time, money, or manpower.

What if I don't sell a physical product?

Every company has wasted or poorly utilized space, even if that space is not within a warehouse. Perhaps you have a file room that can be reduced or replaced with a paperless office initiative, or maybe your floor of cubicles has slowly morphed into a layout that contributes to mess and waste. If you're an IT shop, you can measure space in gigabytes as opposed to square footage. For example, how many databases across how many servers are you running, and is there a way to make better use of that space?

If you have databases or complex machinery, map these out just as you would a physical floor plan. Just how far does one piece of data have to travel to reach its final destination? Is that data ever stored or duplicated unnecessarily? Over time, virtually every system introduces inefficient data processing — it's an unavoidable part of growth and side effect of many people working on the same system. When you measure your database, using Lean tools, however, you can start to recognize when your data becomes cluttered and in need of maid service.

Measuring your measuring with MSA

Measuring the wrong data defeats the whole point. Measurement System Analysis (MSA) keeps your measurements honest, accurate, and expected.

Are you measuring the right data?

Make sure you're measuring the right stuff by running through this checklist:

✔ **Is my data fresh?** If you want to know how customers feel about your product line today, customer satisfaction surveys from last year — or perhaps even last month — aren't relevant. All your data should have a timestamp so you know you're working with the freshest, most relevant material.

✔ **Is my data objective?** It's all too easy to go into a collection or measuring project with preconceived notions of what that data will tell you. This can skew the data you end up collecting, especially when it comes to information like sentiment that isn't strictly mathematical on its face.

For example, if you believe that your employees are as happy as can be, you may feel you can collect feedback directly in one-on-one meetings and overlook the added benefit an anonymous survey may provide.

✔ **How precise is my data?** If you're measuring widget sizes by visually approximating their length, you can't turn around and report accuracy to three decimal points. Your initial measurement units and tools affect the precision of your final numbers.

✔ **Is my data complete?** As I touched on earlier, if you're not measuring all the data points you have on a particular metric, your results will be skewed accordingly. For example, only surveying customers who call in with support requests would likely paint a more negative picture than if you surveyed a random sampling of your entire customer base.

✔ **Am I always measuring the same thing?** For example, if you sell cases of wine, does a quantity of "1" mean one case or one bottle? If you operate in multiple countries, are you always measuring in the same currency? Is an order date the day the customer submitted the order or the day you start processing the order? Defining these terms up front can help eliminate lots of confusion down the road.

✔ **Are my data gatherers honest and committed?** Assigning the wrong people to collect data can also skew your data. For example, an employee who feels her job is threatened by the outcome of a data collection project may not be as thorough as one who understands the importance of accurate information for the future health of the company. Similarly, an intern may simply not understand that skipping over a file here and there or fudging an unclear answer can have far-reaching effects on your business.

Testing your data collectors

The process of making sure everyone measures in the same way is called *gauge repeatability and reproducibility*, also known as *gauge R&R*. The process is a statistical tool that allows you to measure the amount of variation caused by the measurement process, considering both the tool used for measuring and the people performing the measurements.

To carry out the gauge R&R, you test your measurement operators by having them measure the samples multiple times to see how close the results come to the standard measurements and how close the operators are in the measuring process. You also need one expert operator to perform sample measurements under ideal conditions first — these are your standard measurements. After the operators measure all the samples, you're ready to make your calculations:

✔ Calculate the variation for each operator by counting the number of samples for which the operator gets the same measurement value and dividing this number by the number of samples.

✔ Calculate the variation for each operator versus the standard by counting the number of samples for which the operator gets the standard measurement value and dividing this number by the number of samples.

- ✔ Calculate the variation between the operators by counting the number of samples for which the operators get the same measurement value and dividing this number by the number of samples.

- ✔ Calculate the variation between the operators versus the standard by counting the number of samples for which the operators get the same standard measurement value and dividing this number by the number of samples.

You Can't Measure Without Data

Measurement without data is nothing more than a gut feeling. While that data may take multiple forms — a count of customers, a sum of expenses, or a set of narrative responses about customers' experiences — you need to collect it in the right place and ensure that all the data you want to use is comparable (that is, each data point is measuring the same thing or in the same way) in order to make accurate measurements on which you can base business decisions.

Where to pool your data

So, you know what you'd like to measure and how you'd like to go about measuring it — but where does all that data go, exactly? Depending on your business, you may need a single data repository, or, more likely, a few. Choosing the right place to post your data can have long-term ramifications on how easily you can access and manipulate your data in the future.

Your data storage choices

The following are you options for data storage:

- ✔ **Excel:** The tried-and-true resource for collecting and analyzing data, Excel is a no-frills application that can work for almost any company. Entering new data directly into Excel is generally too manual a process for most businesses — you shouldn't be running order fulfillment out of a spreadsheet tab — but with the right training, you can perform most any calculation on your existing data.

- ✔ **CRM:** Customer Relationship Management, or CRM, software has come a long way from serving as a mere electronic address book. Cloud-based CRM systems like Salesforce.com, Zoho, and SugarCRM are basically customizable blank slates that can store, sort, and perform basic reporting functions on data as diverse as patient medication refill schedules to historical inventory fulfillment records. Many organizations can store the majority of their information in their CRMs, and use Excel to perform more advanced forecasting and calculations.

✔ **Off-the-shelf software:** Some companies have made it their sole focus to create software titles that correctly and efficiently measure core business data. For example, you may load historical financial and commission data into Quickbooks accounting software, while you use an inventory management service to track order fulfillment.

✔ **Proprietary software:** If you have unique enough business needs, developing your own custom software can be the best choice for collecting and processing internal data. However, this route is only advised if you have the in-house technical knowledge and skills to develop and maintain it. Outsourcing your core business software can cause irrevocable harm to your business if the external IT staff disappears, moves on, or simply doesn't have a strong grasp of your needs.

Factors to consider

When choosing a data storage repository, ask yourself the following questions:

✔ **How easily can I get data in?** If it takes seven screens to enter an order, you'll aggravate employees, slow response times, and risk inaccurate data as people seek ways to skirt the system.

✔ **How easily can I get data out?** No single system lasts forever or meets 100 percent of your business needs. You need to be able to extract all your data into a non-proprietary format like .csv or .txt files at any time.

✔ **What integration options exist?** The best repositories are versatile, with options to integrate with other systems. Look for systems with Application Programming Interfaces (APIs), which mean a programmer or other software company can write code to let the system update and exchange data with other repositories.

✔ **How secure is my data?** Even if your industry does not require a certain level of data security, like with credit card details or healthcare records, it never hurts to choose the most secure system possible. Look for SAS 70 II compliance, the highest level of security available for commercially available software systems.

Resist the urge to merge

At first it may seem that the best way to analyze your data is to get all of it into the same system, whether that be an Excel spreadsheet or a CRM. Resist this urge. While it may make sense to move data from disparate systems into a single repository, this often leads to double data entry, unnecessary work, and/or hackneyed software "hooks" that detract from the integrity of your functional needs at the expense of your measuring requests.

Instead, focus on complementary data sources. For example, customer order details may fit best in Salesforce.com, while your customer acquisition expenses are in Quickbooks. Technical or security barriers may prevent you from a full-blown sync between the two systems, and even if you can sync, neither system may have robust enough reporting capabilities. At this point, too many organizations turn to the dreaded Data Entry approach in order to get out an accurate customer acquisition cost figure. A better solution is to design a report containing all the right data in the right order in each system that is exportable to CSV, and then create an Excel template that performs the necessary calculations on this combination of reports. You can continue to input customer orders and internal costs as normal, and it will just take a couple minutes to export the right data into the right place when you need it.

How to process archived and handwritten data

If your business has been around for a while (or even if it hasn't), it's likely you've got a treasure-trove of data scattered about in file cabinets, desk drawers, and inboxes. Customer orders, complaint letters, employee evaluations, and even handwritten financial ledgers — all important information that you likely need to keep and refer back to, but in paper form, it's nearly impossible to measure accurately or on an ongoing basis. If you really want to know where your organization stands, you've got to bring those archives into the 21st century.

The idea of converting reams of records into searchable data that can be manipulated may seem like an overwhelming and manual process, but don't fear — there are services and technological advances that can turn almost any document into a file you can measure and monitor.

Optical Character Recognition, known as OCR for short, is a process that automatically converts scanned typed — and even handwritten! — documents into text that you can search, copy, and edit just as you can text that you typed directly with your keyboard. OCR views each character as a separate image, and then electronically "guesses" which character it is. This technology is now sophisticated enough to accurately convert even a hastily handwritten note on the back of a napkin into an correctly transcribed Microsoft Word or Adobe Acrobat file.

To get started with OCR, you want a high-quality scanner or, if the volume of your paperwork calls for it, a third-party mass scanning service. Software titles that can then convert your scanned files into text include Evernote (www.evernote.com), ABBYY (www.abbyy.com), and Adobe Acrobat (www.adobe.com).

Remember, measuring is an ongoing process, not a one-time event. If there's data that continually comes in a non-electronic form, explore ways to get it electronically in the first place (for example, putting a survey online instead of distributing it on paper), or equip your employees with a means to quickly get new data into the system. For example, give your receptionist a desktop scanner customer letters can be scanned as they come in, two or three at a time. Scanning is a much more bearable process when done in tiny bursts once a day than in one big batch.

After you've converted all those handwritten notes and paper files into an analyzable electronic form, you want to make sure you'll still be able to use that data in the future — and much of that depends on the file format in which you save it. The songs coming out of an 8-track may seem as much like music as any other form, but good luck transferring them to a different device to make a playlist for your next run. As a rule of thumb, the most popular file formats — .csv, .txt, and .pdf, followed by .doc and .xls — are most likely to have the best conversion options when they, too, eventually become obsolete.

Where to find new data

Although it's generally up to you to find or seek out data points related to your own organization, it can be difficult or impossible to drum up the right metrics about the market, your competitors, or other external areas all on your own. A third party can often connect you with the data you need to round out an accurate competitive analysis or suss out your product line's real market penetration.

Discovering secondary data sources

Try the following sources for secondary data:

- ✓ **Data.gov:** The central repository for all open government datasets, many of which are available in flat files (CSVs) or even through APIs.

- ✓ **U.S. Department of Commerce:** The U.S. Department of Commerce provides information about business, trade, and economic information from across the Federal Government. Check out the website at www. commerce.gov.

- ✓ **MarketResearch.com:** This source sells market research reports for a variety of industries. It also has the most comprehensive collection of published market research available. Check it out online at www. marketresearch.com.

- ✓ **U.S. Census Bureau:** The Bureau (www.census.gov) gives you free access to all census data about people, businesses, trade, and much more.

- ✓ **DemographicsNow:** This company has numerous tools for both business and consumer markets, such as segmentation, customer profiling, site selection, demographic data, and competitive analysis reports. The company's website is www.demographicsnow.com.

- ✓ **Frost & Sullivan:** This business consulting firm provides industry-specific B2B research and reports for a variety of fields. The online sources are available at www.frost.com.

- ✓ **U.S. Bureau of Labor Statistics:** The Bureau of Labor Statistics (www. bls.gov) is another government resource useful for gathering data on average wages and job responsibilities.

For a more complete guide to finding external industry data, see *Strategic Planning Kit For Dummies*.

Conducting primary research

Primary research involves going directly to the data source, instead of relying on a third party to research and compile the data for you. This method is most often used in market research when you need to collect brand-new data like customer sentiment about a new product line. You can gather these details through customer surveys, one-on-one interviews, and/or focus groups. Websites to help you quickly gather primary research include SurveyMonkey (`www.surveymonkey.com`), Formstack (`www.formstack.com`), and Wufoo (`www.wufoo.com`). There are right and wrong ways to phrase questions in these environments — for the full scoop, see *Marketing Research Kit For Dummies* and *Customer Service For Dummies*.

Decided Whether to Cut Losses or Invest in Archiving Data

Although it's certainly possible to convert just about any existing files, whether physical or electronic, into a current, useable format, it's not always worth the time and expense involved. Understanding what files you must process and what files you can leave as-is (at least for now) can make the process more palatable and, well, more efficient!

Do you need it?

Don't make the mistake of investing time and money archiving or processing old files that you have no intention of measuring. Ask yourself a few simple questions first:

- ✔ **Are you legally required to have it?** If you're audited tomorrow by the IRS or an industry regulatory body, will you be presenting the auditor with a tractor trailer of bankers' boxes or an e-mail with an organized set of attachments? Generally, you should be measuring anything that you're legally required to be tracking, even if the only measurement is "Do you have these required files?"

- ✔ **Do you need to measure it?** Naturally, the data that you need to measure now is the data that needs to be processed first.

✔ **Is it a missing piece of an existing puzzle?** Sometimes physical files contain substantially different data from their electronic counterparts. For example, customers who send handwritten letters are not the same people who fill out a comment form online, and if you're measuring customer satisfaction solely from your electronic submissions, you'll be missing key pieces of data.

✔ **Is it actively referenced?** If your employees are going out to a warehouse or a back room every day to pull a customer's shipping label or order history, those files should move to the front of the processing pack. Not only are you risking inaccurate or lost data, but your employees are likely more aggravated than you realize about having to get up and sift through files every time they get a request.

Do you need it now?

Is this data relevant? Maybe you'll want to archive it one day, but if it's not going to be included in measurements you'll be making in the immediate future, you can save it for another day. For example, you may eventually want to import your customers' entire order histories, but you only need the last 10 years' worth for your current analyses.

Should you even keep it?

Are you legally required to get rid of it? In some industries, you don't want to or can't hold on to certain files after a period of time. If you discover these files in your archives, not only should you shred them right away, but you should put a process in place to remove these files at set intervals in the future.

Chapter 4

I Thought I Saw a Bad Habit: Hunting Down Inefficiencies and Their Solutions

. . . .

In This Chapter

▶ Indentifying the best way to detect inefficiencies

▶ Looking at Lean

▶ Thinking about total quality management

▶ Considering shadowing employees

▶ Understanding Six Sigma

▶ Discovering areas to brainstorming

▶ Finding the right tools for improvement

. . . .

*E*very business has a handful of obvious inefficiencies — perhaps the computers in accounting are slower than molasses, or Machine B in manufacturing seems to break down every other week — but how do you *really* know where your less-obvious inefficiencies lie?

Generally, the farther away you are from a job or department, the less aware you are of the related pain points. I've been in countless offices where the CEO assured me there were no real concerns, and yet a cursory interview with a person on the floor revealed a two-page handwritten "workaround" sheet that he needs in order to get through his day. These internal crib sheets are like a treasure map for inefficiencies.

Beyond the issues recognized by some employees but not others is the more pervasive problem of being unaware of what you do not know. A process that may seem the pinnacle of efficiency to you may be wildly inefficient to someone else with different experience or domain knowledge.

In this chapter, I go through the more formal methodologies — Six Sigma, Lean, Balanced Scorecard, and TQM — for determining where your company can potentially increase its efficiency. Plus, I show you my personal favorite: following folks around for the day to see their workflow through fresh eyes or, as the Japanese Lean experts say, "go to Gemba," a common term used in Lean methodology for going to "where the work happens."

The journey of uncovering 1,000 inefficiencies begins with a single step. In this chapter, I help you choose the right team members to involve in the process to ensure you capture *every* inefficiency you come across. Then I walk through brainstorming potential solutions to each of these inefficiencies, leaving you with a treasure trove of efficiency-enhancing projects from which to draw.

At this stage, you're less worried about picking the right solution or generating a plan, and more interested in rooting through every nook and cranny of your business for potential improvements.

Choosing the Right Methodology

Business people have spent decades working out ways to improve business processes, and some of the more effective methods have been canonized into formal systems and processes that virtually any business can adopt. Which approach fits your business best depends on your size, goals, and company culture — although often, you can take the best ideas from each to compile an exhaustive list of potential internal improvement endeavors.

Balancing the score: Balanced Scorecard

The Balanced Scorecard methodology gives equal weight to four distinct areas of business: customer needs, internal knowledge and education, productivity, and finances. A "balanced" company maintains dashboards of key metrics in each of the four sectors, both to track progress toward related goals and to see where the company stands in objective terms on these measurements.

On a high level, to look for inefficiencies from a Balanced Scorecard perspective, you'll want to brainstorm what's standing between your current operations and the maximum achieveable level of success in each area.

 A much more revealing approach is to actually measure your current organization and assemble initial scorecards. Low scores or growth percentages are the best places to start your inefficiency investigation.

A low score in and of itself is not always a sign of inefficiency, just as there may be significant room for improvement in a metric with a high score. For example, in some highly competitive industries a 1 percent year-over-year growth in new customers is well above average, while in others that same metric would be akin to failure.

Scorecard levels

There are three different levels of scorecards: strategic, operational, and tactical. Each viewpoint can reveal its own set of potential issues.

On a *strategic* level, you consider your company's long-term objectives. Where do you want to be in five years? Why aren't you there now? Consider the landscape between these two points.

On an *operational* level, you measure many of the same (and some new) metrics on an annual basis. Instead of looking five years out, look one year out. What are the biggest hurdles toward achieving those objectives over the next 12 months? What's standing in the way of getting there faster or for less money?

Finally, on a *tactical* level, you review these metrics (and perhaps some additional ones) on a daily basis. If you're just starting out with Balanced Scorecard, you can't do much in the way of comparisons on the strategic or operational levels, but you definitely have time to track the tactical level for a few weeks. This deep-dive perspective is where you find the most insights into inefficiencies as you explore trends that stand out.

Customer needs

The customer dashboard include metrics such as retention rates, market share, number of new customers, customer service complaints, customer service satisfaction, customer response time, average time between orders, average value of each order, and average customer acquisition costs.

The top inefficiencies to explore in this corner include the following:

- ✔ Why are existing customers leaving?
- ✔ Why aren't customers ordering more or more often?
- ✔ Why don't potential customers become actual customers?
- ✔ What are customers complaining about?
- ✔ Why do customers feel dissatisfied about a customer service inquiry?

✔ What takes so long to respond to customers?

✔ What are the costs involved in acquiring a new customer?

✔ Why can't we give the customer what he wants?

Internal knowledge and education

The internal knowledge and education dashboard includes metrics such as employee sentiment about work, employee sentiment about qualifications, access to information, training hours, completion of/scores on certification exams, and career development hours.

The top inefficiencies to explore in this corner include the following:

✔ What are the top employee complaints?

✔ What information can't employees access?

✔ What resources are available for completing necessary education hours or certifications?

Productivity

The productivity dashboard includes metrics such as lead time, process (cycle) time, machine/process downtime, new product development time, time to market, warranty returns, sales returns, time spent servicing accounts, defect rate, process capability, cost of waste, amount of rework, labor costs, research and development costs, marketing/advertising costs, compliance costs, floor space utilization, unused inventory, and forecasting accuracy.

The top inefficiencies to explore in this corner include:

✔ Why does it take so long to get to market?

✔ What causes machine/process downtime?

✔ What causes waste such as defects or rework?

✔ Why do customers make returns? Is our return policy efficient? Should we accept returns?

✔ What are the top issues addressed during account servicing?

✔ What led to existing unused inventory?

✔ Can compliance costs (for example, inspections) be prevented?

Finances

The financial dashboard includes metrics such as revenue, market penetration, gross profit, net profit, revenue per department/division, expenses per department/division, revenues and expenses per product/service line, budgeted versus actual costs, savings, number of shipments, and number of on-time shipments.

 Thanks to tax and accounting requirements, most businesses can assemble retroactive scorecards much more easily than any other kind, which can provide additional insights into expenses, revenue, and savings. The top inefficiencies to explore in this corner include:

- ✔ What are the largest expenses company-wide?
- ✔ What are the largest expenses in each division?
- ✔ What are the largest expenses in each product line?
- ✔ What are the largest expenses in the best-selling product line?
- ✔ What divisions have increased costs over time?
- ✔ What causes delayed shipments?

If you fully adopt a Balanced Scorecard in your organization, tracking metrics over time, then a *dip* (or, if the metric is negative, such as "customer complaints," then an *increase*) in any particular metric is often a red flag that a new inefficiency has been introduced into your organization. Learn more about how to build your own scorecard in *Balanced Scorecard Strategy For Dummies*.

Going Lean

A Lean business is one that maintains an unrelenting focus on providing customer value and an unwavering disdain for waste. Just what is waste — known, in Lean parlance, as *muda*? Any cost or business process that does not create value. Rooting out *muda* in your organization is a key tenet of a Lean philosophy.

Value stream mapping

While you can review the list of the seven types of *muda* below to get your brainstorming juices flowing — and this list is a great place to start — for a deeper dive, construct a value stream map for each of your business processes. On the left, at the start of your map, is your input, such as an e-mail, a customer order, or a piece of steel. Every step on the map represents the next step that input must go through in order to arrive at or become its final destination: the end product or service. A fleshed-out value stream map indicates time and distance at each step, too.

You can write out a value stream map as a list, but it's more fun to draw it out like an actual map!

The seven types of waste

Since every *muda* is an inefficiency by definition, any internal process you identify in Table 4-1 (courtesy of *Lean For Dummies*) is one to add to the list of internal inefficiencies.

You may be thinking that some of these wastes are truly beyond your control. Regulatory demands, accounting requirements, or natural events may be causing these. For this reason, muda is divided into two classifications:

- ✔ **Type-1 muda** includes actions that are non-value-added, but are for some other reason deemed necessary. These forms of waste usually cannot be eliminated immediately.

- ✔ **Type-2 muda** are those activities that are non-value-added and are also not necessary. These are the first targets for elimination.

Table 4-1	The Seven Forms of Waste	
Form of Waste	*Also Known As*	*Explanation*
Transport	Conveyance	Any movement of product or materials that is not otherwise required to perform value-added processing is waste. The more you move, the more opportunity you have for damage or injury.
Waiting	Waiting or delay	Waiting in all forms is a waste. Any time a worker's hands are idle is a waste of that resource, whether due to shortages, unbalanced workloads, need for instructions, or by design.
Overproduction	Overproduction	Producing more than your customer requires is waste. It causes other wastes like inventory costs, manpower and conveyance to deal with excess product, consumption of raw materials, installation of excess capacity, and so on.

Form of Waste	Also Known As	Explanation
Defect	Correction, repair, rejects	Any process, product, or service that fails to meet specifications is waste. Any processing that does not transform the product or is not done right the first time is also waste.
Inventory	Inventory	Inventory anywhere in the value stream is not adding value. You may need inventory to manage imbalance between demand and production, but it is still non-value-added. It ties up financial resources. It is at risk to damage, obsolescence, spoilage, and quality issues. It takes up floor space and other resources to manage and track it. In addition, large inventories can cover up other sins in the process like imbalances, equipment issues, or poor work practices.
Motion	Motion or movement	Any movement of a person's body that does not add value to the process is waste. This includes walking, bending, lifting, twisting, and reaching. It also includes any adjustments or alignments made before the product can be transformed.
Extra processing	Processing or overprocessing	Any processing that does not add value to the product or is the result of inadequate technology, sensitive materials, or quality prevention is waste. Examples include in-process protective packaging, alignment processing such as basting in garment manufacturing or the removal of sprues in castings and molded parts.

Using Total Quality Management

Total Quality Management, or TQM, shines the spotlight on — you guessed it — quality! In a TQM organization, every product, marketing piece, customer interaction, and process needs to be of the highest-possible quality, and anything causing a process to fall short of that benchmark is an inefficiency.

To work backwards from a quality issue and determine the root causes, follow these steps from *Quality Control For Dummies*:

1. **Think of a quality problem in a process that you use every day.**

   Choose something that takes too long, occasionally fails, or delivers faulty products.

2. **Write a statement or brief explanation of what this process does.**

   For example, you can say, "Customers drop off the website and give up trying to place orders because the page takes too long to load."

3. **Create a flowchart of the process.**

   Usually this flowchart follows the Value Stream Mapping process (see Using Lean"). Sometimes, just a picture of the process suggests ways for improving it. The process flowchart should use one "box" for each significant step in the process; this setup alone may point out possible bottlenecks.

4. **Write down the problems with the process, both large and small.**

   State each problem and its undesirable result. For example, the biggest problem is a slow web page (the problem) that causes customers to give up (the undesirable result).

5. **Investigate the potential causes of the problem.**

   Use a fishbone diagram to identify the various inputs to the process. Identify several likely causes you can investigate further. The example chart for the web page would place "slow web page" at the head and each "fish bone" would identify the various parts of the process.

Shadowing Employees

Methodologies such as Lean and Balanced Scorecard can create real, lasting efficiency improvements in your organization, and I encourage you to try to one (or all!) of them on your own efficiency journey. But many people are impatient and don't want to take the time to learn an entire system or track metrics before they can start to improve their organization.

Also, frankly, when you're looking at big picture ideas like customer retention over the next five years, the number of defects per *million* times you touch something, or a warehouse of excess inventory, it's very hard to miss smaller forces that are significant drains on time and productivity. I can usually pick out some low-hanging, easy-to-fix "fruit" just by getting a tour of an office.

Pick an employee — theoretically at random, but the best choice is someone who interacts with other divisions throughout the day — and ask to shadow them for an hour or part of a day.

In order for this to work, you've got to emphasize that you're on a *positive* hunt for ways you can improve their experience at work — and that you are *not* there to check up on them or try to catch them using Facebook.

If you don't have a strong rapport with this employee and the shadowing may spook them, instead have them walk you through their daily responsibilities in "fast-forward."

Play reporter and ask tons of questions. Why is she using that program? What is that button for? Where does this form end up? How did he *used* to do this? What tasks take the longest? What tasks *feel* like they take the longest? This one-on-one method can reveal a laundry list of inefficiencies that, once remedied, will improve morale and the bottom line in big ways.

Just because an issue seems like low-hanging fruit doesn't mean you should attempt to address it right away. There may be farther-reaching consequences of which you aren't aware. Instead, take note of the issues that surface during your shadowing experiments, and then focus on finding the right solutions.

A few small wins can go a very long way toward getting employee buy-in. Identifying and remedying some immediate pain points is a far better motivator for getting people on the efficiency-enhancing bandwagon than a seminar or positive case studies. Invite an employee to shadow you for a while, too — another great way to get workers on board.

Being 99.99966 Percent Sure with Six Sigma

Six Sigma is a results-oriented, mathematically driven process-improvement methodology with a goal of perfect output. Technically, Six Sigma means "3.4 defects per million opportunities," with each opportunity being a touch point in a given product's production process. While technically 3.4 defects is shy of perfection, it's awfully close — and generally light-years closer to perfection than the majority of companies out there.

Some companies have no choice but to perform at Six Sigma (or better!) standards. For example, it's not okay if even one bottle of insulin out of tens of millions makes it onto a pharmacist's shelf at the wrong concentration — someone can die. Similarly, an automotive company not running at Six Sigma would endanger customers' lives with unsafe vehicles. While the custom dresses or business consulting services your own company provides may be less potentially lethal, creating a culture that aspires to this level of quality is attractive to many detail-oriented business owners.

Shutting down the hidden factory

Finding inefficiencies the Six Sigma way means being able to quantify the number of errors or defects at each point in your business processes. Every defect is an inefficiency, and it's then your team's job to closely analyze each defect to determine *what* caused it. (**Hint:** Usually there's more than one force at play.) In Six Sigma, the internal process of fixing mistakes is known as the *hidden factory* (see sidebar).

Learn more about integrating Six Sigma into your business in *Six Sigma For Dummies*.

Business case writing exercise

The use of a Six Sigma business case writing tool helps you identify the problem areas of a business, provide summary description or characterization of the situation, and estimate the potential value of improvement projects.

Exposing the hidden factory

Very few companies can actually achieve Six Sigma (fewer than 3.4 defects per million opportunities) or even Five Sigma (fewer than 233 defects per million opportunities) in their final products, because there are so many critical processes, process activities, machines, people, and materials that have to interact along a chain of causation and span of time.

Here's an example: The chemical properties of the catalyst that is combined with the base material, that is mixed by the processing machine, that is controlled by John, that is inspected by Sally, that is packaged by robots, that is stored in the warehouse, that is shipped to the customer via FedEx — all these have to operate in synch within certain limits of variation if the system is to reliably yield its intended outcomes. Remembering, too, that before any of this, the whole system, including the product itself, was designed by a team of engineers who are by no means infallible.

If any one of the many critical activities is compromised or doesn't function to its expectation, risk and error are propagated throughout the entire system. The system itself is also an opportunity-rich environment for hiding risk and error, because problems arising in one place and time are caused in another place and time, and the space between is extremely difficult to navigate without the proper methodologies, equipment, and people.

Among Six Sigma practitioners, this reality of fixing the results of propagated error is known as the hidden factory or hidden operation. You can almost see the wheels turning, the rework and cover-ups, and the hours and days of wasted time in a company of people who constantly correct mistakes. Every time a corrective action is taken or a machine is re-run, or a warranty claim is processed, you incur unnecessary rework. When you accept these events as "that's just the way it is," you've mentally hidden all these activities from your improvement potential.

This is the hidden factory that runs in the background of all organizations. It is the factory that fixes problems, corrects mistakes, and otherwise wastes both time and money — a company's two most precious commodities. Six Sigma eliminates the hidden factory, and, as a result, returns precious time and money back to the business.

Assemble a team and give each person a supply of blank sheets with the template below printed on them. Each person brainstorms on his own and then submits his ideas.

Template:

> As a company, our _____ performance for the _____ area is not meeting _____. Overall, this is causing _____ problems, which are costing us as much as $_____ per _____.

For example:

> As a company, our <u>response time</u> performance for the <u>customer service</u> area is not meeting <u>the targeted 24-hour window</u>. Overall, this is causing <u>negative online reviews</u>, which are costing us as much as <u>$57,000</u> per <u>year</u>.

Brainstorming Solutions

In most cases, as soon as you identify an inefficiency, you'll have at least one thought as to how to solve it. If the inefficiency lies within your area of expertise, you may have a whole stream of solutions come to you. Naturally, you should capture these initial ideas right away.

It's not always so easy. Often the solution you think of off the bat isn't the best possible option. In other cases, you may have no idea how to begin tackling a problem. This is where some brainstorming strategies for coming up with solutions comes in handy.

Do walkthroughs

Step through the process you're trying to improve, either literally or in your mind. At each step, try to imagine what you may do differently to arrive at a higher-quality or faster result, or how you might replace that step altogether.

This works best if you have significant knowledge about a given area. If your domain expertise is in finance, stepping through a manufacturing process in your head probably won't lead to many breakthroughs. On the other hand, a computer programmer can probably come up with a stellar solution for automating a boring or error-prone internal process for submitting orders to manufacturing via the computer.

Search the Internet

Odds are, someone else has had your problem before. Whether or not they chose the *right* solution is a different story, but reading case studies, blog posts, news articles, and forum discussions can uncover solutions you never would have found on your own.

You can also post your questions or dilemmas online for other people to comment on. Some online business communities are surprisingly helpful. Solid resources include the following:

- **LinkedIn Answers:** www.linkedin.com
- **Quora:** www.quora.com
- **OnStartups:** www.onstartups.com

Look outside the box

Once you've pondered a dilemma for awhile and feel stuck, one of the best things you can do is *stop* actively thinking about it. Go for a walk, go for a drive, file paperwork, seek the Zen on a yoga mat, or find another task that distracts you just enough to keep from overthinking. An idea may hit you when you least expect it. Most of my client breakthroughs happen while working on *other* clients' projects — the experience is just similar enough to keep my gears going but different enough to provide distance.

You can develop an arsenal of inefficiency fighters by simply consuming content. Books, podcasts, magazines, blogs, lectures — all can help get you thinking about your own problems from a new light. One of my favorites is watching TEDTalks — www.ted.org — inspiring, brief talks from the world's leading doctors, researchers, and creators.

Getting Started

Don't worry too much at the start about *how* inefficient a given process is or coming up with the *right* solution to address that inefficiency. It's too easy to think that the first answer someone comes up with is the *best* one, and not allow enough time or involve enough other people to potentially find an even better fit.

Choosing team members to involve

When you decide to make your organization more efficient, everyone needs to at least *know* about the initiative, even if you have so many employees that a company-wide brainstorm would require a football stadium. You need to have a mechanism (see "Capturing and Storing Suggestions"), where anyone can report problems they come across or suggest solutions even if they are not directly involved in any subsequent meetings or initiatives.

Whom you decide to include on efficiency-improvement teams has to do with your company culture. This should not be just "one more meeting" but rather a whole cultural shift toward looking at processes with an eye for improvement opportunities.

If you're up against decades of inefficiencies or even multiple failed past improvement efforts, start small. Brainstorming a smaller list of ideas that ultimately leads to a successful efficiency-enhancing project is superior to brainstorming an exhaustive company-wide list and tiring everyone out before you get to execution.

Once you have a problem statement in hand and are ready to start brainstorming solutions, there's a fine line between having too many cooks in the kitchen, and not having enough outside input. You also have to factor in how much time you are taking out of employees' lives so they can weigh in on these issues. There is a temptation at smaller companies to invite every employee to every meeting, which can become a significant time commitment across a staff that is likely already spread thin.

Don't exclude newer or less-experienced employees' involvement in favor of company veterans. Those veterans are least likely to know anything but the way they do things now, while those with recent outside experiences are probably most aware of your inefficiencies and most able to suggest solutions they've seen elsewhere.

Some of the best suggestions I've come across came from employees' *spouses* — people who have relatively intimate knowledge of your company's inner workings and yet generally also an outside perspective because they work in a different industry.

Consider ways to solicit ideas from outsiders like spouses, vendors, former employees, or even customers.

Capturing and storing suggestions

The best brainstorming session in the world isn't worth much if no one captures the output. It's critically important to store all your generated ideas *somewhere* so you can access them again not just next week, but also in future years when circumstances you can't imagine today may cause people to look back.

Capturing ongoing inefficiencies and solutions

It's impossible to capture every single problem plaguing your business or every single potential solution to those problems, just as it's impossible to root every single inefficiency out of an organization. Instead of fighting this reality, create a culture of continuous improvement and openness to feedback with an internal suggestion box.

We've all worked somewhere with a perpetually empty wooden suggestion box that gathered dust in the break room. Not only is a physical box rather stale, but it makes it hard to catalog ideas — someone ultimately has to type up the suggestions.

Make it easy for people to submit ideas as they have them. Someone on an assembly line may have a sudden thought about how to increase safety, but if your internal suggestion box is online and they don't have easy access to a computer, you're probably never going to hear their idea. In this scenario, a paper and pencil out on the floor would be a perfectly acceptable capture tool.

It's a rare employee who has an idea and then makes the effort to track down a suggestion box if they don't already know it exists. This is particularly true of temporary or substitute workers, who are a wealth of ideas precisely because they have the benefit of seeing how other, similar workplaces handle the same challenges. So, remind them!

Capture tools

Electronic capture tools make the most sense in the majority of environments, because they are both easy to update and searchable. Some tool ideas include the following:

A wiki

Each page may be devoted to a topic area (brainstorm inefficiencies around customer service or requesting time off or worker safety) or to suggesting solutions to a specific issue (ranging from the general "How can we cut costs?" to "Ways to make our customers happier"). Every person in the company should have a login. With the right moderator or spam protection to keep out Internet trolls, you can even open some areas up for public input.

A trouble ticket system

Trouble tickets are traditionally used to submit customer support inquiries or software bugs, but there's no reason you can't use one to track internal efficiency troubles. Each new idea becomes its own ticket, and others can comment on the relevancy of the issue and/or submit suggestions as comments.

Archived ideas

Why hang on to the original brainstormed solutions once you pick a direction? For one thing, the solution you ultimately choose to go with may not prove to be the best fit. An unexpected roadblock may come up — perhaps it costs more than expected, a key vendor goes out of business, or it turns out to be incompatible with existing equipment. If you can easily go back and survey other ideas, you avoid having to start the process over.

If you rule out a potential solution at some point in the future, don't simply delete it from your list. If you erase it from record, here's what inevitably happens: A year down the line, someone else peruses this old project record and thinks, "Hey, they missed a solution!" They then re-add your original, ruled-out solution and in a worst case disrupt the current situation to try to implement this older, less-appropriate solution.

Instead, record *why* you chose not to pursue a given inefficiency or solution. Your future self (and team) will thank you.

Looking at Tools

While I encourage you to grab the nearest writing utensil and piece of paper and start jotting down every potential business inefficiency that comes to mind, this format doesn't lend itself well to branching — that is, to taking hold of one brainstormed thought and letting it guide you to a new chain of thoughts. It's also hard to share a single piece of paper across a group. The following brainstorming tools can aid in your thought process.

Mind maps

You can draw a mind map (effectively a large diagram with bubbles) out on a large piece of paper or on a whiteboard, or use software to construct one electronically. Try programs such as Google Drawing (www.google.com/drive), Omnigraffle (www.omnigraffle.com), or Microsoft Office Visio (http://office.microsoft.com/en-us/visio/).

Start with a single concept in the center bubble, such as "expenses." Draw an adjoining bubble for each expense you think of or that a team member shouts out. Once you've compiled your first list (expenses), draw ideas for eliminating or reducing each expense off that expense's bubble.

Value stream maps

These maps can be visual enough that a newcomer can quickly get up to speed and add their contributions, yet detailed enough to really drill down into specifics for time, distance, and other important metrics. You can start on the left with your initial input and work toward the final output on the right, or go backward. You can't be too detailed — tracking wait times, ship times, dollar amounts, distance traveled, and any other relevant details are all chances to think of new ways to shave off time, costs, or defects.

Affinity diagrams

An affinity diagram is the outcome of an exercise whereby members of the team write their brainstorming ideas onto small, separate pieces of paper or sticky-back notes. Then the team silently groups the individual idea notes into natural categories. The resulting collection of grouped ideas creates an affinity diagram. This modified brainstorming technique has the advantage of gathering all team members' input without the inhibition of criticism.

Chapter 5

Efficiency on Impact: Understanding the Ripple Effect of Change

*J*ohn Donne once wrote "no man is an island, entire of itself" and that same concept applies to every business process. Upgrading a piece of assembly line equipment invariably impacts not just manufacturing, but also accounting, employee sentiment, legal, human resources, and product quality, just to name a few.

Chapter 4 discusses tracking down inefficiencies and brainstorming ways to fix them. In this chapter, I look at the impact of each proposed solution on your whole company. (See Chapter 4 to read up on these solutions.)

This is a step I see organizations overlook again and again, often at great expense. In the grand scheme of things, it's much simpler to check for potential breakages or snags *before* you get started than to try to salvage the situation after you hit a perfectly avoidable iceberg.

Failure to really look at the big picture can have catastrophic outcomes. For example, one client's excited rush to upgrade the accounting software failed to acknowledge the new program's incompatibility with the existing manufacturing mainframe. Post-upgrade, every order had to be *manually* entered into the new accounting software. Morale and productivity took a real nosedive for the three months it took to build a custom middleware solution, at significant expense. All that was needed to avoid this scenario was to ask the IT Department if it had any feedback on the new software.

After you get in the habit of considering the big picture before choosing the route you plan to take, this step becomes second nature. In this chapter, I walk you through the basic steps for vetting any proposal thoroughly, and show you how to capture that vetting process into an easily replicable one for the future.

Finding Out How Inefficiency Negatively Impacts You

Before you get into sussing out the potential new inefficiencies that you may accidentally unleash in pursuit of greater efficiency, take a step back and review the negative impact inefficiencies in all forms are having on you right now.

Inefficiency costs money

According to *Six Sigma For Dummies*, inefficiencies cost many organizations as much as 20 to 30 percent of their revenue each year. Imagine what your company could do it if had 20 percent extra funds to funnel into customer acquisition or research and development.

Sometimes people, equipment, or processes come at a premium. That's perfectly all right — efficiency is not about paying your employees minimum wage and scrimping on product quality.

Inefficiency is when you spend more money than you needed to in order to arrive at the same result. Defective products that need to be discarded, excess inventory, and even long-distance phone call overage fees are expenses that only deplete your bottom line — so get rid of them.

Inefficiency wastes time

You may be able to squeeze every last cent out of a dollar, but there is no squeezing any additional seconds from a day. Every minute squandered is lost forever, never to return. Time spent waiting, whether for a process to finish or for a manager to tell you what to do next, is also time lost.

When it comes to efficiency, time is not just measured in minutes and hours, but also in potential output. A crabby, scared, or underappreciated employee is simply not going to create the same amount or level of work as a well-rested, satisfied, fulfilled one in the same span of time.

Employee sentiment has a great deal to do with making the most of your company's available hours. Measures to make your workplace more enjoyable, cleaner, safer, or even simply less boring can go a long way here.

Inefficiency reduces quality

As process improvement methodologies Total Quality Management and Six Sigma remind us, every defect or missed quality benchmark is an inefficiency. Unhappy employees and older machinery tend to cause more errors than their more efficient counterparts. Subpar quality control processes don't catch errors in time, resulting in defective merchandise potentially reaching customers.

I've never encountered a situation where a business wanted to produce quality results 82 percent of the time, and I've also never met a business that had to settle for such numbers after undertaking efficiency improvements. Correcting inefficiencies across a process can have a major impact on success rates in any business, and get those quality results up.

Inefficiency damages morale

Rote or error-prone tasks are frustrating. If you have to perform them four or even eight hours a day, you will not be particularly apt to go the extra mile or perhaps even to smile.

While I've been the catalyst behind replacing more than one employee with a piece of machinery or an Excel macro in my day, I have to believe that a task that can be replaced with equipment was not particularly fulfilling or engaging. Further, eliminating inefficiencies doesn't always mean letting employees go — they can often be redirected to more interesting *and* meaningful work (really!).

Know what else hurts morale? A lack of trust, which is the direct result of an inefficient project management process. When projects are announced only to disappear into the ether, when milestone after milestone is set only to go by unacknowledged, and when upper management touts dedication to goals that are not aligned with their actions, employees become all the more disenchanted.

An efficient workplace that delivers what it promises to high quality standards is a place where people *want* to work, and that can make all the difference for your sales, marketing, and customer service efforts.

Discovering Inefficiency's Roots

It's been said that those who do not understand their history are doomed to repeat it. This is true when it comes to business mistakes, too. Inefficiencies — particularly severe ones — don't just appear out of nowhere. With 20/20 hindsight, you can often clearly see how your organization ended up making a particular decision or found itself in a given situation.

Knowing how you got where you are doesn't give you a crystal ball for predicting all future inefficiencies, but it does provide some serious insights to aid you in moving forward.

For example, if your computers weren't upgraded for 10 years because the CEO himself doesn't have a computer and didn't understand the difference, delegating future technology decisions to a trusted but more tech-savvy manager can help the company make better-informed choices going forward.

When you find yourself evaluating a business process for improvements or solutions, it can be instructive to work backward and find out how it came to be this way. You can research a given process's history by talking to current or even former employees. If you really want the scoop, look to veteran employees in other departments who may have domain knowledge — particularly the receptionist and the accountant, who usually have the strongest *and* most perceptive memories.

The following sections describe the main culprits I've found behind major inefficiencies.

Not keeping abreast of new technology

This is far and away the most common situation I run across, because it's very hard to know what you do not know. (It's also the biggest benefit to hiring the right outside consultant, who has constant exposure to and experience with tools and processes you may not even know exist.) It's a particular problem in older and/or low-tech businesses with fewer opportunities for exposure to new innovations.

Failing to communicate

When employees or divisions within a company make decisions in a vacuum, it often creates a cascading effect across the entire organization. (Preventing negative cascades is the point of this chapter, in fact.) The sales team switching to a new CRM software meant the support team had to log in to two systems simultaneously to see customer phone numbers. Clearing out the storage room for the cleaners left manufacturing without spokes for a day because they couldn't locate them.

Forgetting your company's history

If this is the year your company goes paperless or switches to electronic billing, it's important that *next* year, everyone remembers this. Too often initiatives conclude or cheerleaders leave the company and those behind slowly forget why a decision was made — or that a decision was made at all.

Preventing Inefficiencies in the Future

Inefficiencies are a fact of business. There will also be *something* to improve. What you should aim to avoid, however, is letting *avoidable* inefficiencies enter (or worse, reenter!) your organization.

Staying informed

You can't know everything about everything, but you can occasionally pick up a business magazine from the newsstand or peruse a productivity blog. Although you should give priority to industry-focused publications, you should also explore unknown territory — checking out the latest tech tools for realtors may indirectly inform you of a new electronic billing service that your medical supply company can use.

Although they're unfortunately often boring sales tactics, newsletters and white papers from your vendors can also give you a heads-up about new features, software titles, or opportunities that can make your business more efficient today.

Empowering your employees

Your employees are not stupid. (Hopefully.) If they are good enough for you to hire them to do their jobs, then they also become the experts at performing those jobs.

You should always give your employees places to submit their ideas for aspects of the company that need improvement or for specific improvements, and encourage them to do so. But you can take this a step further by giving them a bit of room to experiment.

Giving employees the space to try out efficiency improvements on their own is one way to prevent them for waiting for "someone else" to remedy their issues. If Zach thinks that he can get his work done more efficiently by using Gmail instead of Outlook, let him try — with the caveat that he is responsible for reporting back on the results in a meaningful way.

If one of these experiments fails, it's actually a success in a way — Zach feels content that you heard his suggestion and were open to trying it, and you know not only that the switch in e-mail programs didn't work for his position, but *why*. This information can be revisited later in a larger-scale project or if the programs change significantly in the future.

Creating a culture of continuous improvement

This is a lofty goal for many organizations, but that doesn't mean you can't take steps toward it. Efficiency is a mindset and a lens (though not the only lens) through which you can view every business decision. Creating a work environment where this comes naturally, as opposed to being a standalone project, takes time and effort.

The first step is to model this behavior yourself. Are you using efficiency as a factor when making business decisions? Are you talking about efficiency in everyday conversations, naturally? Are you highlighting positive efficiency wins for everyone to hear? After you've started to get into the habit, it's time to instill this attitude into management and, where appropriate, into existing or new formal planning processes.

You can learn more about creating a culture of continuous improvement in *Lean For Dummies*.

Evaluating the Possible Impacts of Change

Every change in an organization has a ripple effect. This is not necessarily a bad thing — these ripples can be positive as well as negative, and proper planning can negate many potential negative ripples — but the key is to be aware of the greater reaction.

Let's take the example of upgrading a piece of manufacturing equipment to a more efficient model. What ramifications might that one change have elsewhere?

- ✔ For the accounting department, the equipment's deposit and monthly installments must be paid on time. It must be amortized on tax returns and added to insurance policies. Budgets may need adjusting to account for more expensive (though presumably less frequent) maintenance and repair services.

- ✔ Employee sentiment changes as the equipment's introduction may cause workers to worry they will be replaced by machines or that additional new equipment will require skills they do not possess. The unfamiliarity may make them concerned for their safety, or having updated machinery may make them feel safer. The new features of the upgrade may also make them happier. The machine may be more enjoyable to operate. It may spark competition or resentment from employees who still have to use similar, non-upgraded equipment.

- ✔ Productivity slows during the first week as employees get used to operating the new machinery. For three hours, the line halts entirely because Henry pushed a button sending the machine into reverse and no one is immediately sure how to switch it back. The defect rate spikes temporarily as the material on the line was damaged when the machine was knocked into reverse.

- ✔ Human resources needs to update employee safety training materials to include the new equipment, and film a new training video.

Again, none of these ramifications are bad, provided you have planned ahead for them. Even Henry's snafu with the reverse button, which we'll categorize under "novice user error," is something that an experienced project manager would have allotted for in a plan. Mistakes are commonplace and not entirely avoidable when learning to use new machines or processes.

Assembling an efficiency jury

Now that you have a solid grasp of the sorts of factors to keep in mind when reviewing possible solutions to your organization's problems, it's time to put together a team and get to evaluating.

The core team to vet solutions is going to be the employees directly involved in the process being improved. If there are a number of employees, assembling representatives from each team can get the ball rolling, with each individual employee being afforded the chance to weigh in on the final decision.

If a particular employee pointed out this problem or contributed a solution, include them in this process, too.

Six Sigma teams include functional representatives to serve as the voice of every support team that may be affected by and/or have input on a given project. Even if you're not using Six Sigma elsewhere, the concept of functional representatives is *key* to vetting a solution effectively.

Performing a cost-benefit analysis

A cost-benefit analysis is a comparative assessment of all the costs to introduce the solution, perform it, and support the changes resulting from it and all the benefits you anticipate from your solution. Cost-benefit analyses help you

- Decide whether to undertake a solution or decide which of several solutions to undertake

- Frame appropriate project objectives

- Develop appropriate before-and-after measures of project success

- Prepare estimates of the resources required to perform the project work

You can express some anticipated benefits in monetary equivalents (such as reduced operating costs or increased revenue). For other benefits, numerical measures can approximate some, but not all, aspects. If your project is to improve staff morale, for example, you may consider associated benefits to include reduced turnover, increased productivity, fewer absences, and fewer formal grievances. Whenever possible, express benefits and costs in monetary terms to facilitate the assessment of a project's net value.

Consider costs for all phases of the project. Such costs may be nonrecurring (such as labor, capital investment, and certain operations and services) or recurring (such as changes in personnel, supplies, and materials or maintenance and repair). In addition, consider the following:

- Potential costs of not doing the solution

- Potential costs if the solution fails

- Opportunity costs (in other words, the potential benefits if you had spent your funds successfully performing a different project)

The farther into the future you look when performing your analysis, the more important it is to convert your estimates of benefits over costs into today's dollars. Unfortunately, the farther you look, the less confident you can be of your estimates. For example, you may expect to reap benefits for years from a new computer system, but changing technology may make your new system obsolete after only one year.

Thus, the following two key factors influence the results of a cost-benefit analysis:

- How far into the future you look to identify benefits

- On which assumptions you base your analysis

The excess of a solution's expected benefits over its estimated costs in today's dollars is its net present value (NPV). The net present value is based on the following two premises:

- **Inflation:** The purchasing power of a dollar will be less one year from now than it is today. If the rate of inflation is 3 percent for the next 12 months, $1 today will be worth $0.97 12 months from today. In other words, 12 months from now, you'll pay $1 to buy what you paid $0.97 for today.

- **Lost return on investment:** If you spend money to perform the project being considered, you'll forego the future income you can earn by investing it today. For example, if you put $1 in a bank and receive simple interest at the rate of 3 percent compounded annually, 12 months from today, you'll have $1.03 (assuming zero percent inflation).

To address these considerations when determining the NPV, you specify the following numbers:

- **Discount rate:** The factor that reflects the future value of $1 in today's dollars, considering the effects of both inflation and lost return on investment

- **Allowable payback period:** The length of time for anticipated benefits and estimated costs

In addition to determining the NPV for different discount rates and payback periods, figure the project's internal rate of return (the value of discount rate that would yield an NPV of zero) for each payback period.

Each support team needs to weigh in on your proposed solutions, so whenever possible, get a representative from each of the following divisions:

- ✔ Information Technology (IT)
- ✔ Legal
- ✔ Human resources
- ✔ Finance
- ✔ Customer support

You don't have to involve your functional representatives in identifying the initial positives and negatives, but they should definitely each weigh in on the impact of the ideas that make it past that phase.

Looking at common areas of impact

Whether your functional representatives need a jumping-off point or if your team is looking for a checklist with which to warm up, the following areas are commonly impacted by organizational change:

- ✔ **Finances:** On its face, how much will this solution cost? How much do you estimate it will save? What are the associated interest, maintenance, repair, warranty, and other ongoing expenses? Are there tax ramifications? How do the long-term benefits compare to the long-term costs? (See the "Performing a cost-benefit analysis" sidebar.)

- ✔ **Human Resources:** Will this solution require the addition or reduction of staff members? Outside consulting or temp workers? Will employee training materials need to be updated? Is it in compliance with OSHA and other regulations?

- ✔ **Legal:** Is it legal? Everywhere? Are there tax law implications? How might this solution impact the chances of being sued? How many hours of legal time are necessary? Do you have to sign a contract?

- ✔ **Quality:** How might this solution increase product quality? Where may it potentially introduce errors or new defects? What existing defects will it remedy?

- ✔ **Customer Service:** How might this solution increase or decrease customer complaints? Warranty returns? The number of customer inquiries? How will it impact response time? How about the quality of customer service interactions?

- ✔ **Customer Sentiment:** How might this solution impact how your customers feel about your organization? About a particular product line or service? Can this lead to bad press?

- **Employee Sentiment:** Will this solution decrease or increase unpleasant work? How do employees feel about it? Will it cause some employees to be treated differently than others? What happens if employees are resistant to this change?

- **Technology:** Is this solution compatible with your current software? Hardware? Machinery? Can you upgrade it? Does it require special tools or software? Do you have the in-house resources to install, maintain, and troubleshoot related issues?

- **Time:** How long will it take to implement this solution? How long before it becomes "second nature" to the organization? How much time will it take or save? What impact will it have on the productivity of those hours?

- **Business Goals:** How does this solution align with business goals? Does it really align or is it a reach?

- **Resources/Skills:** What new skills might this solution introduce into the company? What skills are required to implement it? To maintain it? Do you have those skills internally?

- **Longevity:** How long is this solution expected to last? Can you upgrade? Do you have to upgrade? What are the replacement or upgrade costs? Can equipment or supplies purchased for this solution be resold when a new solution is needed?

- **Downtime:** How long will key employees need to be away from their roles for training? How long until employees are fully-trained? How long will a process be down if the new solution breaks? Is there a backup?

- **Failure:** What happens if this solution doesn't go according to plan? What are the worst case scenarios in terms of cost, time, and sentiment?

Don't forget to consider the impact the status quo is having on each of these areas, too. The new solution should have a net positive impact on the organization relative to a scenario in which you do not adopt that solution.

Predicting the impact of future change

Because the point of this vetting process is to understand the impact of a change on your entire organization, it should look similar from project to project, regardless of the division from which a project originates.

Keep a master list of the functional representatives that you assemble for your first project, and update it as needed during future projects. The *names* of these people aren't important for this list, but rather their roles. You will use this list to make sure every role is filled when vetting future projects.

Additionally, keep track of each impact area that comes up during your projects, whether during the vetting stage or after you implement a project and an unexpected impact surfaces. Some impact areas, such as time and finance, apply to every company across the board. Others may be more specific to your industry or way of doing business.

After you've been through the ropes a few times, this plan will move from a working draft to a reliable checklist. It doesn't have to be intricate — in fact, a basic bulleted list of roles to include and impact areas to consider is all you need here. Keep this list in a central location so everyone can use it in their own planning endeavors.

Setting Up Feedback Channels

After you've decided on the best solution — but *before* you start to implement it — you need to make sure you have mechanisms in place to track its success. After you develop solid feedback channels in the relevant places, they should serve you well for every project going forward.

I can guarantee you that sooner rather than later you'll find that a solution you implemented led to unexpected consequences, didn't perform up to par, or performed well for a while and then fell short in time — no matter how well you planned in advance. You can't plan for all eventualities, but you can definitely plan for not being able to plan for all eventualities.

When you have *one* efficiency-enhancing project on your plate, these results are not so hard to see. But in a few years when you're churning out efficiency improvements right and left, you need to have trustworthy feedback channels to alert you to the first signs of trouble.

"Trouble" can range from reporting confusion over the steps of a new process to an equipment malfunction to an ill employee or a reversion back to the original way of doing things.

The focus is not to create a workforce of tattletales, but rather to hear about those things that *don't* go according to plan so they can be addressed (not disciplined).

Anyone who interacts with your business can be affected by — and is therefore capable of sharing feedback on — your projects. Make sure each of the following has a means of contacting you *and knows to use it:*

- ✔ Internal employees (from CEO to temps)
- ✔ Outside consultants
- ✔ Vendors
- ✔ Current customers
- ✔ Potential customers

Places to gather feedback include the following:

- ✔ Internal wiki
- ✔ Trouble ticket system
- ✔ Internal check-in meetings (especially at the beginning)
- ✔ Website contact form
- ✔ E-mail to the project owner (this requires maintaining an accurate internal list of historical project owners)

There's no point in having feedback channels if no one with any responsibility is on the other end. Someone always needs to be in charge of acting on that feedback or routing it to the appropriate parties.

You need to hammer home to employees that it's okay to ask for help or clarification in times of change. If an employee isn't comfortable asking questions, he's liable to negatively affect measurements of the new solution's success by being slower or less effective than possible, or he may simply revert to the old way of doing things.

Chapter 6

To Efficiency . . . and Beyond: Getting Where You Want to Be

In This Chapter

▶ Getting clear on why you need clear efficiency goals

▶ Picking the best project to start right now

▶ Setting efficiency goals across multiple categories

▶ Planning your next steps after setting goals

Chapter 4 covers how to identify your inefficiencies and brainstorm solutions, and Chapter 5 discusses how to narrow down your best options for tackling them based on their potential impact across your entire organization.

But before you go implementing those solutions, you need to get clear on what the goal is.

In this chapter, I go through the hallmarks of a good goal. Spoiler alert: "be more efficient" is a terrible goal. Your goals need clarity and specificity if you're to know whether you're on the right track and, more importantly, when you're done.

Inefficiencies take multiple forms, and you can capture this by setting multiple types of goals, from financial savings to improved sentiment. Considering different angles can keep your efficiency-enhancing efforts from veering off course by, for example, saving significant money (good) but lowering your service quality (not so good)

I also go over what's often the biggest question I get: Where do you start? It's only after you've acknowledged your problems, vetted your solutions, and set your goals that you have enough information to make the right choice for your company.

Setting Efficiency Goals

You may know what the problem is and have a solution at hand, but unfortunately efficiency is not always as reliable as a math equation. For starters, you rarely have an ironclad guarantee that your solution will *actually* work. And further, how do you even *know* whether it worked? That's where goals come in.

How goals give direction and focus

Neither identifying an inefficiency nor identifying a solution for addressing that inefficiency really captures the *end result* you are trying to achieve. In project management, a project without a stated objective is dead in the water.

Goals tell you where you want to be, and are the metrics by which you can tell when you've arrived (or driven five miles in the wrong direction).

Not only may a proposed *solution* not solve an inefficiency, but it's also very possible that fully addressing a given inefficiency may not realize your ultimate goal.

Say you notice that customer satisfaction has dropped from 95 percent "fully satisfied" to 85 percent "fully satisfied" in this year's annual customer survey. Further investigation shows that average customer support wait times rose from 30 seconds to 9 minutes during that time. Guessing that the inefficiency of long wait times is lowering satisfaction, you employ additional support staff to field phone calls, with a goal to return to at least a 95 percent "fully satisfied" rating at the next review.

The additional staff support reduces average wait times to zero. Awesome — you've eliminated one of the wastes of Lean, *waiting*. The solution worked to address the inefficiency. However, when reviews come in, customer satisfaction hasn't budged.

It ultimately turns out that a new, confusingly worded product manual was frustrating customers and causing an increase in support calls and call times. Eliminating the need to call in at all, not how long customers had to wait on the line, was what ultimately restored sentiment scores.

If the overall goal had not been in place, it would have been all too easy to close this project as not just *complete*, but also as a *complete success*, when it was nothing of the sort.

Clear goals can also make it easier to choose which projects to tackle first or next. It's generally easier for a group of people to prioritize company goals than it is to rank inefficiencies.

What makes a good goal?

You need to be crystal clear when stating your project's objectives. The more specific your project objectives are, the greater your chances are of achieving them. Here are some tips for developing clear objectives:

- ✔ **Be brief when describing each objective.** If you take an entire page to describe a single objective, most people won't read it. Even if they do read it, your objective probably won't be clear and may have multiple interpretations.

- ✔ **Don't use technical jargon or acronyms.** Each industry (such as pharmaceuticals, telecommunications, finance, and insurance) has its own vocabulary, and so does each company within that industry. Within companies, different departments (such as accounting, legal, and information services) also have their own jargons. Because of this proliferation of specialized languages, the same three-letter acronym (TLA) can have two or more meanings in the same organization! To reduce the chances for misunderstandings, express your objectives in language that people of all backgrounds and experiences are familiar with.

- ✔ **Make your objectives S.M.A.R.T., as follows:**

  - **S**pecific: Define your objectives clearly, in detail, with no room for misinterpretation.

  - **M**easurable: State the measures and performance specifications you'll use to determine whether you've met your objectives.

  - **A**ggressive: Set challenging objectives that encourage people to stretch beyond their comfort zones.

  - **R**ealistic: Set reasonable objectives that are achievable.

  - **T**ime sensitive: Include the date by which you'll achieve the objectives.

- ✔ **Make your objectives controllable.** Make sure that you and your team believe you can influence the success of each objective. If you don't believe you can, you may not commit 100 percent to achieving it (and most likely you won't even try). In that case, it becomes a wish, not an objective.

- ✔ **Identify all objectives.** Time and resources are always scarce, so if you don't specify an objective, you won't (and shouldn't) work to achieve it.

Beware of competitive goals. They bring out employees' competitive natures, and the drive to win can, in some scenarios, lead some employees to sabotage others' efficiencies. At best, it will mean individuals and teams are secretive about their processes, which does nothing to encourage efficiency broadly across the organization. You can set a company-wide goal with a benefit (such as a day off or a catered lunch) that extends to everyone, but don't create competitions that pit departments against departments (unless you're at the company picnic!).

Overcoming excuses for not setting clear goals

Excuse 1: Too much specificity stifles creativity.

Response: Creativity should be encouraged — the question is where and when. You want your project's drivers to be clear and precise when stating their objectives; you want your project's supporters to be creative when figuring out ways to meet these objectives. You want to understand what people *do* expect from your project, not what they *may* expect. The more clearly you can describe their actual objectives, the easier it is to determine whether (and how) you can meet them.

Excuse 2: Your project entails research and new development, and you can't tell today what you'll be able to accomplish.

Response: Objectives are targets, not guarantees. Certain projects have more risks than others. When you haven't done a task before, you don't know whether it's possible. And, if it is possible, you don't know how long it'll take and how much it'll cost. But you must state at the outset exactly what you want to achieve and what you think is possible, even though you may have to change your objectives as the project progresses.

Excuse 3: What if interests or needs change?

Response: Objectives are targets based on what you know and expect today. If conditions change in the future, you may have to revisit one or more of your objectives to see whether they're still relevant and feasible or whether they, too, must change.

Excuse 4: The project's requestor doesn't know what they specifically want their project to achieve.

Response: them to come back when they do. If you begin working on this project now, you have a greater chance of wasting time and resources to produce results that the requestor later decides they doesn't want.

Excuse 5: Even though specific objectives help determine when you've succeeded, they also make it easier to determine when you haven't.

Response: Yep. That's true. However, because your project was framed to accomplish certain results, you need to know whether those results were achieved. If they weren't, you may have to perform additional work to accomplish them. In addition, you want to determine the benefits the organization is realizing from the money it's spending.

Who sets the goals?

Who sets a goal has much to do with who is expected to achieve it.

Be sure drivers and supporters agree on your project's objectives. When drivers buy into your objectives, you feel confident that achieving the objectives constitutes true project success. When supporters buy into your objectives, you have the greatest chance that people will work their hardest to achieve them.

If drivers don't agree with your objectives, revise them until they do agree. After all, your drivers' needs are the whole reason for your project! If supporters don't buy into your objectives, work with them to identify their concerns and develop approaches they think can work.

Company-wide goals

Goals for the entire organization, such as overall increases in revenue, customer satisfaction rates, or market share, are usually set by upper management. However, representatives from particular divisions should have a way to weigh in on their practicality or relevance before these goals are formally adopted.

Organizations should be setting broad goals regardless of whether they are involved or even interested in efficiency improvements.

Departmental/divisional goals

Each division or team within a company generally sets goals for projects for which it is directly responsible. It may also need to set goals specific to its own role in company-wide goals. For example, if there's a company-wide initiative to cut costs by 10 percent, then each department needs to adopt that 10 percent metric as its own goal, too.

On a joint project, goals can be set collectively or separate divisions can set their own goals if responsibilities are clearly divided. Usually this is *not* the case, however. You can't, for example, tell accounting to save 10 percent and tell manufacturing to decrease defects by 10 percent independently of one another on the same project — manufacturing needs to be cost-conscious in its solutions, too.

Individual goals

Sometimes inefficiencies are identified on an individual basis. Maybe Marty's output rate is significantly behind his peers', or the accounting department is a single person. In these cases, it's critical that the individual responsible for meeting the goal participates in defining that goal. Simply being assigned a quota or assignment by a manager (or worse, by management two chains above you) is a morale-killer.

There's a difference between individual goals and divisional goals with individual components. An individual goal is one for a specific person, such as "Marissa will close 10 new deals by August 1." A division goal affecting individuals may be "Every person on the sales team will close 10 new deals by August 1," but it does not single out just one person.

When do you track goal progress?

I cover this in Chapter 7, but there's one point that's worth emphasizing right here. You have to *check* on your goals' progress, especially if these goals are long-term, such as an annual increase in revenue or customer retention. If you don't realize you're only 10 percent of the way to reaching your fiscal year until the middle of November, you don't have much time to change course or reevaluate your project.

Unless your project has an extremely short shelf life, it needs multiple deadline checkpoints between the time you start executing the project and the anticipated completion date. Tactical dashboards from the Balanced Scorecard methodology are particularly useful here, as they refresh key project metrics on a daily basis. Learn more about constructing dashboards in Chapter 4 and in *Balanced Scorecard Strategy For Dummies*.

Finding Different Types of Efficiency Goals

"Efficiency" is not a standalone metric. Rather, it always refers to another measure, whether that is money, time, quality, or something else entirely. A well-rounded efficiency-enhancing endeavor includes a number of different types of goals to ensure that the project's spirit is clear to all current and future participants.

Working on a single metric can leave the door wide open for missteps, whether they be accidentally tanking quality in pursuit of cost savings, or missing secondary goals (you want to improve customer service response times *and* customer service satisfaction).

Use the following sections to help your creative juices flow as you brainstorm goals for your company, your division, or yourself.

Monetary goals: What to save, what to earn

Common types of goals related to *money* include the following:

✔ **Spend $X or X percent less**

- Spend $50,000 less on research and development in the next six months.
- Spend 10 percent less in every department this fiscal year.

✔ **Earn $X or X percent more**

- Earn $100,000 more on Product Line A this fiscal year.
- Earn 15 percent more from outside sales next month.

✔ **Increase net profit by $X or X percent**

✔ **Increase billable hours**

- Bill at least 27 hours per week per consultant for the next six months.

✔ **Decrease non-billable hours**

- Reduce non-billable hours to less than 10 per employee per week.

Percentages are better suited for organizations trying to fight financial bloat, but exact dollar amounts are necessary when you have specific budgets or only a certain amount of money in the bank with which to work.

Goals to improve sentiment: Make them love you

Common types of goals related to customer or employee sentiment include the following:

✔ **Increase employee satisfaction with *X***

- Increase employee satisfaction with growth opportunities to 98 percent.

- Increase employee satisfaction with their current qualifications by 5 percent.

- Reach 100 percent employee satisfaction with their current positions.

✔ **Increase brand awareness**

- *Reach 67 percent brand awareness in our target market of 18- to 35-year-old females*

Set stretch goals from Six Sigma

Six Sigma isn't for the mildly ambitious manager or the person who wants to incrementally improve the output of a process. Rather, Six Sigma is for people who want to improve by leaps and bounds.

Six Sigma has repeatedly proven that it produces breakthrough improvement. But to achieve this, you have to combine the power of the Six Sigma method and tools with *stretch goals*, goals that almost seem too aggressive, too optimistic.

Specifically, a stretch goal represents a 70 percent improvement over current performance. For example, if your company's profit margin is 7 percent, you want to aim for 11.9 percent (a 70 percent increase). Or if a certain process or product is producing ten defects per 100 units, you want to reduce that number to 3 defects per 100 units (a 70 percent improvement).

✔ **Increase customer satisfaction**

  • *Reach 98 percent customer satisfaction after support calls by January 17.*

✔ **Increase customer retention**

  • Increase the percentage of renewing subscribers to 50 percent this month

Goals to increase product and service quality

Common types of goals related to product or service quality include the following:

✔ **Increase on-time deliveries**

  • Increase on-time deliveries to 92 percent.

✔ **Decrease defects**

  • Decrease defect rate in labeling to 50 defects per million.

✔ **Decrease rework**

  • Decrease rework percentage in manufacturing to less than 1 percent of production.

✔ **Decrease "no-go's" (products that are unacceptably defective)**

  • Decrease no-go's to no more than 1 per week.

✔ **Decrease variation**

  • Decrease widget width variation to 0.003mm.

  • Decrease widget thickness variation by 50 percent.

✔ **Decrease unused inventory**

  • Decrease unused inventory so it all fits in the storage room.

✔ **Increase the # or % of successful support inquiries**

  • Increase the percent of resolved customer support inquiries by 10 percent.

✔ **Decrease customer returns**

  • Decrease warranty returns by 70 percent over the next year.

✔ **Increase Sigma**

  • Operate manufacturing at Five Sigma next year (or fewer than 233 defects per million opportunities). More on Six Sigma in Chapters 7 and 19.

Goals to shorten response and production times

Common types of goals related to time or speed include:

✔ **Decrease time**

- Lower lead times by 20 minutes.

- Eliminate waiting time between Assembly Lines A and B.

- Decrease Takt time by 10 percent.

- Decrease time from customer order to receipt of product to five business days by March.

- Decrease the time it takes to switch from assembly to packaging by three minutes.

- Decrease production time to under two weeks by December 1.

✔ **Decrease distance**

- Decrease the distance walked by assembly line employees by 10 percent.

✔ **Increase uptime**

- Increase service availability to 99.999 percent.

- Increase support hours by 10 percent.

✔ **Decrease customer support hold times**

- Decrease average customer support hold time to 30 seconds.

✔ **Decrease support resolution times**

- Decrease average support resolution time to 24 hours.

 Goals can also be phrased negatively or neutrally. For example, "Remain #1 in our region for sales" is a neutral goal, where you want to maintain a position rather than change it. Similarly, "Don't reduce customer satisfaction by more than 5 percent" may be a secondary goal for a cost-savings project.

Goals for individual employees and departments

Common types of goals for individual employees include the following:

✔ **Increase certification**

- Increase employee scores on annual safety exams to an average of 92.

- Increase the number of Six Sigma black belts to 12.

✔ **Increase employee interactions**

- The CEO will spend at least one hour per month with each employee one-on-one.

✔ **Decrease safety incidents**

- Have zero accidents next year.

✔ **Increase employee retention**

- Retain each employee for at least one year.

Knowing Where to Start

It's tempting to want to tackle *every* inefficiency all at once, and try to become a lean, mean efficiency machine as quickly as possible. Unfortunately, efficiency doesn't quite work this way.

For one, your organization has limited resources. Taking on more active projects than you have the resources to support is the very definition of *in*efficiency.

Additionally, running too many projects simultaneously can make it very difficult to determine what factors contribute to success (or to failure). This is hard enough to parse out confidently even if you have a single project running across the entire company. Two simultaneous projects can be working in direct opposition to one another, costing much in the way of resources and producing zero in the way of results.

When vetting projects on which to execute, you need to cover two bases. First, is this project both possible and feasible? And second, of the potential projects that pass the first litmus test, which one is most appropriate to start first?

Putting your best foot forward

You can start your trek towards efficiency on the right foot by starting with the right project or small selection of projects.

Decision makers consider the following two questions when deciding whether to move ahead with a project:

> ✔ *Should* **we do it?** Are the benefits we expect to achieve worth the costs we'll have to pay? Are there better ways to approach the issue? Is its objective in alignment with all of our company goals?
>
> ✔ *Can* **we do it?** Is the project technically feasible? Are the required resources available?

Resources to consider include the following:

> ✔ **Can we afford it in monetary terms?** If the money's not in the bank and you can't or won't borrow the necessary funds, you have no choice but to table a goal.
>
> ✔ **Do we have the employee time available?** If your whole staff is already working overtime, then you should tackle goals that increase available time first. You can then use that newfound time for other projects.
>
> ✔ **Do we have the time available to handle training or delays/defects caused during the transition?** Some downtime (or at least *slowed* time) is part of every organizational change. If you're up against the wire to fulfill a client deadline or regulatory compliance project, now is not the time to experiment.
>
> ✔ **Do we have enough team members?** If not, are additional staff members, temp workers, consultants, or third-party vendors available in the market? Can you afford to hire them?
>
> ✔ **Do we know enough?** Picking a technology upgrade project if you have no internal staff members who work in technology requires extra care and trustworthy outside resources. It's possible, but this sort of tricky project is not a good choice for an initial project.
>
> ✔ **Do we have employee buy-in?** I've known few employees to outright embrace change, but there's a difference between hesitance and resistance. If people are dead-set against a project or refusing to participate, you need to pick another project (or get a new team).

Choosing the most efficient execution order

There's no one right answer as to which project you should tackle first, but considering the following criteria will surely bubble a project or two up to the top of your list.

Mission critical

Inefficiencies that put the future existence of your company in peril need to be addressed first. If you can't make payroll next month, all efforts need to be on finding new sources of revenue or ways to cut expenses *immediately*.

Some mission-critical projects are less obvious than having too little money in business checking. For example, an inefficiency may be so frustrating that a key employee (or entire team) is ready to quit over it. Lax record-keeping, lack of an office manager, or a failure to track and encourage training hours may leave your organization facing the loss of required certifications or stiff fines from regulatory compliance agencies. The impending closure of a current vendor needs to be addressed before your inventory depletes.

Low-hanging fruit

Some projects stand out as having short timeframes, big gains, and little risk. These are great places to start, because team members get to see relatively immediate results with a lower chance of experiencing failure their first time up to bat.

Be careful to judge a project's simplicity by *company* standards and not simply your own gut feeling. For example, upgrading all the company computers sounds to many people like a low-hanging-fruit project. After all, you can go to the store, buy a new laptop, and be up and running (and *excited* about it) in a couple of hours.

However, upgrading computers across an entire team isn't that simple. Downtime is involved in setting up multiple machines at once, plus you have to consider the virus software, tracking down software license numbers that no one bothered to write down (so there's a three-week wait period to get new keys from the manufacturer), syncing browser bookmarks, transferring files, ensuring compatibility with existing systems and software titles, and of course training the less-familiar employees on the new operating system and potentially even how to use a somewhat different keyboard or mouse. *Whew.* Unless you work at a computer company (and sometimes, even then), this is actually a *huge* project that requires careful planning.

As a loose guideline, low-hanging-fruit projects are those that someone on the team has successfully completed before (perhaps at another company).

Fast completion

When they're properly planned, some projects have relatively few steps in quick succession. For example, hiring a new team member to address the inefficiency of a customer service team unhappy because they feel stretched too thin can be a straightforward process in companies that hire frequently. (Of course, if you don't have a human resources department, this project may be much slower — so you wouldn't categorize it as a "quick" one.) Human Resources posts a standard job template to a set list of hiring resources, then vets the incoming applications according to established criteria, schedules interviews, and offers the best candidate the position.

Fast projects are often those with solutions your company has implemented before. This may be hiring the 27th customer support representative, or it may be adding an additional article to an established knowledgebase or holding your 172nd customer focus group. Sometimes, the challenge is recognizing an inefficiency, and the solution and resulting execution of that solution are relatively simple, especially if you have recorded the changes and can use them now to your advantage.

Getting it over with

The basic premise of the book *Eat That Frog* by Brian Tracy is that if you have to do something unpleasant — like eat a (presumably unseasoned) frog — then you should do it *first* and get it out of the way. You can apply this strategy to your list of projects by picking the one you and your team are least looking forward to tackling (but that still needs doing, eventually) and putting it front and center.

One project I recommend getting out of the way earlier than later is any solution that involves firing employees. They'll know it's coming the entire time you keep putting it off, and few employees perform worse than those who know they're out the door anyway. They are also likely to quit before you have the chance to fire them, changing the project milestone dates to meet *their* terms instead of your original plan.

Biggest savings

Cost savings potential is the stereotypical default driver of efficiency projects. And with good reason — unnecessary expenses are sheer waste, and as long as you've thoroughly vetted them to check for unexpected side effects, you should get rid of them.

If your organization is cash-strapped, savings is a natural metric by which to determine the project that's next on your plate.

Loudest complaints

Perhaps a project won't save the most amount of money and doesn't involve any quality-improving new equipment for manufacturing, but the underlying inefficiency is such a pain in the butt that removing it would create an audible sigh of relief across an entire division or organization. Pick that one.

Momentum is an underappreciated asset. When you start out with cost-savings measures, even though they may be in the best interests of the company as a whole, most individual employees think, "Great. No raise for me this year." and go through the motions to wrap up the project. If you have an objective they're *excited* about, however, that can change everything. Interspersing harder or boring efficiency-enhancing projects with ones that make a tangible positive impact on team members' lives is a smart way to sustain the efficiency train.

Win over a grumpy employee

They say the squeaky wheel gets the grease, and although we may not like it, this is sometimes a fact of life. I have seen countless projects derailed by a single person who was determined to resist the change, constantly raising objections, making planning meetings drag on past their expected ends, spotlighting every tiny error, and generally making the team's life unpleasant to the point that even the most enthused, engaged employees are now having second thoughts. The project's objective sounded great, sure, but not if it means constantly putting up with Carol.

If you have a Carol in your office, you can't just close your eyes and hope she goes away. In my experience you also cannot try to anticipate her every objection ahead of time — she will always find *something*. Instead, figure out which inefficiency is plaguing her life the most, and consider moving that to the top of the list.

It's important that you don't make any move that may make "Carol" feel her job is in jeopardy, or she will reinforce that wall she has up with steel rods.

Discovering What Comes After You Set Goals

After you've set goals, you've got to *share* them. Write them on the internal wiki, put them up on the wall, add due dates to your calendar, and tie a string around your index finger. So long as you've set an ambitious yet realistic goal (and seeing as you're at the end of a chapter on composing ambitious yet realistic goals, I bet you did!), publicizing that goal adds a hint of public peer pressure to jump-start your execution.

Now, you've got your problems. You've got carefully selected solutions to those problems. You've got goals to know when you've solved those problems. And you know which goals to tackle first. It's time to draft an efficiency execution plan to make sure you reach those goals, on-time and within-budget, which I cover in Chapter 7.

Chapter 7

Efficiently Executing Your Efficiency Plan

So you've come to terms with your inefficiencies, chosen your solutions, set your target goals, and picked your first project. (Or, you've skipped ahead to Chapter 7 without reading Chapters 1 through 6.) Now it's time to get to work!

All of your previous efforts and research now flow perfectly into an ultra-efficient execution plan. In this chapter, I walk you through each step of the project plan, from stating the problem to outlining a completion process for efficiently wrapping up. If you've followed along through the start of this section, you've already done most of the work — now you just need to assemble all those details and divvy out tasks.

As in life (and golf), an important part of hitting your target is follow-through. After you set a schedule and assign responsibilities, you've got to stay on top of progress and deliverables to make sure you're on track. I show you how to account for those future checkpoints up front so they don't sneak up on you.

It's rare for a plan to go off without a hitch, especially if this is one of your first forays into increasing efficiency. I cover how to plan ahead for and even *anticipate* shifts in the wind so they won't detail your schedule or your team morale. And of course, I touch on one of the least-obvious, but most important, components of execution: knowing when you're done.

Architecting an Efficient Execution Plan

A *project* is a temporary undertaking performed to produce a unique product, service, or result. Large or small, a project always has the following three components:

- ✔ **Specific scope:** Desired results or products
- ✔ **Schedule:** Established dates when project work starts and ends
- ✔ **Required resources:** Necessary amounts of people, funds, and other resources

An efficient project execution plan takes you from the initial problem statement on through a finishing process for formally closing up shop. This document keeps all team members on the same page and clear about both what's next and what's expected of them.

When does planning become inefficient?

I'm not going to lie; the amount of work required to efficiently plan a project — let alone efficiently plan an *efficiency project* — can be daunting. This is particularly true when you're first starting out. There are methodologies to read up on and cherry-pick from, new processes to master, brainstorming sessions to plan, and, if you're a human within an organization, an overwhelming number of inefficiencies to tackle.

It's tempting to walk away and stick with the status quo, sure, but an even worse temptation is the one to cut corners and jump right into trying to fix a problem, bypassing the vetting and planning phases in between. This is how efficiency projects get a bad rap.

It can be hard to fully comprehend at first why there's a detailed process between day one and the day work (as opposed to planning) commences. You may try diving in directly and get a perfectly positive result. (And I admit, in some organizations it's hard *not* to improve the situation with very minimal effort.) But you're *lucky*. It's the day a project derails that the full wrath of upper management descends down upon you

for not anticipating a foreseeable obstacle, and the project falls flat on its face because the right supports and team buy-in weren't in place. It's that day that you come clamoring for a team-driven vetting process and never look back.

So, when does all this planning become *inefficient?* When you start hiding behind the plans as a stall tactic because you're nervous to get started or you're afraid of what will happen if things don't work out. If you find yourself rewriting plans to improve the prose as opposed to the content, it's time to quit planning and start executing.

Some methodologies have a different take on the amount of *ongoing* planning that's efficient. In Agile Project Management, for example, planning documentation is reduced to the very bare minimum (known as *barely sufficient*). If the planning doesn't *directly* impact product creation, then it's not encouraged. However, the Agile company still needs an overarching plan and vision, even if it foregoes more detailed plans in its everyday practice.

Writing an entire execution plan as a group will take half a century. You should have had group discussions already that supplied enough details to compose a draft plan on your own. You can then post this document in a central location for final feedback from the rest of the team. Make sure you specify a deadline for giving feedback.

Gathering background information

The start of an execution plan outlines the information you already have in hand regarding the project, the reasons for the project, the desired results, and your assumptions about how you will handle the project.

Stating the problem

If there's no problem, then there's no project. Write down the problem or inefficiency that the project is aiming to address.

Include specific details here to make sure you address the *entire* problem in planning and executing the project. If you leave out a requirement, then your final solution will not be as efficient as it could have been (and will result in a brand-new project).

Clarifying your end result

What does the ideal project outcome look like? Describe it in detail here, using the problem statement as a guide. For example, if the problem is that current equipment is down 20 percent of the time, then the desired end result may be a zero downtime during the three months after installation of new equipment.

In Agile Project Management, this step is known as writing a *user story* — an actual story of what it looks, sounds, or feels like when the end customer is actually using the expected finished product. At the end of a project, you reenact this story to see if it plays out as written. Read more about Agile Project Management in Chapter 19.

Identifying your constraints

A constraint is any limit — chronological, financial, scientific — placed upon your project. Typical constraints include budgets, an external due date, the skillsets of your team members, and the number of hours available in employee schedules for new work, or lack of support from senior management and leadership.

Every project has constraints, and your end definition of success needs to take them into account. If you have a $500 budget or no more than two hours a week to put together a new corporate website, then three pages of text and a basic design template may be all you can achieve. This same outcome would *not* be considered a success if you had six months and a team of four full-time employees to design the new site.

Outlining your assumptions

Every project manager has certain assumptions when going into a project, and it's an excellent exercise to become aware of those assumptions and commit them to paper.

For example, you may take it for granted that the internal legal department will handle your project's contracts at no additional cost. This may be true, or you may discover later that one contract requires a specialized type of law that your internal resource cannot handle without outside, paid help. You may account for some of these assumptions in your risk planning, or they may prove informative to a future project owner or participant.

There's no need to go crazy here — we all know you need oxygen and the business to be open for the project to succeed — but generally every time you think "that's not important" or "they'll just take care of that" in the course of project planning, you should add that assumption to the project plan.

Sample background information segment

Below is a sample execution from a real project I worked on, involving upgrading a manufacturing company's Customer Relationship Management (CRM) software.

✔ **Problem statement:** Our existing customer database software does not track e-mails; has run out of custom fields for us to track which customers we include in which marketing campaigns; is not accessible when sales reps are out in the field visiting clients; and will not run on an operating system newer than Windows XP, blocking our ability to upgrade to new computers.

✔ **Desired end result:** We will have a new customer database system that provides all the same functionality used in the original system, plus e-mail integration, remote access, expanded custom field availability, and compatibility with the newest Windows operating system. The new system will contain all of the old system's data sorted into the correct custom fields. All employees will be able to perform their routine tasks in as much or less time than it takes currently.

✔ **Constraints:** Customer data in the new system must meet certain security requirements as outlined by existing customer contracts guaranteeing privacy. The custom fields in the current system are not used in a uniform manner, so some data will need cleaning. The team using the software is older with limited technical skills. The budget is $5,000 per year.

✔ **Assumptions:** We assume that management will allow us to switch to the new CRM if we can demonstrate the new solution addresses the former system's shortcomings. We assume that we have enough internal technology resources to handle the data import and new CRM customization.

✔ **Risks and uncertainties:** There may not be a new CRM program that meets all of our needs. We are uncertain whether we can export *all* data into CSV files from the former system for importing into the new system.

Acknowledging your risks and uncertainties

Some project outcomes are riskier than others. Risks don't mean you shouldn't forge ahead with your project, but you *do* need a contingency plan if one or more of those risks comes into play. It's always better to plan for acknowledged risk up front than to assume you will just be able to address it if it comes. For example, if a new law may add new compliance requirements to your project, this poses a risk to your timeline. An efficient execution plan would include steps for addressing these new compliance requirements and an amended milestone list.

There's no need to outline risks that apply universally. Yes, your project manager can die or float away during the Rapture, but that can happen to *any* project. Instead, list risks or uncertainties affecting this specific plan.

Secondhand knowledge is also an uncertainty. If your project relies on details that you or a trusted team member did not supply yourselves, these are uncertain until further researched. For example, if a salesperson you meet at a conference verbally tells you how much her software costs, this number is uncertain until you get a formal, written quote from the vendor.

Divvying up the workload

This portion of an execution plan involves identifying individual milestones and assigning them to the right team members. I continue the CRM scenario from the sidebar to provide real-world examples.

Listing all required work and deliverables

Compiling a master list of steps in a project requires thinking critically and in detail about the project. This list is key to the success of the project and should be a step-by-step path directly between the problem statement and the end result.

A Work Breakdown Structure (WBS) can help you assemble a complete list. To create one:

1. **Determine the major deliverables or products to be produced.**

   Ask yourself, "What major intermediate or final products or deliverables must be produced to achieve the project's objectives?"

   Items identified in the CRM scenario include the following:

   - Final CRM recommendation statement
   - Customized CRM
   - Data import map
   - Employee training program

2. **Divide each of these major deliverables in its component deliverables in the same manner.**

   Choose any one of these deliverables to begin with. Ask, "What intermediate deliverables must I have so I can create the deliverable?"

   Example requirements for a *final CRM recommendation statement* include the following:

   - CRM comparison matrix
   - Completed demos for each potential CRM
   - A review of materials for each potential CRM

3. **Divide each of these work pieces into its component parts.**

   Ask, "What deliverables must I have in order to complete this?"

   In order to complete demos for each potential CRM, you must:

   - Compile a list of available CRMs
   - Determine initial selection criteria
   - Schedule or request demos with each CRM

But why stop here? You can break each of these items into finer detail and then break those pieces into even finer detail.

Identifying all roles and responsibilities

Whether you're able to influence the people assigned to your project team, people are assigned to your team without your input, or you assume the role of project manager of an existing team, you need to confirm the skills, knowledge, and interest of your team members.

You can determine the skills you currently have and those that you need by using a *skills matrix*, and then based on this matrix, make the assignments by using a *human resources matrix*.

A *skills matrix* is a table that displays people's proficiency in specified skills and knowledge, as well as their interest in working on assignments using those skills and knowledge. The left-hand column identifies skill and knowledge areas needed to complete the current project, and the top row lists people's names. At the intersection of the rows and columns, you identify the level of each person's particular skills, knowledge, and interests. For each person and skill intersection, you assign two numbers: a skill level (where 0 = no capability and 3 = advanced capability) and an interest level (where 0 = no interest and 1 = interest) in carrying out that skill.

It's absolutely possible for someone to have a skill level of 0 and an interest level of 1. Depending on the situation, this can be a great way to benefit from an employee developing a new skill to contribute to the team.

Based on the completed skills matrix, you can quickly determine which skillsets you have available within your team, and which you need to fulfill via additional team members, outside consultants, or some other source. Not being able to meet all the skill and knowledge needs of a project either becomes a constraint that you account for in the project plan, or a reason that the project cannot begin.

CRM Skills Matrix	Gabe	Josh	Robin	Quinton
Technical writing	2,1	1,0	2,1	2,1
CRM customization	0,0	0,0	0,0	0,1
Data cleansing	3,0	3,1	1,0	3,0

A *human resources matrix* is similar to a skills matrix. Down the left-hand side, you list each task from your *Work Breakdown Structure*. The column headings across the top row correspond to each team member. If a team role is not yet filled, list the role (for example, Accountant) as opposed to the person's name. In each cell intersection, you put the number of hours it will take that person to complete the given task. One task may be assigned to multiple people, with the corresponding number of hours each separate person is expected to spend on that task in his own column.

CRM Human Resources Matrix	Gabe	Josh	Robin	Quinton	CRM Consultant
Compile list of CRMs	0	0	0	0	6
Clean data export file	0	30	10	10	5
Record screencasts	29	0	17	9	13

When you understand the roles that have not been assigned to specific people and the number of hours each role is expected to carry out over the course of the project, you can then begin recruiting additional team members, posting a Request For Proposals (RFP), speaking to a recruiter, or otherwise doing what's necessary to fill those spots.

Working on resource planning

Every project has limited time, money, and other resources. Writing down your resource requirements acts as a helpful checklist for ensuring you *get* those requirements, and this section forms a basis that team members can use for making assumptions (e.g., if the project requires six weeks, they *have* six weeks to work on it!). It also serves as something of an "order form" for other departments and upper management to understand the time, budget, and other support you require to reach your stated goal.

Constructing a schedule

You cannot construct an accurate project schedule in a bubble. Invariably, each member of a project team is also working on *other* projects. Creating an accurate schedule for *your* project relies on obtaining accurate schedules for all *other* projects. If you're just starting out with formally tracking projects, then you have to work off best guesses, and account for this timeline as an uncertainty in your project plan.

A *person-loading graph* is a bar chart with the number of total hours along the left (y-axis) with each week as its own bar (the x-axis). Each employee has his own graph. For a full-time employee, each week would have a bar reaching up to 40 hours. Each week's bar is then broken down into the number of hours spent on each different project that falls under that person's responsibilities. After your organization gets into the habit of keeping these graphs, it's very clear visually which employee has availability each week.

Tracking hours on a daily basis is usually too granular; it's much easier to spend eight hours a week on a project than 1.5 hours a day on it.

Based on the hours estimates from your human resources matrix and each associated team member's person-loading graph, you can work out how many hours each person can work on the project each week, and therefore work backward to determine realistic dates for both the final project delivery date and each major milestone within.

The number of hours you estimated in the human resources matrix earlier does not fit neatly into a 40-hour work week. No employee, anywhere, operates at 100 percent efficiency (meaning they work at peak productivity for every single minute they are at work). There's daydreaming, phone calls, snack breaks, unexpected meetings, and numerous other things that interrupt work.

Although you can increase individual employee efficiency (see Chapter 17 for more on this), you can't get it to 100 percent. Therefore, assuming that an employee who "works" 40 hours a week will actually perform 40 hours of project work in a week is simply asking for project delays.

What if you don't know how long something will take? Make an educated guess based on your team's existing body of experience or any available research. Clearly mark your timeframe as an estimate, and plan ahead for what you'll do if it takes twice (or four times) as long. In other words, don't make any mission-critical dates depend on a timeframe with a high likelihood of variation.

If you're embarking on the launch of a brand-new product line or another project that you know today is likely to change completely before your projected delivery date, consider Agile Project Management. With Agile, you set "sprints" of approximately two weeks each, checking in with your team and adjusting course as necessary between each sprint. For more on the Agile process, pick up *Agile Project Management For Dummies*.

Someone needs to be responsible for following up on each deadline. If initial deadlines go by without acknowledgement, it's all too easy for project members to assume that the project itself has taken a lower priority or, in some cases, stopped altogether. This causes quite a chaotic scene when the entire project is due and most of the members ceased working on it weeks earlier! A successful project has a *closing process* during which the final milestones are accounted for, the project is closed as a success (or failure), relevant details are captured for future reference, and next steps and/or projects are set to further the project's goal.

Beyond accounting for work hours, you also need to set a schedule for checkpoints — including meeting with project members to get updates on project progress, measuring progress towards the project goal, and general team meetings.

Re-visiting the project after a month or so can help determine whether your gains are still as efficient as originally planned. It also helps determine whether the project could have been planned better in certain areas.

Identifying needed resources

In addition to personnel, your project may require a variety of other important resources (such as furniture, fixtures, equipment, raw materials, and information). Plan for these nonpersonnel resources the same way you plan to meet your personnel requirements.

As part of your plan, develop a *nonpersonnel resources matrix*. List each of the project's activities along the left side of the matrix, and each resource required to perform those activities across the top as individual columns. Within each overlapping column, enter the number of hours for which that resource is needed. You can expand this original matrix into additional matrices to show the resource allocation breakdown across weeks or months.

Nonpersonnel Resource Matrix	Printer	Old Server	Recording Studio
Compile list of CRMs	0	0	0
Clean data export file	2	10	0
Record screencasts	1	0	20

There's also financial resources to consider, usually expressed as a budget. A project budget takes three phases:

- ✔ **A rough order-of-magnitude estimate,** which is based on the team's general understanding of a project's needs

- ✔ **A detailed budget estimate,** where you research and ballpark the costs of each task outlined in your Work Breakdown Structure

- ✔ **A completed, approved project budget,** which is adopted into the final project plan. This is basically the final draft of the detailed budget estimate.

Planning for project success

In order to progress efficiently and eventually arrive at the project's stated goal, you need a plan for clear team communication, upholding product/service quality, and measuring success.

Establishing communication

With the diversity of audiences that will be looking for information about your project and the array of data that you will be collecting, it's essential that you prepare a project Communications Management Plan to avoid duplication of effort and to ensure that nothing and no one falls through the cracks.

At a minimum, your plan should specify the following for all project communications:

- ✔ **Target audience:** The people whose information needs are addressed through the project communication. This may be the team as a whole, a subcommittee, upper management, or outside users.

- ✔ **Information needs:** The information that the target audience wants and/or needs.

- ✔ **Information-sharing activity:** The specific type of information-sharing activity to be used to transmit information to the target audience (written reports, presentations, and meetings, for example).

- ✔ **Content:** The specific data to be shared in the project communication.

- ✔ **Frequency:** When the information-sharing activity occurs (can be either regularly-scheduled or ad hoc).

- ✔ **Data collection:** How and when the data for the report are collected.

Ensuring product quality

Delivering a single end product doesn't mean much if you ultimately need a million copies and you had to create 99 defective versions to get to that single desirable one. Your project plan needs to specify what *level of quality* the end product needs to meet. You may express this in terms of Six Sigma ("the new manufacturing process must operate at five sigma") or in other concrete terms.

Continuing our CRM conversion example, our desired end result includes importing all of the old system data into the new CRM. However, since the old system had custom fields that were not always used in a uniform manner, some manual effort is required to read and process that questionable data. Specifying whether you care about importing that data at all, or whether it's an absolute business requirement to port 100 percent of that data, helps determine what resources are needed and when the project is truly complete.

Constructing an audience list

A project's audience is any person or group that supports, is affected by, or is interested in your project. Your project's audience can be inside or outside your organization, and knowing who they are helps you plan whether, when, and how to involve them.

A project audience list is a living document. You need to start developing your list as soon as you begin thinking about your project. Write down any names that occur to you; when you discuss your project with other people, ask them who they think may be affected by or interested in your project.

Suggested audience categories include upper management; requesters, project managers, end users, team members, groups normally involved, groups needed just for this project, clients, collaborators, vendors, suppliers, contractors, regulators, professional societies, and the public.

After you've written a few audience lists, you can construct an internal template that includes the categories of list members and even pre-lists of specific names. In the future, you can start with this list template instead of having to start from scratch. Not only does this save time, but it guarantees that you won't forget certain key roles and names, because they're already on the list!

Expanding Scope

When you first begin a project, you want to be careful of "scope creep" — which is what happens when seemingly small additional results or requirements slowly get added to your original project, ultimately creating a bloated, too-large project that's difficult to execute.

After you've wrapped up a project, however, knowing when (and where) to gradually expand your scope can help ensure that the goodwill and momentum you've built up will live on in a greater way.

Starting with a narrow scope

Naturally, you'd like to operate in a world where everything is possible — that is, where you can do anything necessary to achieve your desired results. Your clients and your organization, on the other hand, would like to believe that you can achieve everything they want with minimal or no cost to them. Of course, neither situation is true.

Defining the constraints you must work within introduces reality into your plans, and helps clarify expectations. As you plan and implement your project, think in terms of the following two types of constraints:

✔ **Limitations:** Restrictions other people place on the results you have to achieve, the time frames you have to meet, the resources you can use, and the way you can approach your tasks.

✔ **Needs:** Requirements you stipulate must be met so you can achieve project success.

Unlimited resources can actually be more of a hindrance than a help. I'm rather fearful for a time when people get to live forever, because I'm not so sure anyone would ever get anything done! Having finite funds, time, and other resources forces you to make decisions and forge ahead.

Even if you had unlimited resources, you should still start your projects with small scopes. You can almost always expand later, but it's hard to view scaling *back* a project as anything but a failure even if the resulting smaller scope is a success.

So, when you're tempted to start off by saving the company $1 million, tackle the first $100,000 instead. Rather than making your first customer-facing event a giant conference with a major headlining musical act, try a casual pizza presentation followed by Q&A. Before switching the warehouse to operate off GPS codes, try to get sales to quit printing purchase orders, and so on.

Seeing where to expand your efforts next

When your project meets or exceeds its targets, the natural thing to do after the confetti stops falling down from the sky is to ask, what next?

Taking the project a step further

After all the brainstorming, measuring, goal tracking, and planning that went into the first round of your project, you probably have a strong grasp right now as to whether there's a round two to be had. Sometimes a project reveals a wealth of inefficiencies of which you've barely scratched the surface, and you'll have ten well-formed project plans simply fly off the top of your head. If this is the case, and there aren't any other constraints stopping you, go for it! Ride that momentum and success far into the efficiency wind.

Other times, you know you stretched every last ounce of effort out of your team just to get this far, and eking out further results (at least via this method) seems far-fetched. If this is the case, then wrap up and look a bit further for your next opportunity.

Continuing efforts in the same department

Perhaps you successfully reduced customer support wait times to zero, but you know of other wait-listed projects in the customer service department. Odds are that much of the work that went into your initial project, including intangibles like a well-oiled team that's now used to working together, can carry you well into an additional project in the same department.

Branching out to another area

Sometimes there are juicier, more beneficial projects in other areas of the company, or you simply may want to spread the efficiency gains around more evenly. You can start fresh on efforts in an entirely different sector of the business, and still use some of the knowledge gained (and perhaps even team members or other resources) from the first project to help subsequent ones succeed.

Trying again if at First You Don't Succeed

Risk is an unavoidable part of *every* project, whether the end goal is increased efficiency or even if you're intentionally setting out to be *in*efficient. It's how you handle the twists and turns that ultimately determine if your project is a success, a wash, or an experience everyone wishes they could forget.

Re-aligning when necessary

So, things aren't going quite as you expected. Changes you thought would bring joy to team members are actually causing them to pull their hair out. The savings you expected to realize didn't materialize, or were eaten up (or exceeded) by some unexpected costs. Training really took two weeks instead of two hours, and quality control measures tanked during that time.

All is not lost! You should continue to hang in there, but you should not hang on to the same project plan. Go back to the drawing board with the new information you've gained from your execution so far and rework the sections of your plan that are no longer true or relevant. One of the real benefits of a well-written plan is that you rarely have to start it over from scratch when you make adjustments.

Realignments don't have to be due to poor results. Sometimes in the course of adopting one solution, you hear of an even better one (or a better one is just hitting the market). This is a good reason to change course, too.

Resetting milestones

Many projects involve doing new work and acquiring new skills in the process. Even a project with deliverables you've produced 100 times can fall behind for a myriad of reasons, ranging from a flu epidemic on a factory floor to a shipyard strike that delays materials.

Instinct would usually have you perform simple addition on the whole schedule. If you're seven days behind on step three, simply add seven days to each subsequent deliverable. Unfortunately, it's usually not that simple. If what you didn't know costs a week up front, odds are it will eat additional time going forward.

Knowing what you know now, sit down with the project team and re-evaluate your milestones. There's no need to get scared and shift your due dates to an impossible-to-miss day next year — aggressive deadlines can be both motivational and sometimes necessary — but you also need to be realistic in light of your existing delays.

Knowing when to throw in the towel

In a successful project, you can stop executing after you reach your stated goal (unless some or all of the processes you introduced are intended to continue indefinitely). In a less-successful project, the finish line is not as clear.

Some indicators that it's time to wrap up a project, regardless of current results, include the following:

- ✔ **A team drained of morale:** Beating a dead horse or a demoralized team never did much good.

- ✔ **Lack of a clear solution:** Resist the urge to forge ahead if your current situation or goal is no longer applicable but you don't have a replacement. You can never arrive if you don't have a destination.

- ✔ **No (or negative) results after exerting real effort:** If your planned solution clearly isn't working to achieve your objective, it's time to try something else.

- ✔ **You run out of resources:** Although there are exceptions to this, namely if your project's performing very well, generally borrowing to get out of debt (by begging for more resources for an ill-fated project) doesn't work.

Realizing When You're Efficient Enough

Projects to increase efficiency have diminishing returns in cases where you can never eliminate that inefficiency entirely. For example, if you achieve a Six Sigma improvement of a 70 percent decrease in assembly defects, a follow-up project that further reduces defects by another 70 percent actually eliminated far fewer defects.

Put another way, say you have 100 defects per month. Improving this by 70 percent leaves you with just 30 defects next month, so a second 70 percent improvement gets you to 9 defects in month three. Let's say we are Six Sigma masters and eke out a third 70 percent improvement — now we're dropped to just 3 defects. As you can see, each improvement is smaller and smaller, even though the efforts to achieve each subsequent improvement were almost certainly greater and greater.

At what point do you say "enough"? This has a lot to do with your organization's goals. (It also has something to do with ethics and the law — there should be no end to improvement efforts to get employee fatalities to zero or prescription drug dispensations to 100 percent perfect.)

For example, most organizations would invest a lot in improving a 60 percent customer satisfaction rating, but be perfectly happy to maintain a 98 percent average without embarking on an improvement project. The potential gains in increasing one additional satisfaction percentile aren't worth the resources involved in executing a project, particularly relative to an organization's other, more pressing needs.

Using Execution Tools

In addition to the tools mentioned throughout this chapter, different business methodologies have additional tools that can aid in the execution of an efficient project. Here are some of my favorites.

Sprint backlog

In Agile Project Management, goals are expressed as *user stories* — literal stories describing how the customer uses or experiences the desired end result. Every iteration (often a two-week period) while a team builds a product has its own *sprint backlog*, a list of stories included in that sprint, the tasks needed to complete each story, and the estimated time to complete each task. Working backward based on the number of work hours in a given sprint, a backlog makes it simple to see which tasks you can fit in now, and which must be tabled for the future.

Burndown chart

A burndown chart is a quick visual representation of the amount of work remaining to meet a deadline. An on-schedule, properly planned project should have a smooth declining line. A flatline or, worse, an incline is a sign that a project is taking too long and needs attention. On the y-axis, chart the estimated number of hours of work left across the entire team. On the x-axis, chart the number of days left until the deadline (with each day as one data point).

Task board

It may sound simple, but a task board is a very clear visual indicator to all team members — and the UPS man — as to how much progress has been made. Divide a wall into four sections: "To Do," "In Progress," "Accept," and

"Done." Each task goes on its own sticky note, and the sticky is placed in the appropriate section and moved as needed. (In the "Accept" stage, the creator feels a task is done, but the project owner or client needs to confirm in order to move it to "Done.")

A3

A3 is a single sheet resolution and planning document; it gets its name from the international A3 paper size. The idea is that on one single sheet of paper, you have all the information you really need about a situation. You design your A3 to fit your needs; however, a typical A3 includes the following sections:

- ✓ Title

- ✓ Owner of the issue and date of the document

- ✓ Background information — "What is the problem?"

- ✓ Current conditions — "What are the current situations related to this issue?"

- ✓ Target condition or goals — "What do we want it to be?"

- ✓ Root cause analysis — "What is the true cause of the issue?"

- ✓ Countermeasures to close gap or reach goal — "What are the actions to resolve this issue?"

- ✓ A plan defining who, what, when, where, and how to measure and verify the implementation of the countermeasures — "What is our plan?"

- ✓ Follow-up actions to ensure the issue is resolved and doesn't reoccur — "How will we track progress, share learning, and handle issues during plan implementation?"

For more in-depth examples of these tools at work, check out *Agile Project Management For Dummies* and *Project Management For Dummies*.

Part III

Increasing Operational Efficiency

The 5th Wave   By Rich Tennant

"We're using just-in-time inventory and just-in-time material flows which have saved us from implementing our just-in-time bankruptcy plan."

In this part . . .

Time to get into the nuts and bolts! This part walks you through increasing the overall efficiency of your business in areas such as finances, customer service, human resources, sales, and manufacturing. Taken together, increasing efficiencies across these areas can have a tremendous positive impact on your entire organization, with a trickle-down effect that can solve additional issues farther down and well into the future.

This part also has a chapter on my favorite topic: process automation. Although there's literally an infinite number of ways you could automate your daily tasks, you'll learn exactly how to implement many of the automations I've found that deliver the greatest return, and you'll know how to automate just about any other process you have running.

Chapter 8

Channeling Henry Ford: Process Automation

. . . .

In This Chapter

▶ Looking at the pros and cons of process automation

▶ Understanding the basic steps to automating any process

▶ Looking at how to improve automation *right now*

. . . .

*P*rocess automation is at the very heart of business efficiency. How can I take a 17-step process and reduce it down to 12? Or down to *two*? How can I eliminate costly human errors by passing certain sensitive tasks on to a computer program? Which tasks should I *never* entrust to a machine? What administrative drudgery can I automate away from my employees' plates?

Some common examples of process automations are:

✔ Automatic sales lead assignments based on zip code

✔ Switching to Web-based customer feedback surveys that perform analytics on the fly and immediately alert you to negative feedback

✔ Switching your website to a system that lets you update text on the fly without involving programmers

✔ Setting up text message alerts every time your company name is mentioned online instead of a manual, after-the-fact search once a week

You can even go as far as using a fully automated warehouse picking and packing system.

Although the umbrella of process automation can certainly include large-scale projects like switching to electronic accounting software, it also includes many seemingly small decisions and changes that can add up to making a huge impact. Every area of your organization undoubtedly has opportunities for improvement — whether that be in error-reduction, time savings, or both — including customer service, accounting, and even your IT department itself (which is usually the one tasked with implementing process automation improvements).

Done right, process automation can alleviate your workforce from huge headaches, ultimately leading to happier, more productive employees. No company wants upper management spending hours on data entry each week, and yet I see that scenario play out in businesses all across the country because the people on the ground see no alternative.

In this chapter, I walk through the positives and negatives to keep in mind as you decide to automate parts of your business, and walk through more concrete details for the most common and effective process automations I come across in my consulting practice.

Discovering the Pros and Cons of Automation

Automation in and of itself is not necessarily efficient *or* even the right choice. The choice to automate a given process or task should always go through at least a basic decision tree, weighing the known benefits and costs. Some of the main pros of automation include the following:

- ✔ At scale, process automation can eliminate the need to hire new administrative employees at significant cost savings.

- ✔ Automation eliminates human error.

- ✔ Process automation lends itself to removing the most boring, busywork tasks. This frees up your workforce to tackle tasks that humans do better than computers.

Whereas some of the cons include the following:

- ✔ Implementing most automations requires some degree of technical assistance, or at least familiarity.

- ✔ Process automation is by definition change, requiring change management (more on this in Chapter 14).

- ✔ Each new automation requires a Quality Assurance (QA) process, which takes varying degrees of effort and time. You need to make sure the outputs of your automation are the same as (or better than) your current human-driven efforts. The last thing you want is to discover in six months that your automated customer service system hangs up on people who press 2!

Automating: Step by Step

The steps for identifying processes in your business that can or should benefit from a more technological touch generally follow the same pattern. Follow the roadmap below to uncover automation opportunities in your organization.

Documenting the current process

The first step in automating anything is ensuring that you have a crystal-clear understanding of how it works in its current incarnation. This helps you understand what parts can be automated and what shape an automation may take. Much of this step can be handled by hunting down inefficiencies in your organization, covered in Chapter 4.

If you've followed the story of Lean in other parts of this book and constructed a value-stream map — a literal, visual map showing how inputs like orders or leads make their way through your organization, ultimately transforming into the end product — then that map doubles as a treasure map for process automation opportunities.

To construct your treasure map, the simplest and most direct way is to walk through the process yourself. (Ideally, find *two* people to walk through separately, under the assumption that one may pick up on a step the other misses.) Follow the process at every step, documenting exactly what transformations the initial input must go through, who touches it, what it waits for, and so on, in order to become the final product.

Pay particular attention to the seven wastes of Lean (overproduction, waiting, transportation, unnecessary processing, unnecessary inventory, excess motion, and defects). These are generally ripe for automation.

At every single step — no matter how seemingly insignificant or quick — in the process, ask the "5 Whys." Why is this step here? In response to the answer, ask "Why?" Repeat five times. This helps you determine if you can potentially do away with the step altogether (perhaps because it's a legacy remainder for a previous process — you'd be surprised at how many of these hang around!), or if you can automate some or all of it.

Gathering requirements

When you know (and have documented) the current process like the back of your hand, it's time to understand the pieces that aren't working, aren't there, and/or people *wish* weren't there.

You can uncover these issues by interviewing people along the way as you construct your initial process map, or by returning after the fact with more pointed questions. The "5 Whys" method also works well here.

The goal here is to find the *minimum* number of steps to get to the *most desirable* end. Ideally your end point in an automated system is even better — not just equivalent to — your existing process.

Pay particular attention to the following:

- ✔ **Errors in the current system, and what level of error (if any) is acceptable.** One way to frame this inquiry is to ask what would happen *if* a given piece of information was incorrect or a step was performed incorrectly.

- ✔ **Boredom in the current system.** What tasks do people loathe the most? What do they procrastinate doing (managers can usually give good insight into this) most often? What tasks seem misaligned with an employee's other responsibilities (for example, a senior manager spending time normalizing spreadsheet data)?

- ✔ **Waiting in the current system.** Are there points when inputs sit around waiting for a human to move or interact with them?

- ✔ **Any manual manipulation, entry, or transmission of data — or anything handwritten.** The need for a pen is usually a good sign of something that should be automated.

- ✔ **Missing pieces.** What do the current process participants *wish* happened or came out that does not? For example, perhaps the customer service manager wishes she had a way to filter all one-star product reviews out the rest of the submissions so she could address them first.

Finding and evaluating your options

This is a common dilemma: You have a good hunch *that* something can be automated, but you're not sure of the best or right way to go about it. Unfortunately there is no single directory of inefficiencies and their solutions. but here are a few strategies you can employ to find the best fit for your needs (the first of which — reading this book! — you've already taken care of):

- ✔ **Ask around.** Definitely seek input from the current process participants, who may have done their own independent research already, but also ask colleagues in other companies (at a Chamber of Commerce breakfast, for example). Sometimes simply learning what *didn't* work for another organization — and why — can shortcut your own research.

✔ **Search the Internet.** Peruse vendor websites peddling potential solutions, but also look carefully for messageboard and forum postings on sites like Quora and LinkedIn, where others in your shoes sought advice for similar problems. This provides a wealth of places to start.

✔ **Hire a consultant for an hour.** After making recommendations for over a decade, I can rattle off the pros and cons of most solutions out there off the top of my head. That's what consultants are for. Don't reinvent the wheel and spend a week getting up to speed on all your options when an hour or two of a consultant's time can help you pinpoint the best solution. After that first hour, it's up to you if you need a consultant to help with the implementation.

Comparing custom versus off-the-shelf solutions

When surveying the array of available tools on the market (which I'm grouping as "off-the-shelf" solutions even though many are available online and therefore never see an actual shelf), it's often tempting to throw up your hands and decide to hire some programmers to build a custom solution that matches your exact business needs.

If you find yourself with this inclination . . . stop right there!

Few things are underestimated more than the amount of time and money that goes into a truly functional custom system, whether that be a custom point-of-sale or even something as straightforward as a custom-built Web-to-lead form. I can count on one hand the number of times this was the most appropriate, most efficient solution for my client in the entirety of my career.

If a given solution doesn't work for your company as-is — perhaps it doesn't integrate with another system you use, or it can't quite replicate the particular way your organization does something — then the next-best thing is to customize an existing solution. To do this, the solution has to offer something called "API access" and the majority of offerings today *do* have APIs.

An API (short for Application Programming Interface) is a technical means for interacting with an existing piece of software or a Web-based application. Although every API is different, you can generally use an API to send information into the system (such as sending a Web form directly into your CRM), display details (such as creating a dashboard of the top open customer support requests), or connect two systems (such as sending sales information directly to order fulfillment).

When you see plug-ins or add-ons available for services, these are built on the API, and if there's an open API, you can build plug-ins for yourself! I've even had clients re-sell their own custom solutions to other companies facing the same dilemma.

Knowing when to tip-toe and when to leap

Some process automations can be integrated slowly, tested by a small group of stakeholders and then released to the company at-large after it's fully polished. Others have to be implemented all at once. In order to prepare yourself and your staff, you need to clearly understand which automations you can introduce piecemeal and which require big leaps of faith.

Judging types of tip-toes

If you're not going to flip the switch overnight, you can start piloting your automation:

- **By yourself.** Few things are more effective drivers of change than top-down examples. If you start using and extolling the virtues of a new process, others will buy-in.

- **With internal change agents.** Who are the internal people most likely to embrace change, take risks, and tolerate some stumbles along the way? They're the people who should test-pilot new implementations first.

- **With external change agents.** In the same vein, you likely have relationships with customers that you know to be open to new ideas and patient with an error or two. If your automation is customer-facing, such as switching to automated invoices, bring these clients on board first. If you're communicative and up front about the possibility for hiccups, you'd be surprised at how this experience — even if it's riddled with errors! — can actually strengthen the bond those customers have with your organization.

Preparing for a leap

Sometimes you can't pilot a change and have to make a change full-stop. If this is case:

- **Give as much notice and training as possible.** Even a perfect new system will fail if no one knows how to use it the first day.

- **Set a realistic timeline.** Too often I have seen overambitious timelines, where in the end the you have to work with a system that is far from properly implemented yet.

✔ **Try to run both systems side-by-side.** Dual data entry is a pain, but it ensures your new process and your old process are delivering the same results or answers. Be honest with employees that the transition will require more work than usual, but the goal is to *lessen* the workload. Set clear dates for when the duality will end.

Getting employee buy-in

You can mandate a change all you want, but employees will find a way to revert back to their old ways if they feel threatened, intimidated, and/or frustrated by the new automations you put in place. Getting employee buy-in can mean the difference between a workforce that embraces rather than resists change. Even more importantly, it keeps the feedback door wide open so you can hear about — and fix! — any issues that come up quickly.

Tips for getting employees to give new process automations a chance include the following:

✔ **Look for low-hanging fruit.** If your first automation projects are ones that genuinely make employees' lives easier, they're more likely to get on board with new automations in the future. Find boring tasks to automate, or look for ways to simplify complex multistep processes. Examples include manually generated reports or math (for example, number of sales per person per week, currently calculated by hand).

✔ **Build excitement.** It can be hard to rally for a Web form, but it's also not helpful to simply send out a drab announcement memo. As much as possible, try to highlight the benefits of the new change and draw positive attention to the people who start using it. This is easiest if *you* have already been piloting the automation.

✔ **Provide ample training.** The new change may make perfect sense to *you* but sound like Greek to others. I don't know about you, but if I had to do my work in Greek tomorrow, my day would be pretty slow and tedious. Having up-front *and* ongoing training resources helps ensure that everyone feels comfortable and not threatened.

✔ **Tolerate mistakes.** Changing the way a process is done and yelling at the first person to make an accidental error is a good way to ensure that no one ever fully adopts the new process (or likes you). You can't tolerate mistakes indefinitely, but you should make it clear that you want people to dive in and try, and there will be supports in place when necessary.

Finding Automations You Can Implement Right Now

Although your organization undoubtedly has processes you can automate that are specific to your industry or corporate culture, there are some automation opportunities I find in nearly every place of business. The following pages are an overview of how to implement these automations in your own company.

Converting your website into a Content Management System (CMS)

A *Content Management System (CMS)* lets you — or anyone else at the company with the appropriate permissions — update pages on your website without needing to learn any HTML code. Today's top CMSs have entire ecosystems of developers and designers so you can do much more than just change the occasional sentence. You can rearrange elements on a page, add functionality such as photo slideshows and password-protected file downloads, and much more, all with very minimal training.

A CMS eliminates the waste of "waiting" by letting you and your staff update your own website immediately, in-house.

Two of my favorite website CMS options are:

- **WordPress (**www.wordpress.org**):** With both a hosted and a self-install version, WordPress is an open-source CMS with a giant ecosystem of plug-ins, developers, custom themes, and training materials. Because it's open-source, you can hire developers relatively easily to build any additional customizations (ranging from design tweaks to custom functionality), and because it's so popular, it's easy to find both experienced users and training options. Although it's traditionally considered to be a blog platform, there's nothing stopping you from using it for your entire website.

- **Drupal (**www.drupal.org**):** Also open-source, Drupal is the powerhouse CMS behind many large well-known sites, including many government portals. You can take advantage of existing plug-ins or build your own.

The actual process of *converting* your existing website to a CMS can be a bit of a process, but done right, it will ensure that you can change not just content, but the entire design and architecture of your site with little-to-no outside technical intervention going forward. In other words: It's well worth it!

- Decide if you love your current website design, or if it may be time for a change. To keep your current design, you need to hire someone to convert the design into a WordPress theme. To change, you can hire a custom WordPress theme designer or purchase a ready-made one at sites like `www.themeforest.net`. WordPress also maintains a directory of free themes at `www.wordpress.org`.

- Determine which parts of your site need to be updated through the CMS interface, as opposed to the raw code of the site. The answer here is usually "all," and WordPress's default functionality lets you change things like page titles and headings fairly easily. It also separates out "widgets" (small sidebar sections used for sets of links, images, and news announcements) from article content. However, an experienced WordPress designer can make this workflow even easier and make it almost effortless to add in article sidebars, calls to action, ads, and other content items.

- Give each potential updater his own WordPress account and set permissions accordingly. For example, you may want marketing to be able to edit only the "Marketing" section of the site although your own personal account can change anything, anywhere.

When it's in place, you can edit any page on your website as though it's a Word document — making text bold, adding hyperlinks, adding new articles, and so forth.

Scheduling meetings automatically

Does the following sound familiar? You need to meet with Tony and Alex. You e-mail out a time. Tony responds with an alternate time, which Alex subsequently can't make. By the time a mutually agreed-upon time is found, you realize you've accidentally booked a different meeting in that spot.

Scheduling is a tremendous waste of time, and it doesn't have to be that way. An increasing array of calendar services can allow other people to book appointments with you automatically, during times you specify. You just have to show up.

Scheduling application options include the following:

- TimeBridge (`www.timebridge.com`)
- ScheduleOnce (`www.meetme.so`)
- Some applications like Microsoft Outlook and Salesforce.com offer appointment booking options.

To use an automatic appointment-booking service:

- ✔ Install or connect the service with your existing calendar. Most solutions work with all major calendaring options such as Outlook and Google Calendar.

- ✔ Set the hours during which you are available for meetings. The calendar integration automatically blocks out times that you are already booked!

- ✔ Send your custom calendar link to anyone with whom you need to meet.

- ✔ The other party suggests one to three times that they are also available. Until you confirm one of these times, all of them are marked as busy to new appointment bookers.

- ✔ You confirm a time. It's added to both parties' calendars, and you just have to show up.

Getting your OCR on: Turn printed papers into full-text searchable files

OCR, or *Optical Character Recognition,* refers to the process by which a computer recognizes and translates text on a page. In short, it lets you scan printed documents *and even handwritten notes* and convert them into full-text-searchable computer files that you can edit, copy and paste, and otherwise treat exactly like any other document you typed from scratch. OCR can turn your entire organization in a paperless one, eliminating data entry and increasing document discoverability.

My personal favorite scanner is the Fujitsu ScanSnap, which comes in Mac and PC versions and includes OCR software. This scanner has a small footprint and is ideal for keeping on an individual employee's desk. Ultimately, any quality document scanner can be used in conjunction with OCR software like Evernote (www.evernote.com), ABBYY Fine Reader (finereader.abbyy.com), or Iris (www.irislink.com).

There are also websites that will OCR your documents on a one-off basis. You can upload a PDF or even an image file, such as a GIF or a JPEG, and get back a text document. Search online for "free OCR." Each site differs in the exact file formats it accepts and creates.

To convert anything from a napkin to a receipt to a lengthy contract into a full-text-searchable PDF:

- ✔ Run the paper through a scanner.

- ✔ Run the resulting file through OCR software or an OCR conversion website.

- ✔ Search and copy text from your file to your heart's content. (Make sure to keep a backup!)

Signing up for an e-mail service

E-mail can be much more efficient than just checking off a bunch of names in your address book and sending a group message. Today's e-mail services can automate and enhance many of your electronic lead and customer communications, freeing your team up to focus on the human aspect of this process, such as writing compelling copy and deciding how often to send particular messages.

E-mail services differ in cost, functionality (for example, some offer integrated A/B testing capabilities, automatically splitting your mailing list into random groups to let you test whether one subject line encourages more opened e-mails than another), and volume (some are aimed at small lists of 500 recipients while others can handle e-mailing millions). The right e-mail service can also offer automatic unsubscribe links and lessen the number of your messages that wind up in spam filters.

My favorite e-mail services include the following:

- ✔ MailChimp (www.mailchimp.com)

- ✔ MadMimi (www.madmimi.com)

- ✔ ExactTarget (www.exacttarget.com)

So what can you automate with an e-mail service? Some ideas include the following:

- ✔ Sending automatic e-mails at set intervals to potential customers with useful information

- ✔ Following-up with leads after a certain number of days of silence

- ✔ Tracking which recipients actually open your e-mails

- ✔ Using A/B testing to find the subject lines and e-mail content that drives the most sales

Writing an Excel macro

An Excel macro is basically a recorded series of actions. Say you export a report each week, and then manipulate it in a few ways each and every time: you bold the headers, replace the salesperson abbreviations with full names, filter out dead leads, and sum some columns. This is a lot of manual work that can be automated with a macro. Define a macro once, and then you just have to hit "play" on subsequent reports to watch all of these tasks carry out like magic on their own — much more efficiently.

There are two ways to define, or write, a macro in Excel:

- ✔ Record a macro by pressing the "record" button and carrying out each of the tasks you need done, such as bolding text or filtering columns.

- ✔ Write Visual Basic code from scratch (or search online for sample code and modify it as needed). Although you probably need a programmer to do it this way, I encourage you to at least *look* at the Visual Basic code and see if you can manipulate a thing or two.

Learn more about Excel macros in *Excel 2010 For Dummies*.

Some of the most common time-saving Excel macros I've seen include the following:

- ✔ **Complex find-and-replace.** For example, if you have to regularly replace nicknames or abbreviations with full names.

- ✔ **Visual formatting.** You may regularly take raw data and make it "pretty" — a macro can handle all your formatting, colors, and so on literally with one click.

- ✔ **Data normalization.** Perhaps your raw data always comes in with a date format you can't use for a subsequent data import. A macro can automatically apply a formula to each date to convert it to the right format *and* make sure that date is in the spreadsheet as a hard value (not just a formula, which makes it harder to copy and paste).

Creating an electronic form

Printed forms are the bane of my existence as an efficiency consultant. I want to collect them all and burn them in a giant bonfire. If you have printed forms — whether *internally* or externally — it's time to flip the switch to put them online. Electronic forms eliminate data entry errors and enforce validation (for example, nothing's stopping you from putting "Neener-Neener" in the phone number spot on a written form, but you can easily make a rule to only allow numbers in an online form). They also can perform analytics and send alerts on the fly, helping you _act_ on the information you receive in a timely and efficient manner.

You can use electronic forms for

✔ Letting new customers sign up for your product or service in lieu of having to call in.

✔ Accepting client payments in lieu of having your sales team take them over the phone.

✔ Collecting customer feedback after they sign up, interact with support, or cancel, and alerting you to negative experiences right away.

✔ Surveying internal employees about their job satisfaction and automatically tallying the results.

✔ Collecting new lead information off your website and automatically submitting it to your CRM, avoiding any manual data entry.

Some of my favorite form services include FormStack (www.formstack.com), SurveyMonkey (www.surveymonkey.com), and Wufoo (www.wufoo.com). Each service differs in the third-party integrations it supports and the actual form design features.

Automating your notifications

Notifications are something that most companies are simply _missing_ as opposed to doing inefficiently. You need to know when your company is mentioned in the press so you can highlight it to your staff (or respond appropriately to controversy). You should know immediately when customers leave negative reviews so you can reach out quickly and stave off a bigger public relations problem. And you can also benefit from knowing when people ask questions about your company or industry so you can be the first to respond (and hopefully consequently earn their business).

The tools I use every day for notifications about this very book include the following:

✔ **Google Alerts** (www.google.com/alerts) send you an e-mail when the keywords you specify appear in blog posts and news articles. You can specify the frequency and quality of alerts.

✔ **If This, Then That** (www.ifttt.com) lets you set up custom alerts across a variety of channels. The basic premise is "if this happens, then do this!" For example, when a competitor posts a new article to its blog, they send you a text message. When a negative review of your company appears on Yelp, they call you. If your stock price dips, they call _and_ text you.

Common efficient notifications include the following:

- ✔ When someone mentions your company (or a competitor) online
- ✔ When there's a review of your company on Yelp
- ✔ When an industry organization posts new content or makes an announcement
- ✔ When someone asks a question related to your product/service line on LinkedIn that you can answer

Signing your contracts electronically

Signing contracts is one of those small, routine tasks that actually eats up considerable resources. You need to send the original document, print it, sign it, scan it, or physically mail it back, and then wait for receipt of a version signed by the other party. Electronic document signing is not only legal, but it eliminates virtually all these steps, letting you sign contracts and other important documents in under a minute. Here's the process:

- ✔ When you create an account on one of these sites, you upload the document in need of a signature. You can even save copies of documents you sign frequently, such as new customer onboarding paperwork.
- ✔ Fill in your signature, today's date, and any other fields with their drag-and-drop interface.
- ✔ After you sign, send a special signature link to the other party, who is prompted to login and also electronically sign her name.
- ✔ After both parties sign, you both receive an electronic copy of the final paperwork. Voila!

Top providers of electronic document signing tools include Docusign (www. docusign.com) and Echosign (www.echosign.com).

Chapter 9

The Bottom Line: Financial Efficiency

*A*s an owner or manager of a business, you get paid to make profit happen. Of course, you should be a motivator, innovator, consensus builder, lobbyist, and maybe even sometimes a babysitter, too, but at the end of the day, the purpose of your job is to make and improve profit and earn an adequate return on the capital investment of the business. No matter how much your staff loves you (or those doughnuts you bring in on Mondays), if you don't meet your profit goals, you're facing the unemployment line.

Competition in most industries is fierce, and you can never take profit performance for granted. Changes take place all the time — both changes initiated by the business and changes from outside forces. Maybe a new superstore down the street is causing your profit to fall off, or political unrest in the country where one of your products parts is manufactured required switching suppliers at the last minute at twice the cost. Without analyzing the root causes, too many businesses fall in the trap of assuming that the best, most efficient solution is to run a sale and slash prices. Maybe price cuts and giant balloon creations will keep your cash register singing, but making sales does not guarantee that you make a profit. Profit is a two-headed beast: Profit comes from making sales *and* controlling expenses.

Financial efficiency is not about finding the cheapest employees, parts, and services while charging the maximum price that the market will bear. As I point out many times in this book, no single decision in your business is made in a vacuum. Cheap supplies often mean shoddy end product quality, which will likely lead to fewer customers and therefore lower profits in the grand scheme of things. Every financial decision needs to be made in light of its potential impacts on other areas of your business. That said, most businesses I consult for have a slew of low-hanging fruit when it comes to everyday expenses that can be lowered or eliminated.

In this chapter, I walk you through a number of small steps you can take toward realizing large financial gains, while making sure you've got your foundation — efficient financial management skills covered.

Examining Financial Efficiency

Financial efficiency is more complex than simply comparing dollars in and dollars out. Here's an illustration of this point with an example of a hypothetical financially efficient CEO:

> Eli is the CEO of a major distillery that ships to nearly every state and over 20 countries. As the cost of packaging and shipping is a significant part of his overall expenses, he has a designated employee spend a day each month getting up to speed on the latest policy changes of UPS, FedEx, USPS, and local foreign carriers. As a result, when USPS changed the package dimensions for its economy rate, Eli knew about it within days and was able to order new packaging right away, while his competitors were forced to swallow higher rates.

> The focus of Eli's company is high-quality spirits. He's put time and energy into cultivating relationships with his suppliers, and he's not going to leave them for a marginally cheaper rate. Eli is clear about this policy, so he cultivates goodwill with his partners, which benefits his business more than constantly shopping around for 50 cents off grain.

> For overhead costs, that's a different story. He has an app on his iPhone that lets him remotely control his equipment so he can turn the thermostat down on warm weekends when no one is there. Employees use their own cellphones for work, and he pays a portion of their bills. Ultimately, this means he's able to get in touch with them more easily, and he saves money in the process.

> Eli uses the Salesforce.com CRM to keep track of his leads, customers, and contracts, and he hired a developer to build a custom integrated application that tracks his inventory and shipping. Keeping all these details in one place makes accounting a breeze, because he can export his income and expenses directly into his accounting software. If anyone has a complaint about Eli's financial efficiency, it's his accountant — for being able to bill only a few hours a month!

How efficient are your expenses?

It's easy for expenses to creep out of control over time, especially those that are outside your core areas of expertise (for example, a grocery store may not be on top of the latest computing technologies and prices). Asking yourself the following questions can help track down some runaway costs:

- ✔ **When was the last time you reviewed your electric bill?** The larger your physical space and infrastructure, the more opportunities you have to drastically lower this bill. In fact, many private companies have released tools and even *games* to help residential and commercial customers lower their electric bills. Ask your utility if it offers *Green Button*, a way to download your energy usage data and even connect it with some of the aforementioned tools so building managers can track and try to reduce usage over time. There are also devices you can install to turn off lights automatically on weekends, when people leave the room, or even remotely via your mobile phone. My favorites include Leafully (`www.leafully.com`) and Melon Power (`www.melonpower.com`).

  Don't let efforts to curb energy usage unintentionally encourage employees to leave the office early. If all the lights go out at 6 p.m., it's hard to stay late to meet a deadline or work flexible hours.

  You can also take an analog approach here: posting small signs over light switches and incorporating "turn off the lights" in end-of-day checklists go a long way toward changing behavior.

- ✔ **When was the last time you reviewed your other overhead expenses?** It's easy to focus on expenses directly related to the product or service you create, and to just assume that the foundational costs — phone bills, Internet connections, printing/copying costs — are efficient as-is. Making a company policy to review these on an annual basis can keep these expenses from reaching runaway peaks.

  The Digital Government Strategy for the federal government of the United States recommends a "Bring Your Own Device" policy, where employees are partially reimbursed for using their existing personal computers and mobile phones for work, citing lowered costs and increased productivity.

- ✔ **What's your expense approval process?** If the answer is "we don't have one," it may be time to create a process — even if it's only one or two bullet points. Typically, an approval process dictates a certain price point, under which employees or departments can make purchasing decisions without approval, and over which approval is required.

  Every approval process should *require* a market price comparison. Although cheaper is not always (or often) better, it never hurts to know where your chosen purchase falls on the pricing ladder. Far too often, I see business people pay way too much for a service solely because they weren't aware of the cost of other options.

Never make it a policy to purchase the lowest-cost option. In fact, I've seen a few companies institute a policy that explicitly *rejects* the lowest-cost choice.

✔ **Do you understand the Total Cost of Ownership for your equipment?** The *actual* cost of most equipment far exceeds its sticker price when you start to factor in future required costs. The sum total of the equipment's costs for the entire time you own it is its *Total Cost of Ownership (TCO)*.

Consider buying a printer. The cost of the printer does not end when you walk away with the printer itself; there are toner cartridges, paper, cables, maintenance contracts, and potentially additional software to purchase as well. Before buying a printer, you should do some back-of-the-napkin math to determine if paying a little more up front ultimately leads to a lower cost overall (because, for example, one manufacturer sells significantly cheaper toner cartridges).

✔ **How do you recognize which expenses are tax-deductible?** This is a particular issue for small businesses where you report your business expenses as deductions on your personal tax return. I've seen companies with dedicated accounting departments that scramble to collect receipts in *boxes* when tax time rolls around, and this is a completely unnecessary cause of stress and waste of time. This gets even more complicated when you depreciate assets (which means you spread the deduction for the cost of expensive equipment over multiple years).

✔ **How are you processing payments?** A sneaky hidden expense is the expense of processing customer payments. This includes payroll expenses for the people handling incoming payments and collection agency costs, as well as actual fees for bank accounts, merchant accounts, and credit card terminals. Knocking even 0.1 percent off your credit card processing rates can put serious money back in your organization's pocket.

✔ **Who is in charge of keeping expenses in check?** Researching competitive pricing is a task that is rarely "owned" by one person in the company. Decision-makers may assume that accounting handles it, or may simply not think about price when comparing other features. If there's no one you can designate in this role, then you at least need to take steps to include cost-checking measures in your project-planning templates (more in Chapter 7).

A bigger problem here is as a company grows, two or more departments may make the *same* purchase independently, when they could have collaborated to lower or eliminate the cost of the additional purchases. It's one thing to add extra seats to one software contract, and another to purchase two different systems that do the same thing.

When comparing costs and potentially switching to different equipment, software platforms, or even health insurance providers, don't forget to consider the cost of switching. For example, if you change health insurance providers every year, you may put employees with chronic illnesses at risk of being rejected or receiving lower benefits. This change may also cause all your employees to have to switch primary care providers, breeding significant resentment. I'm not saying you can never switch providers — in fact, if your employees have lots of negative feedback, it may be wise to switch! — but you need to keep the big picture beyond mere dollars and cents in mind.

How efficient are your prices?

If you're charging too much — or not enough! — your pricing is not efficient. Get to the bottom of your pricing efficiency by asking yourself the following questions:

- **What determines your pricing?** The vast majority of companies I work with have no real answer to this question. Do you?

  Even if it's too late to change your core pricing, understanding why it is what it is (even if that understanding is *because it sounded like a good price*) can change the tone of future price-changing conversations. For example, if cutting a list price by 10 percent means you'd sell at a lower cost than your cost to *produce* that service or item, that's a problem. If that same price cut still leaves you with a 90 percent profit margin, it may be easier to swallow.

- **At how many different prices are you selling the same product or service to different customers?** In businesses where the owner has a direct hand in sales, or where managers have a great deal of pricing leeway, it's all too easy to find yourself billing hundreds of customers at hundreds of different rates for the exact same thing. An ambitious salesperson feels he can get a 10 percent markup on Customer A, while a manager eager to close a deal offers a 40 percent discount to Customer B.

  Although it's ultimately your choice to offer this sort of pricing flexibility, this is wildly inefficient if you have someone *manually* tracking the price differences, and/or if this variation impedes your ability to increase prices in the future if your raw costs go up. Find out how different prices are recorded and billed in your accounting department. You should also run through a hypothetical scenario where you need to increase prices by 10 percent. Is this a matter of a few keystrokes by an accountant, or does it *give* your accountant a stroke?

Consider whether your accounting or billing software lets you "grandfather in" existing customers, which means you can choose to continue offering them their current rate while charging new customers a different one.

- ✔ **Who approves discounts?** A corollary to the above question, you need to codify how much leeway individuals have to change pricing. Usually, these policies consider the total original price (for example, sales people cannot offer discounts on contracts over $5,000 without manager approval) and the percentage or dollar value of the discount (for example, sales people can offer discounts of up to 10 percent on their own, but require approval for greater discounts).

If you have an approval policy, make sure the person with authority to approve the discounts is easily accessible. If it takes two days to approve a contract, you may lose the entire sale, which is the equivalent of offering a 100 percent discount!

- ✔ **Where do you store price lists?** You need a single source for current pricing and all current, past, and planned sales and discounts. Internal employees can't be expected to maintain a list of potential discounts off the top of their heads, and this leaves the door open for both honest mistakes and abuse — particularly if the purchasing customer attempts to use a fraudulent coupon or promotion code.

- ✔ **How do your prices compare to your competition?** Rates that are wildly lower *or* higher than everyone else in your sector likely mean you are leaving money on the table. If they're far lower, you may be able to raise your rate with less resistance. On the other hand, if they're far higher for comparable services, you are probably missing out on customers who can't afford you.

- ✔ **Do you offer volume or prepayment discounts?** If your company is just starting out, a discount for prepayment (for example, 10 percent off if you pay for a full year up front, instead of monthly billing) is a smart way to increase your initial cash flow. Volume and prepayment discounts also work because your costs are generally lower in both arrangements: It costs less to generate a large order and it avoids the costs of frequent billing to receive an annual payment.

In consulting, volume discounts can also make good financial sense because you don't have to spend time or money tracking down additional clients to fill those additional hours.

How efficient is your budget?

Budgeting, when done right, is an important part of an efficient *and* responsible financial strategy. You can check the health of your budget process with the following questions:

- **Do you have a budget?** Some organizations resist budgeting because they feel they can't accurately predict their future expense needs or income. This is a fair point in volatile or new businesses, but it's not a reason to eschew budgets. You need to understand how much you *can* spend or you may find yourself facing a stack of bills you literally cannot pay.

  Budgets don't have to be carved into stone. You can set relative targets and update a budget as a living document (in a spreadsheet) as you take in additional income. The point of a budget is to make sure you pay attention to individual expenses and that you don't exceed your ability to pay at all.

- **Does every department have the same budget?** This is a sign that those budgets were not set thoughtfully. It's rare for every department to have the same expense needs, and it's destructive to assume that they do.

- **How is next year's budget determined?** Is last year's number simply carried over? Is there a change request process? Are last year's expenses analyzed to determine whether individual departments spent their budgets responsibly?

  Never reduce budgets on the basis that last year's budget was not spent in full. This invariably leads to one result: Every department will spend every last allocated dollar regardless of whether they actually need to, which equals a tremendous amount of waste company-wide. I've been hired more than once not because a group was concerned about increasing its efficiency, but because it had to find something to spend its budget on or it would lose those dollars in subsequent years.

- **Do departments have input into their own budgets?** I'm constantly surprised to find otherwise-democratic organizations assign budgets in dictator fashion. I suggest having each department suggest its own budget for final review, rather than the top-down approach of sending each department a prepared budget and asking for feedback (or, worse, not accepting feedback!).

- **How well did each department — and the company as a whole — stay within budget last year?** This is the single-best signal as to whether your budgets are accurate. Wildly exceeding budget is also a *big* problem because it places the entire organization at risk for literal bankruptcy.

- **Where is the budget tracked?** This should be as transparent as possible. If everyone in the company can see that marketing is already past its annual budget and it's only March, that can stem the flow of cash better than a litany of meetings and administrative policies.

- **Is your budget flexible?** An ironclad budget can get in its own way if an emergency situation, or even a large cost-savings measure, comes up a couple months after the budget was set. You need to have a "side door" policy for approving changes in a documented and responsible way.

Conducting an Expense Analysis

For a manager to analyze a business's profit behavior thoroughly, they need to know which expenses are *variable* and which are *fixed* — in other words, which expenses change according to the level of sales activity in a given period, and which don't. The title of each expense account often gives a pretty good clue. For example, the cost of goods sold expense is variable because it depends on the number of units of product sold, and sales commissions are variable expenses. On the other hand, real estate property taxes and fire and liability insurance premiums are fixed for a period of time.

Separating variable and fixed expenses

You should always have a good feel for how your operating expenses behave relative to sales activity. But separating variable and fixed operating expenses is not quite as simple as it may seem. One problem that rears its ugly head is that some expenses have *both* a fixed cost component and a variable cost component.

A classic example was the "telephone and telegraph" expense (as it was called in the old days). Businesses had to pay a fixed charge per month for local calls, but long-distance charges depended on how many calls were made and to where. Modern communication networks using cellphones and the Internet are increasingly flat-fee. In any case, accounting should separate the fixed and variable cost components of expenses for reporting purposes.

Variable expenses

Virtually every business has *variable expenses,* which move up and down in tight proportion with changes in sales volume or sales revenue. Reducing variable expenses means more money in your pocket every time you make a sale.

Here are examples of common variable expenses:

- The cost of goods sold expense, which is the cost of products sold to customers
- Commissions paid to salespeople based on their sales
- Franchise fees based on total sales for the period, which are paid to the franchisor
- Transportation costs of delivering products to customers via FedEx, UPS, and freight haulers (railroads and trucking companies)
- Fees that a retailer pays when a customer uses a credit or debit card

Cost of goods sold is usually the largest variable expense of a business that sells products. Other variable expenses are *operating* expenses, which are the costs of making sales and running the business. The sizes of variable operating expenses, relative to sales revenue, vary from industry to industry. Delivery costs of Wal-Mart and Costco, for instance, are minimal because their customers take the products they buy with them, so they only have to focus on deliveries to a relatively stable number of warehouses. Other businesses deliver products to their customers' doorsteps, so that expense is obviously much higher (and dependent on which delivery service the company uses — FedEx or UPS versus the U.S. Postal Service, for example).

Fixed expenses

Fixed operating expenses include the different costs that a business is obligated to pay regardless of changes in sales levels. As an example of fixed expenses, consider the typical self-service car wash business — you know, the kind where you drive in, put some coins in a box, and use the water sprayer to clean your car. Almost all the operating costs of this business are fixed: rent on the land, depreciation of the structure and the equipment, and the annual insurance premium don't depend on the number of cars passing through the car wash. The main variable expenses are the water and the soap, and perhaps the cost of electricity.

Fixed expenses are the costs of doing business that, for all practical purposes, are stuck at a certain amount over the short term. Here are some more examples of fixed operating expenses:

- Gas and electricity costs to heat, cool, and light the premises
- Employees' salaries and benefits
- Real estate property taxes
- Annual audit fee (if the business has its financial statements audited)
- General liability and officers' and directors' insurance premiums

Be careful not to overreact to a temporary downturn in sales by making drastic reductions in your fixed costs, which you may regret later if sales pick up again.

Margin is your operating profit before fixed expenses are deducted. Don't confuse this number with *gross margin,* which is profit after the cost of goods sold expense is subtracted from sales revenue but before any other expenses are deducted. Your attention should be riveted on margin per unit, and you should understand the reasons for changes in this key profit driver from period to period. A small change in unit margin can have a *big* impact on operating earnings.

Increasing margin can have huge, long-term *negative* impacts on your business if you don't consider potential cost savings in light of your *entire* organization. Outsourcing customer service may shave something off the bottom line, but ultimately lead to plummeting customer satisfaction scores and lost business.

Lowering your expenses responsibly

I can't emphasize this point enough: simply slashing expenses is *not* (necessarily) efficient. In fact, this behavior is why efficiency sometimes gets a bad rap. Recall that every decision has a ripple effect across your organization. Making responsible choices to save money means ensuring that your cost-saving measures don't mean you're ultimately paying *more* in the way of product quality, customer satisfaction, and/or time.

Gathering up the books

The process for analyzing expenses isn't secret or complex: Start by pulling out past years' expense receipts.

If you're committed to expense reduction, or if you have a relatively small number of expenses, you want to go through every single one. If you want to start with a sampling, you can either start with the largest expenses, or with the largest *category* of expenses (see the next section).

For the biggest potential cost savings, focus on variable expenses (which you can separate from fixed expenses as described in "Fixed expenses") first, because lowering those costs means you save *every* time you produce or sell a product.

For the fastest cost savings, focus on fixed expenses. Your list of fixed expenses is probably much shorter than your variable ones, and needs review less often. You can (and should) literally keep a checklist of fixed expenses with the last date you reviewed it, so you can keep an eye on them at least once per year.

Categorizing expenses

Categorizing your expenses has two main benefits. One, it lets you create a pie chart so you can understand at a glance where the majority of your money is going. The biggest piece of the pie is usually the place to start hunting for inefficiencies and cost savings first. Second, it makes filing taxes much simpler and faster if your expenses are already aligned to IRS expense categories. Should you ever be audited, it also makes it easier to pull your records and justify your deductions.

Allegedly, if your business spends an unusually high amount in a given category as compared to other businesses in your sector, the IRS is more likely to audit you. If you are rushing to categorize expenses last-minute, you increase the risk of miscategorizing or, in extreme cases, simply lumping all expenses into a single umbrella category and potentially showing an unusually high number, triggering an audit.

You can find a list of expense categories on the Schedule C tax form. Most major accounting software also has this list.

Some accounting software contains all the typical Schedule C categories in addition to a myriad of other categories. This can make it harder to reconcile come tax time.

Implement a streamlined accounting process that automatically enters each tax-deductible expense into your accounting system as it's spent (or reimbursed). Categorize each expense *in the moment*, rather than waiting until you file taxes to group expenses by travel, office supplies, and so on. On-the-spot categorization takes a few seconds that you hardly notice; all-at-once categorization takes hours that you deeply resent.

Finding out if you're paying too much

The easiest way to review an expense is to identify other providers and compare your current rate to the rates they are offering. You can usually accomplish this with an Internet search or a phone call.

There's no secret trick here, except that you have to know and *remember* to shop around for better rates on your expenses. Here are some common cost savings I help clients uncover:

- **Lowering costs by changing your packaging.** Shipping costs are based on *both* weight and package dimensions; if you have nonstandard dimensions, you often pay additional processing fees. There's also potential savings in buying packaging materials in bulk or from different vendors. Remember that using sub-par shipping materials means your product falls apart or gets soggy, so don't go *too* cheap.

- **Full-time positions you can switch to contractors.** Swapping *the same* employee from a salaried spot to a contractor (who does not receive benefits and who pays his own taxes directly, saving your organization significant money) isn't bound to work well, because that individual will probably be resentful and quit.

  However, you can look forward and determine if certain positions or departments are better served with contractor positions. This is an important consideration for time-limited positions that too many organizations reflexively hire on permanently when they really only need a year of work.

This may sound harsh, but I'm a big believer in setting employment expectations all around. Salaried employees have an expectation that their job will be around for years to come. Contractors know that they are only guaranteed employment up until their next contract. Hiring salaried employees for short-term needs costs you more and sets incorrect expectations on both sides.

✔ **Software you can move into the Cloud.** Software is something you install on a single computer and that you can only access from computers on which that software is installed. When you move to the Cloud, you can access your information from any Internet-enabled computer or device. Not only are Cloud services generally more efficient and easier to customize than software titles — not to mention, you never have to upgrade services that live in the Cloud, eliminating a whole class of upgrade fees and IT expert hours — but they're also generally *way* more affordable.

✔ **Custom software you can move to vendor-supplied titles.** As recently as a few years ago, it was often more cost-effective (and simply felt better to many executives) to hire contractors to build custom software to handle routine business processes like accounting, human resources, or inventory and fulfillment. Today, not only are there powerful options in the Cloud to handle all these needs, but they come complete with something known as an API, which lets a programmer build customizations and integrations on top of the standard platform.

In practice, this means you may be able to enjoy a much more affordable base platform and hire a development team for a relatively small number of hours to build out the "last mile" between that system and your existing internal systems. You no longer have to personally worry about maintaining servers, programming upgrades, or writing statements of work to cover new feature requests. If this isn't your organization's core competency, you are better off using another company that *only* focuses on building the best accounting/inventory/sales service and using your newfound free time to focus on *your* core competency.

If you're considering switching services or software titles, don't forget to account for the hidden costs: data transfer, customization, training, downtime, and initially less-productive employees as they learn a new system.

Make sure you compare *actual* rates and not promotional rates — for example, most Internet providers offer a very low rate for the first six months, and then bump you to a much higher one.

Internet- and software-related expenses are particularly likely to drop significantly in price over a short period of time. Avoid signing multiyear contracts, and pay particular attention when contract renewals come up to whether you have cheaper alternatives. It's also helpful to simply get a number of employee eyeballs on your expenses for a "gut check." There is no exhaustive directory in which you can look up the price you "should" pay for a given service, but individuals within your organization may have particular domain knowledge to know whether certain costs are within (or well out of) range.

Call your current providers once per year to find out if there's a better rate or package that can save your business money. This strategy works on everything from getting a lower corporate credit card interest rate to negotiating better supply costs because your purchase volume has increased.

Making Your Accounting More Efficient

Aside from understanding whether your expenses are as low as they can be without negatively affecting your business, and whether your prices are as high as they can be without chasing off customers, it is important to understand whether you are spending too much money or time on the actual accounting process.

Technology is your friend here more so than in many other areas. There may be great arguments (many of which I make myself) for letting humans answer the phone or process sales, but I have yet to hear a convincing reason to let humans manually type up receipts or do accounting longhand. Remember the days of sitting with page upon page of giant green ledger paper on the kitchen table and manually adding up line after line (on those calculators that printed)? You never have to go back to those tedious, error-prone days again.

Looking at accounting software tools

It would be possible, although not very likely, that a very small business would keep its books the old-fashioned way — record all transactions and do all the other steps of the bookkeeping cycle with pen and paper and by making hand-written entries. However, even a small business has a relatively large number of transactions that have to be recorded in journals and accounts, to say nothing about the end-of-period steps in the bookkeeping cycle.

When mainframe computers were introduced in the 1950s and 1960s, one of their very first uses was for accounting chores. However, only large businesses could afford these electronic behemoths. Smaller businesses didn't use computers for their accounting until some years after personal computers came along in the 1980s. But, as the saying goes, "We've come a long way, baby." A bewildering array of accounting computer software packages is available today.

There are accounting software packages for every size business, from small (say, $5 million annual sales and 20 employees or fewer) to very large ($500 million annual sales and up and 500 employees or more). Developing and marketing accounting software is a booming business. You can go to Google or Yahoo and type "accounting software" in the search field, but be prepared for many, many hits. Except for larger entities that employ their own accounting software and information technology experts, most businesses need the advice and help of outside consultants in choosing, implementing, upgrading, and replacing accounting software. If I were giving a talk to owners/managers of small to middle-size businesses, I would offer the following words of wisdom about accounting software:

- Choose your accounting software very carefully. It's very hard to pull up stakes and switch to another software package. Changing even just one module in your accounting software can be difficult.

- In evaluating accounting software, you and your accountant should consider three main factors: ease of use, whether it has the particular features and functionality you need, and the likelihood that the vendor will continue in business and be around to update and make improvements in the software.

- In real estate, the prime concern is "location, location, location." The watchwords in accounting software are "security, security, security." You need very tight controls over all aspects of using the accounting software and who is authorized to make changes in any of the modules of the accounting software.

- Although accounting software offers the opportunity to exploit your accounting information (mine the data), you have to know exactly what to look for. The software does not do this automatically. You have to ask for the exact type of information you want and insist that it be pulled out of the accounting data.

- Even when using advanced, sophisticated accounting software, a business has to design the specialized reports it needs for its various managers and make sure that these reports are generated correctly from the accounting database.

- Never forget the "garbage in, garbage out" rule. Data entry errors can be a serious problem in computer-based accounting systems. You can minimize these input errors, but it is next to impossible to eliminate them altogether. Even barcode readers make mistakes, and the barcode tags themselves may have been tampered with. Strong internal controls for the verification of data entry are extremely important.

- Make sure your accounting software leaves very good audit trails, which you need for management control, for your CPA when auditing your financial statements, and for the IRS when it decides to audit your income tax returns. The lack of good audit trails looks very suspicious to the IRS.

Processing payments efficiently

Efficient payment processing involves both *automated* systems as well as a *variety* of methods. Much as many of us would like to move away from checks altogether, almost every business I run into has at least a handful of customers that insist on mailing in payments, whether they are a cute grandmother who has been a customer for 40 years or the biggest client contract in the bunch who somehow hasn't managed to adopt electronic bill payments. Processing payments efficiently means choosing the best payment method for a given situation, even if that means you use more than one. Options include the following:

✔ **Credit card terminals.** In the traditional way that retail storefronts to collect payments, you can swipe or type in your customers' credit cards and print a receipt on the spot. This method continues to work fine if you are a retail shop, but is inefficient if you use the terminal to process website or phone orders.

✔ **Website payments.** Even if you don't have an online store, you can still accept online payments. Major providers include Google Checkout, Amazon Payments, and PayPal; you can send clients invoices and they then pay you with their credit card using one of these services. Not only does this keep payment card industry (PCI) compliance in *their* hands and out of yours, but it can sometimes reduce the friction of making a payment if your customers already have their payment information stored on these services. With services like PayPal's Virtual Terminal, you can also manually enter customers' card numbers if you receive them on printed bills or over the phone.

You can also create an online payment form that accepts the aforementioned payment methods using a form creation service like Formstack (www.formstack.com) or Wufoo (www.wufoo.com). These include dynamic options so you can actually use these forms to *accept* orders and charge the corresponding amount.

Some payment caveats

If you accept credit card payments, you need to be aware of PCI compliance regulations — security requirements that you *must* follow, or face huge fines. For example, you cannot print your customers' full credit card numbers on receipts. For more on the PCI compliance regulations that apply to your business, check out www.pcisecuritystandards.org.

Never e-mail credit card numbers! This is inherently insecure behavior. Accepting payments from 10 different sources rapidly becomes inefficient if they are not all connected to a central accounting system that tracks amounts due and payments received. Sending a "past due" invoice to a client who paid via text message two weeks prior creates bad will and undermines your relationship.

✔ **Mobile payments.** If you are out in the field, such as at a tradeshow or fair, you can use a mobile payment method like Square (www.square up.com) to swipe customer cards. Square sends you a tiny device you attach to your mobile phone. You swipe the cards, have customers sign with their fingers, and Square sends you the funds within a few days. The future!

✔ **Text payments.** Major banks and merchant accounts are increasingly offering the ability to send and receive payments via text message. Interestingly, this is the *main* way many people in the developing world exchange funds, and the First World is just now starting to catch up.

Managing accounting automatically

Although every organization has its own comfort and ability level when it comes to process automation, there's *no* excuse for generating routine accounting material like invoices and receipts by hand. Every major accounting software and online merchant account includes the option to auto-create invoices and receipts. (If yours does not, that's a really good sign that it's time to upgrade or switch.) Some of my favorite tools include the following:

✔ **Harvest (**www.harvestapp.com**):** This is both a web-based and a mobile app, so employees who work by the hour can track billable time from anywhere and autogenerate client invoices. You can also set it to create and e-mail invoices automatically at set intervals. This is what I personally use to bill clients.

✔ **Conga Composer (**www.appextremes.com**):** If you use Salesforce.com as a CRM to track clients, you can also autogenerate invoices, receipts, and just about any other document by using Conga Composer to create Microsoft Word and Excel templates. You can then generate documents for a whole list of clients, or on a one-off basis with a custom button.

✔ **Microsoft Word mail merge:** You can insert merge fields into an invoice template you create yourself in Microsoft Word, and then auto-fill those fields based on an Access or Excel database. This isn't ideal, but it works in a pinch if the alternative is truly doing it by hand.

Receipts and invoices are a great place to highlight news, important information, or other information about your business. For example, you can include a reminder that customers can check your 24/7 online knowledgebase for customer service assistance at the bottom of your receipts. Even if they don't need help at the time, that little note can help remind them to check your self-help resources when they *do* need assistance, lowering *your* customer service costs.

Chapter 10

Efficiency, at Your Service

*T*hese days, all you hear about is how you need to be customer-focused by listening to the customer and delivering what they want when they want it with high reliability at a competitive price. Literally hundreds of articles, books, blogs, and white papers, not to mention the thousands of opinions, perspectives, comments, and contributing seminars are generated every year on the subject. Happy, satisfied customers will return and share their thoughts with others, which will make the difference between whether you stay in business or not.

However, in all the excitement of determining how *effectively* you are satisfying your customers' needs and expectations, very little is actually focused on how *efficiently* your organization is operating in order to enable these high levels of customer service performance. Yet, inefficient customer service when taking orders or addressing complaints can and will bankrupt a company faster than any other type of failure. Focusing on how efficiently you service your customers and capitalizing on those best practices will enable your company to be consistently competitive.

In this chapter, I give you some helpful ideas and best practices to ensure that you are operating at peak efficiency as you satisfy and delight your customers.

Discovering the elements of Efficient Customer Service

What is customer service efficiency? How can you determine what "efficient customer service" is? In order to answer these questions, first you need to define what customer service efficiency looks like.

Consider several key questions in evaluating how efficient your organization is with respect to effective customer service:

✔ How efficiently your customers access your products and services — is it easy, simple, fast, error free, user friendly, and cordial?

✔ How efficiently your company processes information, related to:

- Order fulfillment, delivery, confirmation, and tracking
- Customer information — buying tendencies, interests
- Self help, Frequently Asked Questions (FAQs)
- Response to questions, inquiries

✔ How efficiently your company tracks and executes change management of:

- Customer and market desires, new requirements
- Product and services — changes in design, development, creation, provision, delivery, and effectiveness

✔ How efficiently your company manages financial aspects, such as:

- Billing — is it easy, simple, fast, error free?
- Customer accounts — tracking, reporting, customer access

One common way to determine efficiency in customer service is to look at how easy it is for customers to find and buy your products and services, and contact you if they have any questions. In other words, how easy are you to reach?

 Another way to determine efficiency is to look at how easily customers can locate, purchase, confirm, track, receive, and complete their orders without any assistance. How well can they find answers to key questions regarding your products and services totally by themselves at their convenience, not just during normal business hours?

Of course, when customers do contact you, another measure of efficiency is to determine how well you respond to them in terms of timeliness, accuracy, and issue resolution.

Becoming customer-centric is a process that requires focus, effort, and action in certain strategic areas. In the following sections, I discuss each of these six key strategic areas and show you how to implement them. For more on the subject, check out *Customer Service For Dummies*.

Taking a top-down approach

Most business owners, executives, and senior managers, when asked, nod their heads in complete agreement that excellent customer relations are the cornerstone of a successful business. In the final analysis, however, what matters isn't what you say, it's what you *do*. A manager's actions can greatly enhance the staff's commitment to providing improved service.

For example, executives at a well-known communications company take complaint calls in the customer service department once a month. They personally follow up on the calls they answer until the issues are resolved. This allows them to keep the pulse of current issues and have a real understanding of what their team experiences on a daily basis.

Asking for feedback (And actually using it)

Many companies mistakenly assume that they know what their customers want. One of the first and most important steps in becoming customer-centric is taking steps to find out — rather than just assuming that you already know — what your customers want and expect of you.

You need to discover whether you're meeting, and hopefully exceeding, their expectations. You can put your fingers on the pulse of your customers' experience by conducting surveys and forming focus groups.

After you gather and analyze the data, be sure to close the loop by reporting any appropriate findings back to the people you surveyed.

Educating everyone, everywhere

Your front-line staff has the greatest amount of interaction with your customers. Many times, however, these are the workers within the organization who receive the least amount of education.

In this context, *education* means formal classroom-style training in which the objective is to build skills and awareness in specific areas of service excellence as well as any *general improvement activities,* including coaching sessions, team problem-solving meetings, and so on that illuminate the importance of service in those staff members' specific jobs.

Creating customer-centric systems

In my work, I see that *in-focused systems,* systems that work favorably for the company but unfavorably for the customer, serve as the fulcrum on which a successful move toward being customer centered rests. Companies must be willing to examine and change these systems to become more customer-centric. Until the inherent service problems caused by such systems are resolved, any service improvements are limited.

The prospect of creating customer-centric systems can be overwhelming. Part of the problem lies in the tangled web of procedures, policies, and actual technology that make up the systems and act as a blueprint for the way a company does business. Although obviously indispensable, these systems can help or hurt your customers and staff, depending on how they're designed.

Quality groups or service-improvement teams work well when developing procedures and processes. They empower the entire staff to take ownership of the new procedures and processes and ensure that staff members who are the closest to the customers and know the most about the issues are an integral part of brainstorming service solutions. Remember that changes in processes and technology need to be based on customer and employee feedback. After you've gathered feedback, you can use quality groups to design the new procedures and processes.

Developing consistency

Friendliness, courtesy, responsiveness, and accuracy are worthy goals, but how do you achieve them, given that they mean different things to different people?

If you ask ten people what being friendly to a customer means, you'll more than likely receive ten different answers. You have to quantify *service quality* by developing specific, objective, and measurable service standards that translate service quality into specific behaviors and actions. *Service standards* provide a basis for the objective evaluation of staff performance and ensure consistency of treatment for customers across the board.

You must clearly communicate to your staff the behaviors that are required to meet these standards.

Recognizing excellence every chance you get

In a company's culture, what gets recognized and rewarded is what gets done. Every recognition program needs to have three important elements:

- **A formal recognition program:** Formal recognition can be department-, division-, or company-wide. It needs to provide rewards for the individual or team that best fulfills specified service criteria. The rewards can include cash, movie tickets, vacations, lunch with the CEO, and so on.

- **An atmosphere of informal recognition:** Casual, everyday acknowledgment of staff that's often expressed by the manager's spontaneous gestures is what I'm talking about here. It can be in the form of thank-you notes, pizza parties, sharing customers' complimentary letters, and so on. Never underestimate the positive motivating force of recognition.

Knowing the Criteria for Effective Service Standards

Seven criteria make a service standard effective. I recommend that you review your current standards against this list and revamp the ones that need it. Effective standards need to be as follows:

- **Specific:** Standards tell service people precisely what is expected of them. Customers don't have to guess about your expectations or make anything up.

- **Concise:** Standards don't explain the philosophy behind the action. Instead, they get right to the point and spell out who needs to do what by when.

- **Measurable:** Because actions in a standard are all specific criteria, they are observable and objective, which makes them easy to quantify.

- **Based on customer requirements:** Standards need to be based on customer requirements and not just your industry's standards. Fulfilling your customers' expectations gives you an advantage over competitors that do not.

- **Written into job descriptions and performance reviews:** If you want employees to adhere to the standards, then write them down and make them part of each employee's job description and performance review. Using standards as a management tool gives them more credibility.

✔ **Jointly created with your staff:** The best standards are created by management and staff together based on their mutual understanding of customer needs. You may want to consider using quality groups as a vehicle for having members of your staff come up with service standards.

✔ **Fairly enforced:** Standards that are enforced with some people and not with others quickly erode. Company-wide standards require everybody to conform to them, including the top brass. Department-specific standards apply to everyone within that department, including the manager.

Developing Service Standards in Four Simple Steps

The key to developing service standards is organizing the process into bite-sized pieces. In this section, I discuss each of the four steps for developing standards.

Step 1: Defining your service sequences

Viewing your business as a series of separate but connected interactions can help you define and understand what I call *service sequences*.

Service sequences are to your business what chapters are to a book. They're a way of conveniently subdividing the aspects of your service so you can discover specific customer encounters that require standards. For example, if you're in the hotel business, your basic service sequence may go something like this:

Reservations

Check in

Use the room

Check out

Step 2: Mapping out the steps

After you break your business services up into various chapters, choose one area that needs improvement (as indicated by customer feedback). You need to map out the major steps that make up that particular customer encounter chronologically (like the paragraphs within a chapter). For example, the check-in sequence for a hotel includes the following steps:

1. **Guest approaches the front desk.**
2. **Desk clerk asks for the guest's name.**
3. **Desk clerk pulls the guest's reservation from the file (hopefully).**
4. **Desk clerk asks what form of payment the guest will use.**
5. **Guest is given a room key and directions to the elevator.**

In this encounter, no value is added to the basic interaction. It simply is an accurate, step-by-step process that probably reflects how every hotel in the world checks in a guest. Thus to be able to add value to the guest's experience of staying at this particular hotel, you need to define key experience enhancers.

Step 3: Determining your experience enhancers

For each individual step of your service sequences, ask yourself:

> *What general service qualities will enhance the customer's experience of doing business with my company during this step?*

As your guest approaches the front desk in the first step of the check-in sequence, your actions are critical, because they make an immediate first impression on the guest. Two of the most important general service qualities at this point are being friendly and attentive to the guest.

Make sure you carry out this same procedure for each step of each service sequence you want to improve until you determine the key experience-enhancing qualities for each step.

Step 4: Converting your experience enhancers into standards

After discovering how you can enhance the quality of service in a given sequence, you can then rewrite the step-by-step interaction by converting your general service qualities into the three types of service standards: personal, product, and procedural. In the hotel example, you can rewrite the sequence for checking in a guest to reflect these important standards:

- ✔ **Promptness:** When more than three people are waiting in line, call the desk supervisor for assistance.

- ✔ **Friendliness:** Smile at the customer as he or she approaches the front desk, make direct eye contact, and say "Good morning," "Good afternoon," or "Good evening."

- ✔ **Recognition and attentiveness:** Use the guest's name as soon as you know it.

- ✔ **Initiative:** Ask the guest whether he or she would like a wake-up call in the morning.

- ✔ **Quality assurance:** Call the guest within 15 minutes of checking in to make sure that everything in the room is satisfactory. Once at Canlis, a restaurant in Seattle, the host actually called my *table* to check and make sure everything was to our satisfaction. That was quality!

Evaluating the Effectiveness of Your Service

Customer service is a broad term. When trying to determine how effectively you are meeting the needs and demands of your customers, several areas need to be analyzed. The following sections look at each.

How effective are your self-help resources?

One way to determine the effectiveness (and efficiency, of course!) of your self-help resources and processes is to have someone not familiar with your products and services attempt to use them, first alone, and then with some additional guidance in testing specific customer-centric aspects.

The things to assess is whether the customer is actually able to get to the desired information easily and quickly, obtain accurate information without undue searching, and if the customer can subsequently use this information in his/her decision-making regarding placing an order or requesting special customer service.

An easy to way to see if this is effective is to review calls or queries in to customer service, and see how many of them are related to how useful and effective the self-help systems and resources are. If you are experiencing frequent calls for clarification, further explanation, or for information normally found on your self-help resources, it is a good indication you may not have a very effective (or well-marketed) system, and may want to revisit this valuable customer service resource.

The old adage is true: "You never get a second chance to make a first impression." So, if your customers get completely lost trying to help themselves the first time using your (inefficient) self-help services, the likelihood they'll contact you again is very small and you may have lost a customer.

How efficient are your customer service responses?

Do your customers' inquiries get resolved within a few minutes of asking a question or submitting a request? If they are required to ask multiple questions, or have to be routed to different specialists in order to be able to adequately respond, this raises questions as to how efficient your customer service response process is.

Through what is called *awareness building,* you, as a customer service provider, need to survey customers in order to get a good idea as to how efficient your customer service responses are. The following sections look at how to survey customers. For more on awareness building, pick up a copy of *Customer Service For Dummies.*

If you've already invested some time in improving the quality of service your company or department is providing, much of your effort still may be focused on other priorities and goals, such as generating revenue, cutting costs, and budgeting — with more attention going toward quantitative rather than qualitative aspects of the company.

This first phase of implementing your service strategy is designed to help you build awareness throughout your company (from top to bottom) of the overall importance that service plays in your company's future. The main activities that I recommend in this phase are as follows:

- ✔ **Conducting formal surveys of your customers to assess overall satisfaction levels and determine the main customer-service issues.** Benchmarking your starting point before you begin any service improvement program is essential. Various methods you can use to gather feedback include the following:

    - Telephone interviews
    - Online surveys
    - Face-to-face interviews
    - E-mail surveys
    - Complaint-analysis tools
    - Lost-account surveys
    - Focus groups

If you haven't done your customer research, stop dead in your tracks; go no further. Don't waste your time by moving on to other phases before you actually know what your customers and staff think.

Defining Your Customer Service Goals

I am always amazed at how often companies talk about their number one goal of satisfying customers, but they don't establish customer service goals. Without goals for customer service, there can be problems between organizational departments. Take sales and manufacturing, for example, where sales is focused on making every customer happy, whereas manufacturing is focused on getting what the customer ordered delivered on time. These can conflict, depending on what is important to the customer, be it delivery or response, and can result in conflicting actions being taken on behalf of the customer, which can create barriers and ultimately result in both late delivery and a dissatisfied customer.

Finding out why you need customer service goals

To get a better understanding of why goal setting in customer service is so important, it is first critical to review the fundamentals of goal setting. Following are the main reasons to set goals whenever you want to accomplish something significant (for more on the subject, pick up *Managing For Dummies*):

✓ **Goals provide direction.** To get something done, you have to set a definite vision — a target to aim for and to guide the efforts of you and your organization. You can then translate this vision into goals that take you where you want to go. Without goals, you're doomed to waste countless hours going nowhere. With goals, you can focus your efforts and your team's efforts on only the activities that move you toward where you're going — in this case, opening a new sales office.

✓ **Goals tell you how far you've traveled.** Goals provide milestones to measure how effectively you're working toward accomplishing your vision. If you determine that you must accomplish several specific milestones to reach your final destination and you complete a few of them, you know exactly how many remain. You know right where you stand and how far you have yet to go.

✓ **Goals help make your overall vision attainable.** You can't reach your vision in one big step — you need many small steps to get there. If your vision is to open a new sales office in Prague, you can't expect to proclaim your vision on Friday and walk into a fully staffed and functioning office on Monday. You must accomplish many goals — from shopping for office space, to hiring and relocating staff, to printing stationery and business cards — before you can attain your vision. Goals enable you to achieve your overall vision by dividing your efforts into smaller pieces that, when accomplished individually, add up to big results.

✔ **Goals clarify everyone's role.** When you discuss your vision with your employees, they may have some idea of where you want to go but no idea of how to go about getting there. As your well-intentioned employees head off to help you achieve your vision, some employees may duplicate the efforts of others, some employees may focus on the wrong strategies and ignore more important tasks, and some employees may simply do something else altogether (and hope that you don't notice the difference). Setting goals with your team clarifies what the tasks are, who handles which tasks, and what is expected from each employee and, ultimately, from the entire team.

✔ **Goals give people something to strive for.** People are typically more motivated when challenged to attain a goal that's beyond their normal level of performance — this is known as a *stretch goal.* Not only do goals give people a sense of purpose, but they also relieve the boredom that can come from performing a routine job day after day. Be sure to discuss the goal with them and seek feedback where appropriate to gain their commitment and buy-in.

Setting time goals: How much can you save without impacting service?

When you think about time goals in regard to customer service, most people immediately think: "On-time delivery! Of course! What else is there?" But, as you will see, time goals for customer service go beyond just delivering on time. Efficiency associated with on-time delivery is just one aspect. Think about every activity associated with customer service, from initial call or Web contact through issue definition, resolution, confirmation, and completion. Each of these activities, along with dozens more related to customer service, has a time goal in terms of how fast they get acknowledged and addressed, or how long customers must wait to be served, or how long it takes to complete a request.

The following guidelines can help you select the right customer service goals — and the right number of goals — for your organization:

✔ **Pick two to three goals to focus on.** You can't do everything at once — at least, not well — and you can't expect your employees to, either. Attempt to complete only a few goals at any one time. Setting too many goals dilutes the efforts of you and your staff and can result in a complete breakdown in the process.

✔ **Pick the goals with the greatest relevance.** Certain goals bring you a lot closer to attaining your vision than do other goals. Because you have only so many hours in your workday, it clearly makes sense to concentrate your efforts on a few goals that have the biggest payoff rather than on a boatload of goals with relatively less impact to the business.

✔ **Focus on the goals that tie most closely to your organization's mission.** You may be tempted to take on goals that are challenging, interesting, and fun to accomplish but that are far removed from your organization's mission. Don't do it. (At least, not without acknowledging that they're removed from your mission.)

✔ **Regularly revisit the goals and update them as necessary.** Business is anything but static, and regularly assessing your goals is important to making sure that they're still relevant to the vision you want to achieve. Put in quarterly or midyear review schedules. If the goals remain important, great — carry on. If not, meet with your employees to revise the goals and the schedules for attaining them.

Avoid creating too many goals in your zeal to get as many things done as quickly as you can. Too many goals can overwhelm you — and they can overwhelm your employees, too. You're far better off setting a few significant goals and then concentrating your efforts on attaining them. Don't forget that management isn't measured by one huge success after another. Instead, it involves successfully meeting daily challenges and opportunities — gradually but inevitably improving the organization in the process.

For customer service goals, then, think of defining time goals in the language of the customer, and what they value. The real key is to design efficiency into those key processes and policies that deliver to these goal above all else.

For example, if "timely response to my question on the first call" is a key customer service goal, then you should have systems and processes that enable your customer service reps to respond in a timely manner, with all of the requisite information necessary for a successful response on the first call.

You can quickly see that you need to balance necessity with cost-to-implement in order to design creative, innovative ways that enable a great response while managing expenses effectively. Be careful about designing processes and systems that may enable your desired response, but at a cost-prohibitive price.

Think of the way your company currently responds to customer service requests. In today's web-based business environment, whole companies buy and sell products and services in a completely virtual environment, using web-based software and systems to provide product and service information, take orders and payment, track shipments, and confirm receipt — even to track customer service issues themselves. Can you capitalize on this and other technology to enable a better, more efficient customer service experience?

Be careful here. You must always remember the customer service goals, and be sure not to compromise them on behalf of cost savings. If user friendliness or cordiality is critically important to your customer, you want to be careful automating every transaction. Always enable connectivity to a live person who can provide assistance. It may cost more, but ensures that your processes are in line with your customer service goals.

Setting quality goals: Providing the best possible customer service

How your customers define customer service quality will be based on what is important to them. For example, some people want to find an answer quickly on their own, but others may want one-on-one reassurance. The former person may be frustrated to have to call during business hours, but the latter person may feel unappreciated if she has to self-service on your website.

Setting quality goals is directly dependent on what your customer values, and can change from one customer to another. Having said that, however, some standard performance expectations are universal. No one likes to wait on hold for 30 minutes. Remember, a quality resolution is not always about offering a 10 percent discount if the issue was not related to cost, but rather to quality, delivery, or accuracy.

Finding out how efficient your customer relationship management is

CRM (Customer Relationship Management) is the acronym that customer-service professionals are using today. CRM is simply the marriage of process and technology for tracking every contact point that customers have with your organization.

Many companies find a CRM to be overwhelming at first. I have yet to find a company that can really derive benefit from a CRM out of the box (without some degree of customization). However, if you take the time to do it right, valuable lessons can be learned from CRM — lessons that can improve your bottom line, such as discovering specific and often unspoken customer needs that enhance both loyalty and sales.

Measuring Customer Service Efficiency

So, what determines *efficiency*?

When you call to confirm an order, you want confirmation within one minute or less. If you go online, you want easy, one-click confirmation capability. Better yet, you want an e-mail proactively confirming your order, when it is shipped, when you can expect it, and telling you of anything that comes up to delay or affect your order. Not a problem, right?

For a company, efficiency also implies simple, effective systems to enable customers to have this capability.

So, how do you measure customer service efficiency?

Start by considering what is important to the customer, in terms of service: Reliable, receptive, timely responses come to mind, along with simple, effective, and easy-to-use self-help tools. This is easy to envision, because everyone's someone's customer. You want these things from the businesses you buy products and services from and interact with frequently.

These kinds of characteristics are what are called Key Performance Indicators, or KPIs. They indicate whether service is performed at a desired level, as measured specifically to established targets or goals. For example, timeliness in response is a KPI, which can be measured by tracking the percent of incidents that had a response within 24 hours. Ease of use and simplicity may be measured in tracking the number of screens and clicks required to complete a request. Resolution may be measured through tracking issues or questions resolved within two days, or by method of resolution.

As you can see, KPIs can be measured different ways, depending on the organization's customer service approach and goals. After you have identified the customer-defined measures, then you can review the policies, processes, and systems that you have in place to enable these goals to determine how efficient they are. Processes that provide for rapid response and resolution can be measured in terms of how much effort was required per each customer interaction, or dollar value settled, or by percent escalated for resolution. The internal efficiency measures would be selected to best represent performance against key business performance KPIs such as cost, resources, time, and any operational expense and/or capital investment required.

Gathering info about your customers' satisfaction levels

You have many ways to gather customer information about their satisfaction. One common way is to review your customer service inbox. If a customer is dissatisfied with what you've provided in terms of quality or service, they are likely to send a letter or e-mail to let you know about the issues (after chewing out some managers, of course). No doubt, you have a method for dealing with customer complaints and the issues that arise from time to time within your company. The Balanced Scorecard customer leg is ideal for tracking these issues.

Here are other common ways you can gather information from customers:

- Evaluate communication at call centers and help desks.
- Check out product-return centers.
- Interview field service reps and technicians.
- Conduct surveys and send out questionnaires.
- Hire a third party (consultants, websites).
- Hold discussions with focus groups.

Zeroing in on the right customer measures

How do you measure your customers? Do you get a ruler and size them up, or do you count them out one by one? Most companies already have some data and information on their customers, and we're sure you do, too. That's well and good, but the first thing you need to ask when beginning the customer scorecard is if your data and information include the *right* measures. Do they really reflect what your customers think and how they feel about your products or services? Do they focus on the critical few things that are truly important to customers? In short, does your data measure what you really need to measure?

You can take many different approaches to measure your customers, but the key is to find the critical ones that are important to you and your company so that you can hit the right mark and avoid costly mistakes. The following sections work to help you identify these proper measures and weed out the bad ones. I also assist you in implementing the tracking measures, and I list the common mistakes you want to avoid at this stage of the process.

The measures you select depend on where you are in your organization. A strategic-level customer scorecard, for example, will have measures that comprise high-level objectives, such as customer retention and loss rates and profit and revenue per customer. Customer scorecard measures at the operational and tactical levels will be more specific. For example, you can measure what it is about your product or service that drives retention, profit and loss, or revenue measures at the strategic level. Such measures usually focus on things like quality, cost, and speed of delivery.

So whom do you survey? This would seem to be obvious, but it is actually not so easy. Certainly you want to ask your customers, right? But which ones? And at what level within your customers? You need to ask those customers that have some knowledge about your customer service processes, likely because they have had to avail themselves of your services at one time or another.

When you consider the best way to ask your customers, surveys come to mind almost immediately. This is because surveys provide immediate, up-to-date feedback. However, conducting a survey requires that you already understand your customer's needs and expectations.

Having a customer-focused company means you must understand what your customers want and expect from your business and then evaluate how well you're meeting those desires and expectations. An often overlooked yet vital tool for accomplishing those tasks is the survey. Surveying helps you

- ✔ Gather specific feedback about how satisfied your customers are with the level of service they receive.
- ✔ Provide an initial benchmark against which you can measure future progress.
- ✔ Make changes, based on your research, to the way you do business.

Surveying Staff and Customers

If you've already decided to survey your customers and you're reading this chapter to find out the next step, don't stop there. The importance of surveying customers is obvious to most companies; however, I believe that a staff survey also is an essential part of the surveying process.

I recommend that you survey your customers and staff simultaneously (or at least not too far apart), because often the issues that come to light in your customer responses directly correlate to situations described by your staff.

For example, in a survey I conducted for a software company, the majority of customers reported dissatisfaction with the way they were treated when they called the technical support department. In the corresponding staff survey, several technical support representatives complained that their call times were so closely monitored that they felt pressured to give incomplete answers to one customer so they could move on to the next caller. By observing both sides of the problem, the company was able to make some immediate changes for the better.

How often to measure your customer service efficiency depends on how frequently information is updated, coupled with how available staff and customer input is. For example, you may want to automatically record the date and time of every customer service transaction in order to get an idea of the average cycle time, and of any peaks and valleys through the day. To track resolution performance, you may want to capture this information daily. But you may want to survey staff only once or twice a year, since you are looking for process performance improvement opportunities in that case, and therefore can collect this type of information more infrequently.

A good rule of thumb is to define the frequency of measurement as dictated by how quickly you can respond and adjust or correct the customer service process being measured in order to improve the customer experience.

Figuring Out What Type of Survey You Need to Do

The type of survey that your company chooses depends on your purpose for doing the survey. Are you looking for some insight into why you've lost market share? Are you interested in getting a general idea of how your customers feel about your company? Maybe you've been experiencing high staff turnover and want to get to the bottom of the problem. Here, I discuss some basic types of surveys that you may want to consider and why they may or may not be right for you.

Random customer survey

The *random customer survey* is a tried-and-true, good old-fashioned, all-around survey that's used by companies that want to measure overall customer satisfaction and highlight any widespread service problems. Random surveys involve selecting a percentage of your customers; contacting them by phone, e-mail, mail, or in person (or a combination of these approaches); and asking them to evaluate the service they receive from your company. If your company has never conducted a survey, or hasn't done one in a long time, a random survey is a good place to start.

Company-wide attitude survey

The *company-wide attitude survey* helps you assess three areas that are critical to forging strong links in the chain that determines the service your customers receive.

The company-wide attitude survey almost always is implemented through a confidential questionnaire that is sent out to all staff members and managers. If your company has never conducted a staff survey, or has morale problems such as high turnover, I strongly recommend a company attitude survey.

How satisfied are your staff members with their jobs?

Nothing can tarnish the service your customers receive faster than coming face to face with an employee who has a resentful attitude about his job or your company.

This attitude can be caused by many things, but I find the most common are:

- ✔ Not feeling listened to or appreciated
- ✔ Feeling overwhelmed by an ever-increasing workload
- ✔ Inadequate job training or support
- ✔ Lack of teamwork between departments
- ✔ Poor supervisors or managers

Although none of these situations can be corrected overnight, a survey can help highlight common problem areas and put them on the table for discussion.

Do you have open channels of communication?

I've yet to deal with a company that didn't have communication problems. The question is: How serious are those problems? If, for example, your staff members feel disenfranchised because they have no formal avenues for giving feedback to upper management, then their frustration will be taken out on customers. A staff survey can help you assess how well you're establishing open channels of communication and where room for improvement exists.

Do employees feel a sense of teamwork throughout your company?

Is each person within your company an island unto themselves? If the coffee pot runs dry, does the last person using it brew another pot? If a customer calls in and reaches the wrong person, is she treated with care and concern or is she transferred randomly into telephone hyperspace? A staff survey can help a great deal with identifying and correcting teamwork deficiencies throughout your company.

Lost account survey

This type of survey is excellent whenever your company wants to know why it has lost a particular customer or group of customers. Using this survey, interviews are conducted (usually by telephone or in person — rarely e-mail) with customers who no longer do business with your company.

One of the greatest benefits of the lost account survey is that you're often able to discover specific reasons why customers left. You can also let the lost customer know that you're sorry that he's no longer doing business with you and that you're interested in learning from your mistakes. Understanding the customer's reasons for leaving helps you make improvements for future customers.

Because you're catching the customer at a critical moment, you may have an opportunity during the interview to save the account by using *bounce-back initiative,* which means responding to a service problem by doing something extra as a way of apologizing to the customer.

Depending on your industry, isolating the customer's actual moment of departure isn't always easy, and without that information, recovering a customer before it's too late can be difficult, because you may miss your window of opportunity to take timely and effective actions. If you're able to catch the customer in time, I recommend that you prevent the person who originally was responsible from contacting the customer. To maintain objectivity, you can instead have someone who has no previous contact with the customer conduct the interview.

Target account survey

Rather than doing a random survey of your customer base, you may want to do a more targeted and focused survey of a particular group of customers. For example, if 80 to 90 percent of your business comes from ten customers, you may want to create a survey that is specifically targeted to them. The advantage of a targeted survey is that it is limited in scope, precisely focused, and can be specifically designed for a particular group.

I especially recommend this type of survey when you want to improve service for a particular segment of your customer base.

Focusing on future customers

While taking a look at your existing customer base, you also need to be keeping your eyes on the future. Ask the following questions pertaining to your business and industry:

✔ Where are your markets heading?

✔ What new trends are emerging in your industry?

✔ What's the state of technology, and how will it impact your customers and your business?

✔ Can you identify ways to leverage what you currently do and move into other markets to gain additional customers?

Customer exit survey

On-the-spot interviews conducted with customers as they exit from your place of business are great for assessing their immediate opinion of the service they've just received. For example, at one time or another, you've probably been stopped by someone with a clipboard in hand as you left the supermarket. That person probably asked whether you had a moment to answer a few questions about the service you received at the store that day. These *customer exit surveys* are a cousin of random customer surveys, with one important exception: They catch the customer immediately after he or she receives the service. Doing so provides you with specific, accurate, and immediate feedback while the experience is still fresh in the customer's mind.

I recommend this type of survey whenever your customers physically visit your place of business to use services or purchase products.

Communicating with Customers

What do you tell your customers? Do you talk with them regularly? About what? How much do you actually know about what your customers want, their plans, goals, or strategies? How much do you factor in?

If you don't know the answers to these questions, don't be surprised. Many managers focus so much energy on pleasing the customer they often don't really know what the customer's own plans and goals are. It is more about just being sure to give the customer what they want. Sound familiar?

But in the realm of customer service, there is much to be gained toward developing greater efficiencies, both short term (in the processes that deliver value to the customer) and long term (in the planning for future products and services). It is vital not only to communicate with customers, but also to develop a two-way dialogue so you can come to a greater understanding of what they want and why, and how you can fulfill those wants and needs.

Communications with customers should always be approached as a partnership, sharing each other's goals and common interest in your products and services. The long-term benefit will be a better understanding of each other's needs, as well as developing a shared trust and common purpose.

Communicating and establishing relationships: Two common threads

The incessant tasks that make up your day are the *functions* of your job. Thinking that all the paperwork, e-mails, memos, and meetings are the whole story is tempting, but if you look a little deeper, you find two common threads that link together the fabric of everything you do at work, regardless of whether you're a plumber, a teacher, or an IRS auditor.

The first common thread is communicating with other people. Although plumbers may spend most of their day alone under a sink with only a wrench for company, their communication skills are what count when they explain to you what the problem is and what it will cost to fix it. A teacher's ability to make a subject utterly fascinating or boring has a great deal to do with the way he or she talks about it. Even the IRS has instituted customer communication improvement programs during the past few years! The bottom line is that everyone, regardless of whether they work alone or in a group, uses some form of communication to get their jobs done.

Communication isn't just about talking. It's also body language, writing, and, in today's world, online interaction. *Customer Service For Dummies* offers some valuable techniques for enhancing your communication skills.

The second common thread of the workplace routine is establishing relationships with other people. *Relationship* usually refers to a personal connection, such as a friend, spouse, or family member. However, in the service game, the word relationship means connecting with another person to accomplish something. Go back under the sink and visit with your seemingly solitary plumber and you discover that he or she has relationships with customers, vendors, and fellow plumbers. The same applies to the schoolteacher, who not only has relationships with the students but also with their parents, fellow teachers, and school administrators. IRS auditors likewise have relationships with tax accountants, citizens, and the United States government. (Now that's a lot of relationships.)

Building relationships to last

Many years ago, service gurus counseled senior executives to create customer-centric organizations. Becoming customer-centric often meant moving away from an intense focus on product development to placing an equal amount of emphasis on relationship development. After all, even great products fail occasionally, and a strong bond between company and customer can overcome most problems.

If you're a business owner today, you still need to develop trusting relationships with your customers. The differences between today's business world and the business world of the past are the tools that you have at your disposal. A courteous voice on the telephone and a friendly face across the counter still are important; they're just so expensive nowadays that they have to be rationed. Replacing these luxuries are software and hardware that can be as rewarding to your customers as they are to your company's bottom line when they're designed, integrated, and used with a focus on customer service.

Staying close to your customers

Customers rarely describe doing business over the Internet as a warm and fuzzy experience. The absence of face time is, for many, the downside of today's Internet-heavy service environment. And yet, never before have businesses had the opportunity to be in such close and direct contact with their customers. The Internet enables your company to be in direct communication with all your customers — regardless of where they reside on the planet — as long as they have an Internet connection.

You can assess individual customers' needs, apologize, say thank you, ask for input, and suggest new products or services suited to each one of them rather than to an entire demographic group — all online. Think of the Internet as a direct line to your customers and a new, exciting opportunity for any company that knows the value of listening and staying close to its customers.

Actively communicating with your customers can be very beneficial for both sides, and provide a continuous dialogue so you can better understand their needs and how to fulfill them.

You can also establish a customer "dashboard" specific to customer service, and make it available online so that your customers can be constantly informed as to their order and delivery status, and of any changes that can arise. For helpful hints and guidelines on how you can do this, take a look at *Balanced Scorecard Strategy For Dummies*.

Setting up efficient communication channels

A key component for customer communication is to set up channels for dialogue and exchange of information, and provide for customer service whenever needed. These channels can and should take on several forms, in order to provide flexibility, and feed into the ticket system and knowledgebase for future analysis:

- ✔ **Phone** — You can establish multiple telephone connections: one that will support customer service inquiries and requests, and another to enable free discussion of key strategies, plans going into the next year, and key initiatives that will impact (and hopefully benefit) your company as well.

- ✔ **E-mail** — Establish a customer service e-mail address, to enable customers' flexibility in reaching you with any requests or inquiries of a specific nature.

- ✔ **Website** — Establish a clear, simple, easy-to-use ordering system that is web- or source-based, with provision for both contact with questions and live chat capability. You can also integrate a third-party case management tool such as ZenDesk (www.zendesk.com) or UserVoice (www.uservoice.com).

- ✔ **Text** — Establish, similar to phone, a contact number where a customer can text with specific desires, or inquire about a product or service or existing order. Apps exist today especially suited for this purpose, and you will distance yourself from your competition by providing this additional channel.

- ✔ **Facebook, Twitter, and other socially based web media** — Establish regular lines of communication, blogs, and extra channels enabling customers to comment and ask key questions.

- ✔ **Paper-based** — If your customer base calls for it, you may need to offer a paper-based ordering option for people who need or choose to interact this way.

You will need to monitor these regularly, to ensure their continued efficient utilization as needed, and that they indeed feed your information-gathering systems for future analysis.

Keeping in mind the importance of timeliness

Timeliness is perhaps the most important gauge with which a customer evaluates value. Referring to more than just on-time delivery (which is important enough), timeliness also deals with response time to an order, question, or request, and how long it takes to answer a call or respond to changes or adjustments to orders or customer service requests.

Everywhere, companies are being judged on the basis of whether they deliver on time, respond promptly to customer service calls, or quickly and effectively deal with any issues that may come up. Practically every company measures on-time delivery as a KPI, and people are judged by whether they are on time to work or to meetings. In fact, timeliness is an ingrained component of our society and how we interact.

Timeliness is so critical, it plays a vital role in determining how efficient your customer service is. As you survey your customers, look for any indication that there may be an issue with timeliness, and if you find it, attend to it immediately. Maintaining a reputation for being on time and prompt in response has many positive benefits, spilling over into better performance, greater customer retention, and growth.

Routing messages efficiently

One key component that plays an important part in customer communication is the efficiency by which messages are routed, from the customer to the right area. Messages should move as quickly and effectively as possible, with the least number of stops, if any, along the way.

Routing is usually built in to most messaging systems, though it may be non-obvious. A phone tree can direct callers to the right department by having them dial the right number. A web form can send e-mail to different people in your organization based on the topic selected in a drop-down.

If you have an actual customer support center, make sure the escalation policy is clear and in writing. At what point do they escalate a call to someone else, such as a manager? Who exactly do they call to handle technical problems they can't solve, or refund requests.

Handling Customer Service Issues with Grace

Responsiveness is the most important aspect of customer service efficiency, especially when handling customer service issues. The following sections show you how to demonstrate to your customer's that you care.

Following up with your customers for adjustments

Unfortunately, rather than follow *up* with customers, many companies foul *up* with their customers. That's good news for you, especially if the ones who are fouling up with them are your competition and you're the ones who are following up with them. It's a sad and sordid tale about the number of companies that don't validate the conclusions they reach about their customers and what they think they know. It's almost like they were marksmen who follow a process of "ready, fire" while skipping "aim" entirely. As any good marksman will tell you, you hit the target consistently only when you follow the process in the right order: ready, aim, fire. And I know you want to be one of those who are hitting the mark of customer satisfaction consistently.

In order to hit the bull's-eye like a true marksman, you have to validate your data and information with your customers. Doing so enables you to adjust your aim based upon new information, and finding out this new info is as easy as asking the following questions:

- ✔ Did we get this right?
- ✔ Is this what you're talking about?
- ✔ Is this what you want?
- ✔ Are we on the right track?
- ✔ Did we miss something?

You also need to keep your customers informed about what you've learned and the changes you make as a result of your new knowledge. If you do, you can manage the information they get and keep them thinking about you and your company. After all, they will think about you when it comes time to buy your service or product in the future. So keep your customers informed by doing the following:

- ✔ **Putting out company newsletters or putting valuable information on your website.** Both are excellent ways to keep you customers informed about what you and your company are doing.

- ✔ **You can use newspapers and journals to generate a buzz about new products and services and about how you're dealing with issues that are important to them.** Let them know they matter to you and that you care about them.

- ✔ **If a customer has a complaint, send them a personal letter, letting them know you are working the problem and you appreciate their business and will work hard to solve their issues.** When solved, send them another letter, letting them know it's solved and what you've done to correct it.

  Yes, I said a *personal letter!* Not one of those boilerplate, cookie-cutter kind of letters that get e-mailed out en masse that has all of the personality of a pet rock. I know, it takes time to do this, but put yourself in their shoes. Getting a personal letter makes you feel special, and isn't that how you want your customers to feel — special?

Picking out the analytics you should be measuring

As customer service has evolved, so have the metrics and resulting analysis. Today, the metrics and analysis you should be conducting is very different than what you did even 20 years ago.

Today's analytic focus should be on a myriad of customer components, focused to enable a much more predictive than reactive ability, to allow a company the ability to conduct

- ✔ Process modeling
- ✔ Predictive modeling
- ✔ Rule definition
- ✔ Business intelligence
- ✔ Knowledgebase decision logic

Key analytics may include but not be limited to the following:

- ✔ Customer behavior trends, profiles that dictate certain back office activity levels
- ✔ Customer segmentation and type definition (including demographics and other differentiators) to enable an understanding and potential predictability of purchasing and customer service trends that correlate to specific characteristics

✔ ROI based on customer service experience and population, defining costs and resourcing optimization, potential for linear programming to assign resources in the best interests of the company

✔ Additional business intelligence (part of knowledgebase) to include scorecard/dashboards, online analytical processing, decision making, and automated recommendation drivers

✔ CRM predictive customer buying models

✔ Portal-based customer service tools

✔ Intelligence surrounding the customer services issues handled, including demographics, type and size of customers, and purchasing habits. This includes the number of contacts that were required to resolve an issue, by type

✔ Chronic, repeating issues, and reactive tasks conducted by customer service affecting efficiency

Choosing a Ticketing System

Picture your company: You are taking a lot of orders in multiple ways (for example, phone, e-mail, snail-mail and over-the-counter) and you're providing customer service in all those different ways, too. Sounds crazy, right? Yet in order not to lose opportunities to support customers that want to order and receive customer service in different ways according to their needs and business models, many companies try – and fail – to be all things to all people. What can you do to support such a complex business model? Streamline all of your customer service interactions through a single system that tracks and manages information coming through e-mails and other means, as well as all communication related to service tickets, and provides for time and resource management in responding to customers.

In customer service circles, this is known as a Ticketing System. A Ticketing System provides for a standard method to track and manage all communications, service tickets, and resolutions, and helps assign time and resources according to defined priority, while enabling real-time reporting and response. While such a system is vastly superior to any manual-based tool, not all ticketing systems are created equal. You must first understand several aspects, and determine what would be the best fit for your business needs:

✔ **E-mail and communications management** — although most do this well, some also back up records, which may be of use for archival requirements, as well as enabling a more secure system in case of a failure or crash.

✔ **Business Needs** — you will need to define how complex your situation is, how much you want to control versus enabling self-service capability for your customers, and whether you have any requirements for highly secure systems.

✔ **Type of system** — After you determine your e-mail and communications management characteristics, and the level of complexity for your business needs, you will want to select the type of system most appropriate to your needs. This involves understanding some of the capabilities of a Ticket System currently available off the shelf versus web-based versus specific software programming:

- **Web-based systems** provide for tracking and management, can be expanded to manage multiple databases, and provide greater support to self-service capabilities. Most have APIs, which allow developers to build additional capabilities or integrations on top of them to customize them to your exact needs.

- **Software programs** come as a program that has to be downloaded onto every computer, but can work in environments that have limited Internet access.

Several help resources are available on the Web to help you in selecting which Ticketing System is best for your needs. Service and support ticketing systems enable you to manage your e-mail and communication with customers in a standard, timely, and responsive manner, integrating the services required, and providing for FAQ and other information needed by the customer (including a knowledgebase).

Many of the systems have a cost associated with them, determined by size, user base, and other factors. However, there are a couple that are free and provide limited capability as well. The key will be to continually assess the system for its usefulness and compatibility with your business model and customer service needs and goals.

Presently several ticket systems are referred to on websites, and are provided here in no particular order. Each needs to be assessed against your organization's needs and goals:

✔ ZenDesk

✔ User Voice

✔ Get Satisfaction

✔ Salesforce.com Support Cloud

Helping Your Customers Help Themselves

Customer service has shifted over the last 40 years to a much more customer-driven system. From a customer service efficiency perspective, the idea is to help the customer help themselves in every aspect of their customer experience, from selection, ordering, receiving, and billing, to any need that may require additional information or clarification.

This reduces the need for a company to staff at the levels required in order to answer the phone, allowing for concentration in key areas, and utilizing the instant messaging capability for customers who want to converse with a live person, through the IM window, while they are still in the order page.

For customers, the idea is to make it easy to navigate and to resolve any question or query or concern that may come up.

So, how well do you enable your customers to "self-help" regarding their ordering and customer service needs? There are conflicting schools of thought on this, where one side believes that the customer should have total access to all pages and resources in order to be able to process his/her order. The other side believes that customer service will always extend to helping the customer with a live person for any and every task the customer wants to perform.

So, how does your company feel about this? The answer will define your self-help customer service process, so make it carefully.

Creating a knowledgebase

A *knowledgebase* is a searchable directory of solutions, help articles, past cases, and other materials that current customers (and even employees) can use to find answers to their questions. This is a tool that provides for intelligent information storage and interpretation where customers are troubleshooting specific issues. A knowledgebase can complement a help desk by enabling the customer to determine what is wrong, troubleshoot the issue, and determine the correct resolution all without having to call in to customer services at all. This software works in conjunction with a search engine to enable the widest possible search capability for root cause and problem resolution.

Creating a knowledgebase helps in determining chronic repeatable customer service issues or opportunities for improvement, because you can run reports on the search terms visitors enter and how many hits each article receives. Many knowledgebase platforms, such as Microsoft's, incorporate some degree of voting so end users can rate whether a particular article is helpful or not.

Providing online tools

Tools to help with customer service efficiency, along with a ticket system and knowledgebase, include:

- Help — Frequently Asked Questions (FAQs)
- Phone, text, and e-mail — automated proactive messaging
- Instant messaging with online customer service representatives

This is just a partial list. You should explore what options are available to you and your customer, what systems you share, and how you can mutually benefit through collaborative communication best practices.

Knowing When You've Succeeded

You can determine how successful your customer service is in many ways — some related to your overall customer service performance as well as through incoming information from customers regarding their service and satisfaction levels. Much of this can be provided via a dashboard, as discussed previously.

The important thing here is to look for ways to determine the level of how successful your customer service efficiency is, and use this information on a regular basis by building in continuous improvement practices to make your customer service experience better.

Chapter 11

Ready, Aim, Hire:
Human Resources Efficiency

. . . .

In This Chapter

▶ Understanding what HR efficiency is

▶ Setting goals for more effective processes

▶ Assessing your HR efficiency

▶ Looking at best practices for hiring and firing

▶ Thinking about efficient scheduling

▶ Using the tools for HR efficiency

. . . .

*T*he greatest costs in almost any organization center on one thing: its people. Salaries, benefits, and the costs associated with recruiting and training employees all add up to a significant amount of money. This makes it especially important for executives and managers to optimize the human resources (HR) processes and to make them as efficient as possible.

The bottom line for the importance of human resources efficiency comes down to this: if you hire efficiently, you can largely avoid having to learn about how to *fire* efficiently. Despite the stereotypes of business executives being cold or unfeeling, I have never once met one who got any pleasure out of letting someone go. (That's often what they hired me to do on their behalf.) Sometimes, avoiding hiring a full-time employee for a temporary assignment — or avoiding hiring someone *at all* — is the most efficient choice.

In this chapter, I look at many different aspects of HR efficiency, including onboarding, setting HR goals, measuring employee sentiment and effectiveness, hiring and firing, alternative scheduling, HR tools that can improve efficiency, and more.

Knowing What HR Efficiency Looks Like

Companies today are smaller, leaner, and not as hierarchically structured as they were 20 years ago. But the most significant change in the organizational makeup of most companies has less to do with the infrastructure and more to do with the fundamental *nature* of jobs — and the working arrangements of the people who hold those jobs.

What's happening, in short, is that you can no longer think of today's workplace as the specific building or piece of real estate where employees perform their jobs. You also can't think of a job as an activity that starts at 9 a.m., ends at 5 p.m., and lasts through to retirement. Today is the age of the telecommuter and the virtual office. Thanks to wireless connections, the Internet, video conferencing, mobile phones, and other technology tools, many businesses can run efficiently even though the key players almost never meet face-to-face.

To maximize HR efficiency, you need a strategy in place to help ensure that workers bring the necessary skills to the table and that they are smoothly integrated into the existing work environment.

How efficient is your hiring process?

People generally assume that when hiring decisions go wrong, the fault lies with bad judgment during the interview process. However, this view is simply far too simplistic.

The traditional hiring notion of "finding the best people to fill job openings" has been replaced by a much more dynamic concept. It's generally referred to as *strategic staffing,* which means putting together a combination of human resources — both internal and external — that are strategically linked to the needs of the business and the realities of the labor market. An efficient hiring approach takes into account the immediate and long-term needs of the business, as opposed to the specs of a particular job.

Table 12-1 shows the difference between the traditional approach to hiring and the strategic staffing model.

Table 12-1	Paradigms: Old and New
Old Staffing Paradigm	*Strategic Staffing*
Think "job."	Think tasks and responsibilities that are keyed to business goals and enhance a company's ability to compete.
Create a set of job "specs."	Determine which competencies and skills are necessary to produce outstanding performance in any particular function.
Find the person who best "fits" the job.	Determine which combination of resources — internal or external — can get the most mileage out of the tasks and responsibilities that need to be carried out.
Look mainly for technical competence.	Find people who are more than simply "technically" qualified but can carry forward your company's mission and values.
Base the hiring decision primarily on the selection interview.	View the selection interview as only one of a series of tools designed to make the best choice of hiring.
Hire only full-time employees.	Consider a blend of full-time and temporary workers to meet variable workload needs.

As a leader, you need to look at your company's overall priorities and determine their staffing implications. Equally important, you need to make sure that any staffing decision clearly supports these business priorities. You're not simply "filling jobs." You're constantly seeking to bring to your company the skills and attributes that it needs to meet whatever challenges it may face.

How efficient is your onboarding process?

An effective *onboarding* program consists of supplemental efforts taken early in a new employee's tenure to help him build a better understanding of your organization's culture, his job responsibilities, and how they tie into company and departmental priorities. Onboarding goes beyond mere practicality and acknowledges that what new employees learn in their first few weeks has long-term effects on their ability to tackle the challenges of today's faster-paced business environment. In other words, starting out on the right foot is even more important than employers ever thought.

Depending on your company's size and the complexity of the work, an onboarding program can last from several weeks to several months. It covers matters related to training, scheduled milestones, mentoring programs, and interactive meetings where employees can ask questions about corporate or departmental initiatives.

How efficient are your employee policies?

In the 21st century, a workplace that's free of hazards, sexual harassment, and discrimination is no longer considered a "benefit." It's something that employees have every right to expect. In recent years, federal, state, and local government agencies have been using their powers of enforcement to ensure that workers are protected.

Government-mandated regulations touch almost every aspect of the human resource function, including safety and health, equal-employment opportunity, sexual harassment policies, pension reform, and environmental issues.

There's also a growing body of research (combined with my own anecdotal experience) that you can get greater productivity and loyalty from your employees when your corporate policies provide them with greater autonomy and freedom. Treat your employees like children — requiring doctor's notes on sick days, demanding that their bodies be in chairs not one minute after 9 a.m., and dictating rather than discussing projects — and you will get child-like returns. Empower your employees and you will get empowered results.

With all of these external demands — compounded by a company's own policies and procedures — it's easy for employee policies to become inefficient and actually serve as *obstacles* for high-performing organizations. You should never have more policies than you need. For years, department store giant Nordstrom famously distilled its employee policies down to just one page.

Examining HR Goal Setting

If you created a list of the most important duties of management, "setting goals" would likely be near the top of the list. In most companies, senior management sets the overall purpose — the vision — of the organization. Middle managers then have the job of developing goals and plans for achieving the vision senior management sets. Managers and employees work together to set goals and develop schedules for attaining them.

Goals provide direction and purpose, helping you see where you're going and how you can get there. And the *way* you set goals can impact how motivating they are to others.

Putting people first when setting HR goals

Consider two aspects of contemporary business. On the one hand, in order to thrive, your organization must be diligent, competitive, and keenly focused on bottom-line results. But at the same time, most of the companies that earn respect and profits know that nothing is more critical to attaining their goals than a workforce that feels not only engaged, but also *valued*.

The cornerstone of a great place to work is trust built on open, engaged relationships between management and employees. Only from that foundation can employees feel the profound sense of engagement that marks a great company. Here are some things to consider when setting HR goals:

- **Employee well-being as a core value.** Without exception, companies known for their "people-friendly" HR policies have adopted the notion that employees are a cherished asset — and need to be treated accordingly.

- **A reasonable commitment to job security.** Though even the most employee-friendly businesses in today's marketplace can't guarantee life-time employment, companies that place a high value on the personal well-being of their people tend to view massive layoffs as a last resort, not a reflex response to a business downturn. This has a flip-side as well: do not hire people you *know* you only need for six months as employees. Being clear when people do *not* have job security is hugely important.

- **People-friendly facilities.** Virtually all businesses today are obligated by state and federal law to provide a safe working environment. Employee-friendly companies, though, go above and beyond, creating facilities and introducing policies that far exceed legal requirements.

- **Sensitivity to work-life balance issues.** A company's ability to attract and retain employees with the expertise it requires relates increasingly to the "human" side of the everyday working experience — the general atmosphere that prevails in the workplace. This includes, in particular, the extent to which company practices help people balance the pressures they face at work with the pressures they have to deal with at home.

- **A high degree of employee autonomy.** Employee empowerment in employee-friendly companies is more than simply a catch phrase; it's one of the key values that drive day-to-day company operations. The rationale behind true employee empowerment is that most people work harder and do a better job when they're accountable for their own decisions and actions, as opposed to simply "following orders."

- **Open communication.** Managers have a vital role in explaining to employees how their individual goals support organizational objectives, and a two-way dialogue helps staff understand how overall business priorities should affect their work.

✔ **A sense of belonging.** To be truly productive, people need to feel "good" about being a part of an organization. The more people feel comfortable with being who they are at work, the higher their morale, the greater their contributions, and the more their creativity is unleashed.

Choosing the right HR goals

Human resources management is all about people: finding and recruiting them; hiring them; training and developing them; paying them; retaining them; creating an environment that's safe, healthy, and productive for them; communicating with them; and doing whatever is reasonably possible to find that delicate balance between what best serves the basic needs of employees and what best serves the market-driven needs of the company. This chapter is about performing these functions as effectively and efficiently as possible.

When choosing the right HR goals for your organization, it's important to think strategically. No doubt you've heard the term *strategic thinkers*. But what does it really mean?

At their core, strategic business thinkers try to look ahead, attempting to anticipate which issues and information will be most relevant. They don't look at their work merely as a series of tasks or simply react to events; they also examine trends, issues, opportunities, and long-term needs — and shape what they discover into policies and recommendations. To borrow from the restaurant industry, strategic thinkers do more than cook; they help shape the menu.

Measuring HR Efficiency

Although many things in a business are qualitative in nature and cannot be measured precisely, HR efficiency is a quantitative element and as such can be measured precisely. In this section, I cover two areas vital to measuring HR efficiency: measuring employee sentiment and measuring effectiveness.

Measuring employee satisfaction

In many cases, particularly if your company has fewer than 50 employees, you don't have a hard time getting a good read on the general atmosphere in the workplace. You're able to personally make your way around offices and work areas enough to observe how employees interact with one another, how they feel about the way they're treated by senior management, and whether morale is rising or falling. But if your company is larger, periodically conduct a more rigorous employee survey. Here are some tips:

✔ Watch your timing. Don't conduct surveys during holidays when many employees may be taking days off. Avoid exceptionally heavy workload periods.

✔ Think carefully about your objectives before crafting your survey questions. What do you want to find out? What do you intend to do with the information?

✔ Share survey objectives with employees, but do so in language that's relevant to them. In other words, instead of using HR terms such as, "We want to assess employee attitudes," tell them, "We want to hear your thoughts since we merged with Company X."

✔ Before you unveil your survey to the entire company, test it out on a small group of employees to see whether your questions are appropriate and what you can refine.

✔ Assure employees that their comments are confidential. This is a key step.

✔ Communicate to employees the results of the survey on a timely basis and take action, as appropriate, when employees make recommendations. Let employees know how their input has affected company policy.

To gain valuable ideas about improving your working conditions and making the workplace more inviting, consider conducting exit interviews with employees who have resigned or are otherwise voluntarily leaving your company. (People you've had to fire, although they are potentially the most candid of all, are not good subjects for two reasons: They're unlikely to cooperate and, if they do, their input will probably be overly negative rather than constructive.)

Measuring employee effectiveness

All performance appraisal systems are driven by the same objective: to establish a systematic and efficient way of evaluating performance, providing constructive feedback, and enabling employees to continually improve their performance.

The basic ingredients in all systems are pretty much the same: setting performance criteria, developing tracking and documenting procedures, determining which areas should be measured quantitatively, and deciding how the information is to be communicated to employees. Where the different methods vary is in the following areas:

✔ The degree to which employees are involved in establishing performance evaluation criteria

✔ How employee performance is tracked and documented

✔ How performance is rated and how it's aligned with corporate priorities, objectives, and goals

✔ The specific types of appraisal tools used — in some cases, for example, certain approaches are more appropriate for evaluating managers and professionals than other employees

✔ The amount of time and effort required to implement the process

✔ How the results of the appraisal are integrated into other management or HR functions

✔ How the actual appraisal session is conducted

The following section offers a brief description of performance appraisal methods most commonly used today.

Goal-setting, or management by objectives (MBO)

In a typical MBO scenario, an employee and manager sit down together at the start of an appraisal period and formulate a set of statements that represent specific job goals, targets, or *deliverables.*

In the case of MBO, goals, targets, and deliverables should be as specific and measurable as possible. For example, instead of "improve customer service" (too vague), try something like "reduce the number of customer complaints by 5 percent."

This list of targets becomes the basis for an action plan that spells out what steps need to be taken to achieve each goal. At a later date — six months or a year later — the employee and the manager sit down again and measure employee performance on the basis of how many of those goals were met. I suggest meeting every 2–3 months, as it's very common for internal and external forces to influence goals set as long as a year ago.

Essay appraisals

Though less popular than it was a few years ago, the *essay approach* still has merit. It can be quite useful for a supervisor to periodically compose statements that describe an employee's performance during the appraisal period. The statements are usually written on standard forms, and they can be as general or as specific as you want. A supervisor may describe an employee's performance in terms of his or her ability to relate to other work-team members.

These written statements can either be forwarded to the HR department or can be used as one element in an appraisal session. Any written evaluation also needs to include more measurable evaluation tools, such as rating scales applied to specific objectives, tasks, and goals.

Critical incidents reporting

The *critical incidents method* of performance appraisal is built around a list of specific behaviors, generally known as *critical behaviors,* which are deemed necessary to perform a particular job competently. Managers, the HR department, or outside consultants can draw up the list. Performance evaluators use a critical incident report to record actual incidents of behavior that illustrate when employees either carried out or didn't carry out these behaviors. You can use these logs to document a wide variety of job behaviors, such as interpersonal skills, initiative, and leadership ability.

Job rating checklist

The *job rating checklist* method of performance appraisal is the simplest method to use and lends itself to a variety of approaches. To implement this approach, you supply each evaluator with a prepared list of statements or questions that relate to specific aspects of job performance. The questions typically require the evaluator to write a simple "yes" or "no" answer or to record a number (or some other notation) that indicates which statement applies to a particular employee's performance. More often than not, the responsibility for developing the list lies with the HR department.

A more sophisticated variation to this method is to establish a *weighted rating system* in which a number is used to reflect the relative importance of each criterion being evaluated. The weighted variation presents a clearer picture of how employee strengths and weaknesses measure up against the priorities of the job.

Behaviorally anchored rating scale (BARS)

Behaviorally anchored rating scale (BARS) systems are designed to emphasize the behavior, traits, and skills needed to successfully perform a job. A typical BARS form has two columns. The left column has a rating scale, usually in stages from Very Poor to Excellent. The right column contains behavioral anchors that are the reflections of those ratings.

If the scale were being used, for example, to evaluate a telephone order taker, the statement in one column may read "1-Very Poor," and the statement in the right column may read, "Occasionally rude or abrupt to customer" or "Makes frequent mistakes on order form."

Forced choice

Forced-choice methods generally come in two forms: paired statements and forced ranking. In the *paired statements method,* evaluators are presented with two statements and must check the one that best describes the employee; it's either one or the other. In the *forced ranking method,* a number of options are listed, allowing the evaluator to select a description that may fall somewhere in between the two extremes.

Ranking methods

Ranking methods compare employees in a group to one another. All involve an evaluator who asks managers to rank employees from the "best" to the "worst" with respect to specific job performance criteria. The three most common variations of this method are as follows:

- **Straight ranking:** Employees are simply listed in order of ranking.

- **Forced comparison:** Every employee is paired with every other employee in the group, and in each case, the manager identifies the better of the two employees in any pairing. The employees are ranked by the number of times they're identified as the best.

- **Forced distribution:** The employees are ranked along a standard statistical distribution, the so-called *bell curve.*

Multi-rater assessments

Multi-rater assessments are also called *360-degree assessments.* The employee's supervisors, co-workers, subordinates, and, in some cases, customers are asked to complete detailed questionnaires on the employee. The employee completes the same questionnaire. The results are tabulated, and the employee then compares her assessment with the other results.

Hiring and Firing

Your challenge as a manager is to figure out how to not just find the best candidates for your job openings, but also convince them that your company is the best place to work. You also need to be able to fire an employee when, no matter how much you try to help someone succeed in your organization, that person's employment at your firm just isn't meant to be.

The lifetime earnings of the average American worker are calculated at approximately $1 million, so hiring (and firing) really is a million-dollar decision!

Knowing the importance of clearly documenting HR policies

Even if your company has only a handful of employees, keeping your basic procedures and policies well documented is always a good practice. Whatever effort may be required to get basic company information in print and on a password-protected part of your intranet can save you time and grief down the road. The following list gives advice for creating a procedures manual:

✔ **Separate company policies from job-specific procedures.** Try to make a distinction in your employee manual between policies that apply to everyone in the company (general hours, payroll, vacation, and so on) and procedures that relate specifically to how people do their individual jobs.

✔ **Keep it simple.** Employee manuals don't need to be literary works, but they do need to be clear and concise. Use plain English and try to avoid overly formal, bureaucratic wording and phrasing. You may want to consider hiring a professional writer to polish your final draft.

✔ **Pay attention to legalities.** Here's some scary news: Anything that you put in writing about your company's policies or procedures automatically becomes a legal document, and someone may use it against you in a wrongful dismissal suit. Play things safe. Make sure that an expert in employment law reviews the manual before you publish it.

✔ **Control the distribution.** Every employee who receives a manual should sign a document that acknowledges his receipt of the manual and that he understands its contents. Keep the signed form in the employee's personnel file. You may need it in the event of a disciplinary proceeding or lawsuit.

Knowing what to include

Most policies and procedures manuals follow the same general format. What differs from one company to the next are the specifics. The following list gives you a look at a typical table of contents for a policies and procedures manual:

✔ Welcome statement by CEO

✔ Equal Employment Opportunity (EEO) policy statement (including sexual and other forms of harassment)

✔ Company history and overview

✔ Employment at-will (if applicable)

✔ Company mission statement and values

✔ Essential company rules, such as work hours, business ethics, smoking, dress code, sick days, and so on

✔ Performance appraisal procedures

✔ Disciplinary procedures (you must have a lawyer carefully review this section)

✔ Health, safety, and security rules and procedures, including a fire-exit map

✔ Benefit, pension, and deferred-income programs

✔ Parking and transportation information, including maps

Playing it safe

Whatever else your employee manual does, make sure that it doesn't do any of the following:

- ✔ Make promises you can't keep
- ✔ Publish procedures you don't follow or can't enforce
- ✔ Say anything that someone may construe as discriminatory
- ✔ Use the phrase "termination for just cause" without specifying what you mean

One last piece of advice: Always include a disclaimer that emphasizes that the manual is a general source of information and not for anyone to construe as a binding employment contract.

Setting up an efficient onboarding process

Your onboarding program can be as elaborate as a six-week combination training and boot camp or as simple as a series of scheduled one-on-one conversations between the new employee and a manager or HR staffer, or something in between. Whatever form you take, however, you want to give it structure.

You need to provide a schedule, and everyone involved needs clearly defined roles. You want the individual elements of the program *weighted.* In other words, a logical and strategic connection between the importance of a particular issue or topic and how much time you devote to that issue or topic must exist.

The first day: Ease anxieties

Even though new employees have likely been on your company premises previously during the interview phase, their experiences on the first day of work will leave a lasting impression, even from the minute they walk into the building or onto the job site. You need to offer a first-day welcome to begin the process of making them feel at home. Following are tips for you — or the individuals' bosses if you're not supervising the new hires — to remember:

- ✔ Alert the receptionist or security guard (if you have one) that a new employee is arriving and make sure that this person greets the newcomer warmly.
- ✔ Arrange for someone (you, if possible) to personally escort the new hire to his work station or office.

- Personally introduce the newcomer to other members of the working team.

- Give the new employee a company roster with names and phone numbers of people to contact, along with their job titles.

- Encourage current employees who haven't been formally introduced to the new hire to introduce themselves and offer to help in any way they can.

- At some point during the day, meet with the employee to take up where the last interview left off. Let them know how glad you are to have them on board and that you will be providing a comprehensive introduction to the company and the job within the next few days.

- Schedule a lunch with the new employee and his manager on the first day.

- Make every effort to have the employee's work station set up before he arrives, with a computer, e-mail access, a phone number, and basic supplies. It frustrates me to hear stories of new employees waiting as long as two weeks to actually be able to *begin* work because they don't have basic tools! A "new hire" checklist can help streamline the onboarding process for every new employee.

The first week: Discover more about the company and the job

You probably gave the new employee plenty of information about your company while recruiting and interviewing. Even so, the first few days on the job are the best time to reinforce that information and build identification with the company. At the very least, a new employee should know the following:

- Your company's basic products or services

- Size and general organization of the company

- An overview of your industry — and where your company fits into the overall picture (Who's your chief competition?)

- Your company's mission statement (if you have one) and values

- Department goals and strategic objectives

- The corporate culture

Second week and beyond

A key part of the onboarding process is early follow-up. You or supervising line managers should meet with employees at predetermined points: two weeks after the first day on the job, a month after, two months, or at intervals that work best for each job's complexity and changeability. These times are when you check in with new team members to find out how things are going for them. How well do they understand the company and their roles? Do they have any questions that have not been answered? Inquire especially as to the value of training programs. Are they helpful? Do they address the right areas? Are they worth the time being spent on them? What future developmental experiences would employees like to see?

These follow-up meetings are also a good time to hear their assessment of the onboarding process thus far.

Hiring — and firing — best practices

When it comes right down to it, your organization's success depends in large part on the quality of the people you employ. Recruiting and hiring the very best people — and terminating the ones who aren't performing — are among the most powerful ways of improving both the efficiency and the effectiveness of your business. In this section, I consider hiring — and firing — best practices.

Hiring the best

People are the heart of every business. The better people you hire, the better business you have. Some people are just meant to be in their jobs. You may know such individuals — someone who thrives as a receptionist or someone who lives to sell. Think about how great your organization would be if you staffed every position with people who lived for their jobs.

The following list presents some of the best ways to find candidates for your positions:

- **Internal candidates:** In most organizations, the first place to look for candidates is within the organization.

- **Personal referrals:** Whether from co-workers, professional colleagues, friends, relatives, or neighbors, you can often find great candidates through referrals.

- **Temporary agencies:** Hiring *temps,* or temporary employees, is routine for many companies. The best part is that when you hire temps, you get the opportunity to try out employees before you buy them.

- **Professional associations:** Association newsletters, magazines, websites, blogs, and social networking sites are great places to advertise your openings when you're looking for specific expertise, because your audience is already prescreened for you.

- **Employment agencies:** These are a good, albeit pricey (with a cost of up to a third of the employee's first-year salary, or more), alternative.

✔ **Websites and blogs:** If you don't already have a great recruiting page on your company website, you should. In addition to this baseline item, also consider setting up company blogs where employees can describe what they do and how they do it.

✔ **Social networking sites:** Two sites in particular deserve your attention if you hope to broaden your search for good candidates: Facebook (www.facebook.com) and LinkedIn (www.linkedin.com). You can run ad campaigns on Facebook to target the individuals you're hoping to hire by college, geographic area, and even hobbies. (In fact, you can run a campaign that shows your employment ad to people who work at your competition!)

✔ **Traditional job-hunting sites:** A number of job-hunting sites have become popular with people looking for new positions. This makes them good platforms from which to pitch your own job openings. Some of the most popular include CareerBuilder.com (www.careerbuilder.com), Monster.com (www.monster.com), and Craigslist (www.craigslist.org). You'll likely have to pay to post your jobs on these sites — prices vary.

Five steps to better interviewing

Every interview consists of five key steps:

1. **Welcome the applicant.** Greet your candidates warmly and chat with them informally to help loosen them up. Questions about the weather, the difficulty of finding your offices, or how they found out about your position are old standbys.

2. **Summarize the position.** Briefly describe the job, the kind of person you're looking for, and the interview process you use.

3. **Ask your questions (and then listen!).** Questions should be relevant to the position and should cover the applicant's work experience, education, and other related topics. Limit the amount of talking you do as an interviewer. Many interviewers end up trying to sell the job to an applicant instead of probing whether a candidate is a good fit.

4. **Probe experience and discover the candidate's strengths and weaknesses.** The best predictor of future behavior is past behavior, so exploring applicants' past experience can be very informative. Asking your candidates to name their strengths and weaknesses may seem clichéd, the answers can be very revealing.

5. **Conclude the interview.** Allow your candidates the opportunity to offer any further information that they feel is necessary for you to make a decision, and to ask questions about your firm or the job. Thank them for their interest and let them know when they can expect your firm to contact them.

Firing underperformers

Involuntary terminations — firings or layoffs — are seldom pleasant experiences for either manager or employee, but I promise you this: it's *more* unpleasant for everyone involved if you wait too long to let someone go. Involuntary terminations come in two types:

- ✓ **Layoffs:** A *layoff,* also known as a *reduction in force,* occurs when an organization decides to terminate a certain number of employees for financial reasons. For example, your company loses several key contracts and the revenue that was projected to come with them. To stay afloat, your firm may have to reduce payroll costs through layoffs.

- ✓ **Firing:** Employees are fired when they have no hope of improving their performance, when job descriptions need to evolve and the people in the jobs aren't able to evolve along with them, or when they commit an act of misconduct that is so serious that termination is the only choice.

An 1884 Tennessee court decision (*Payne v. Western & A.R.P. Co.,* 81 Tenn. 507) established the termination-at-will rule within the United States. This rule said that employers have the right to terminate employees for any reason whatsoever — including no reason — unless a contract between employer and employee expressly prohibits such an action. However, more than 100 years of court decisions, union agreements, and state and federal laws have eroded the ability of employers to terminate employees at-will. The federal government, in particular, has had the greatest effect on the termination-at-will rule, particularly in cases of discrimination against employees for a wide variety of reasons.

At-will still exists on a state-by-state basis, and some companies require prospective employees to sign a statement confirming termination-at-will when they're hired. Be sure to check your local regulations.

Federal regulations, such as the Civil Rights Act of 1964, the Equal Employment Opportunity Act of 1991, the Age Discrimination in Employment Act, and others, prohibit terminating employees specifically because of their age, race, gender, color, religion, national origin, and other federally mandated exclusions. Double-check any local and state regulations, too. To ignore these prohibitions is to invite a nasty and expensive lawsuit. Even the mere appearance of discrimination in the termination process (or anywhere else in your firm) can get you into trouble. In fact, most former employees — by some estimates, up to 90 percent — who bring wrongful termination cases to court today win their cases.

People generally agree, however, on certain behaviors that merit firing. Some of these behaviors are considered *intolerable offenses* that merit immediate action — no verbal counseling, no written warning, and no reprimand or suspension, just immediate and unequivocal termination. They generally include these behaviors:

✔ **Verbal abuse of others:** Verbal abuse includes cursing, repeated verbal harassment, malicious insults, and similar behaviors.

✔ **Incompetence:** Despite your continued efforts to train them, some employees can't perform their duties at an acceptable level of competence.

✔ **Repeated, unexcused tardiness:** If an employee continues to be late to work after you warn him that you won't tolerate this behavior, you have clear grounds for termination.

✔ **Insubordination:** The deliberate refusal to carry out one's duties — is grounds for immediate termination without warning.

✔ **Physical violence:** Most companies take employee-initiated physical violence and threats of violence very seriously.

✔ **Theft:** Most companies that catch employees engaging in this nasty little practice terminate them immediately and without warning.

✔ **Sexual harassment:** Unwelcome sexual advances, requests for sexual favors, and other verbal or physical conduct of a sexual nature on the job are intolerable offenses in many organizations and subject to immediate termination.

✔ **Intoxication on the job:** Although being drunk or under the influence of drugs on the job is sufficient grounds for immediate termination, many companies nowadays offer their employees the option of undergoing counseling with an employee assistance program.

✔ **Falsification of records:** Falsifying records is another big no-no that can lead to immediate dismissal.

Keep in mind that just because you *can* terminate an employee immediately for any of these offenses doesn't mean you *should*. For example, if an employee doesn't know how to do his job, you may decide to provide additional training opportunities instead of terminating him.

When it does come time to fire an employee, these guidelines can help you make this difficult transition a little easier:

✔ **Make it clear when expectations aren't being met.** Bring up your concerns and the reasons behind them. It's unfair (and frankly, wasteful) to fire someone without giving her the opportunity to improve. Give specific feedback and an exact date by which you expect to see a change.

✔ **Offer a 0 percent increase as a raise.** Typically, in this approach, the person quickly falls in line or ends up leaving of his own accord. Either way, your problem is solved.

✔ **Act quickly to dismiss.** When all is said and done, if someone isn't working out well, the sooner you deal with the situation, the better it'll be — for the employee, yourself, and the workgroup.

✔ **Follow through quickly.** Don't hem and haw, or threaten to fire someone repeatedly and not actually do it. When it comes time to let someone go, rip off the Band-Aid.

✔ **Watch your timing.** I suggest firing someone at the end of the day or over lunch. Being let go is a source of shame, and there's no reason to call attention to the matter by forcing someone to pack up his desk in the middle of the afternoon and walk through the building while everyone stares.

Your employees know full well when a member of their team is not performing up to par, and they look to *you* to see whether that behavior will be tolerated. Constantly giving someone second chances creates a company culture where people stop striving for excellence. If Joe still has a job and it's common knowledge that he actually calls his dad to do his work for him, that does little to motivate others to go the extra mile. Firing people quickly is better for your *entire* organization.

Outsourcing: Pros and cons

Outsourcing is the practice of turning over an entire function (shipping, payroll, benefits administration, security, computer networking) to an outside specialist. In many cases, the outside firm's employees or consultants work side by side with a company's regular employees. In some cases, a function may be moved to a remote location miles away from your office — even occasionally out of the country. This latter approach, often referred to as *offshoring,* has grabbed headlines and generated much economic and political debate in recent years.

Companies usually outsource to save time and money, either because of necessity or choice. Necessity is the driving factor when a company's business demands outstrip its ability to handle a particular function without investing heavily in new equipment (or a new facility) or bringing in a large number of new employees. Choice is the driving factor when companies want to focus all their internal energies on those operations that contribute directly to their competitive advantage — and outsource those that may only be necessary for a discreet period of time or specific function.

You need to grasp the implications of outsourcing so that you can help provide strategic counsel throughout any hiring process — and contribute to decisions about whether to use this alternative in the first place. After all, any outsourcing effort inherently carries a demand not just for one discreet hire, but for many people — and your input about how to conduct an effective search for skilled contractors or consultants is extremely valuable.

Seeing Beyond 9–5: Alternative Scheduling

One of the most popular management concepts of recent years has been the scheduling concept known as *alternate work arrangements.* Broadly speaking, an alternate work arrangement is any scheduling pattern that deviates from the traditional Monday-through-Friday, 9-to-5 work week.

Flexibility is the basic idea behind alternate work arrangements. You give employees some measure of control over their work schedules, thereby making it easier for them to manage non-job-related responsibilities. The business rationale behind the concept is that by making it easier for employees to deal with pressures on the home front, they'll be more productive when they're on the job — and less likely to jump ship if one of your competitors offers them a little more money.

Alternate work arrangements are generally grouped into the following general categories:

- **Flextime:** *Flextime* refers to any arrangement that gives employees options on structuring their work day or work week. In the most extreme (and rarest) form, employees decide for themselves not only when they work, but also for how long. More typically, though, employees working under flextime arrangements are expected to be on the job during certain core hours of the work day. They're given the opportunity to choose (within certain parameters) their own starting and quitting times — as long as they work the required number of hours each day.

- **Compressed work week:** Under this arrangement, employees work the normal number of hours but complete those hours in fewer than five days. The most common variation of the compressed work week is the so-called 4/10, in which employees work four 10-hour days instead of five 8-hour days. Watch out for the legal number of breaks per working hours/day.

- **Job-sharing:** As the term implies, *job-sharing* means that two part-time employees share the same full-time job. Salary and benefits may be prorated on the basis of what proportion of the job each worker shares. Apart from the obvious consideration (both people need to be qualified for the job), a successful job-sharing arrangement assumes that the employees sharing the job can work together harmoniously to make the arrangement work.

- **Telecommuting:** Telecommuting refers to any work arrangement in which employees — on a regular, predetermined basis — spend all or a portion of their work week working from home or from another non-company site.

✔ **Permanent part-time arrangements:** The hours in these arrangements usually vary from 20 to 29 hours per week, with employees sometimes given the right to decide which days they work and how long they work on those days. The key attraction of this arrangement is that the employees may be entitled to company benefits, albeit on a prorated basis.

In theory, alternate work arrangements offer a win-win situation. Many studies have shown that flexible scheduling policies improve morale and job satisfaction, reduce absenteeism, cut down on turnover, and minimize burnout — and with no measurable decline in productivity. The process needs to be carefully thought out, but it has huge rewards when implemented correctly.

The biggest hurdle with flexible work arrangements is ensuring that it does not disrupt communication. It's easy to overlook the ambient awareness that simply sitting in the same room (overhearing phone calls, chatting in the elevator, hearing the conversations that happen just after a meeting) creates. For tech-savvy teams, having an open online chat room to ask questions or even share funny mustache pictures can do the trick. In other cases, you may need to have one day or half-day each week that everyone must be in the office together, with flexible time arrangements for all other days.

Looking at HR Tools for Efficiency

There are a variety of tools available for making an organization's HR function more efficient. In this section, I consider a few of the most effective.

Processing résumés more effectively

The ability to process résumés effectively is a key element in improving human resources efficiency. This means quickly separating the best candidates from the worst. Based on résumés alone, you'd think that all your candidates are such outstanding prospects that you can hire them sight unseen. Anyone who does any research at all into how to look for a job knows, at this point, how to write a résumé that puts him in the best light. And those who don't know how to write a great résumé can now hire people who do know.

Before diving into that pile of résumés, consider the following observations:

✔ No job applicant in his right mind is going to put derogatory or detracting information in his own résumé.

✔ Many résumés are professionally prepared and designed to create a winning, but not necessarily accurate, impression.

✔ Reviewing résumés is tedious, no matter what. You may need to sift through the stack several times. Keep your eye drops handy!

Reading between the lines

Now that more and more people are using outside specialists or software packages to prepare their résumés, getting an accurate reading of a candidate's strengths simply by reading his résumé is more difficult than ever. Even so, here are some of the characteristics that generally (although not always) describe a candidate worth interviewing:

- ✔ **Lots of details:** Though applicants are generally advised to avoid wordiness, the more detailed they are in their descriptions of what they accomplished in previous jobs, the more reliable (as a rule) the information.

- ✔ **A history of stability and advancement:** The applicant's work history should show a steady progression into greater responsibility and more important positions. But don't go by job titles alone; look at what the candidate did. Assess how important the work was to the company involved.

- ✔ **A strong, well-written cover letter:** Assuming that the candidate wrote the letter, the cover letter is generally a good indication of his overall communication skills. Look for specifics that indicate he wrote the letter for you, and that he did not just copy the same verbiage for 20 other applications.

Watching out for red flags

Résumé writing is a good example of the Law of Unintended Consequences. Sometimes what's not in a résumé or what's done through carelessness or mistake can reveal quite a bit about a candidate. Following are some things to watch out for:

- ✔ **Sloppy overall appearance:** This is a fairly reliable sign that the candidate is lacking in professionalism and business experience. I have actually seen applicants include photos of themselves drinking at parties with their résumés (many times!). Those get filtered out first.

- ✔ **Unexplained chronological gaps:** Such gaps in an employment history may mean one of two things: The candidate was unemployed during these gaps, or the candidate is deliberately concealing certain information.

- ✔ **Static career pattern:** A sequence of jobs that doesn't indicate increasing responsibility may indicate a problem — the person wasn't deemed fit for a promotion or demonstrated a lack of ambition. Exceptions occur, however, especially for workers in highly specialized fields.

- ✔ **Typos and misspellings:** Generally speaking, typos in cover letters and résumés may signify carelessness or a cavalier attitude. In a Robert Half International survey, 76 percent of U.S. executives said that they wouldn't hire a candidate with even one or two typographical errors in his résumé.

✔ **Vaguely worded job descriptions:** Perhaps the applicant didn't quite understand what his job was. Or perhaps the job responsibilities didn't match the title. Before you go any further, you probably want to find out what a "coordinator of special projects" actually does. You want to see job descriptions that indicate how crucial the job is to his company's success.

✔ **Weasel wording:** Phrasing such as "participated in," "familiar with," "in association," and so on can indicate that the applicant may not have the actual experience he's claiming. Did the applicant actually work on that vital project, or did he merely run errands for someone who did? A sentence doesn't need to be untruthful to be misleading.

✔ **Job hopping:** Although cradle-to-grave employment is by no means the norm today, a series of many jobs held for short periods of time may signal an unstable or problem employee or a chronic "job-hopper." Be sure to look at the whole picture of employment history. People do leave jobs for good reasons and should be prepared — and willing — to tell you about it.

Setting up a job board

No doubt, you're already familiar with many of the benefits of the Internet as a recruiting tool: access to a much larger potential candidate base and a relatively low-cost way to manage the process of hiring and continually attracting future employees. Literally thousands of job boards cover virtually every industry, profession, educational background, experience level, ethnic group, and much more. If you haven't already done so, consider setting up a job board as a part of your company's website.

A miraculous tool, but there's no free lunch

One of the Web's huge appeals is its ability to help you locate qualified candidates at extremely low costs. However, it can also become a nightmare if not managed properly. For starters, the Internet has the potential of dramatically increasing the number of responses to your job ads. Many HR managers report they have great difficulty even keeping track of submissions. Even small companies can receive hundreds of resumes from a single ad, depending on the position and job market. Some HR professionals, or their staff members, still manually read through or at least scan each résumé.

If your budget allows, however, you can improve your organization's efficiency by creating computer protocols that flag certain qualifications to help you narrow down résumés. These electronic codes enable your computer to rapidly sort through résumés by designating certain terms, words, credentials, or any other information. You can set a filter for an accounting position, for example, to eliminate candidates who lack a CPA credential.

Keep in mind, though, that you should create these protocols carefully, taking time to talk extensively with line managers about the experience and credentials that really matter for a position. Otherwise you may inadvertently eliminate viable candidates. As a rule of thumb, only set filters for jobs that you have already successfully filled at least once.

Quality in, quality out

In a marketplace with so many possibilities, you want to make sure that your job ads attract the best and brightest candidates. You've got to design ads that stand out, and, as a medium, the Internet is certainly no exception to this rule.

You're only as good as your website

The Internet has dramatically changed the quality of applicants' research. Just as you're now able to find out more about candidates who may be applying from all over the world, job seekers in turn can uncover in-depth assessments and facts about your company. The implications of these changes are:

- With information now so much more accessible then ever, you want to make sure (to the extent that you can) that your company's website accurately showcases your firm's strengths and range of capabilities. After all, you want the best people to be drawn to your company, and a website that's outdated, difficult to read, or lacking relevant information can reduce your chances of luring top-notch candidates.

- Don't be surprised at how well prepared candidates are when you get to the interview process. You also need to be prepared and raise your expectations for the discussion. The topics you cover can relate more specifically to business priorities and issues affecting your company.

Tracking paperwork

The days of file cabinets overflowing with folders and random sheets of paper are now officially over. Tremendous efficiency gains can be had in any organization by using the power of computers, the Internet, and the Cloud to store and track HR paperwork. And there's one thing that puts all this—and much more—together in one place: HR software.

The scope, flexibility, and versatility of HR-related software — or Human Resource Information Systems (HRIS) — continues to accelerate. The new generation of software, for example, not only produces and tracks routine HR paperwork such as employee data, evaluations, rewards and disciplinary actions, and training, but it also integrates that data with information relating to career development and assessment.

It's a given that all software decisions should be driven by the strategic and operational needs of the business — as opposed to the capabilities of the software. This axiom takes on special significance when you're considering buying software that will combine and integrate functions that currently operate as separate tasks. Regardless of how elegantly the software is designed, how easy it is to use, and how fast it runs, the system must ultimately produce a business payoff. The following list provides a general idea of features that normally differentiate one product from another:

- ✔ Response time
- ✔ Integration with other systems (such as your CRM – which many of my clients use directly to manage hiring and HR paperwork)
- ✔ Scope of search capabilities
- ✔ Report and audit capabilities
- ✔ Internet and intranet compatibility (I recommend Cloud-based solutions).
- ✔ Scanning and OCR capabilities
- ✔ Security and self-service capabilities

Chapter 12

Streamlining Your Sales Process

*Y*ou can have the most ruthlessly efficient expense reduction plan in the world, but if your company doesn't also *sell* efficiently, you're going to shutter.

An efficient sales process doesn't mean reducing your company to its bare bones and firing your inside sales team in favor of a commission-only third-party sales organization. Sales is a core part of every organization, and should be managed and executed from inside the organization (though for a variety of reasons, a supplementary external salesforce may make sense, too). The key is to create a rich and well-organized sales experience both for leads and your sales staff.

What does a rich sales experience look like? For starters, you have to empower your potential customers with choices and information. Creating useful information that helps drive new customers to your door — known as inbound marketing — is about as efficient as it gets.

Having motivated, energetic sales employees is more important in sales than most anywhere else. In most cases, they're the first impression your customers ever have of your product and your organization, and first impressions can make or break deals. An efficient sales staff has the tools and resources available to close sales without drowning under piles of paperwork or red tape. The more time sales staff spends constructing contracts and waiting for approval, the less time it has to actually close sales — an action necessary to the very life of your company.

Finding Out How Efficient Your Sales Process Is

In short, an efficient sales team generates the most revenue *for the long haul* — for the least amount of effort. It's not efficient to swindle a customer for a single upfront payment if that ultimately means you lose future business with that customer and everyone that customer knows. Similarly, spending a year to close a high-value deal is not usually the most efficient use of your time.

Check out the following sections to get an idea of where your business is operating efficiently and where it could benefit from new tools or ideas.

How efficient is your lead generation?

Generating sales leads is a crucial part of building your business. Discover how strong your lead generation is by answering the following questions:

- ✔ **How do you capture referrals?** As auto industry mogul James Yerage says, "your next sale is coming from the one you just made." If you have no mechanism for requesting or capturing referrals, you're leaving money on the table. Depending on your industry, there's a myriad of opportunities and tools for finding out who else may be interested in your offering.

- ✔ **If you search the Internet for your company name or product category, do you come up?** The Internet is an increasing source of incoming leads across every sector. If your potential customers can't find you online (or find someone else first!), they may never become customers.

- ✔ **Do you capture leads on your website?** Your site (you *have* a website, right?) needs to be informative, certainly, but it also needs a big call to action. Lead capturing doesn't have to mean someone literally signing up to indicate they want to buy — it can also be giving their e-mail to get a free trial, joining an e-mail list, RSVPing for a webinar, or requesting a relevant white paper.

- ✔ **Do you maintain records of past customers and leads?** Too many people think of old leads as totally dead. Although *some* certainly are, the others may be your most qualified future customers — they already indicated interest, and factors beyond your or their control, such as a lack of budget or a contract with a different vendor, may have been what was standing in the way before. You need to keep a log of past leads and customers and make sure you peripherally keep in touch with them. Leads that contact you again after two or more years are certainly not unheard of.

✔ **If you buy leads, do you track the Return on Investment (ROI)?** Never assume that a set of leads is worth anything just because you paid something for them.

✔ **Do you know how to A/B test?** A/B testing means slightly varying some aspect of your sales process — maybe the day of the week you call, whether you call or e-mail, the subject line of your e-mail, and so on — across different customers and see if one is more effective at closing sales than the other. Big companies like Google are ruthless about A/B testing and know exactly what font sizes, colors, and ad placements get the most eyeballs and clickthroughs (and therefore generate the most revenue).

✔ **Do you know how your last five customers found you?** Knowing where your recent and/or best customers found you can help you know where you need to be in order to get even more customers like that.

✔ **What efforts do you take to upsell your current customers?** Most organizations have *some* way to generate more revenue from an existing customer base, whether that's new product upgrades, warranties, consulting services, or additional donation pledges. This is part of your sales process, too!

✔ **What information do you collect on an initial lead?** As a rule of thumb, you should collect only the absolute minimum amount of information you need up front. The more information you request, the fewer the number of responses you will receive. For example, start with just an e-mail address, and then find ways to collect even more details as your interactions grow.

How efficient is your lead nurturing?

After you have potential customers interested, how are keeping their attention? See how you fare with the following questions:

✔ **What sorts of *information* do you provide for potential customers?** Information is power. The more details you can provide for your leads, the more reasons they'll have to sign up — and the less time your sales team will have to spend answering redundant questions or filtering out leads that are clearly not good fits for your product.

✔ **How long does it take for a sales lead to get a response from you?** If your competitors respond before you, they stand a better chance of winning the sale.

✔ **Can leads indicate a contact method preference?** Most people have a preferred means of interaction. For example, I loathe voicemail, but I love text messaging and e-mail, so those are the best ways for companies to contact me. Asking your leads how they like to be contacted, and actually contacting them in that manner, increases the chances they'll see and listen to your messaging.

✔ **Do you track mailing list unsubscribes?** Not only do you need to make sure (it's a legal requirement) that you remove people from your list who request removal, but this is a great opportunity for an exit interview. Why are they unsubscribing? What could you have done (or not done) to keep them?

✔ **What hours is your sales team available?** You don't necessarily need to be up 24/7, but you should at least make your hours clear so leads know when they can and cannot expect to reach someone. You never want a potential customer's first interaction to be with your voicemail.

✔ **Can customers sign up and make purchases on their own?** Humans are impulsive. If the only way I can gain access to your product or service is to sign up for a guided tour with a salesperson two days from now, odds are I am going to walk away and never let you know I was there. (In fact, if it's actually me, I can *guarantee* I'm going to move on to a competitor that offers instant access.)

✔ **Do you track duplicate leads?** If a lead is halfway through the sales pipeline with Joe, and then Mary cold calls her, it looks (at best) like your company is disorganized. You also don't want to treat a "new" lead *like* a new lead if the person was actually in your pipeline two years ago.

✔ **Who checks the company e-mail address?** I'd say at least 50 percent of my client base has a generic company e-mail listed on its website that *nobody ever checks*. Find out, and make sure those e-mails are going to a real person.

✔ **What percentage of your sales leads open the e-mails you send them?** If you don't know, you need to start using an e-mail marketing tool that can tell you.

✔ **How do you rate your leads?** If you wish you had more leads, this isn't a problem — but if you have too many leads to process in a timely manner, you need to find ways to make the most valuable ones bubble to the top. Setting internal criteria for what makes the best lead (for example, companies with 5 to 25 employees, or who are looking to buy in the next 30 days versus the next year), coupled with qualitative feedback from your sales team, can lead to rating system as simple as "warm" and "hot."

✔ **How do you assign your leads?** "Whoever answers the phone first" is a wrong answer here. Incoming leads should be distributed throughout your sales team, ideally for specific criteria such as territory, product interest, or company size.

✔ **Do potential customers have a consistent point of contact?** When possible, let the original salesperson see the sale to its close. Interacting with four different employees makes the sales process more impersonal than it needs to be, and easily leaves the door open for confusion, mistakes, and even missed upsell opportunities.

✔ **Can customers sign up for demos/trials on their own?** No matter what you're selling, you should be able to offer an online demo, a video, or at the very least an attractive flowchart to walk interested parties through the process. Requiring that they contact you to learn more means you never actually end up talking to many potential leads.

✔ **Is there a notification when a lead reaches a certain age?** It's all too easy to forget some leads as the phone rings, your e-mail inbox fills up, and the boss calls another meeting. You should make sure every lead has an "age" and the appropriate parties are alerted if too much time goes by since the last point of contact.

How efficient are your sales teams?

Ask yourself these questions as you assess the efficiency of your sales teams:

✔ **What keeps two salespeople from working on the same lead?** A central sales database can help make it clear which salesperson owns which lead, preventing duplication, confusion, and lost sales (not to mention lost time).

✔ **How do two team members share information on the same lead?** Sometimes one salesperson has valuable information on a lead that they are not working directly. More often, a *past* salesperson has information on a lead in their e-mail inbox or notepad, which future salespeople have no means of accessing. Again, a centralized sales database can help surface these past interactions long after individual salespeople move on.

✔ **What is your sales team's attitude about sharing information?** Hoarding leads and information is common in highly competitive sales environments (and, interestingly, is something I see in almost every non-profit). How may you encourage more collaboration? Are company sales goals or bonus policies actually inhibiting collaboration that can lead to greater sales?

✔ **Do you have a CRM?** A CRM, or Customer Relationship Management tool, is the single greatest tool for increasing sales efficiency. It offers a central place for storing lead and customer details, archiving e-mail/phone interactions, integrating management approvals or hot lead alerts, and much more. The best CRMs can be customized to match your exact, most efficient business processes.

Never adapt your business process to meet the requirements of a piece of software!

✔ **Do you have an autodialer?** In phone-heavy sales environments, you lose a lot of time manually dialing numbers. You also lose some "rhythm" which can be important when you're in the sales call "zone." An auto-dialer calls leads and customers in succession (running off a preset list), alleviating the need to dial manually.

✔ **Do you know what time zones your sales leads are in?** Calling people at their office when they're already home for the day isn't an efficient use of time, especially if you don't realize time differences are the issue.

✔ **Do you A/B test your sales methods?** There's certainly an art to sales, but you can measure the effectiveness of a given art with careful A/B testing. More on this later.

✔ **Do you have sales scripts covering multiple scenarios?** By no means should your staff read off of scripts, but these are a valuable tool for getting new salespeople up to speed, for reminding experienced salespeople of key talking points, and most importantly, for testing which types of pitches and approaches are most effective.

✔ **What ongoing training do you provide to your sales team?** Quality ongoing sales training can keep best practices and strategies at the forefront of your sales team's minds. Quality ongoing *product* training is equally important. Nothing is worse than having a salesperson without expert knowledge.

✔ **How does the sales team reach leads while they're on the road?** If salespeople work weekends, travel frequently, or even spend time visiting local customers, they need a means of accessing and updating the company's lead database remotely.

✔ **Do you have sales quotas? How often are they met?** Having quotas is not inherently efficient or inefficient, but if your team almost never meets their quotas, that's a sign of underlying inefficiencies in either sales prospecting or quota-setting.

✔ **Do you give bonuses for sales performance? How often are they earned?** Again, it's less about whether you have bonuses, and more about whether anybody actually feels they can stand a chance at earning one.

✔ **Does sales interact with current customers?** Can (and do) they check in with the people they sold to, or does the relationship end abruptly?

✔ **How are upsell opportunities handled?** Who (if anyone) upsells to existing customers?

✔ **How do sales incentives align with company goals?** This one requires some careful thinking and often the benefit of some bad experiences. If you were trying to *manipulate* current sales incentives, how would you do it? How can you plug that hole?

✔ **What sales collateral do you make available?** The more quality collateral — pamphlets, websites, white papers, demo videos, and so on — you provide to your sales team, the easier time they will have closing deals.

✔ **Does sales interact with customer support?** If issues arise during installation or onboarding that put a sale at risk, does your sales team have a chance to save the situation? Do they even *know*?

✔ **Are feature requests tracked?** Often, leads will indicate they *would* sign up if you only had a particular feature or offering. You need to make sure this information is captured by sales and passed on to the appropriate people who may be able to make those features a reality.

✔ **Can a salesperson e-mail his entire list of leads?** If not, you're probably not using an efficient central database.

✔ **Can a salesperson take his entire list of leads and leave for a competitor?** Although it's entirely possible to actually *do* this with most modern database systems, the important part is the audit trail. If you can see who is downloading what data, you can pinpoint times when salespeople access or move information they shouldn't, and take appropriate action. Trying to prevent downloads from happening is an exercise in futility, because if someone can access leads at all, they can find a way (even if it means photographing the computer screen) to take it with them.

✔ **Who owns your sales contacts?** An experienced salesperson will likely be reluctant to join your company if it means you will gain ownership of his Rolodex.

At the same time, a salesperson can't expect to be able to take your entire organization's aggregate leads with him when it comes time for him to move on.

✔ **Do you know about CAN-SPAM?** Your company faces legal action and fines if you e-mail people without permission and/or don't give people a way to unsubscribe from your e-mail lists.

✔ **Have you ever cleaned your leads?** A "dirty" lead can be someone who moved away, is deceased, or changed her last name; a duplicate; or even a bounced e-mail address. It's particularly important to clean your leads if you do direct mailings, because every dirty lead becomes at least one dollar right down the drain.

✔ **If you need to, can you transfer leads out of your current system and into a new one?** Portable data is a key tenet of efficiency. Your cutting-edge system of today is the dinosaur of the next decade. Much of my work is legacy migration, which is a largely avoidable problem if you never assume you will use the same system in perpetuity.

✔ **Are there security measures in place for handling sensitive lead data?** The greatest of all inefficiencies is being sued by a potential customer for mishandling her private information or credit card details.

✔ **What, if anything, does sales have to wait for in order to close a deal?** Remember that according to Lean, all waiting is a waste. How can you speed up a salesperson's ability to finalize a deal?

Setting Sales Goals

Sales efficiency is all about maximizing your long-term sales revenue. Since there's almost never a governing body hanging around to tell you the exact number of potential customers you have and the exact number of dollars you can potentially earn this year, much of this maximization comes from how you stack up against your sales goals. Ultimately, efficient and carefully thought-out goal setting sets you up for the greatest chance of sales success.

How to set realistic sales goals

Setting realistic sales goals is part logic and part luck. The goal needs to be ambitious enough to motivate your employees and avoid leaving potential revenue on the table, and yet not so pie-in-the-sky that no one can reach it and everyone is therefore demoralized.

You can set sales goals for your company in much the same way you can set other goals, using the SMART method Make your goals:

- ✔ **Specific:** "Sell more" is certainly a goal, but it's a lousy one. Sell how much more? And more what — units? Dollars? Net or gross? Nothing short of a specific number and unit of measure will do here. In sales, you should also define exactly what state the sale needs to be in by the deadline. For example, does an e-mail from a lead that says "Sign me up!" count, or does the first check have to have cleared the bank?

- ✔ **Measurable:** In addition to specificity, you need to make sure you can actually measure progress towards a goal. In sales, if you give each salesperson a goal to sell 100 units, but you have no way to know who is ultimately responsible for each goal, then this goal is not measurable. You'd have to either change the goal to a team goal, or find a way of assigning sales to individuals.

- ✔ **Attainable:** It's one thing to put giant audacious goals up on your wall and visualize them in the shower every morning. It's another to hold your sales team accountable to them. If you currently sell 100 units a month, maybe you can sell 125 a month — but moving your goal to 1 million a month is not achievable, to the point that few would even attempt sales that month.

- ✔ **Realistic:** Along the lines of attainability, your sales goals shouldn't require your team members to work 100-hour weeks. The best goals stretch and challenge us — they don't put your best people on medieval torture racks.

- ✔ **Timely:** "Sell 100 units" is specific — but *by when?* Selling 100 units in an hour is a whole different task than selling 100 units over the course of a year. Give a very specific time frame. I encourage you to include a time of day (e.g., by January 17 at 5 p.m.) where possible for additional clarity.

What to consider setting sales goals

The exact specifications of your goals have much to do with your industry, your business values, and your organizational culture. As you contemplate what your sales goals look like, or review your existing goals, keep the following considerations in mind.

Sales needed to keep the door open

Although the many companies that shutter their doors each year are a testament to the fact that there's no guarantee you *can* sell enough to stay afloat, understanding how much you need to sell in order to meet your financial obligations is an incredibly important metric. Start here. Your sales *goals* can't be lower than this point.

Not all goals are monetary

Remember that sales goals can extend beyond dollars and cents. Consider complementary goals such as number of units sold, number of leads generated, number of upgrades, number of upsells to existing customers, and/or a minimum number of customer interactions each month.

Carefully consider what unintentional negative behaviors your goals can encourage. For example, if you set a goal of 100 minutes on the phone each day, I've seen logs proving salespeople simply called a 1-800 hot line and left the phone on hold for an hour. A variety of goals and units of measure can encourage healthy sales habits and real sales.

Time to close

If your average sales cycle takes six months, your sales team has little wiggle room to double closed sales in the next three months. Don't set them up for failure.

Percent closing

In the same vein, if your team has never closed more than 2 percent of deals over the last two years, setting a goal to close 20 percent of sales next month is not realistic. An exception: If you radically overhaul your sales process, launch a new product line, or experience a similar change of external events, a big jump *is* possible — but audacious goals should only be set as bonuses, not something on which your team's rent payments will depend upon.

Market size

It sounds obvious, but I've seen organizations overlook this in their frenzy to make sales. You can't sell to 1 million female joggers in Maine if there are only 200,000 of them. It's also nearly impossible to capture 100 percent of any market, so keep your total market size in mind when setting figures.

Company versus team versus individual goals

You need different goals for the company as a whole versus the sales team specifically and versus individual sales people. Setting team goals versus individual goals can lead to wildly different behaviors, and you need to keep this in mind. Individual goals can pit people against one another, but team goals can discourage any one person from going the extra mile. Your organizational culture has much to do with which type is the better fit, and many organizations find that setting a team goal with specific individual responsibilities is the best compromise.

Seniority

A more experienced salesperson has a bigger Rolodex, more deals in the pipeline, and generally a higher chance of succeeding than new team members. Putting the two on a level playing field may be unfair. At the same time, offering more senior salespeople higher commission rates or bonuses can motivate the new folks to want to become senior, too. "Senior" doesn't have to be defined in years — it can be akin to an airline frequent flyer program where you gain status based on your sales in the last two years.

Setting discount floors

If your sales people have the capacity to offer discounts, be careful of how this privilege can be abused to meet sales goals. For example, to hit a goal of 100 units, someone can offer your product at a 95 percent discount in order to close the deal — ultimately *costing* you money.

Previous sales figures

Your past sales numbers (and/or your competitors' past sales numbers) are a North Star in terms of what your team is capable of. Don't expect that simply moving the goal out a few million miles will be all your team needs to reach it.

Motivation

A good goal motivates — it should be encouraging your team members to make that one extra phone call at the end of the day or stretch that one extra bit to win a potential client over. It should not cause them to become desperate animals on the last day of the month, trying anything and everyone to get another close.

Get feedback from your sales team as you develop goals. Don't assume, as I've seen happen many times, that including your salesforce in goal discussions would lead to easy-to-reach goals. Quality sales people are fueled by a challenge and want to see the company for which they work succeed. Trust in your team and honor their feedback, and they'll deliver even better results for your entire organization.

Looking at Sales Commissions

If you decide that sales commissions make sense for your organization, you've done the easy part. Now the hard part: actually *defining* the commission structure, and then keeping track of it.

Setting efficient and clear commission policies

An unclear commission policy is *literally* expensive, because you either pay for the lack of clarity in hard dollars or, if you choose not to reconcile the difference expected by your employee, goodwill. Making structural decisions up front and documenting them helps keep everyone on the same page. Ask yourself the following questions when coming up with your commission structure:

✔ Do you pay *only* commissions, or do salespeople receive a base rate with commission on top of it?

I have found a combination of base and commission to work effectively in most sales organizations. Salaried salespeople miss out on the potential high returns of commissions, although commission-only salespeople are typically very stressed out. You want your employees hustling for status and a nice car, not food and a roof over their kids' heads.

✔ When are commission payments due to the salespeople? How often are they paid? Particular clarity is needed for sales that close near payment due dates. For example, if commissions pay out the 15th of every month, do sales that close on the 14th pay the next day or the next pay period?

✔ What happens to existing salespeople when you change commission rates? Are they grandfathered in on their old rates, or do they switch to the new ones?

✔ Is the commission based on net or gross sales?

✔ What event triggers a commission? For example: a signed contract or a cleared check?

✔ Does the commission percentage change based on certain deal factors, for example, the amount of the sale? For example, do sales over a certain amount earn a higher commission percentage?

✔ Is the exact commission percentage dependent upon the payment method? For example, do check payments lead to a higher percentage than credit card payments? (Remember that check payments often require more work from your accounting staff, so there's a hidden cost there.)

Maintain an open door policy to answer questions and get feedback from your sales team about commissions. Don't present the current policy as set in stone.

Tracking sales commissions

Many popular accounting and CRM software titles offer commission tracking, and in a pinch, you can always track commissions in a spreadsheet. When choosing the right tracking tool for your organization, ask the following questions:

- ✔ **Does it integrate with your accounting system?** Integration is especially important if you only pay commissions on payments received (as opposed to sales made). If there's no integration, the commission tool by default requires double data entry.

- ✔ **What happens when you change commission rates?** If it retroactively changes the commission rates, all of your historical payment amounts will be off.

- ✔ **Can salespeople see their own progress?** Not only is it motivating to see your sales and commission figures rise, but any salesperson worth their salt would be meticulously tracking their commissions *anyway*. Giving them access to real-time figures saves this duplication of effort.

- ✔ **Can it respect minimum and maximum rates?** This is important if you cap commissions.

- ✔ **Does it keep a history?** New commission payments shouldn't overwrite past ones.

- ✔ **Does it handle bonuses?** Ideally, it will calculate bonuses on its own based on logic you enter — you shouldn't have to manually calculate and/or enter bonus payments.

Discovering the pros and cons of quotas and commissions

A quota is a minimum number (or dollar amount) of sales that a person has to reach during a set period of time, such as a month. Commissions are a percentage of each deal (on either the gross or the net sales amount) that a salesperson is entitled to after closing a deal. Depending on the nature of your particular organization, quotas and/or commissions may make a great deal of sense, or no sense at all.

In evaluating whether one or both systems is the right choice for you, consider these pros and cons. Some pros include the following:

✔ Commissions tie income to payroll, which can help a business avoid the unfortunate situation of not having enough income to pay its employees.

✔ Commissions make your sales team direct stakeholders in each and every sale. When incentives are structured properly, they encourage salespeople to go the extra mile to find and nurture leads, and to close sales.

And on the cons side, consider the following:

✔ Quotas and commissions that are too much of a stretch create stress in your salespeople. When your next mortgage payment is dependent upon your ability to close your next sale, you are apt to cut corners and you are certainly going to come across as desperate. Customers can smell desperation and will react in one of two ways: fleeing, or taking advantage. Neither is good for your business.

✔ When the goal is simply to close a sale, commissions and quotas can lead salespeople to drop a lead like a hot potato the moment they convert. You can hedge against this behavior by integrating sales goals that involve good post-sale care and attention.

✔ When there's a particularly finite lead pool, quotas can lead to serious competition within the team — which can be good *or* bad.

✔ Commissions can cause "small potato" clients to be ignored or overlooked as everyone focuses on the bigger revenue opportunities. On the flip side, a quota of "17 sales" can be met by closing 17 small potatoes and ignoring the more difficult, bigger-value sales.

Ultimately, whether quotas or commissions are a good fit for you has everything to do with how they are structured. Following the SMART guideline discussed in "How to Set Realistic Sales Goals" can help you set commissions that work well for the business *and* for the salespeople.

 Just starting out? Pay some experienced salespeople a fair salary for a few months (or longer, depending on your average sales cycle) on a contract basis, and use their success as a baseline for where to set your initial goals.

When it's time to hire your own full-time labor force, if you can't hire a full crew of experienced employees, consider hiring one experienced salesperson to act as a mentor to a new, less-experienced group.

Measuring Sales Efficiency

Knowing how efficient your organization's sales are is partly about setting SMART goals and reaching them, but there are also other efficiency measures to consider within sales. For example, you can measure and improve many aspects of your sales process by A/B testing individual variables; you can track your sales progress over time by forecasting and then comparing actual and forecasted figures; and you can see how your sales stack up to your competitors.

Implement A/B testing

A/B testing in its purest form involves changing *one* variable in a scenario, holding all other variables equal, and seeing which leads to the better outcome.

What does that mean?

Shopping websites use A/B testing all the time. For example, the website will look exactly the same to two different visitors, except each visitor will see a different headline. If Visitor A buys and Visitor B does not, A/B tracking programs make note. Over time, if significantly more people who see Headline 1 buy than those who see Headline 2, the website starts to use Headline 1 all the time.

The website can then continue A/B testing its headline by comparing the new headline against additional headlines, to ultimately try to find the one that is most effective at driving sales.

A/B testing never stops. It's a valuable tool for constant, gradual improvement in the sales process.

A/B testing in sales

In sales, it can be hard to change only a single variable at a time, but that doesn't mean it's not still a worthwhile exercise. Some of the variables you can test include:

- E-mail subject lines
- E-mail content
- Time of day you send an e-mail or place a phone call
- Greeting when you answer the phone
- Scripts (which I use loosely here to mean *talking points* since, again, you should not read from a memorized script!) during a phone call

How to A/B test

The exact method to A/B test depends on what tools you're already using to communicate with sales prospects, and what variable you're specifically measuring. Options include the following:

✔ Add custom fields. (You can also add an additional column to an Excel spreadsheet, if that's where you're keeping leads.) Give each script, greeting, and so on its own unique ID (as simple as E-mail-1, E-mail-2) and indicate in this field which you use with each lead.

Make sure you keep a key for the master e-mails and greetings so you know which ones are most effective!

✔ Use an e-mail list or newsletter service with built-in A/B testing such as MailChimp (www.mailchimp.com), ExactTarget (www.exact target.com) or ConstantContact (www.constantcontact.com). This automatically divides your list, sends a different subject line or e-mail body to each half, and reports back on which half was opened the most. Integration with a CRM can give you a full-circle approach to see which clicks ultimately lead to sign-ups which lead to sales.

Make sure you have a large enough sample size before making any fundamental changes based on A/B testing feedback.

Set up sales forecasting

If you want to forecast the future—next quarter's sales, for example — you need to get a handle on what's happened in the past. So you always start with what's called a *baseline* (that is, past history — how many poppy seeds a company sold last year, where the market futures wound up last month, what the temperature was today).

Unless you're just going to roll the dice and make a guess, you need a baseline for a forecast. Today follows yesterday. What happens tomorrow generally follows the pattern of what happened today, last week, last month, last quarter, last year. If you look at what's already happened, you're taking a solid step toward forecasting what's going to happen next.

You can choose from several different forecasting methods, and it's here that judgment begins. The three most frequently used methods, in no special order, are moving averages, exponential smoothing, and regression.

Method #1: Moving averages

Moving averages may be your best choice if you have no source of information other than sales history — but you *do* need to know your sales history. The underlying idea is that market forces push your sales up or down. By averaging your sales results from month to month, quarter to quarter, or year to year, you can get a better idea of the longer-term trend that's influencing your sales results.

For example, say you find the average sales results of the last three months of last year — October, November, and December. Then you find the average of the next three-month period — November, December, and January (and then December, January, and February, and so on). Now you're getting an idea of the general direction that your sales are taking.

Method #2: Exponential smoothing

Exponential smoothing is closely related to moving averages. Just as with moving averages, exponential smoothing uses past history to forecast the future. You use what happened last week, last month, and last year to forecast what will happen next week, next month, or next year.

The difference is that when you use smoothing, you take into account how bad your previous forecast was — that is, you admit that the forecast was a little screwed up. (Get used to that — it happens.) The nice thing about exponential smoothing is that you can take the error in your last forecast and use that error, so you hope, to improve your next forecast.

If your last forecast was too low, exponential smoothing kicks your next forecast up. If your last forecast was too high, exponential smoothing kicks the next one down.

The basic idea is that exponential smoothing corrects your next forecast in a way that would have made your *prior* forecast a better one. That's a good idea, and it usually works well.

Method #3: Regression

When you used regression to make a forecast, you're relying on one variable to predict another. For example, when the Federal Reserve raises short-term interest rates, you may rely on that variable to forecast what's going to happen to bond prices or the cost of mortgages. In contrast to moving averages or exponential smoothing, regression relies on a *different* variable to tell you what's likely to happen next — something other than your own sales history.

Many accounting and CRM programs ship with native forecasting tools. If you can export a sales report to Microsoft Excel, you can also perform any of the three forecasting analyses outlined previously with the free included Analysis ToolPak.

Run a competitive analysis

Knowing where your competitors stand on key metrics and how their sales processes work can provide valuable insights into how you may be able to improve your own organization and processes.

Just keep in mind that your most successful competitor is *not* necessarily a representation of the biggest possible success in your industry. They may be wildly inefficient themselves! If anything, they are a marker for the minimum you can achieve.

What to compare

You can learn much both from your competitors' successes and their failures. When you can find this information, pay particular attention to the following:

- ✔ How many current customers they have
- ✔ How many leads they generate
- ✔ How large their salesforce is
- ✔ How their salesforce is paid
- ✔ The frequency and content of their e-mails
- ✔ Their selling points, slogans, phone greetings, and other sales verbiage

How to gather information

If your competitors are public companies, you can access much of the information about their customer base, revenues, and even future goals in their public filings. Look on their website or search the U.S. Securities and Exchange Commission's website at www.sec.gov. There may be additional data available at www.data.gov, particularly localized portals such as cities.data.gov, counties.data.gov, and states.data.gov.

For private competitors, this task is a bit harder, but you can still find out a lot by looking online. Press releases, although they are not guaranteed to be 100 percent factual, can give you a good idea of the number of employees and/or customers, and of new product offerings.

In either case, you can learn much of what you want to know about their sales processes by simply calling up and pretending to be a customer. If you feel this is dishonest, know that *they* have almost certainly called *you* posing as a customer before. It's an incredibly common practice, and in most cases it's relatively harmless. (This does not work well in cases where the only possible deal is a multimillion dollar contract that takes a year to close. That's a poor use of your time and a waste of their salesperson's time.)

You should also sign up (under an anonymous e-mail address) for your competitors' mailing lists, demos, and other online materials. Knowledge is power here!

Discovering Tools and Technologies to Increase Sales Efficiency

It may never be appropriate to replace the human interactions usually involved in creating a sale, but that doesn't mean there isn't also a place for technology in the mix.

Choose the right Customer Relationship Management (CRM) database

I make it no secret that I'm a huge fan of CRM systems. Today's CRMs are hardly the static electronic address books of yesterday — they're a whole ecosystem of applications and plug-ins that let businesses from psychiatrists to multi-site manufacturing firms track, automate, integrate, and predict nearly every aspect of their workflows. The right CRM can not only keep your sales details straight, but it also can drive more sales faster and integrate sales into other areas of your business such as accounting and fulfillment.

When choosing a CRM, keep in mind the Total Cost of Ownership. This term refers to the lifetime cost of a product or service, including setup fees, consulting costs, maintenance, the cost of the (dedicated) person(s) using it, and annual subscription fees for as long as you expect to use it. If Total Cost of Ownership seems high, compare it to the potential cost of not having a CRM — which are almost inevitably higher.

Some questions to ask when choosing your next (or first!) CRM include the following:

- **Do you hire programmers to build your own CRM or choose an existing solution?** The answer to this question in all my years of consulting has *never* been to build your own CRM. Most companies do not have the internal resources to create or maintain such a system, and if you do, their resources are better spent on tasks that are *not* reinventing the wheel. You can, and probably will, use IT staff to build additional customizations or integrations on top of an existing CRM.

- **Is the CRM on an internal server or in the Cloud?** "The Cloud" refers to services that exist entirely online, which means you can access them from any computer, or even a mobile phone, with the right password. You never need to upgrade software that's in the Cloud or install software on your computer.

  Internal CRMs require installing software on each computer, and generally require IT services for installing and upgrading a network across your company so people can share contact details. If a computer crashes, all that data is lost.

Go with the Cloud! CRM software that you have to install is not worth the IT expense, and you can't access data securely from home or on the road.

✔ **What integrations do you need? What are available?** If you've already constructed some Lean value-stream maps, you have a good understanding of how information flows through your business. How exactly does customer information flow from when it first becomes a lead to when the final payment is made? Which parts are clearly CRM domain and which, such as order fulfillment and accounting, are not? Can the CRM you're considering integrate with those other areas, either through an existing third-party application or a custom-developed solution?

✔ **Is there an API?** API, or Application Programming Interface, refers to your ability to build on top of an existing system — such as to have it "talk" to your manufacturing mainframe, sales forecasting tool, or website. An API is critical for being able to customize a CRM beyond simply making custom fields.

✔ **What training and consulting resources exist?** The default configuration of today's top CRM tools is most efficient for exactly no businesses. Some degree of customization is necessary to really get the most bang for your buck — and unfortunately sometimes the trade-off for a highly customizable system is that there's a lot to learn. You can ease this learning curve with the right consultant, or, if you have the time to learn, the right training resources.

Popular CRM applications include Salesforce.com, SugarCRM, ZenDesk, and BatchBook.

Enhance your phone system

If your sales process is mostly phone-based, there are tools out there to help make calling faster and higher quality.

Auto dialers

Manually looking up and dialing phone numbers for each sales call is a huge waste of time in aggregate. An auto-dialer puts that time back in the hands of your salespeople by automatically dialing a new customer the moment your employee hangs up the phone from the last call.

Look for an autodialer that meets your needs, such as one that integrates with your CRM tool, can create lists of calls based on your criteria (for example, you would want to exclude leads by time zone toward the beginning of the day to avoid waking people up!), and can pause between calls for a set period of time (say, five minutes) so your salespeople have time to write up notes or take care of follow-up actions.

You also definitely need a means of pausing the autodialer for lunch or quick breaks. This may seem obvious, but some systems don't have this built-in!

Quantity does not always mean quality. Your sales team is better off making 20 high-quality sales calls per day than 100 mediocre ones.

Quality control recordings

"This call may be recorded for quality assurance purposes" feels like the standard greeting for most automated phone systems. Although you should check with your legal counsel before implementing call recordings, they are generally helpful both for making sure your salespeople (as well as your customer support staff) are providing the level of service you expect *and* for protecting yourself from "he said, she said" arguments if legal disputes arise.

Make your marketing more efficient

Efficient marketing can easily be its own book, but there are a couple high-level concepts to keep in mind to make sure your marketing is just as efficient as your sales process.

Inbound marketing

Inbound marketing is the idea that instead of using the traditional sales process where you identify and reach out to potential customers, you should invest time and energy in making yourself easy for potential customers to find *you*.

Inbound marketing has taken off in the Internet age where consumers (both individuals and businesses) are increasingly looking online for information and options to solve their problems. How can you put yourself in front of these people when they are searching for a solution to a problem that *you* can solve?

Forms of inbound marketing include publishing a blog with useful information for your industry; publishing useful articles in other blogs or publications (that just-so-happen to point back to your website); posting informative articles and white papers on your website; interacting with people in your industry on Twitter; and answering related questions on websites like Twitter, Quora, and LinkedIn.

Inbound marketing is very different from putting advertisements for your company on other websites. It's about helping to inform potential customers about issues and questions relevant to their needs, and therefore establishing yourself as an authority on the matter. If you're the perceived authority, people are more likely to sign up for more information, demos, and so on, and ultimately purchase from you.

A/B testing

You can extend the idea of A/B testing (discussed earlier in this chapter) out much further in your marketing campaigns across the analog and digital worlds.

Additional variables to test include print advertisements (content, headlines, placement, day of the week, publication); direct mailings (type, timing, and messaging); paid search keywords (compare multiple keywords); and banner ads (websites on which they were placed, image used, colors).

One tried-and-true means of A/B testing different campaigns is to use unique promotion codes. For example, run two different ads in the newspaper on two different days, with a different "coupon code" listed on each. You can track the success of the ads by seeing how often each code is redeemed. A more tech-savvy version of this has you listing different URLs in each advertisement, and tracking which URL is visited more.

Selling via Call Centers

After you reach scale, selling over the phone (or increasingly, through a website) requires a dedicated call center full of employees who focus on, well — calling customers! Done right, a call center can be a great asset — but done wrong, you can be scaring off most of your potential customers and not even realize it.

In-house versus outsourced call centers

The answer to this question depends mostly on your available resources. If you have the physical space, the money for equipment, the available local workforce, and the related managerial experience — feel free to set up shop inside your organization. If this description just overwhelmed you, then it's probably best to find an outsourced call center.

Note that outsourced does not *have* to mean out of the country. There are many large call centers available within the United States.

Effective call center scripts

Providing effective, A/B-tested scripts is exponentially more important when you start to scale your calling efforts. If your company is new, you should literally try out some phone sales and see what sorts of approaches seem to work. (Everyone should have experience directly selling their own product or service, even if their day-to-day responsibilities are not in sales.)

After you have a call center, it's easier to continue to A/B test scripts. Just remember to try to change only *one* variable at a time. For example, it's not valid A/B testing to give Joe one script and Josslyn a different one because the resulting sales differences may be because of *Joe and Josslyn* and have nothing to do with the scripts themselves.

Most major call centers can work with you on developing script best practices and decision trees that help guide the people answering the phone through your leads' potential questions. Look for a call center that will dedicate a few employees to your organization instead of spreading your organization's calls across the whole staff, as this helps individuals gain actual experience with your company and your leads.

Escalation policies

Even if you use a call center for *most* sales calls, odds are there are some that you want to funnel back internally. For example, you may want to handle sales in excess of $1 million yourself. You may also want to handle angry leads or answer particular questions. (You definitely want to be available to answer questions that your call center's decision tree doesn't address!)

An escalation policy helps the call center determine which calls to handle itself and when to pass these calls on to you. When in doubt, err on the side of forwarding calls to yourself. You can always modify the policy later and be more lenient with the calls that the center is allowed to handle — but you'll kick yourself for years if you realize you left the call center to handle calls that it wasn't prepared for.

Quality assurance

As with all things outsourced, it's important to keep an eye on the quality of the calls being made. This is not to say that the call center employees are necessarily providing *bad* quality calls, but you have to remember that your company, products, and services are new to them, and they are inherently less prepared to answer questions and close sales than you.

Watching quality by comparing sales numbers between the outside call center and internal sales calls, and by listening in on a random sampling of calls, can help you identify issues or points of confusion and clear them up right away.

Generating Sales Efficiently and Legally

Following a few best practices will help keep your organization's sales robust *and* legal.

Using Referrals

Word-of-mouth marketing remains *the* best way to generate leads and close new sales. Hearing your best friend recommend a car salesman who treated her well and gave her a fair price can immediately circumvent your doing *any* research on competitors and instead go straight to that same guy. Yet, most businesses completely take word-of-mouth for granted and focus very little, if any, attention on referrals.

You can also *ask* for referrals, and at multiple points during and after a current sale. If you collect feedback on a sales experience, ask if there's anyone else to whom you should reach out. On your website, add links to easily e-mail a given page or blog post to a friend or share it on major social media sites like Twitter and Facebook.

Make sure your customers' last impression of you is a lasting one. Even if you haggled for a bit too long on price or there was a hiccup in shipping, if the very last experience a customer has with you is a positive one, then they're more likely to remember you fondly *and* talk about you positively with the people they know. Giving your customers a pleasant, memorable sales experience is the easiest and cheapest way to generate referral sales.

Complying with e-mail laws

In the United States, commercial e-mail — in other words, e-mails you send to potential customers — falls under the CAN-SPAM Act. Violations of this law can lead to tens of thousands of dollars of fines, and paying fines is never efficient. To comply with CAN-SPAM, you must

- ✔ Clearly identify your e-mails as advertisements.
- ✔ Provide a means for recipients to opt-out of all future e-mails from your organization.
- ✔ Honor all opt-out requests within 10 days of receipt.

For full information on complying with this law, visit www.ftc.gov.

Collecting preferred contact methods

No one cold calling me will ever make a sale, no matter how badly I may need their product or how good a price they are offering. This is because I hate phone calls and don't answer calls from numbers I don't recognize. On the flipside, I read most every e-mail I receive, and am very likely to clickthrough to learn more about something that catches my eye. As the number of products and services available grows, and as it becomes easier to reach customers, more and more people are going to be like me — only they may *hate* e-mail and prefer phone calls, or like e-mail before 6 p.m. and prefer phone calls afterward.

If you're going to stand out among the crowd, you need to understand how each of your customers prefers to interact and adapt accordingly. Never present a potential customer with a form asking for four types of contact information. Instead, ask for the *one* type of contact information they want you to use — and then use it. If that means you send tweets to certain leads, then you tweet — simple as that.

Tracking time zones

Most businesses are competing in an increasingly global marketplace. Your next customer may be coming from down the street, or from an entirely different hemisphere. Don't assume that they're in the same time zone (or even speaking the same language). One good way to make a bad impression is to accidentally call a lead at 2 a.m. and wake them up, because you didn't realize they were in Hawaii.

Many CRM titles offer time zone-tracking capabilities. You can also get pretty close by searching online for a script that matches countries or states to time zones. You may be an hour off on some, but you can reliably avoid middle-of-the-night phone calls with minimal extra effort.

Keeping the human touch

Although the right balance between automation and human interaction is ultimately up to your specific business, a fully automated sales process is generally *not* the most efficient option. Even if you sell a web-based service that customers can demo and sign up for on their own, and even if it has an extensive library of FAQs, you should still have a human around to answer questions. You can also write your messaging in a "human" way.

Chapter 13

Up to My Gears in Efficiency: Manufacturing Efficiency

Manufacturing is the process of creating something. A work of art is a unique creation. It is manufactured but since it is a one-of-a-kind item, it is not an exactly repeatable item. However, most manufacturing concerns the creation of multiple identical items. The goal is to make them identically perfect and at an identical low cost. This is accomplished through identifying the best way to do something and then documenting those steps so future work can follow the same actions.

Efficiency is the creation of something of value with a minimum of waste. Waste takes many forms, some of them not obvious. Obvious forms of waste include scrap material, reworked goods to remove defects, idle workers, or energy wasted from equipment left running for no good purpose. Less obvious waste is waiting time for approvals, for materials, for tooling changes, and so on.

A problem with making your company more efficient is that process improvements are islands of improvement in a vast sea of effort. A change in one place to improve efficiency may create more inefficiency elsewhere. To be truly efficient, every process of the company must be examined for improvement opportunities.

Discovering What Efficient Manufacturing Looks Like

Most manufacturing processes are inefficient. An efficient manufacturing process minimizes waste of the people, machinery, and materials used to create something of value. I say *minimize* waste since no process is 100 percent efficient (and it may not be cost effective to make it so). There is always some element of waste. Management's goal is to identify and minimize the wastes that it can control.

Waste is not just in the factory. Successful companies seek out waste in all its forms throughout the organization. Some companies squeeze the last few cents out of a manufacturing process only to turn around and waste dollars in shipping inefficiencies. This is due to the human nature of focusing on what we know best and not looking for opportunities in areas we know least.

A holistic approach to manufacturing efficiency examines every step of the process from customer contact all of the way through final product delivery. It also looks at all the back office processes that support manufacturing to ensure they are operating at peak efficiency.

How does your quality stack up?

As a child, you probably heard the story of *Goldilocks and the Three Bears.* Just as Goldilocks wants the soup, the chair, and the bed to be "just right," your customers want something that fits their needs.

You measure quality by how well a product or service conforms to the customer's desired specifications. Quality isn't a statement of the value of a product. Although one bear's soup is too hot for Goldilocks, and one bear's soup is too cold, the food is all high-quality soup for the intended diners. Goldilocks finds the teeny, tiny bear's soup to be "just right" because she happens to share the same taste in soup as that bear, not because that bear's soup is any "better" than the others.

The idea that insufficient value is bad is easy for everyone to understand. If I ask for a ladder that holds 300 pounds (let's say I'm very strong), and the ladder you sell me holds only 250 pounds, I'm going to have a problem with the quality of your ladder. I will incur a cost (a medical cost!) that you created because you sold me, in my opinion, a ladder of poor quality.

The impact of providing too little quality is such an important concept in the field of quality control that it has a formal name: *cost of poor quality,* or *COPQ.* COPQ consists of all the costs that result from producing a poor-quality product or service. This expense consists of the following:

- ✔ Cost of improving the actual product or service to fill the gap between what the customer wants and what you currently offer
- ✔ Cost of materials you added to the product or work you put into the service before the customer rejected it
- ✔ Cost of lost labor and resources you need to fix the poor-quality product
- ✔ Cost of potential lost market share (you may lose orders to competitors that offer better quality)
- ✔ Cost of getting rid of the poor-quality product rejected by a customer (because you can't resell it)

 Calculating COPQ for your organization helps you determine the potential savings you can gain by putting quality process improvements into practice. Calculate your COPQ in four steps:

1. **Identify all activities that are necessary only because of poor quality.** Conduct a brainstorming session with people familiar with the process to identify all tasks that workers perform solely to fix quality problems, such as inspection, rework, repair, and returns.

2. **Determine where in the production process these activities occur.** In other words, you look at which production steps cause the quality problems.

3. **To calculate the total cost of poor quality, identify the percentage of effort that each corrective activity consumes in its part of the production process; multiply by the total costs in that area.** For example, if workers perform 10 percent of the effort in a production area solely to fix quality problems, 10 percent of the entire cost of that production step is the cost of poor quality for that area.

4. **Sum the cost of poor quality for each area to get the total for your organization.** Sadly, the COPQ for most companies ranges from 15 to 25 percent. Reducing this value can increase the quality you provide to your customers, increase employee morale (being on a winning team), and improve profits.

How efficient is your manufacturing process?

The most important part of any process is the result — the finished product or service that you produce or deliver. The Rolled Throughput Yield (RTY) is the number of finished units a process produces the first time through without any rework. RTY is an indicator of the number of units that go into a process compared to the number that come out complete at the end. The higher the RTY, the more efficient the process.

The RTY is mathematically related to the Sigma level, but explaining natural logs (mathematical logs, not big wooden sticks) isn't something for this *For Dummies* book (sorry for the curious!).

Unfortunately, life isn't as simple as a one-step process. Imagine a three-step process in shaping wood:

- ✔ In the first step, 100 pieces of wood enter the process, but the workers make only 95 properly for the second step. The workers didn't cut the other five pieces according to specification, so the pieces are discarded.

- ✔ The second step takes the output from the first and makes additional cuts. Of the 95 pieces that enter the second step, only 98 percent (93 pieces) are fit to pass on. The other two pieces are discarded.

- ✔ The third step takes the results from the second and drills some holes into the wood pieces as a finishing touch. Of the pieces that enter the third step, 99 percent (92 pieces total) are delivered as finished products and one piece is discarded.

So, you calculate the Rolled Throughput Yield by multiplying the percent of good material that leaves each process step. Here are the results for the wood example:

Step 1: 95 ÷ 100 = 0.95 (95 percent)

Step 2: 93 ÷ 95 = 0.978 (98 percent)

Step 3: 92 ÷ 93 = 0.989 (99 percent)

RTY: 95 percent × 98 percent × 99 percent = 92 percent

The total RTY is 92 percent. Out of 100 pieces of wood that enter the process, only 92 acceptable ones come out.

After calculating the RTY, you need to consider the money lost in buying the other eight pieces of material and the labor lost by working on the material lost in the third step. Now, consider the impact of a 20- or 30-step process. How much would you save by improving a process with so many steps? That's where Six Sigma comes in.

Consider the example of filling in a home loan application form with 30 blanks. If customers experience a 99-percent success rate for filling in each blank, you'd calculate the RTY by multiplying 99 percent times itself 30 times. The result is a 74 percent chance of a customer filling out a form correctly the first time. Not a very efficient process! Imagine the cost of reworking all the defective forms to clear up the bad data in the blanks.

Manufacturing Goal Setting

Most companies embark on their quality journey in response to a problem. These problems may be internally identified during business processes or externally identified by customers. After the original problem is resolved, the next logical step is to apply this effort to other problems. With limited resources, where should the company look for its next worst quality problem? Before hiring a quality staff and hanging up posters exhorting "Zero Defects," take the time to identify the goals the company intends to realize from its program. This will focus the team on areas of the greatest manufacturing "pain."

A company needs to set goals for everyone to work toward. You may set goals to reduce customer complaints, have faster delivery times, or reduce reworked goods. Here are some traits of goals and tips for using them:

- Choose goals the organization can easily measure, and make sure managers regularly give employees feedback on their progress.

- Visit companies that are the "best in class" to see what they've done to improve product quality — a technique known as benchmarking. How does a top-rated restaurant provide top-notch service? How does a five-star hotel handle its reservations? How does an overnight express-delivery company keep its aircraft in the air at all hours? With benchmarking, you learn from others so one day you'll be good enough for others to come visit you!

- Select goals that are challenging enough to encourage improvement, though not so lofty that workers become discouraged. You can't fix a company overnight.

- Compare goals and results to both previous work done by the company and to work done by other companies.

Setting clear manufacturing goals

Manufacturing goals are derived from customer requirements. A desire for a lower price drives manufacturer efficiency. A requirement for faster delivery may drive agile manufacturing for making smaller lots, each with a different variation. Some goals are in response to moves by your competitors. As the auto industry demonstrates, high quality products are necessary just to stay in business. Take care that your goals do not have unintended consequences!

Your organization doesn't exist to provide you with a paycheck (although you may think it does) or to give you something to do during the day. Your organization exists to provide some product or service to your customers!

Without customers, your company would cease to exist. Any number of competitors are just waiting for the chance to swoop in and take your place if you don't meet your customers' needs and expectations. Identifying your customers' likes and dislikes so that you can continue to provide them with the products and services they need is critical to the survival of your organization (and to the delivery of your paycheck).

In quality control, the phrase *voice of the customer* (VOC) describes the customers' needs or requirements. This phrase embodies both the needs and requirements that customers have explicitly stated and those they may not have told you about. Actively seeking the voice of the customer provides benefits beyond your immediate quality concerns, including the following:

- Demonstrating to your customers that you care
- Gaining important intelligence about what your competitors are doing, both right and wrong
- Providing information about products or services your customers didn't know you provide
- Reinforcing the importance of the voice of the customer to your employees
- Making your customers feel that you're more than just a vendor; you're a partner that helps them meet their needs

Understanding the trickle-down effect of manufacturing changes

Solving a quality problem can be personally satisfying. People naturally like to take pride in the value of their efforts, and no one wants to be associated with sloppy processes and poorly performing products. Everyone wants to be on the winning team. Management teams who reward quality improvement efforts with positive attention and public praise will find employees offering suggestions for process problems.

This in turn (with encouragement) leads to employee empowerment to address simple issues in their own work areas. The key to empowerment is risk assessment. If the employee's suggestion requires a $250,000 capital improvement, then that must flow through the usual capital suggestion list. However, most employee suggestions involve basic things like the following:

- ✔ Fix my scanner gun — why is it broken for months?
- ✔ Rearrange a work cell for easier work flow.
- ✔ Purchase higher quality material to reduce rework (cost of material goes up but overall process cost goes down).

Employee suggestions must be weighed against the likelihood and impact of the failure. If it involves a simple change with minimal cash outlay (usually some labor), then it can be approved at a low level. It is not unusual for efficiency problems to be caused by a single manager's decision (or whim) not to address a situation. A bit of executive awareness usually solves this.

A positive executive attitude toward quality improvement will slowly trickle through the company based on management actions. A small success here or there provides local examples that things can change. Ask each worker, "what obstacles interfere with your daily work." If the first few suggestions are respected and hopefully resolved, then many more will follow. The workers become happier and the company becomes gradually more efficient.

Employee perception of quality improvement programs is important. A negative trickle-down effect comes from quality improvements that eliminate jobs. For example, if the quality of a process is improved so that its output requires very little rework, then the people who used to rework the defects will no longer be needed in that role. This can ripple out among the workforce and make them fearful that a quality improvement is a smoke screen to cut jobs. Where possible, redeploy displaced workers. The overall result will be to reduce the fear of "quality improvements."

Manufacturing Efficiency Improvement Methods

Process improvements methods reflect the industry in which they were first conceived. Still they can be easily adjusted to most office, service, or manufacturing situations. They follow a logical progression and need not be exclusive. Consider borrowing the pieces you want from each to create the solution that is unique to your own situation.

✔ **Six Sigma** is an excellent process for rooting out the cause of stubborn process problems that everyone says, "That is the way it always has been, and will always be." Six Sigma is a time-consuming technique that seeks leaps in process improvement. Before applying Six Sigma, see if 5S and Lean resolve the problem first.

✔ **Lean** is a way of examining all company process and removing the non-value added steps. Over time, processes become bloated. Business environments are always changing with new products, changed emphasis within the facility, and so on. Every step in a process is another opportunity to make an error. Workers alter processes to meet their personal whims, to fulfill management requests that may no longer be needed, or worse, try to suit customers' needs when no customer has ever ask for those (unnecessary) changes. Applying Lean techniques simplifies processes by removing unnecessary steps.

✔ **Agile Manufacturing** reflects the reality that companies cannot afford to keep large inventories of finished goods sitting around. Agile is a way of approaching the manufacture of small lots in quick response to customer needs.

✔ **5S** is the first place that most companies start. A successful workplace organization program often speeds up processes since the workers are not stepping around things and everything is in its assigned location. Of all quality programs, this is the easiest one for employees to understand and also, through 5S, the employees take ownership of their own work environment.

✔ **Total Quality Management (TQM)** empowers employees to make small changes throughout the organization, and to recommend large changes for management review. TQM is a quality approach that emphasizes executive presence and support to establish a quality culture throughout the company. Employees are trained in basic tools and empowered to use them. TQM is likened to thousands of small quality improvements adding up across the organization.

Six Sigma: Eliminating variability in your manufacturing process

Everyone has had a job where some part of it has never worked right — a persistent problem that annoys everyone but doesn't seem to have an obvious cause. From time to time, someone tests a solution, but nothing seems to work. If a company has a stubborn problem — something that employees have to work around — then Six Sigma may be the answer to their prayers.

Six Sigma is a collection of quality improvement techniques that identify the root causes of problems in production or service-delivery processes. It uses quality-analysis techniques and a broad application of statistics to pinpoint the process inputs that cause the undesired outputs. The techniques work to minimize the variation of inputs and produce more consistent products.

Some quality improvement techniques, such as the Total Quality Management (TQM) method, seek to make small improvements that add up over time to a big improvement. Six Sigma, however, focuses on break-through improvements. It's the best tool for fixing those stubborn, they've-always-been-this-way problems.

A *sigma* (σ) is a statistical indication of variation. Statistics is a technique used to make a judgment about an entire group of people or items based on only a few. The study of statistics isn't for everyone; however, just as an understand-ing of electronics isn't necessary to use a PC, an understanding of statistics isn't necessary to grasp how Six Sigma works its magic within your company.

Lean manufacturing: Emulate the Toyota Production System (TPS)

The elimination of waste is one of the keystones of Lean processes. To elimi-nate waste in your processes, you need to understand how to identify waste. The Toyota Production System (TPS) is based on the idea that there are seven kinds of waste in a manufacturing process. As a result, their descrip-tions and many of the examples rely on manufacturing processes. With the evolution of Lean and other quality improvement techniques, the business world has transitioned to looking at the overall supply chain, service indus-tries, and other areas for waste.

Examining a supply chain simply requires looking outside the four walls of a factory and recognizing the movement from facility to facility, utilizing differ-ent forms of transport. When you look at a production facility, the product flows from machine to machine and process to process; the end result is the delivery of a quality product to the customer. The same is true of a service. The product may not be as visible, but the process still involves a flow that ultimately adds value. Waste is still waste, whether it exists inside a small workstation or around the world.

Some experts add an eighth type of waste: the underutilization of skilled employees. Why use the time of a skilled (and expensive) tradesman, man-ager, or data-processing technician for performing simple clerical work? Every employee must do some portion of simple documentation, but in some cases, paperwork can consume a skilled person's day.

The seven types of waste are defined in Chapter 1.

Agile manufacturing: Responding more quickly to change

Agile manufacturing provides products tailored to their customers' needs on a short order-to-delivery cycle. An Agile organization can quickly shift from making one thing to another. To do this requires involvement of every part of the company, such as materials management, personnel management, accounting, executive support, and of course, the shop floor personnel. Agile manufacturers use technology to communicate and to maintain databases of common part information and design drawings. To be consider an Agile manufacturer, each of these functional areas must quickly respond to the customer needs to begin creating high quality products.

Most manufacturers use large fixed conveyors and machines to fabricate and assemble their products. They focus on optimizing their existing processes for higher quality and lower cost. They are not focused on building 50 of one thing and then 400 of something else. An Agile manufacturer can quickly shift with changing customer requirements and can fulfill requests for quick delivery of important components. They use simple techniques such as smaller machines on wheels, portable unpowered conveyors, and wide-open factory space where the equipment can be quickly rearranged to meet the needs of the job.

Agile manufacturers have their own limitation. They do not produce cellular telephone one day and washing machine the next. Instead they focus on product or technology *families*. This enables them to use the same technical staff across a range of products. Agile manufacturing is suitable to producing expensive items and is not viable for providing commodity products.

This concept is not isolated to small companies. The Toyota Production System emphasizes agile manufacturing for process quick changeover. If you recall "waste of over production," rapid changeover processes enable small lots. Small lots improve quality through the quick identification of problems (detect trouble on a lot of 50 units instead of 5,000).

5S: Removing clutter from manufacturing

The 5S method is the Japanese concept of housekeeping. 5S is a methodical approach to eliminating waste in time and materials. Its philosophy is that a simplified work area operates more efficiently, cheaply, and safely. The belief is that a sloppy workspace is, by its nature, filled with waste: wasted time looking for items, wasted costs in excess materials and tools, wasted space, and so on. The five *S's,* loosely translated into English, are Sort *(Seiri),* Straighten *(Seiton),* Shine *(Seiso),* Standardize *(Seiketsu),* and Sustain *(Shitsuke).* 5S's mantra is "only what is needed, in its proper place, clean and ready for use."

Using the 5S method in your company has a variety of benefits, but you also need to be aware of some disadvantages before you decide to move forward. The pros of 5S include the following:

- ✓ **5S simplifies processes.** By examining workflows in a department, removing the need to work around clutter, and making needed material easy to find, you greatly simplify processes.

- ✓ **5S increases materials visibility.** The same material is now always located in the same marked places. The materials stock person can see when materials are running low and address the situation before you run out.

- ✓ **5S reenergizes the workforce.** 5S is an employee-driven program. Employees organize the work areas, and they decide what stays and goes; the result is cleaner, more efficient workspaces.

- ✓ **5S improves quality of management.** The work in progress is more visually obvious now that the clutter is gone. Incoming materials are always in the same places, and you can tell when they're running short. Finished goods are always in the same places, and you can tell if they're on schedule.

- ✓ **5S improves the quality of changing over to occasional production runs.** You plan the locations of processes and materials and mark their locations on the floor, which reduces confusion and improves product quality.

The 5S process can flop if your company lacks the courage to promptly resolve questions. Additional disadvantages of introducing 5S to your company include the following:

- ✓ People develop a comfort level for the way things are today, whether the methods are efficient or wasteful. Radically changing practices can be unsettling to people who live their lives within daily routines. People may resist giving up their secret stashes of parts and tools.

- ✓ Cleaning up a mess that took years to create takes time. Your organization needs to clean up the entire facility.

- ✓ The results of 5S fade away without management support to maintain the initiative.

TQM: Improving quality in manufacturing environments with infrequent change

TQM is more than a few data-analysis tools; it's a cultural attitude toward everything "quality." It provides customers (internal and external) with the products and services that best satisfy their needs. TQM is a combination of the following:

- **Quality culture:** This concept is a company-wide value system in which workers focus on improving the quality of everything they do. Workers discuss possible improvements at every meeting and in every report.

- **Quality strategy:** Strategy involves a published plan with specific techniques and measurable goals for sustainable quality improvement.

- **Process improvement tools:** Employees use these tools to support the program.

- **Continuous quality improvement:** This concept means that every worker in the company feels empowered to improve their individual processes and is encouraged to recommend changes to larger processes. Each person takes ownership in order to make products right the first time and to stop bad products from reaching the end of the line.

Total Quality Management (TQM) is a company-wide, proactive effort to improve quality. *Total* means that all business functions (engineering, production, marketing, and so on) focus on defining and fulfilling (the ever-shifting) customer needs. Each company tailors TQM to fit its circumstances. The unifying theme is to "do the right things, the right way, the first time."

Total Quality Management requires your company executives' ongoing commitment to change. Rather than being the duty of a "quality department" in some distant, dark back room, quality improvement becomes everyone's business. To be considered *total,* quality has to permeate all levels of the organization. Here are the TQM principles:

- **Management commitment:** Quality improvement must be a daily topic. Meetings have to include time for asking, "How can we improve this process?"

- **Employee empowerment:** Resolving something on the spot is much faster than going through the tedious steps of getting endless approvals. Empower employees to immediately address problems they can resolve, and reward them for passing issues beyond their control up the leadership chain.

✔ **Fast action:** Management should quickly review suggestions for quality improvements. Every day an idea sits in the inbox leads to another day's worth of defects. Base decisions about changing workflow on data collected at critical points in the process. Data should be the basis for decisions; you shouldn't rely on whims of the moment.

✔ **Customer focus:** Keep the products in sync with ever-shifting customer demands. Yesterday's optional feature is today's requirement. A customer can be either the person purchasing the final product or the next person working in a process.

✔ **Continuous improvement:** Processes and products are never good enough. You can always make improvements — to make the product better, reduce its cost, or improve a process's efficiency.

Evaluating Potential Manufacturing Improvements

Project selection is an important part of your quality program. Picking the wrong project results in a lot of time wasted for minimal impact. Poor projects are usually selected because a manufacturing manager does not want the quality improvement program to interfere with current production.

Begin with some research into the company customer complaint files, equipment maintenance logs, existing quality audits, and even Help Desk tickets. Next arrange a brainstorming session that gathers ideas from the various department managers.

Determine which quality improvement to start your program with through the use of a simple ranking matrix. In this example, begin with the name of the improvement. Next assess the problem's quality impact to determine whose solution would provide the greatest benefit:

✔ Rank the impact on the "Critical TO" categories of Cost, Delivery and Quality from 1 to 5 with 1 being low impact and 5 being high. It is not unusual for a problem to impact several of the categories in some way.

✔ Calculate a "Pain" Score by adding all of the values together.

Then assess if you have the resources to tackle a particular problem. In this section, you are looking for projects that may be easy to complete. Rank the capabilities from 1 (low) to 5 (high) in the following areas:

✔ **Technical People Available:** Can you get time from the local subject matter experts?

✔ **Process Business Criticality:** How critical is this process to the company's ongoing financial health?

✔ **Time Required:** How long do you think it will take to resolve this issue? Some are quick hitters if you focus on them for a short time.

✔ **Potential Payback:** What is the overall benefit to the identified impact areas if you are successful?

Calculate a *Capability Score* by adding the values in the Capability section together. For an overall score, add the Pain Score to the Capability Score.

Creating this matrix offers several immediate benefits. First, everyone is talking about quality and applying it to the company. Second, some enterprising managers will latch onto one of the problems not selected for the first round and tackle it themselves. Now, if the executives can just maintain this high level of enthusiasm!

Part IV

Increasing Employee Efficiency

The 5th Wave   By Rich Tennant

"A large part of our success is based on our ability to resolve conflicts before we get to work."

In this part . . .

Ultimately, your organization is only as efficient as your employees. Once you have operational overhead in order, you need your employees to work quickly and accurately to fulfill their responsibilities. This part covers giving your employees the resources and training they need to be their best, with an eye towards change management, knowledge capture and transfer, internal communication, project management, and ways to keep meetings from draining team morale. There's also a specific chapter on improving efficiency on the individual level, from mastering keyboard shortcuts to developing a trustworthy task management system.

Chapter 14

I Love You, You're Perfect, Now Change: Change Management

● ●

In This Chapter

▶ Introducing change in a nonthreatening way

▶ Determining where to start

▶ Getting employee buy-in

▶ Combating resistance to change

● ●

*E*very other chapter of this book – and every chapter of every other book on business efficiency and productivity – is useless if you don't get change management right. This may sound harsh, but it's true. No matter how easy or positive you perceive your proposed change to be, if you go about implementing it in the wrong way, you risk your organization pushing back and resisting (or outright *rejecting*) your proposal. This effectively cements your inefficiencies in place.

Change is rarely binary; that is, either on or off. Successful change means a 100 percent adoption of the new process (or a 100 percent cessation of the old process). Three employees following the new shipping procedure and 17 following the former procedure easily leads to greater chaos than the original system ever caused, and the natural reaction to this chaos is to revert back to the status quo.

Although change management can be more art than science, there are still some undercurrents that I've found successful across projects spanning single individuals to multiple federal government agencies. Remember these strategies, and you'll be well-equipped to move your organizational efficiency forward in a way that unites, rather than alienates, your team.

In this chapter, I go over the importance of effective change management and change management best practices, and show you how you can make everyone on your team a successful change agent.

The Importance of Change Management

Whether it's a big change (like taking a different job, having a child, or moving into a new home) or a small change (like buying a new pair of shoes or upgrading to the latest phone), when it's your idea, you're motivated. You determine the effort, the risk, and the rewards. You balance the equation — and you're willing to go for it!

Now alter one critical element of the scenario: The change is no longer your idea. Your mother told you what job to take. You can only afford one kind of phone. You have no choice but to move to a new home. Immediately, you don't feel the same sense of participation. You don't feel in control. You're not sure where it will all lead. Fear, doubt, uncertainty, and perhaps even anger enter the picture.

Getting everyone onboard

Helping everyone in your organization understand and embrace necessary changes — feeling participatory in the process as opposed to persecuted — is the hallmark of a successful change manager. There is no magical incantation. It takes real work — work that people usually don't like to do.

Change can and will happen on its own, whether you want it to or not. You need to get at the helm of a change management project if you want to have a say as to what the end result will be.

Change is a lot easier to implement in your organization if it has the support of senior management. Likewise, change is less likely to be successful if people think that not everyone in the organization agrees that the change is necessary — for example, management disagrees about the nature of the change. So if senior management supports a change, make sure that everyone in the organization knows this. Actions count more than words. Consider a vice president of a major corporation who spent $10,000 on a stone wall decoration in his rented office when the company was telling employees to conserve cash. When word got out, the employees were less interested in finding creative ways to preserve the bottom line.

How to be a change manager

Thinking about the ways you can introduce and manage change can help keep negative reactions at a minimum.

Consider these principles for managing and introducing change:

- ✔ **Agreeing on the goal of the change:** Make sure that you, and the people around you, have a shared understanding of where you're heading. Everyone aiming at the same target goes a long way toward institutionalizing a change.

- ✔ **Communicating fully:** It's all too easy to forget to communicate new changes to the plan, intentions, goals, or even personal understandings. Consider what platforms are most natural for you to share your thoughts with, such as written e-mails or an internal blog, and incorporate that method into your change management communication strategy.

  Giving bad news remotely (for example, through e-mail) doesn't help you manage people's reactions, and you won't really know whether people understood the message correctly. Meeting face to face can be challenging, but it provides an entirely different level of understanding.

- ✔ **Considering the impact:** Throughout the change process, think about who's affected by the change and what it means to them (in addition to the other areas of the company that may be affected). Read more about this in Chapter 5.

- ✔ **Involving key people:** Wherever you can, involve affected people in change decisions and get their support and input.

  Change that's imposed on people is more likely to fail than if you involve people in deciding the way in which change will be introduced.

People are wary of the unknown; you can reduce their worries with communication and involvement. The more people who are involved with a change, the more help you can get with the things that need to be done.

As a manager or leader, people look to you for guidance during a change process. The leadership style you adopt during change absolutely affects the success of the change.

It takes time for people to work through the change process, so don't expect to get immediate acceptance of any change you announce.

You're likely to feel comfortable when you think that you understand and have some control over the things that happen to you. Changes at work can plunge you into the change-reaction cycle, reducing your feeling of being in control. People are generally reluctant to lose control, which leads to resistance. When you understand the change and how it will affect you, you feel more in control of the process, and you are apt to see the change as less threatening.

Don't try to convince "The Resistance." Focus your efforts on the people who are more open to change; the others will eventually follow.

Ways to Introduce Change

The way in which you introduce and manage change has everything to do with how your employees react to it. The type and scope of the change, the environment in which it's being introduced, and the personalities and backgrounds of the people who need to be brought on board all play a role in the way you should broach a new change.

Attitude change is more likely to be successful if people are actively involved in the changes and not just passively told what is happening.

For example, if you're introducing performance-related pay, people are likely to be scared that they're going to lose pay under the new system. Make sure that people receive the message that they may receive significantly more money if they meet transparent metrics.

Repeat positive messages and successes. People are more likely to remember bad news (the risk that pay will drop under the new system) than good news (that pay will rise for high performers). Repeating positive messages can help employees keep a positive attitude about the new changes.

Combating resistance to change

In general, people resist change for a few key reasons. Understanding each of these reasons and preparing yourself with effective methods for defending against or accommodating them is what makes the difference between a smooth transition and a needlessly difficult one.

Common reasons for resisting change include:

- ✔ **Fear:** Change stirs varying levels of fear in individuals, often in unexpected ways. A new piece of time-saving and defect-reducing equipment may make an entry-level worker fearful that she will lose her job to a machine. Bringing in a consultant to better document work processes can stir concern that there's a witch hunt underfoot for any little mistake an employee has made. Moving from a familiar piece of software to a Cloud-based service tool can cause an employee to worry that he lacks the training and experience to keep up.

  The best way to address fear is to be open about it up front. If you intend to replace line workers with equipment, don't bring in the equipment and then hide in your office until you hope the workers quit on their own. If you don't intend to replace them, say so, openly. If your process documentation is not a covert operation to find employees who are on Facebook during the day, then say so — even explicitly eliminate that reporting option from the consultant's expected deliverable. If you hear about or anticipate concern about a lack of training, provide some proactively. I've seen more than one confident employee learn a thing or two in training!

✔ **Resentment:** When employees resent change, it's usually a sign that they feel the change is being imposed upon them by others in the company, and that they feel excluded from the decision-making process.

It's rarely feasible to include every member of an organization at the planning table, but that does not mean you can't still put a nearly finished plan out for feedback. More importantly, you need to give people the chance to become familiar with the expected change and their expected contributions. See "Invite everyone on the bandwagon" later in this chapter for more on socializing your ideas throughout the company.

In larger organizations, having departments nominate a point person to attend planning meetings and report back to the group with updates can be an effective way to involve the greatest number of people without having to hold meetings in a football stadium. This creates a feeling that every person got to participate, even if they did not.

✔ **Confusion:** You may understand how your proposed change gets your organization from here to there, and the equipment or technology you choose to get there may make perfect sense, but that doesn't mean anyone else shares your sense of clarity. As in most things, people resist what they don't understand. Not understanding how a change will take place, and/or not understanding his role in the process, is the perfect recipe for an employee who refuses to adapt.

Information counteracts confusion. Be clear about every step involved in the change process. Never assume that employees will understand the reasoning behind your decisions — and don't assume they'll proactively ask you about them, either. You are the one who needs to be proactive in the change communication process.

Sometimes managers get caught up in explaining the "how" of a new process and forget the "why" Reducing a 17-step process down to seven steps is not a compelling reason for a department to stay late for a month. Understanding that the new process increases product quality by five percent and eliminates a potential choking hazard can turn that conversation on its head and make people happy to pitch in. Similarly, if budgets are tightening, it's counterproductive to tell employees that everything's fine and expect them to get on-board with sudden cuts or cost savings measures. When everyone understands that they can do something to keep the company in the black, however . . . that's when I've seen the very best of people come out.

✔ **Lack of Resources:** Employees are measured by the results they can achieve relative to their responsibilities. This measurement does not take into account whether that employee has enough resources — namely, enough time — to reasonably reach all of their milestones.

When you're feeling overwhelmed with deliverables and expectations, the last thing you want to hear is that there's yet another change underfoot, a new process to learn, or a new tool to master — even if there's a perfectly logical argument that ultimately the change would save you time.

This can be a tricky form of resistance to manage because it's often entirely legitimate. To successfully get the overwhelmed employee on board, you need to be transparent about the amount of new work that's expected; the length of time they will be expected to take on this new work; and the real benefits you expect them to realize in terms of increased future efficiency.

Downplaying or shrugging off the work involved in incorporating a change is the worst thing you can do here. They know it's there, you know it's there, and this attitude will undoubtedly leave them feeling unheard and burdened. Do whatever you can to help make the workload more bearable, whether that's extending a deadline on another project; bringing in temp workers; starting a different project first that will free up some new hours; flexible work scheduling; overtime pay; or even scrubbing in to help yourself! Nothing says change management like the managers helping out with the real, on-the-ground work.

Considering older employees

The workforce is getting older as people are living longer and retiring later. This means more veteran employees within your own organization, as well as an increasing number of older individuals available on the job market. Employees who have been through the ups and downs of your company over the years are an asset in and of themselves, but they can also present unique change management challenges. Some best practices for working with them include:

- ✔ **Respect their experience:** Older workers have experiences that you can leverage to make the organization more efficient. Most problems are not new or unique to your organization; older workers are more likely to have seen similar issues in their past experience and have valuable input into what works and what doesn't. Using their experience will also make them feel like valuable members of the team.

- ✔ **Accommodate technical shortcomings:** Although age is not a reliable indicator of whether a person is technical or not, the longer an employee has been in any one organization, the less likely they are to have exposure to alternate systems and technologies. However, they are likely to know the inside of the organization like the back of their hand. Pairing more experienced employees with new hires with complementary skillsets can bring out the best of both worlds.

- ✔ **Don't break the law:** It's against the law to discriminate against employees (or potential employees) on the basis of age. Don't try to skirt this by implementing overly complicated technical systems to try to push out older employees. Instead, provide training for employees of *all* ages when you need your workforce to adapt to new technologies.

- ✔ **Listen:** Older workers tend to be good at spotting pretenders, who tend to do a lot more talking than listening. Listen to their concerns about any changes being made, and make sure to take those concerns into account.

Helping nontechnical employees adapt to new technologies

Communicating a change management plan that involves adopting new technologies to nontechnical employees requires special consideration of their place and role in the organization. These employees are most likely to resist change because they fear for their ability to adapt to an increasingly technological workplace or they are afraid that they will be out of work and unable to support their families after being replaced by machinery.

Some tips for communicating change to nontechnical employees include:

- ✔ **Highlight the benefits in nontechnical terms:** Just because employees need to learn new technical skills does not mean they currently understand what those skills look like. I consistently run into employees in administrative roles – where you would expect a level of tech savvy — who can barely operate their PCs. Start bringing them on board by describing the outcome and benefits in terms of deliverables ("you no longer have to hand-write these shipping forms") instead of simply pointing out the new process ("start printing these labels instead of writing them").

- ✔ **Use their language:** Telling your shipping department you are adopting a new CRM or building middleware is likely the equivalent of giving a speech in another language. Break down any jargon. If in doubt, break it down further.

- ✔ **Provide ample training:** You need to provide quality, ongoing training that covers the new tools and skills you expect your employees to adopt.

Change Management Planning

A written change management plan provides two key benefits: it serves as a literal roadmap from your current point to 100 percent integration of the new changes, and it is a convenient and effective format for communicating your intentions and expectations to the entire organization. Often, the process of simply putting together the plan brings to light new ideas and concerns that otherwise may have been realized too late in the process.

Components of a successful change management plan

Successful change management requires careful planning. Chapters 7 and 19 cover designing successful execution plans in greater detail. At a high level, a change management plan includes these components:

- ✔ **Documenting the change process:** Keep a written copy of the change process in a central location, such as a company wiki, so it is available to everyone involved.

- ✔ **Assessing the readiness for change:** This can include assessments of the organization as a whole, departments, sponsors, and the culture of the organization.

- ✔ **Planning for communication:** Pay careful attention to what should be said, who should say it, and when it should be said. Your initial communications should build awareness within the organization of the need for change and inspire support for the changes.

- ✔ **Training the management team:** Most employees are only concerned about their immediate supervisor, so it's critical to ensure that all members of management support the change and are consistent in their communication to employees.

- ✔ **Training employees:** You may need to provide training in specific areas so that employees are adequately prepared to support the desired changes.

- ✔ **Creating sponsor roadmaps:** Sponsorship from management is critical for changes to be successful; they must be an active and visible part of the change process.

- ✔ **Planning for managing objections:** Nobody "likes" change, so you need to have plans for identifying and managing resistance. (See "Combating resistance to change.")

- ✔ **Collecting data and feedback:** Getting and acting on feedback is a key part of any successful change process. Employees will be more supportive of the changes if they feel that they have a say in the process.

- ✔ **Recognizing successes:** Celebrating wins early and often helps to reinforce the changes in the organization.

Change management examples

Numerous companies have effectively implemented change management plans to improve their organization. Arguably, any company that has stuck around for any length of time must have some degree of change management competence. Some examples of successful change management projects include:

- **British Airways:** In 1981, British Airways decided that in order to survive long-term they would need to become more efficient. Their new chairperson, John King, imposed changes including the closure of several routes as well as the selling off of the cargo service business and planes. The company also laid off 20,000 staff members as part of the change. But before making these changes, King made sure that everyone understood the reasons for the restructuring through clear leadership and communication.

- **America Latina Logistica (ALL):** In 1995, Brazil began privatizing its rail system. One part of the network became ALL. Like the rest of Brazil's rail system, ALL was a mess, with a deteriorated infrastructure and not near enough money to fix everything. To move the organization to a sustainable financial position, the new President of ALL, Alexandre Behring, set four clear and simple rules that guided how money was to be spent throughout the organization. He also limited the number of corporate priorities each year to five, and instituted a process where employees at every level met with their boss to set team and individual goals for the year. Within three years, the company was profitable.

- **Apple:** No one can deny the overwhelming success of Apple under the leadership of Steve Jobs. A key to Apple's success was Jobs's ability to communicate to his employees the need for change, and his positioning Apple to profit from giant innovative leaps.

Change Management Best Practices

You directly influence the success of change initiatives through your behaviors, decisions, and communications. As the face of the organization, you have the challenging role of leading the organization to success in spite of your own personal reaction to the change. In this section, I look at what you can do to make the unknown more transparent and advance your organization's efficiency.

Keep the feedback loop open

People need to be informed and they need to be heard. Make communications clear, consistent, multidimensional, and frequent. One-time declarations don't make a transformation. Instead, develop a communication strategy to support your implementation plan. This communication plan needs to be a two-way effort. One part is what you want to say; the other part is what your employees want you to hear.

In the beginning of a change, it's better to over-communicate than under-communicate with people. Your team needs to know what it's in for. Supplement any formal communication plan with informal communications. Nothing can derail a change movement faster than misinformation and water cooler rumors. In the absence of information, people fill the blanks with speculation and fear, and that leads to irrational and potentially destructive behavior.

Communication does not end with letting people know what *will* happen. This is only the beginning. Keeping a feedback loop — in which employees are free to come to you or their manager with questions, suggestions, and concerns — is what ultimately keeps the process of change on track. Even the smallest of changes can have unexpected complications. Open communication means hearing about these issues when it's early enough to fix them; top-down directives mean hearing about them after staff quit or the assembly line shuts down.

Invite everyone on the bandwagon

People need to feel heard before they will support a change effort. Simply presenting a new plan or idea for feedback — even if no one says a word in response — makes it infinitely easier to get those same people to adopt that change, as it feels more like *their* decision than a top-down mandate.

Avoid a company culture where some people are viewed as change agents and everyone else is viewed as (or feels like) soldiers simply carrying out those agents' orders. Empowering every individual in your organization to feel like a change agent means you have an enormous number of allies who can proactively notice and potentially remedy inefficiencies. Total Quality Management (TQM), which you can read more about in Chapter 1, really furthers the idea of empowering all employees to see themselves as change agents.

When it's time to make a change, socialize your suggested solution as much as possible. This means posting draft plans on the company-wide wiki; mentioning it in a status meeting with an invitation for people to come to the next project meeting or to join the mailing list; and ultimately creating an open company culture where information flows freely from top to bottom, and across departments and sites.

The power behind socializing a change *before* it starts is simply to get people comfortable with the idea. Let me use the analogy of a recipe. Imagine if someone simply read you a recipe, line by line, and you needed to execute each step before hearing the next. As each new ingredient comes up, you have to run to the store. Because you did not know you'd need melted butter, you waste time waiting for your frozen stick to soften. Worse, you have no idea until many steps in (and perhaps not even then!) what it is you're even cooking! Without the chance to review the recipe ahead of time or provide feedback on your preferred tastes, you can find yourself spending an entire day making Brussels sprouts brownies — yuck.

Socializing does not mean everyone has the ability to change the plan, or that your planned change needs to be caught up in endless feedback grid-lock. Instead, it means that when the key decision makers have composed an execution plan, everyone that it may affect needs time to review it, become familiar with it, and feel like they have the opportunity to speak up if they have a serious concern.

Whatever you communicate, be prepared to back up the message with actions. If you say that you're going to do something by a certain date, do it, or explain why it didn't happen. Historically, across every organization, proposed changes have a reputation of never seeing the light of day. Prove this stereotype wrong.

Fix pain points first

This is the single-most effective change management strategy I've ever found, and it's the one I suggest you turn to *first* again and again. Since it enhances efficiency and tends to make employees happier, it's almost hard to do this too often.

Essentially, when you pinpoint a larger project or inefficiency you want to tackle, look for the parts that cause employees the greatest frustration; are the most tedious, slow, or boring; are the most error-prone (requiring frequent human intervention to correct); or are the most time-consuming. Fix these *first*, and then present the larger proposed solution. This starts to build trust, demonstrating that you are aware of pain points, committed to reducing them, and most importantly, that you are *capable* of making positive changes instead of just talking about it.

Common pain points that are generally well received include:

- ✔ **Data entry:** Nobody (even a Type-A personality like me!) enjoys rote data entry. Explore whether online forms, fillable PDF forms, an outsourced data entry team, or bringing in temp workers or interns can help reduce the data entry burden on staff. (Remember to tread carefully if the staff member's main responsibility is data entry work).

- ✔ **Spreadsheet manipulation:** Recording a macro, learning a handful of Excel formulas, reorganizing (or instituting!) a central database, or sometimes simply ensuring that everyone works off the same template with the same column headers can eliminate many hours of headaches. This is particularly relevant for employees responsible for generating status reports — you are more likely to get these reports if you make it as easy as possible to generate them.

- ✔ **Required participation:** Getting rid of a stale standing meeting or committee doesn't just free up an hour on the calendar, but it can downright lift a dreaded burden off employees' shoulders.

- ✔ **Working 9 to 5:** Although it is not traditionally considered a pain point, I'm a fervent believer that you get better results and cooperation from employees who are given greater autonomy. If you trust them to be adult enough to make their own decisions about catching their son's baseball game, making a dentist appointment at 10 a.m., or simply catching a bit of extra sleep after a long night, you stand to gain exponentially by getting your employees' most productive hours and best feet forward.

You can use the goodwill and free time you accumulate by eliminating pain points as a sort of currency which you can then apply toward future projects that have fewer (or no) immediate gains for the employee. For example, if you can save Nathan 20 hours each year by automating his most-detested task – combining every department's annual result reports into a master deliverable – then he may be much more willing to put in five hours on a project that will save *another* department (but not him) time.

Don't confuse eliminating a pain point with eliminating job security. Automating a few hours of tedious work away from a busy knowledge worker is a far cry from automating half of an assembly line worker's job. The former is likely to be grateful; the latter is likely to be fearful (of losing his job).

Chapter 15

Before You Get Hit by a Bus: Knowledge Capture and Transfer

• •

In This Chapter

▶ Understanding how and why to capture knowledge

▶ Looking at ways to transfer knowledge

▶ Updating knowledge

▶ Ensuring employee support

▶ Checking that you've got what you need

• •

After I put out any pressing inefficiency fires, one of the first thought exercises I engage in with clients is: "What happens if you get hit by a bus tomorrow?" What *would* happen? In most cases, the true — and somewhat terrifying — answer is: This business would cease to operate.

As business owners and managers, we all want to believe that *we* are the secret ingredient to success — our competitors can move in next door, copy our process step for step, and undercut our margins by ten percent, but without our preexisting relationships, charisma, and secret sauce, they can never replicate what we have.

Although I'm not denying this is true to varying extents, when taken too far this attitude of secrecy, coupled with our natural inclinations to never write things down, can also cripple us. And it doesn't take something as drastic as being hit by a bus — you can simply want to take a day off. If you're the only person with the key to the front door or the password to the server, you can't stray too far. If your employees feel like they're operating partially in the dark, morale suffers. If your company doesn't have a process for sharing knowledge, every resignation or retirement costs that much more, and every new hire requires that much more effort to bring on board. In this chapter, I discuss the importance of spreading this knowledge around so that your business survives your being hit by the proverbial bus, even if you aren't.

Capturing Institutional Knowledge

Fostering a culture of sharing isn't just for nursery school — it's also a tenet of efficient organizations. Capturing and disseminating accurate information about your core business processes and each person's role within those processes not only helps keep your company running like a well-oiled machine, but it is also one of the best ways to stop future inefficiencies in their tracks.

The following are some benefits to sharing important knowledge within your organization:

- ✔ **Increased efficiency savings:** My career as an efficiency consultant actually began in technical writing — I would document a client's 30-step process and then not be able to help myself from pointing out that steps 17 through 25 (and a couple administrative assistants, while they were at it) could be replaced by an Excel macro. The single-best way to suss out potential efficiency savings is to write out a step-by-step process and then look for unnecessary steps.

- ✔ **Increased company-wide communication:** When the right hand knows what the left one is doing, everyone benefits. In many companies, especially larger ones, manufacturing is a total mystery to the sales team, and vice versa. In some extreme cases, this lack of knowledge leads to resentment, with manufacturing assuming that the sales team eats pizza and watches YouTube videos all day while they do the "real" work. Capturing what the sales team really does and making that information accessible to everyone can clear up or prevent such scenarios.

- ✔ **Less damage when employees leave:** Rick is your top sales guy. If Rick retires or leaves for another position, the last thing you want to discover is that Rick's client contacts are entirely in his head. A thorough capture process ensures company-critical knowledge is retained by the company even as employees shift in and out.

- ✔ **Faster onboarding:** When your policies and processes are well-documented and you have a strong coaching and mentoring program, getting a new hire up to speed is a quick and nearly painless process.

- ✔ **Smarter, empowered employees:** The best way to learn is to teach. When your employees teach one another, they all become stronger at what they do. Better yet, when they can access training materials and answer their questions on their own, they'll be more productive and self-sufficient overall.

- ✔ **Ability to uncover your team's weaknesses:** If no one can capture a process correctly, or if key team members capture information incorrectly, this is a clear sign of a knowledge deficiency. After it is uncovered, you can take steps to remedy these weak spots before they become big problems.

✔ **Easier value-stream mapping:** If you follow (or aspire to follow) Lean (see Chapters 1, 2, and 19 for more on Lean), you know that part of the program is creating a visual representation of each of your processes, with input coming in on the left and output leaving on the right. At each step along the way, you identify factors such as time, quality, and cost. If you start with well-documented processes across your company, constructing value-stream maps is a cinch.

Knowing what information to capture

Knowing what kind of information to capture is just as important as knowing how to capture it in the first place. It won't help your organization's efficiency to, say, document where your favorite lunch spots are. Focus on information that is necessary to keep your business operating.

Institutional knowledge you should document includes the following:

✔ **The official and unofficial responsibilities of each member of your team:** This can be broken down by role ("Mary's Executive Assistant is responsible for updating the company-wide vacation calendar") and by person ("Karen is responsible for organizing the office Christmas party").

✔ **Contact information for all vendors, employees, customers, and sales leads.**

✔ **A complete sourcing list, including historical information about past vendors:** If you now get your corrugated boxes from Easton Boxes instead of Arnold's Box Emporium, why? If the accounting department needs t-shirts for its kickball league, does it find its own vendor or is there a company-approved source?

✔ **Repair information for both proprietary company equipment/software and company assets such as printers and molds:** Don't just include the manuals, but also any "insider" information such as a preferred support rep's name or that unique way Dan kicks the Coke machine to get it to give back your quarter.

✔ **Customer service policies:** These should include an escalation tree ("if I can't solve this customer's problem, where do I go?"), suggested scripts, solutions to common (and where possible, uncommon) problems, and official policies (see *Customer Service For Dummies* for more ideas).

✔ **The complete step-by-step process by which your company creates each one of its products and services.**

✔ **The complete step-by-step routine of each employee:** These should be for both everyday and infrequent tasks (such as the HR process for terminating an employee or the actions/arrangements to complete when taking new employees on board, from ordering a chair to providing their

IT profile.). Include deadlines where appropriate, such as annual filing deadlines with the IRS.

✔ **The complete step-by-step process by which your company finds, qualifies, and closes new sales.**

Choosing your capturing process

Capturing knowledge effectively is a more nuanced process than simply asking your employees to write things down. Not only do you have to convince everyone that this is a worthwhile endeavor (more on this later in the chapter), but you also need to make sure you're capturing the real picture — and accurately.

Self-documentation

The most common capture method by far, this process involves every team member and department taking responsibility for documenting their own processes. Your team can generally begin this process right away, and since no one knows what Rob does better than Rob, each employee is the most qualified one to document the role he occupies.

The downside to relying on self-documentation is that people are easily blinded by familiarity. If Kim's spent the last seven years typing Ctrl + 642 to launch the customer search screen in her company's custom software, it may honestly never even occur to her to write that down — leaving Kim's replacement the following year at a total loss for how to search for John Doe's order history.

With no outside input, it's all too easy to skip steps or flat-out do things wrong (especially when it comes to new employees). Having a good documented procedure in place also avoids processes becoming increasingly inefficient when passed on from one employee to another or given to a different department. This is the effect of the so-called "water cooler rules" – where Mary once heard from Jim that she couldn't print double-sided, and this eventually becomes codified in all her work despite it not actually being required. You need some plan in place, especially in the beginning, to confirm this documentation is accurate.

A responsible manager also cannot overlook the possibility of fraud or intentional omissions, especially in positions that are competitive with others in the company. For example, the secretary who is paid by the hour is unlikely to share her computer efficiency tips, which would ultimately lower her paycheck. You can keep problems like this in check somewhat by members of the same circle or department cross-checking one another's documentation, and/or combining self-documentation with job shadowing (coming up next).

Job shadowing

Instead of asking each employee to document his own work process, have them document one another's. On designated days or in designated shifts, have each employee walk another through their workflow. It's the shadowing employee's responsibility to then record the steps taken and what he learned.

The benefit of job shadowing is that it's easier to capture a complete picture when teaching steps to someone unfamiliar with the process. Since there's active teaching going on during the capture process, the odds are good that the resulting documentation will transfer that information effectively.

WARNING!

The downside to job shadowing is that it can be a lengthy and misrepresentative process. The employee being shadowed may feel uncomfortable having someone looking over their shoulder all day, and the mere presence of another person will have an effect on how they perform their duties. The risk of employees hoarding information is partially, but not entirely negated with shadowing — they can't hide any steps truly necessary to complete a task, but there's nothing making them share best practices, either.

My preferred method In most organizations is to have folks start out with self-documentation, and then use job shadowing to refine and clarify that information, ensuring that it can be used as a reliable training tool for future employees. I found that team sessions (whole team or a few chosen ones) get you great results, as they are not only documenting the current process steps, but also capturing "best practice" at the same time.

Outside help

If your budget allows for it and your team is open to the idea, hiring an outside technical writer or team to come in and begin the documentation process can alleviate much of the capture-related workload for your employees.

An outsider's objectivity can lead to a more thorough collection of steps and details, because they aren't influenced by institutional knowledge. "Everyone" may know that only Judy handles clients with accounts over $2 million, but the technical writer doesn't — so he can bring details like that to light and commit them to paper.

However, hiring an external person or team to capture data doesn't help your internal team become familiar with your chosen knowledge repository or tools, and it doesn't get them in the habit of recording processes or making changes. If you do choose this process, you'll need to pay close attention to the transition when this external team departs to make sure your knowledge-capturing efforts don't stop there.

The job-swapping game

If your company culture isn't too formal, one of the most effective *and* fun ways I've seen to kick-off a knowledge-capture project is to have employees swap roles with people in other areas of the company.

To start, you need your employees to either self-document their daily workflow, or designate a day for them to show their temporary "replacement" the ropes and vice versa. On the designated swap day, each person uses the supplied captured knowledge to try to perform that person's real job. Afterward, people share feedback and ask questions, all in an effort to improve that documentation.

Obviously the extent to which this game works depends on the nature of your business. In a hospital, janitorial probably should not swap with neurosurgery. But why couldn't janitorial join the interns on rounds? Or the neurosurgeons shadow some nurses? Get creative. The real point is to see whether someone else can understand and follow the steps outlined to do a given person's job, or if there are holes and/or points of confusion.

Not only does this activity do wonders for opening up lines of communication across departments, but it can also shed light on new inefficiencies. The folks handling order fulfillment may never think twice about the packing slips they receive from sales, but when Meghan from sales tries her hand at fulfilling orders for the day, she immediately sees that the 30 minutes she spends each morning writing personal notes to customers on those slips is a waste because they actually get shredded instead of being included in the packages. Further, a tech-savvier team member may recognize a way to generate an e-mail template to send these packing slips directly to order fulfillment, skipping the printer entirely.

Some companies really have fun with this idea, dressing up as the person they're "replacing" or holding trivia games to see which department knows the most about the others.

Choosing the right tools for capturing knowledge

The best tool for capturing knowledge within your organization has everything to do with the particular process you're capturing. Popular capture tools include the following:

✔ **Screencasts:** A screencast is basically a video of your computer screen. Using special software, hit "record" and carry out your tasks on-screen. You can then edit, caption, and/or add voiceover to create a complete tutorial. Check out Techsmith's SnagIt software or the entirely web-based Screenr.com.

   • *Best for: Capturing processes that involve software or websites.*

✔ **Video:** Although you should bring in a video crew for the most important video shoots, such as factory floor safety training, a cellphone camera can do the trick for some cases. Some employees in "thought" roles like managers or sales leads enjoy recording short videos of themselves relating best practices or strategies.

  • *Best for: Physical processes that are easier to show than tell, such as operating machinery, or brief best-practice shares.*

✔ **Interactive Courseware:** Develop your own online training courses that step learners through specific content and (optionally) test their progress throughout. Software titles like Articulate Storyline and Adobe Captivate let you create highly interactive courses with videos, images, and sound effects.

  • *Best for: Material that doesn't change frequently (as this form of capture is hardest to edit), and material you need to track/test employees on for compliance purposes. This makes a great first impression for onboarding new employees.*

✔ **Flow Charts:** Construct a flow chart that shows how to move through a process with multiple decision trees along the way (like a "Choose Your Own Adventure" book for business processes).

  • *Best for: Outlining multi-step processes, such as how to handle a customer service call.*

✔ **Mind Maps:** The ultimate organizational thinking tool. You can compare your Mind Map to a real map with the center of a city representing your most important idea. The main roads that come off represent your main thoughts. The secondary roads represent your secondary thoughts, and so on. Use color, special images, and/or shapes, and a long list of boring information can be turned into a colorful, memorable, and highly organized diagram.

  • *Best for: A planning tool, forming the basis of a new process or an improvement to an existing process.*

✔ **Dry Erase Boards:** Sometimes the best way to step through a process is to draw it out. Photograph the finished image and post a high-resolution version for future reference.

  • *Best for: Nonlinear thought processes, especially when worked on by multiple people.*

✔ **Text Editors:**

It's hard to go wrong with a basic text editor like Microsoft Word, TextEdit, or even Notepad.

  • *Best for: Anything that doesn't require a visual component (although you can embed images in most word processing programs and websites).*

Don't forget to consider the ways in which your team will consume this information. A video with critical audio instructions is useless on a loud factory floor (or on a silent factory floor with no means of playing video!). Consider compromises like closed-captioned video footage.

Transferring Knowledge

Knowledge transfer can take many forms. After you've captured information, you want to make sure that all your employees can access what's already available; that you can effectively communicate this information to new hires; and that information passes from employee to employee instead of leaving or dying with a single person.

Creating a coaching program

A supportive internal coaching program helps ensure that employees at all levels are continually learning from their more experienced peers. If it is done right, both parties in a coaching relationship benefit from the arrangement.

Depending on your company culture, a coaching program may be some informal pairings within a department to check-in on goals, or it may be a highly structured relationship with regular goal-setting, check-in appointments, and assessments.

Mentoring new hires

Help your newest hires get up to speed with a mentoring program. Remember that a mentor is not (necessarily) an employee's manager, but rather someone able and willing to show him the ropes.

When choosing mentor pairs, it's important to ask for volunteer mentors rather than pick names from a hat. Some employees are just more naturally suited for the role than others, and the last thing any employee needs is a grumpy mentor who isn't interested in the responsibility. Give new mentor/mentee relationships a brief but firm timeline (say, three months) so they have an easy way to part ways if the relationship doesn't work out.

Show-and-tell coaching

One coaching method is "show-and-tell coaching," as described in *Managing For Dummies*:

1. You do, you say. Sit down with your employees and explain the procedure in general terms while you perform the task.

2. They do, you say. Now have the employees do the same procedure as you explain each step in the procedure.

3. They do, they say. Finally, as you observe, have your employees perform the task again as they explain to you what they're doing.

To be successful, your processes have to be front and center. A company-wide e-mail with a link to a third-party feedback tool doesn't pass muster. I suggest launching one or two processes at first, and only adding more once those initial efforts are part of everyday company life.

For more on coaching and mentoring strategies, check out *Managing For Dummies*.

Sharing knowledge electronically

Sharing knowledge doesn't have to — and in fact, shouldn't — always be a structured, scheduled process. There are also tools available for disseminating knowledge electronically on an as-needed basis such as:

- ✔ **Content Management System (CMS) or Learning Management System (LMS):** These platforms make it easy for anyone to write, edit, and post articles to a central website without needing to learn any code. WordPress and Drupal are free, open-source Content Management Systems that include rich text formatting, video embedding, and full-text search. For more of a focus on learning and assessments, try an LMS like Moodle.

  - *Best for: Just about everyone can benefit from a CMS-driven knowledgebase. You may also choose to use both types: a CMS for everyday knowledge and an LMS for material that follows more of a syllabus format and involves testing, such as employee sexual harassment training or safety training.*

It seems like every IT Department I've ever run into wants to build its own Content Management System (CMS). Say no! The top CMS titles on the market are free, easy to install, and feature-rich. There's no need to reinvent the wheel here unless your company has truly unique needs.

✔ **Wiki:** A wiki is basically a living document — one single version that updates for everyone when a single person edits it. The most famous wiki is Wikipedia.org. A wiki's built-in revision history ensures that you can see which employees made what changes over time.

  • *Best for: Collaborative information that updates occasionally or frequently, or that requires group commenting. A wiki with granular security settings can help you limit editing access to those with direct involvement.*

✔ **Microblog:** A cross between a non-time-sensitive article posted on a CMS and the immediate nature of a chat room, an internal microblog lets employees post quick questions or comments that others can respond to over time. For example, Customer Relationship Management (CRM) platform Salesforce.com has a built-in microblogging service called Chatter so users can leave notes for others on customer records. Twitter is a public-facing microblog; you can roll your own private microblog internally with Status.net.

  • *Best for: A company where an organization-wide chat room would be too crowded, empty, or disruptive, but which still wants an easy means of internal communication.*

✔ **Chat:** Chat rooms let employees ask questions and interact in real time. With the right team, the ability to quickly get answers and resume work can be a real time saver, but it's also easy for company chat rooms to devolve into time wasters. A logged chat room coupled with managers who set good examples of responsible chat room use can help prevent it from becoming a virtual water cooler.

  • *Best for: High-tech companies or virtual teams.*

Whatever tools you choose, always lean toward ones that record information in a searchable way. For example, an internal knowledgebase where multiple people can post answers to questions lets others immediately find those answers via search in the future. On the other hand, those same answers posted in an unlogged chat room are lost forever.

Keeping Knowledge Fresh

Initially capturing the right information is only the start of the battle. After you have version one in place, it's now your team's responsibility to keep that information updated over time. If there's one thing that every business has in common, it's that things change — all the time.

From my perspective, the moment a documented routine contains a single inaccurate or missed step, you may as well not have it at all. If your team can't trust the information they find, they'll revert right back to keeping personal notes on stickies next to their keyboards and making mental notes, further eroding the completeness of your system. In a worst-case scenario, a well-intentioned employee following incorrect instructions can cost your company serious money.

Capture and transfer isn't a one-time event — it's a constant process that you need to slowly massage into your company's core culture.

There are two main ways to keep your employees engaged with knowledge capture and dissemination: Make it easy, and make it integrated. Take a look at how.

Making updating easy

The more steps it takes for an employee to update a single step in his documented routine, the less likely he'll ever be to make that change. Whenever possible, choose a central repository like a wiki or a content management system (CMS) that lets everyone view and collaborate on the same documents at the same time.

Make sure the system you choose keeps a revision history, so you can see exactly who made each change. This is important both for accountability purposes and for rolling back if someone accidentally deletes a page.

Offer a selection of capture methods where possible. Some people may prefer typing something out, but another feels more comfortable taking a quick screen grab. Some individuals want to draw out a flow chart by hand, but others wouldn't let you pry Omnigraffle out of their cold, dead hands. So long as the handwriting's legible and it gets the job done, let them do their own thing.

Sometimes you may have to make allowances for certain employees' attitudes or limitations. Good old Stan, bless his heart, is one of your best salesmen but types 5wpm. Perhaps you can pair Stan with an intern who can make updates for him. Although you should be firm that all employees participate, there's some wiggle room for exactly what shape that participation takes.

Don't forget to make both your capture tools and your captured output accessible to all employees. Some may require special equipment or assistance. Beyond accommodations such as blind employees needing screen readers, consider less-visible disadvantages, such as dyslexic, illiterate, or English-as-a-second-language employees.

Integrating updates

Your company's central knowledge repository should not be relegated to a figurative (or literal) back room. Bring it front and center. For example, post pertinent information like schedules and meeting agendas on the repository so every employee gets in the habit of visiting it daily. Highlight new or novel articles in company newsletters and, importantly, in regular conversations and meetings.

It takes practice, but it's critical in the beginning to think about knowledge capture in all your decisions. When a committee recommends a change, publicly remind them to update the relevant documentation and share it with the group. When Shipping and Receiving gets a new piece of machinery, someone needs to record the new asset and its associated training materials.

Most importantly, use and update the information yourself. What knowledge can you share with others in the company? What steps do you go through to make a decision? Modeling this behavior on a management level creates a positive trickle-down effect throughout the entire company. (Plus, your employees are probably more curious than you realize to learn what it is that you do behind that closed door.)

Getting Employee Buy-in

Starting your knowledge capture and transfer journey off on the wrong foot with your employees is the biggest mistake I see people make. If your team is scared or annoyed by this change, it will never get off the ground, no matter how many prizes for the best tutorial you dangle in front of them or how many outside consultants you bring in to do the job. Luckily, I've seen many organizations successfully transform from secretive cubicle silos to cultures of collaboration.

Including everyone from the start

The worst thing you can do is begin by hiring an outside technical writer or consultant and announce to your team that they will be job shadowing everyone and writing down what they're doing. People will panic that their jobs are in jeopardy. Even the most productive, Type-A employee (in fact, *especially* those employees!) frets that they aren't quite as organized or by-the-book as they can be. Having an outsider observe them under a microscope for an entire day is the single-best way to exacerbate these concerns. Employees will call in sick, quit (I've seen it happen), or — perhaps worst of all — lie.

When watched like this, most people revert to the most basic of chores, reorganize their desktops, and call clients they know to be dead or on vacation just to pass the time.

If you do get to the point where you call in capture reinforcements, it has to be because your team members *want* you to. I've seen this work best when someone internal suggests/requests a shadower, and then only for those folks who want to work with them. This changes the shadower from a menace to a time saver. For the others, they're responsible for documenting their own processes up to the same standards. So long as they rise to the occasion, they don't have to be shadowed if they don't want to be.

Getting your whole team involved at the start may be as small as asking people to test out different capture tools and provide feedback. Even if someone never downloads a single trial, simply having the opportunity to provide input goes a long way toward earning buy-in. If your organization is large, you can seek volunteers for a committee that makes decisions about which tools and processes best fit your needs. Make sure everyone knows how to contact committee members with suggestions, complaints, and other feedback.

Framing capture as a benefit, not a chore

From day one, you need to be clear about what your expected benefits of knowledge capture are, and communicate those to your team. If you're not sold, your employees will never be.

At the beginning, capturing and disseminating knowledge is a lot of work for everyone. Few people realize just how many responsibilities they have until they have to commit them to paper (or a Word document), step by step. One of the best things you can do up front is to acknowledge this. Don't brush it off as "a few extra minutes a day," because then that's exactly how much time people will devote to it. Give people permission to take the extra time to document and share, and make sure everyone sees you and other executives taking the time to do it too. If someone feels their job is in jeopardy if they "waste" time teaching something to a fellow employee, or that they're expected to stay late to write documentation, they're going to resist, silently or otherwise.

 Keep your quality expectations in check. It would be awesome to have a complete video training library with professional voiceovers and a description so rich with searchable keywords it would make Roget proud. However, if you don't have the budget for an in-house video production team (and who does?), you'll have to make do with some lousy screencast audio and the occasional passive voice creeping into your step-by-steps. It's much more important to encourage accurate, complete information than high production quality.

What are the main benefits for employees? For starters, when everyone contributes their part, everyone will have a wealth of information from which to draw. No more waiting on other people for answers to questions they can now answer themselves from the company knowledgebase, or worrying about misremembering or misrepresenting a company policy to a customer.

Well-organized internal information also means an end to the drudgery that is version management. I have actually been on a phone call where someone non-ironically referred to version 166 of a spreadsheet. That would make anyone die a little inside. A strong knowledge capture program alone wouldn't prevent those 166 rounds of editing, but it would prevent everyone from downloading that same file 166 times from their e-mail.

Some employees may really come to embrace training and mentoring, or someone may go the extra mile in creating engaging or amusing training material. Not only can (and should) you publicly highlight and praise these individuals, but you should also find ways to increase these employees' responsibilities in these areas. If she's interested and good at it, putting Stacy in Accounting in charge of that department's training and mentoring program (coupled with some financial compensation in recognition of the extra work) will make Stacy happy, lighten the load of her less-enthused co-workers, and lead to a better-quality overall program. Win, win, win.

Being Assured You Got It All

So you've got an institutional library of processes, best practices, and contact information — but how can you be sure your company will be okay if that much-hyped bus runs you over?

For one, you can commit to actively measure your knowledge capture and transfer both now and going forward. The Balanced Scorecard approach is particularly well-suited for this, as one of the four corners of the scorecard is knowledge and growth. (Check out *Balanced Scorecard Strategy For Dummies* for the full scoop on constructing your own scorecard.) Metrics for measuring this category include the following:

- **Employee satisfaction:** When you survey your team members, do they feel fully equipped to do their jobs? Do they feel others are secretive or possessive about their processes or customers? (Make sure you conduct these reviews in an anonymous manner to get honest feedback.)

- **Pages viewed/updated:** If you're using an electronic repository like a wiki for managing documentation, you can track how often people create new pages or view/edit existing pages. Every organization will develop its own baseline normal for these figures, but "zero" is a reliable sign that something's wrong.

Never give an incentive or reward for the "highest" number of edits or changes. You'll lose hours of productivity to people switching semicolons with commas or adding superfluous data. The goal is the most accurate information, not the most edited information.

Aside from measuring, actually using the information you collected in your company's day-to-day activities is the best way to find and plug holes. Example ideas include:

- ✔ Set new hires loose on your collected knowledge before starting another training program. What questions do they still have? What steps or concepts are they missing?

- ✔ Sit down and read documented material yourself. (In a large company, select a random sampling.) Does it make sense? What questions does it bring up for you?

- ✔ Make the job swapping game (see sidebar) an annual tradition to ensure your documentation is up to snuff.

Just as efficiency is a journey and not an exact destination, so too is your knowledge dissemination process. If you — or your accountant, or your VP of Engineering — doesn't make it into work tomorrow, there will be some requisite readjusting and missed steps no matter how many safeguards you put in place against it. But with an open culture of communication and knowledge transfer, you can trust in something bigger than a perfectly documented system: that your remaining employees have the experience and tools at hand to make things right again on their own.

Chapter 16

Fine-Tuning Internal Communication

*I*nefficient internal communication doesn't just lead to incorrect information changing hands — it can also suck hours of employee productivity each week as people are forced to wade through piles of unnecessary information to get to the details they need to do their work. Clear internal communication also goes a long way towards supporting clear *external* communication with sales leads and current customers.

Efficient communication includes both the act of communicating — talking to the right person at the right time with the right words — and also the communication itself. In this chapter, I walk you through developing an internal style guide that can ensure that even outside contractors can communicate your company name and main talking points correctly. There's also a huge benefit in storing many forms of communication for future reference and re-use, such as in a customer support knowledgebase.

Finding Out What Efficient Internal Communication Looks Like

Lucy kicks off her day in a stand-up meeting, where each person in her department gathers in the corner and gives a brief verbal overview of what he hopes to accomplish that day. She then settles in at her desk to write the script for a training video for their newest piece of equipment. Since she needs to concentrate, she blocks her morning off on her shared company calendar so everyone can see they shouldn't disturb her.

Is that new equipment model the SvPG III or the SvPG3? She can never remember, but a quick peek at the company style guide reminds her — SvPG3 it is.

At a certain point she can't quite decide which title she likes best. She posts both her ideas in the company's internal chat room. When she checks it again, two people left ideas for her.

At lunch downstairs, the whole company is invited to hear Gina talk about the engineering department's ideas for revamping the widget line. Sounds interesting, but Lucy has a bunch of errands to run today on her break. She can always watch the video online later.

While at lunch, Lucy saw an adorable Hello Kitty beach towel that would be a great retirement gift for Lauren. When is Lauren's retirement party, again? Lucy checks her "off-topic" e-mail folder for the latest messages from the internal off-topic mailing list to find the party's date/time.

At 4:45 p.m., fifteen minutes before she's due to head home, Lucy gets an e-mail alert reminding her to submit a daily status report. She clicks the link to the update form in the e-mail and enters a few sentences about what she accomplished that day. When she hits Send, a copy of the report is logged on the company intranet (where anyone can read it) and e-mailed to her direct manager.

Performing an Internal Communication Checkup

There's no right or wrong answer here — this checkup is designed to get your brainstorming juices flowing as to areas in which you can increase efficiency in your organization.

How are your employees currently communicating?

Which of the following methods do your employees use to communicate with one another?

✔ Meetings

✔ Calling one another on the phone

✔ Text messaging

✔ Microblogging (e.g., Twitter, Chatter, Status.net)

✔ Individual e-mails

✔ E-mail mailing lists

✔ Handwritten notes

✔ Chatting in public spaces (e.g., the water cooler)

✔ Video chat (e.g., Skype)

✔ Chat room (e.g., Campfire)

✔ Instant messaging (e.g., gChat)

✔ Wikis

How would you convey the following communications?

✔ The company-wide all-hands meeting on Friday at 4 p.m. needs to move to 3 p.m.

✔ The baby shower for Jenny in Accounting will be on Thursday. Someone needs to bring a cake, and someone else needs to bring a vegetable platter. Everyone needs to give Gloria their $20 contribution by Tuesday at 10 a.m.

✔ You need to have a meeting with the sales team today.

✔ You've followed all the steps in the company knowledgebase, but you still can't solve a customer's technical problem. Help!

✔ You need to be left alone from 10 a.m. to noon to finish writing a research article.

✔ One of your top customers, Susan Mann, died in a car accident yesterday.

✔ Your team's latest logo was chosen as Freshest New Look by a top design blog.

- The IT Department is launching a new company website in five weeks.

- You need someone (anyone, really) to send you Amy Johnson's e-mail address, which you seem to have misplaced.

How does information travel within your organization?

Try this exercise to find out. Tell one randomly selected employee that there will be a company-wide meeting in the conference room at 2:30 p.m. Ask them to spread the word. See what percentage of the staff appears at the meeting. Have each attendee write down (anonymously, if appropriate) how he/she heard about the meeting.

Review what opportunities you *give* employees to share knowledge with these questions:

- **What is the current process for submitting status reports?** Having a set schedule and format for delivering status reports increases your chances of employees keeping each other and management informed, and ensures that the most important information is shared in a consistent manner.

- **When was the last time your company asked an employee to share the knowledge gained at a recent training or conference with the rest of the company?** Having an employee share insights gained from professional development with others in your organization is a great way to spread the knowledge—and it also ensures that the employee spends his or her time at the event thinking of ways to apply what he learned to your organization.

- **How did that employee share what they learned with others at the company?** A debriefing with their manager may seem like an efficient downloading of information, but a casual brown bag lunch or a more formal presentation would get that new information out to the entire company.

- **How often *can* employees lunch together? How often *do* they lunch together?** Informal lunches can be key to cross-departmental communication. Once I stopped a $300,000 project because I happened to be standing next to someone in the lunch line who was discussing having finished building the exact same thing that was about to be procured!

- **What opportunities do members of different departments have to interact (e.g., company picnics, committees, company-wide meetings)?** The more chances employees from multiple departments have to interact and even simply learn each others' names, the easier it will be for departments to communicate about important issues.

Keeping Track of Internal Communication Efficiency

Measuring internal communication efficiency may sound like a tall order, but it's quite possible. You can collect and evaluate metrics such as employee responses to surveys and conduct occasional communication experiments.

Paying attention to employee sentiment toward communication

An organization with truly efficient internal communication would receive positive responses from employees on all the following questions:

- Do you feel other members of your team/department know what you do all day? A "no" answer here or on the following two questions indicates that you need more communication between employees and departments.

- Do you feel people from other teams/departments know what you do all day?

- Do you feel your boss knows what you do all day?

- Do you feel pestered by requests for information? If so, that information should be moved to an internal resource like a knowledgebase. Key information should not reside in employees' minds alone.

- Do multiple people regularly ask you for status updates? This can be avoided by implementing a single status update system.

- Do you feel satisfactorily recognized for your accomplishments? If not, then good work by employees may not be communicated well internally.

- If you need complete peace and quiet one afternoon to finish a project, how would you secure that peace and quiet? Every organization needs a clear way for one employee to communicate this need to others without making a big fuss. *Not* communicating is an important consideration, too!

- How do you think others on your team would feel about your request for an interruption-free afternoon?

- How many times are you interrupted during the day? (Encourage employees to keep a tally on a random day.) Clear guidelines for different communication channels minimizes interruptions, as non-urgent inquiries are almost never appropriate to interrupt someone.

The following exercises will help you understand just how well you and your team know what other team members are doing and more importantly, *why* they are doing it.

If any of the responses are unsatisfactory, you know you have room to improve when it comes to sharing individual and team status updates. Try some of the following techniques:

- Choose an employee at random. What did they do yesterday? If you don't know, how would you find out?

- Choose two employees from the same group or department. Have each one write an explanation of what the *other* person does. Do not let them ask for help, search e-mails, and so on.

- Choose two departments. Have each one write an explanation of what the *other* department does. Team members can collaborate on this response, but should only use their existing knowledge — no peeking.

How clear is your company language? Efficient communication requires that everyone means the same thing when they use the same word.

In other words, if you use a term like "account manager" in an e-mail, does everyone understand that to mean the same thing? Answering any of the following questions incorrectly — or not even having an answer — is a sign you can use some communication guidelines (see "Create a Style Guide" later in this chapter):

- What is the correct way to write your organization's name?

- In the last 50 communications your team sent out, how many times was the organization name written incorrectly (e.g., with different capitalization or spacing)?

- In your company, what do you call:

    - A person who responds to customer support requests?

    - The person assigned to a specific customer account?

    - A person who solicits new business?

How efficient is internal company e-mail communication? On a given day, track (or have your assistant track) the following metrics:

- How many internal e-mails did you receive?

- How many of those internal e-mails did you *need* to receive?

- How many of those internal e-mails were not directly related to work (e.g., discussion of the weather, weekend plans, office parties)?

✔ How many internal responses did you *not* need to read (e.g., responses to earlier threads, off-topic notes, or single-word agreements, cc's)?

✔ Of all the e-mail subject lines, how many would you classify as "clear" versus "unclear"? (Define "clear" as a subject line that lets you accurately predict the content of the e-mail.)

✔ How many internal phone calls did you receive? How many would have been better suited as e-mails and vice versa?

✔ How many internal written notes (e.g., memos, phone messages) did you receive? How many would have been better suited as e-mails?

✔ How many times did someone approach you at your desk without a prior appointment?

You should also have employees or a sampling of employees track the same numbers.

Measuring how long it takes information to move

At a random time (it's important *not* to announce this ahead of time), send a company-wide e-mail asking each person to respond as soon as they read it to indicate they received it. You may even say this is a test of the e-mail system to encourage responses. Based on the send times, record how long it takes your team, on average, to read e-mails. Repeat this measuring exercise every time you disseminate an important message.

Improving Cross-Departmental Communication

In many organizations, communication within the same team or department already works well, because the close proximity and intimacy lends itself to a certain ambient awareness that keeps everyone on the same page without much effort. However, communication between two separate departments is an entirely different matter, and a great deal can be gained from having open communication channels *throughout* a company, too.

I've had people argue with me that the sales team and the folks on the manufacturing floor don't need to communicate much because they have nothing to do with one another. So why does the left hand need to know what the right hand is doing? For starters, they're all part of the *same* company. This means they should have shared goals, from wanting to create products of the highest possible quality to, at their most basic, wanting the business to keep its doors open.

Understanding the pitfalls of closed communication

John Donne said "No man is an island, entire of itself" and the same applies to a company's departments. Ultimately the decisions made by sales *do* impact things on the manufacturing floor, and vice versa. If there are no lines of communication currently open, then the amount of energy required to figure out the right person to talk to when an issue does arise is often too great for any one employee to muster.

For example, say a purchase order comes into the printing department for 144 *gross* (that's 20,736 units) of custom stickers. Since there are 144 units in one gross, this quantity seems like it may be an error, and the customer may have meant *one* gross of stickers. If Monica in shipping has never even met anyone in sales, she's probably *not* going to track down someone in the sales department to double-check this. After all, she's just printing what it says on the sheet, and it's not her problem if it's wrong. When it surfaces that the quantity was a mistake, the company is out the supplies, ink, and staff time it took to print 20,592 unnecessary stickers.

However, if Mary has a preexisting relationship with Joan in sales, she wouldn't hesitate to pick up the phone and give her a call to check this order. The two may even enjoy getting to catch up for a moment. Nurturing casual internal relationships like these can often lead to employees solving or even preventing small issues on their own before they become problems, which is a key to efficiency.

Encouraging collaboration

Although sales and manufacturing may seem like distant cousins, many departments are much more closely intertwined. Take customer service and marketing. Invariably, customers with questions about your latest promotion are going to contact your customer service team — so *it* needs to be informed of the marketing department's plans ahead of time. Further, if a number of customers are confused, customer service needs to convey this to marketing so it can explain future promotions more clearly.

Success story

The first Startup Weekend GOV, a 54-hour-long hackathon hosted at Seattle's City Hall, was a great testament to the lasting power of simply getting different departments in the same room.

The City of Seattle, King County, and the State of Washington each publishes publicly available data, ranging from restaurant food safety ratings to crime rates and bus routes, online. They wanted local technology companies to integrate this data into their products, helping to create new jobs and generate revenue from open data. However, not many people were using it.

These online datasets are maintained by a company called Socrata, which also runs government data powerhouses like `www.data.gov`. Socrata wants the governments to keep publishing more datasets and for more technology companies to consume that data.

Finally, the local technology companies and programmers certainly wanted to create jobs and increase their revenues. However, most didn't know that the datasets were available, and those who did were unclear about the legalities surrounding using the data or, in some cases, needed technical assistance to connect to it. Others had ideas for new datasets they'd like to work with, but had no idea how to request such a thing. To these programmers, "the government" was an unknown group of people who probably wouldn't even meet with "little guys" like them.

After the governments teamed with Socrata and invited the local tech community to City Hall for a weekend-long programming competition, all that changed. On Sunday afternoon, you saw Seattle's Web Manager Bruce Blood deep in conversation with a team about how the city processes citizen reports of graffiti or potholes. A private citizen casually standing in line for dinner next to Washington State's CIO Bharat Shyam suggested a new dataset he'd like to see, and they exchanged e-mails. In the future, if folks ran into a technical hurdle, they knew they could ping Chris at Socrata or Carter at Twilio with questions instead of feeling like the companies were unapproachable.

Whether or not their projects lived past the weekend, the relationships — however brief or casual — lived on, and the former barriers to communication collapsed. All it took was a single shared experience to open the doors.

 Communication that is clear and exchanged via the appropriate channel improves efficiency. You want everyone on the same page about which forums are appropriate for which communications. For example, it's okay if employees have personal conversations in the break room during lunch, but not in the customer support chat room in the middle of the afternoon.

Sharing status updates and other important information

Simply getting individuals and teams to give regular updates on what they're doing is a huge efficiency win. The "ambient intimacy" from reading others' status updates helps ensure that everyone is on the same page without needing to call extra meetings or write formal status reports every month.

Regular status updates should be brief and largely informal. Just a few sentences each day about what a particular employee did is all you need to keep the left hand in sync with the right one.

Standup meetings

Like the name implies, a standup is a meeting where everyone literally stands together and gives a brief verbal update of what they accomplished the day before and what they plan to do today. These are usually held at the beginning of the day. Each update is 30 seconds or less.

Best for: small teams in physical proximity.

Status update forms

If team members work hourly, such as consultants, they can also log their hours for the day in this form. In addition to asking for a few sentences about what a person accomplished that day, you can also include a custom field or two as necessary, such as asking for questions or feedback on a given topic. Create your own custom submission forms using Formstack, www.formstack.com; Wufoo, www.wufoo.com; or FormAssembly, www.tfaforms.com.

Best for: everyone.

If you want regular status reports, make it clear when you expect them. Once a day by 5 p.m.? Once a week on Fridays? Encourage every employee to set an e-mail or text message reminder on their calendar to submit their report. The e-mail reminder can even include a link to the status update form.

Mailing lists

When a team is working collaboratively on a project and many e-mails go back and forth, it's more efficient to move those communications to an e-mail mailing list. Not only does this make it a piece of cake to filter project-related messages, but it also makes it simpler to search archives for a particular project and to ensure that team members don't get left out of individual status update e-mails. Outsiders who are interested in what a group is doing can review the mailing list archives or even subscribe and ensure they're kept in the loop.

Best for: companies that e-mail frequently and/or have a large number of employees.

Microblogging

A microblog is a cross between a blog and a chat room — individuals post brief messages, including interactive messages like questions or requests for feedback, but there's no expectation of immediate replies like in a chat room or instant message client. Other participants can read messages and leave their own as their schedules permit.

Best for: technology-heavy companies, or teams that require regular brief interactions that can otherwise prove interruptive. A microblog lends itself to more frequent updates than once a day.

Sharing new knowledge

Beyond sharing what they're doing, you also want employees to share what they know. This is particularly true when your company funds part or all of a training course or conference pass—it only makes sense that you give the employees who attend the chance to share what they learned with everyone back at the office.

Let's do lunch

Invite all interested employees (from executives through janitorial) to have lunch while listening to a particular speaker. This is usually someone internal with knowledge to share, although there's nothing stopping you from inviting relevant (or even irrelevant!) outside speakers. The speaker doesn't have to take up the whole hour and you should encourage questions/discussion. Unsurprisingly, participation jumps when you bring in lunch. Videotape speakers and post the material online for everyone to view or refer back to.

Best for: casual debriefings that people can opt in or opt out of as they see fit, such as updates from conferences or beta product demos.

Blog it out

Whether internal or external, blog posts written by employees can cover information that is too brief or too complex for a talk over lunch. You can ask for submissions from every team/department on a regular basis, which keeps everyone thinking about ways to educate others about what they do, or post submissions as they come in. Appointing a given writer (or two) on each team will increase the chance of getting articles in. Well-written blog articles are also a smart way to establish authority with customers, so consider making at least some posts public.

Best for: topical information that lends itself to article form.

Wiki while you work

Information posted on an internal wiki remains there for current and future employees to access as needed, until/unless another employee changes it. Wikis can be great for historical reference — for example, if a team keeps notes on a wiki as they evaluate choices for a new software platform, they can return to those notes in two years when they need to reevaluate.

Best for: snippets of knowledge, feedback, and even useful links/articles that are somewhat timeless, or that you need to log for historical purposes.

Form committees

The term "death by committee" can certainly be true, but when done right, a committee really can be an efficient means of communicating internally. Generally, you can eschew Robert's Rules of Order and formal agendas in favor of a casual environment where members from different teams can give oral updates, ask questions, or ask for feedback.

Best for: companies large enough that departments do not interact regularly, casual updates and recommendations (as opposed to mission-critical decisions, which may call for specific teams/committees on a per-project basis).

The key to a good committee is to include volunteers (as opposed to appointing people), and to lower the amount of work required to participate. Be crystal clear about the purpose of the committee and the expectations of each participant. For a communication-enhancing committee, asking each member to give a five-minute update on his department's current projects is a start, but it's even better if he brings current questions or concerns to the table for a group brainstorm.

Looking at Internal Communication Best Practices

It's one thing to offer internal communication tools, and another to use them efficiently. Although this sometimes happens organically, often putting guidelines into words helps bring everyone onto the same page. The same is true for creating a style guide, an essential tool for ensuring seemingly small communication details — like phrasing your company tagline properly — are not overlooked.

Setting usage guidelines for each channel

Knowing when to pick up the phone, when to send an e-mail, and when to draft a memo is far from common sense. Not only do norms change from company to company, but they can be different across offices, departments, or even individuals.

Creating a department or company standard is a good approach, but don't forget to involve your people! You are not only receive the buy-in needed to implement your new guidelines quickly, but also are able to capture best practices.

 When possible, let each employee indicate their preferred means of being contacted on a central employee directory page. For example, Julie's profile may say "Call with questions from 2–4 p.m." but George's may say "I never answer my phone without an appointment; please e-mail me to schedule a time."

The following suggested guidelines are ones I've seen work successfully in many different organizations. These are guidelines, not rules — obviously airline pilots should not e-mail their co-pilots in the middle of flights, and in some cases a bullhorn may actually be the best way to communicate a message to a particular team.

Pick up the phone

Phone calls are for urgent inquiries where not having an answer is holding up key business processes such as a critical sale or a product release, or for emergencies that halt productivity (e.g., calling tech support because the server is down or calling accounting because a payroll check bounced).

E-mail

The issue with e-mail is not so much *what* is e-mailed as *who* receives each message. Messages for specific groups or on specific topics (especially *off* topic) are better suited for internal mailing lists than a constant string of one-off messages.

If you can only get your team to adopt one e-mail guideline, make it this one: use the "To" field for people who are on a need-to-know basis, and the "CC" field for everyone else. This allows recipients to easily set e-mail filters to bubble messages in which they are on the "To" line up to the top, and then survey the others as time permits.

Instant message

The instant response time of an IM makes it a great way to get quick answers to questions, but can also quickly devolve into a web of private internal chat rooms. In the workplace, IM really needs to be for work-related queries only.

If employees want to chat about other topics, and your company culture is okay with that, then employees need to use separate, private IM accounts for those conversations.

Have some face time

If your workplace allows this kind of behavior in the office — which I think is *the most* disruptive and should therefore be watched *most* carefully — then you absolutely must provide your employees a way to deflect potential visitors, whether through a sign, a silly hat, or other means. At least with a phone call, you can choose not to answer if you're working on something with higher priority. This is akin to having your neighbors show up at your door at all hours expecting you to feed them dinner — wildly inappropriate in our personal lives and yet something we seem to tolerate in the workplace.

Microblog

Best for messages that are time-sensitive in terms of days, not hours. For example, you can post that you're off at a conference for the next four days. If the microblog is attached to other software, such as the Chatter microblog integration in Salesforce.com, it's useful for casual unstructured notes like "Mrs. Brown hates being called in the morning."

Leave a note

This is a little old-school, but it's the last resort for employees who do not have access to e-mail and/or phone — a dwindling breed, but that is actually part of a handwritten note's charm. As they become a rarity, they feel more personal and are very effective for notes of encouragement in particular ("Loved the talk at lunch today!")

Creating a style guide

I cannot tell you how many companies I have consulted for that do not consistently write *their own names* correctly. Take a fictional company called "NorShore Adventures, Inc." If some employees use "Norshore" but others write "Nor-Shore" or "Nor Shore," this is a cry for internal communication help — and specifically, for a style guide.

A style guide is an official resource, like a dictionary, for how your company spells, capitalizes, or refers to related words and phrases.

There are a few official style guides out there, such as the *Chicago Manual of Style*. Although they are fun for a select group of grammar sticklers (myself included!), these tomes have more practical use in most organizations as a doorstop than as an official resource. These style guides are simply too long and overwhelming for most employees, so it's best to make your own.

An efficient internal style guide should be as brief and clear as possible while covering any confusing terminology. This style guide is equally useful for internal and external communication; you shouldn't require separate versions. Your style guide should cover:

- ✔ **The correct spelling, spacing, capitalization, colors, and font/size for your company name and logo.** Include file versions of your logo in the right format/size when distributing the style guide electronically.

- ✔ **The names of any products and services your company offers.**

- ✔ **The correct way to refer to job positions.** Are your account managers "Customer Evangelists," "Opportunity Advisors," or simply "Account Managers"?

You don't need anything special to create a reliable style guide — a word processing program or, if it will be posted online, a basic wiki will do the trick. If the guide isn't published as a "living" document on a shared file server or wiki, make sure to have a distribution plan for when you make changes or additions.

You may want to think about putting out a (few) Microsoft PowerPoint templates with your company style on it, to be used company-wide internally and externally.

Looking at effective (and ineffective) e-mail policies

E-mail is almost always an organization's internal communication Achilles' heel — I've never seen a company that couldn't benefit from an efficiency overhaul of their e-mailing tools and policies. Because e-mails are free to write, easy to check, and arrive immediately, it's all too easy to send too many or pay too much attention to your inbox. In aggregate, this creates a huge productivity drain on an organization.

Encourage e-mail

Despite its own faults, e-mail is still almost always preferable to other forms of communication. I still get clients all the time who dictate letters and then *print them out and mail them.* Forgetting the cost of postage for a moment, this is terribly slow *and* discourages a response. If you receive a printed letter, you probably feel like you have to respond in kind, and by the time you get around to it, two weeks have passed. This also applies to printed memos that get distributed through interoffice mail.

Since a recipient can, at least theoretically, decide when they want to check their e-mail messages, e-mail is less intrusive than a phone call because the person you're messaging can delay the interruption until they're ready. In the same vein, it's much faster and clearer to read an e-mail than to listen to a voicemail. Walking up to someone's desk is the *most* intrusive form of communication because it denies the person the choice of whether or not to engage.

Know when to wiki

Never collaborate on a project, whether that be an advertising flyer, a database schema, or a potluck menu, over an e-mail thread.

After you get about six messages deep, the process becomes totally unwieldy, and it takes twice as long just to parse out who made which changes.

Make it easy for employees to generate wikis when they need to collaborate. A single group e-mail with a link to the wiki is all that's needed to kick off the process, and everyone will have an equal chance to contribute. They will also be equally appreciative of not having to scroll through a 60-message-long thread just to get to Revision 32.1b.

Create mailing lists

When every individual sending an e-mail is left to their own devices when it comes to filling the "To" line with addresses, you open the door both to unnecessary people being included and to necessary people being forgotten.

Mailing lists mean you send a message to one single address and it is then routed to the appropriate list members. Topical lists make it easier to filter messages, especially off-topic ones. For example, Microsoft has a mailing list for moms to swap nanny recommendations and parenting tips.

The real benefit to using mailing lists is the autonomy it gives each recipient. For example, Mary can subscribe to a digest-only version of the "off-topic" list, meaning she gets a single e-mail at the end of each day containing all of that day's e-mails. In practical terms, this means her phone doesn't buzz every time someone volunteers to join the company Relay for Life team. She can also choose to subscribe, or unsubscribe, to different departments' lists depending on her current job needs.

Improve your subject lines

Instead of trying to overhaul your employees' e-mail habits overnight, focus on subject lines. A clear subject makes a world of difference when determining which e-mails to address first, or which ones to read on your phone instead of waiting to return to your computer.

Troy Lavinia, CEO of Mosaic Research Management in New York City, encourages his team members to indicate a priority number at the start of each internal e-mail subject. "My employees are on the phone most of the day, and when they have a break in-between calls, they need to be able to quickly see which e-mails are most important. This ensures mission-critical tasks don't fall through the cracks, without anyone feeling pressured to read every e-mail during those precious few free minutes."

It's not how often you check, it's what you check

Lately the fad in productivity has been limiting the number of times you check your e-mail in a given day, usually to an absurdly small number like "two." Twice a day may be an acceptable frequency if you are a coal miner with no reception underground. For everyone who has ever compulsively hit "refresh" hoping for a response to an e-mail you sent 30 seconds ago, limiting access to your inbox just creates anxiety.

Some people find it very helpful to switch off the ever-so-tempting *ping* notification of a new mail coming in. If you are a compulsive "refresher," it will not distract you immediately from what you are doing.

Making open-door communication policies

Venture capitalist Paul Graham wrote a now-famous article titled "Maker's Schedule, Manager's Schedule" highlighting the differing needs of the two groups when it comes to time. A maker — a programmer, designer, architect, writer, and so on — requires large, uninterrupted blocks of time in which to work. In contrast, a manager's day tends to be a succession of meetings with brief interludes in between to answer e-mails and tackle smaller tasks.

If you put a maker on a manager's schedule, they will not be able to perform effectively, because they will never have a block of time long enough to work.

Just as important as giving your employees better ways to communicate with one another is giving them the tools and allowance to *not* communicate for periods of time. This is particularly important in an open office with cubicles or shared desks.

People are often afraid of being perceived as standoffish or mean if they announce that they need everyone to leave them alone for the afternoon so they can get some work done. You need to provide them with the explicit permission to take time for themselves if they need it, and a corporate culture that supports this attitude too.

Different approaches work for different office environments and attitudes. In one particularly whimsical example, programmers at a tech startup wore funny hats when they needed uninterrupted time to work out bugs or write new code. A different take on this would be a small sign on each desk with "red" or "green" on either side, to indicate whether that person is open to being approached. More formally, you can offer a quiet room for employees to relocate with laptops, or have periods of time blocked out company-wide or on individuals' calendars as interruption-free.

Looking at Different Communication Tools

The right tools can have everything to do with how efficiently your team communicates. If your office has a slow Internet connection, employees will be more likely to pick up the phone than e-mail. If there's no shared file server or Intranet, then people have no choice but to e-mail a spreadsheet back and forth to make changes.

As you introduce each new communication channel into your organization, be clear about its intended usage. Telling everyone there's now an internal chat room and not providing any further context pretty much guarantees that it will devolve into a place to share cat pictures. However, providing that chat room for the IT department and making it clear from the start that its purpose is addressing quick, topical questions can lower the number of cat pictures significantly (or at least increase the ratio of productive chat to funny cats).

Check out the following communication tools, or research online for other options:

- ✔ **Wikis**
  - MediaWiki: www.mediawiki.org
  - PBWorks: www.pbworks.com
  - Google Docs: www.google.com/docs
- ✔ **Chat Rooms**
  - Campfire: www.campfirenow.com
  - HipChat: www.hipchat.com
- ✔ **Message Forums**
  - phpBB: www.phpbb.com
  - vBulletin: www.vbulletin.com
  - QuickTopic: www.quicktopic.com

✔ **E-mail Mailing Lists**

  • Google Groups: `groups.google.com`

  • GroupServer: `www.groupserver.org`

✔ **Microblogs**

  • Chatter (part of Salesforce.com): `www.salesforce.com`

  • Status.net: `www.status.net`

  • Hall: `www.hall.com`

  • Jive: `www.jivesoftware.com`

✔ **Blogs**

  • WordPress: `www.wordpress.org` (self-hosted) or `www.word press.com` (hosted)

  • Joomla: `www.joomla.org`

  • Drupal: `www.drupal.org`

Chapter 17

Helping Employees Be More Efficient

· ·

In This Chapter

▶ Measuring employee efficiency

▶ Figuring out what some employees really do all day

▶ Comparing productivity systems

▶ Discovering the best time and task management techniques

▶ Finding individual efficiency enhancements you can implement today

· ·

*E*mployee efficiency is the baseline of all other efficiency projects. If an individual isn't organized enough to keep on top of her responsibilities — or worse, doesn't know quite what her responsibilities are — then your organization will never be able to effectively execute a project on which she works. Since individual inefficiency is usually systemic, this has a huge ripple effect across your organization.

Personal inefficiency can range from employees who are blatantly lazy to (more common) those who are simply don't know that there's a different, more efficient way to accomplish their tasks. Addressing a lack of knowledge about best practices, techniques, and tools is an endeavor *every* organization can benefit from.

In this chapter, I help you identify some common inefficiencies I see on a micro level — many of which you may recognize in your own work life! And of course after I suss these inefficiencies out, I'll help you reduce or eliminate them. This requires a two-pronged approach — I have many specific suggestions that can remedy these issues, but I also want to show you how to come up with or discover new solutions to address the more unique scenarios you may come across.

No one is 100 percent efficient 100 percent of the time — not even me! Zig Ziglar is known for saying "motivation is like showering — recommended daily!" I feel this same way about efficiency enhancements and best practices. Rereading this chapter and seeking out other personal productivity resources (including other *For Dummies* books such as *Thriving in the Workplace All-in-One For Dummies* and *Successful Time Management For Dummies*) on a regular basis are small investments of time that will pay dividends in saved hours and dollars.

Figuring Out What an Efficient Employee Looks Like

The best way to explain efficiency in an employee is to illustrate it with an example. Take a look at an average day in the life of Bradleigh, an efficient employee.

When Bradleigh gets to the office, the first thing she does is load her task management app, which pre-sorts her tasks by due date, priority, context, and mood. Try as she might, Bradleigh's no morning person — so reading a white paper or writing a speech feels like a tremendous chore at the start of the day. Since she knows this about herself, she starts out focusing on the smaller, easier items on her list, like going through her e-mail, completing a required human resources online training course, and submitting an expense report.

Around 10 a.m., Bradleigh walks over to the break room and chats with Bryce about another co-worker's upcoming wedding. No one — including Bradleigh's manager — takes issue with this time, because Bradleigh's proven she can be trusted to deliver on her commitments without being micromanaged. The brief respite from work gives her the mental refresh she needs to tackle some serious Excel action when she gets back to her desk. Without this trust, which she established by consistently meeting her deadlines and keeping up her communication, her co-workers may have resented this midmorning foray, impeding their ability to work well together.

Back at her desk, Bradleigh practically flies through her next task, catching up with current clients. A report in her CRM shows her exactly which customers she hasn't connected with in the last 60 days. She clicks on each name, types a single word ("backintouch") and her text expansion program automatically inserts her check-in paragraph template. She customizes it slightly to suit each customer, and hits send. Her clients would feel just as appreciated if she'd typed that same paragraph ten separate times, but this way, she composed those messages in a fraction of the time.

Mark wants to meet Bradleigh to talk about a new project. Thanks to Bradleigh's scheduling program that integrates with her calendar, Mark was able to suggest a couple of times when he was sure she was available, and Bradleigh confirmed the one for 10 a.m. the next day. (She prefers morning meetings so she can get more work done in the afternoon when she's more alert.)

After lunch, Bradleigh needs a couple hours to concentrate on writing an important speech. She takes advantages of one of the quiet work rooms at the end of the office, where she knows no one will bother her until she emerges. Since speech writing is pretty intense, she uses the Pomodoro Technique, which she learned about a recent brown bag lunch about productivity at the office. Every 20 minutes, she takes a five minute break, during which she walks around the room. After two hours, her speech is done, and since she met all her deliverables for the day — and her task software automatically sends that update to her manager — she can head home early.

How efficient are your employees?

What follows are questions that you should ask yourself in order to get a sense of how efficient your employees really are. The answers to these questions may vary wildly from department to department and from employee to employee, so I encourage you to survey widely.

Don't make a beeline for the people you think of as well-organized or ask for volunteers (which creates a self-selecting group that's more organized than the norm). You want to learn more about how a wide range of employees are functioning on a daily basis. Try these questions:

- **Do employees even track tasks?** In too many organizations, employees keep their tasks in their head (and occasionally on a sticky note). Even if they claim it's working just fine for them, mental task lists are not efficient.

- **Do employees and managers have visibility into one another's tasks?** If task lists live in vacuums, as opposed to in a software or web-based program with sharing enabled, then employees have to do double-entry duty: keep their own system updated *and* update team members of recent progress.

- **How are delegated tasks tracked?** Other people often forget their deliverables (especially if they're not very efficient to begin with!). An efficient employee tracks requests made of others and knows when to follow up, as opposed to forgetting about the deliverable altogether.

- **Do employees keep tasks in a central location?** The Beatles may have been here, there, and everywhere, but tasks should not be. If it makes contextual sense to have a few different task lists (for example, keeping a folder in your e-mail program of messages that require a response, as opposed to manually writing down each needed e-mail response on a separate list) then there should still be one central location referencing the sub-lists. Otherwise, things can and will fall through the cracks.

✔ **When was the last time you audited how employees spend their time?** Keeping detailed timesheets every day is not a good use of time (unless you need to for billing or regulatory reasons), but that doesn't mean you should *never* do it. Just as it's good to log everything you eat and every step you take every once in awhile, sometimes it's good to have an unannounced day on which every employee marks how they're spending their time in five-minute increments. The results are often eye-opening.

✔ **Are project plans broken down into specific tasks?** An execution plan doesn't need the same degree of detail as an individual employee's task list, but "launch a new product" is a wildly too-large "task" in desperate need of further breakdown. As a guideline, projects should be broken down into sub-tasks just far enough to assign them to individual people. It's then their responsibility to break it down further as necessary.

✔ **Are employee tasks sorted by context and mood?** A task list is infinitely more helpful and efficient if it empowers its owner to get things done better and/or faster. I explain more about the power of mood, context, and other task "meta data" later on.

Select an employee's task list at random:

- **How many of the first ten tasks can she complete in under 30 minutes?** When a single item takes hours to complete, you develop a natural aversion to it, because in today's workplace it's nearly impossible to commit to an uninterrupted block of time of that caliber.

- **How many of the first ten tasks are clear to you?** Even if he is a subject matter expert and you are not, a well-written task should still be clear to you. I'm a huge believer that vague tasks cause a sort of mental resistance — you're more likely to tackle "Write a 400-word press release on the new employee incentive program" than "Write article," even though the actual work involved is identical.

- **What's the EV of these ten tasks?** Calculating a task's Earned Value (EV) helps keep every project on time and on budget, and when you get in the habit, it makes future accurate project planning much simpler. More on this calculation later.

✔ **How do employees submit status reports?** The more automated this process, and the more ingrained into their existing task systems, the better.

✔ **Ask an employee at random to compose a new e-mail. Did she use the keyboard or the mouse/trackpad?** If she used her mouse or trackpad, she hasn't mastered her e-mail program's keyboard shortcuts — "compose" being one of the most basic keystrokes. This means she's literally losing time every time she writes an e-mail, and in aggregate, that time can really add up.

✔ **Visually survey your employees' desks. Are they generally messy or cluttered?** Although I have yet to see a desk that's both messy *and* efficient, an empty desk is usually not a paragon of efficiency, either. The 5S process can help increase the efficiency of personal workspaces.

✔ **Do employees have forms or templates for repetitive communications?** Text expansion software and web form creators not only save hours of digging around in your computer archive to copy and paste an e-mail from last month, but they also help ensure consistent communications throughout the organization.

How does your organization empower employee efficiency?

Employees can't reach maximum efficiency on their own — they need guidance *and* support from their organization. Without the company behind them, when a lone employee tries to make improvements, she's often shamed or drowned out by others who don't share her motivations. (Or worse, a well-meaning employee leads her team on an efficiency wild goose chase, with lots of lists and little actual productivity.)

Ask yourself the following questions to evaluate how supportive your company is of employee efficiency:

✔ **Can an employee refuse a meeting?** If employees aren't allowed to protect their own time, others will invade that time — even if they mean well. Although the degree to which someone should be allowed to decline meetings varies depending on his role, there should always be an explicit mechanism in place so an employee can make sure he has enough time left after meetings to actually get his work done.

✔ **Can an employee refuse a task?** A corollary to the preceding point is that an employee can't be efficient if she is at the beck and call of everyone else. If her only role is company concierge, then maybe that works — but if she's at the mercy of seven superiors' requests and *still* expected to post five articles to the corporate blog today, she's going to burn out quickly.

✔ **What resources are available for an employee who needs uninterrupted time to complete a task?** Many people think this has more to do with the office layout, but it actually has everything to do with the office *culture*. An employee who can't get the quiet and/or interruption-free time necessary to write that important sales proposal or finish that code will be frustrated, behind schedule, and probably not perform as his best. If there's no quiet area in the office, they may need permission to escape to a coffee shop, home office, or even a hall closet if that's what they need to be efficient.

✔ **Do employees have time to plan?** A few hours each week spent staying organized, planning the weeks ahead, and taking stock of one's responsibilities is *always* worth it. Without this time, it's possible to work for years only to get into work one day and suddenly find yourself wildly off track (whether that means the company missed the boat on a new technology or you simply missed the chance to move into your preferred position). A company culture that doesn't support planning — which means never chastising employees for taking the time to clean up and get organized, and never considering this "free" time as opposed to productive time — is one that's constantly putting out fires instead of shooting up fireworks.

✔ **What training or productivity resources do you offer for employees?** It's a rare employee who proactively seeks out efficiency-enhancing techniques, even if he really *wants* to be more efficient. It's up to the organization to provide resources and that includes the *time* to consume them.

✔ **What outsourcing options are available for employees?** Sometimes outsourcing tasks makes much more sense than an employee doing the work directly, particularly as hourly rates go up. A workplace that expects the CEO to do his own data entry is not an efficient place to work. That CEO should be setting an example and outsourcing that work to someone with a lower hourly rate.

✔ **Is money available for purchasing organizational supplies and/or software?** If it's up to employees to get their own index cards or purchase their own CRM seats, they probably will not do it. Even a very small budget can go a long way.

✔ **Are your existing technologies, such as a CRM or online support desk, customized for your organization?** It's extremely rare for something like a Customer Relationship Management (CRM) system to work for *anybody* right out of the box. If you don't invest some up-front resources in customizing it to the nuances of your particular organization, I can guarantee you're leaving some employee efficiency on the table. Plus, you may regret leaving customizing for later. After your employees get used to work-arounds, it's harder to change back to a more efficient way.

Measuring Individual Employee Efficiency

It's hard to know if you're empowering or improving employee efficiency or where to focus your initial improvements if you don't know how efficient your employees are *today*. For most employers, especially in larger organizations, the first step is figuring out what certain employees actually *do* and then figuring out how long it takes them to do it.

Figuring out what every employee does

Not knowing what an employee *really* does all day is in no way an implication that he's not highly efficient and/or extremely talented. It may just be that his responsibilities have shifted since you hired him, or perhaps that he was hired before you came to the company. Sometimes employees perform specialized roles, like computer programming or architectural drafting, that may seem like Greek to you. You don't have to be able to step into their shoes tomorrow, but you do need to get a better idea of what's going on.

So how do you figure it out? Start in human resources and ask for a job description to get a general idea. Then sit down with the employee (and his manager, if applicable) and ask him to explain his actual responsibilities to you. A bulleted list works fine. What tasks is he responsible for on a day-to-day basis? How about a regular basis (e.g., an accountant filing quarterly taxes)? What target(s) is he moving toward with his work?

A lighthearted and honest approach works much better here than simply scheduling a formal meeting to discuss job responsibilities. And whatever you do, don't go into the meeting with the assumption that someone is inefficient, even if you're pretty sure they are. You may think you're highly approachable, but your employees may not, especially if they don't work closely with you. This kind of meeting can spark some serious and unnecessary fear.

Does an employee's description of her own work jive with the official HR write-up? Probably not! Most employees' responsibilities extend far beyond their initial role descriptions. This is a perfect opportunity to modify the descriptions to better capture an employee's responsibilities in a way that can positively benefit the employee and the company. Frame your questions so that he understands that a clear description means he gets the credit and visibility he deserves for all his work (and if he ever leaves, the company will have a better idea of what it will take to find a replacement).

Some strategies for getting to the meat of an employee's responsibilities include:

- ✔ Using the "5 Why" method. When your employee explains one of his roles, ask "Why?" In response to his explanation, ask "Why?" again. Repeat until you've asked "Why?" five times. This is one of the fastest ways to bring potential inefficiencies or areas of concern to light immediately.

- ✔ Asking what the biggest pain point in his day is. Be purposefully vague — pain to him may be the task that takes the longest or is the most boring. Be clear that your intention for asking is to help *alleviate* that pain, not to chastise him.

After asking about the biggest pain point, ask more specific follow-up questions about the most time-consuming and/or mind-numbing tasks.

✔ Where possible, asking him to demonstrate certain tasks. Again, use the "5 Why" method to try to suss out unnecessary steps right away. I've been amazed at the many tasks I discover that continue to be done long after they ceased being necessary, because "it's always been done that way."

Discovering where time is really spent

Actual tasks and responsibilities aside, there's *always* room for productivity improvement in someone's day. Since you can't improve what you can't measure, it's important to take a baseline of how an employee's day (or week) is spent. A number of analog and digital tools are available to help track this information. Most people are shocked when they see how their day is *actually* spent, and that sort of self-awareness is a powerful first step when it comes to effecting change.

I recommend having employees first track time *without oversight*. In other words, Joyce is the only person who sees her own initial tracking information. Empower her with the space and time needed to handle some initial remedying on her own. It's embarrassing to have someone look at your "first draft," as it were, and employees are liable to lie to protect themselves. If Joyce realizes she spent two hours of personal time on a day when she had other projects due (something she genuinely may not have realized without tracking it), she may self-correct and be wary of online window shopping at work going forward.

Of course it's best to pair this private time tracking with some resources, whether they be workshops, an outside consultant, some productivity blogs, and/or a small budget for tools/coaching. For example, an employee may realize that five hours a day is too much time to spend in his e-mail program, but not know how to shorten that time while still keeping on top of client requests.

Track different days of the week during different weeks to get a more accurate representation of how time is really spent. A single week is not necessarily indicative of how every week is spent.

When employees have the chance to remedy obvious shortcomings on their own, then you can start to request the occasional time-tracking sheet or use administrative accounts for computer tracking software. I cannot stress enough how important it is to *not* use these tools as a way to chastise or ride individual employees. It's not fun to yell at someone for being on Facebook and it's horribly demeaning to be yelled at for it. (Of course, if someone is on Facebook *all day*, that's another story. I have yet to see this in a real work environment, though.)

Instead, what you should do is look for general trends that you can investigate remedying. E-mail is an obvious one. If your team is spending half their day in Outlook, there's a goldmine of potential efficiency savings with the right training on e-mail filters and keyboard shortcuts. You can then literally monitor the resulting time savings and use that as a benchmark if, over time, teams start falling back into old habits and some new intervention is necessary.

If an individual employee is an outlier — say Max spends three hours in your CRM while the other 17 team members spend only two — then this is worth investigating *objectively*. I've seen situations where this indicated that Max was the only one doing his job properly and the 17 others were slacking off, and I've seen situations where this indicated Max needed help with typing or a more accessible monitor.

Some tools you can use for individual time tracking include:

- ✔ **RescueTime** (www.rescuetime.com) is a software program you can install on each employee's computer. In keeping with the above recommendations, it lets individual employees see very detailed information about how they are spending their computer time (with the option to input non-computer activities) while aggregating results for company admins.

- ✔ **Emergent Task Timer** (davidseah.com/productivity-tools/) by designer Dave Seah is a printable form that lets individual employees mark their activities in 10-minute increments.

- ✔ **Any daily calendar template** available at your local office supply store or printed from a calendar program. It should go down to 15-minute increments, and employees fill it out by hand. A timer can help remind people to input their current activity at every quarter hour.

Make sure *you* time yourself — you may be just as surprised as to where your time really goes!

Don't use firewall software to block certain websites that you consider to be unproductive, and don't forbid employees to check their personal e-mail or look at Twitter while at work. Treating your employees like children isn't the way to encourage them to go the extra mile when the time comes. Further, no one can be 100 percent productive 100 percent of the time. As long as your employee is getting her work done, does it really matter if she spends her breaks on Facebook instead of simply staring into space? Focus on results, not on how many minutes a week are spent on shopping websites.

Sometimes, sites that appear unproductive are actually useful. For example, industry events or client information may be posted on Facebook pages, and your employees will miss out on these details if you unilaterally block the site.

Looking At Popular Productivity Systems

Productivity is more than a lengthy checklist. Different practitioners have developed various productivity systems over the years, with diverse organizations and personality types gravitating toward the ones that suit their individual needs.

In my experience, few people are diehard devotees to any given system. Instead, they cherry-pick the parts that work best for them from multiple systems.

Understanding the basics of the most popular productivity programs can help you decide where to start. When you give one system an honest chance, it will likely be very clear to you which parts help and which parts may need further tweaking to better serve your needs. Frankly, you can use *every* concept listed here in concert to create a truly powerful and flexible personal productivity system.

I encourage you to try out the following tactics yourself (after all, *modeling behavior* is one of the key components of a successful change management plan), and to share these resources with your employees. Every employee may find their own particular rhythm from the systems.

Increasing personal efficiency takes planning time. If you don't give your employees the time to learn and implement, the permission to make some initial mistakes, and at least a tiny budget to get the tools they need, then none of the following will work.

Getting Things Done: Powering productivity through context

Created by David Allen, Getting Things Done — known as "GTD" by its practitioners — is a productivity methodology intended to help you get more done in the same amount of time by pulling together many of the best time-tested productivity strategies into one system. GTD's basic premise is that you need to develop a *trusted* system, and that this trust enables you to do more faster and with less stress. For example, a trusted system means that you don't have to worry about whether you did something (because you trust that you have an accurate record) or whether you're going to remember to do something (because you trust that if you capture it once, it will make it onto your radar at the right time).

Assigning contexts

When you "get things done," every task is assigned a *context* to indicate the location or tools necessary to actually complete this task. Assigning a context enables two productive behaviors:

- **Batching:** You lose flow, and therefore time, if you make a call, then read an article, then make a second call, then read an e-mail, then make a third call. Making three phone calls in a row is a more effective way to complete this same group of tasks. When you clearly indicate the phone calls you need to make with a "calls" context, you can run through all the calls you need to make at once.

- **Focusing on the tools at hand:** If you don't *have* your phone, you can't very well make phone calls. With a normal task list, this means rereading your entire list each time you're ready to do something new, scanning for a task that you *can* complete in spite of your lack of dial tone.

    This is not an efficient use of time or mental capacity. You already wrote the list, so why reread it every time you need a next task? Contexts allow you to filter your task list by the tools at hand. Hide phone calls and expose tasks you can do on your computer or while out running errands, instead.

Example contexts include "phone," "e-mail," or "grocery store." I use a generic "errands" context and keep that list separately in my phone, so I can consult it whenever I am headed out the door to see if I can stop and take care of one of these tasks on my way somewhere else.

One particularly important context is "Waiting On," which is where you keep tasks that you can't personally tackle because you're waiting on someone else for an action or a response. When you perform your weekly review (explained next), pay particular attention to the "Waiting On" tasks to see if you now need to follow-up with the other person. I use a "Waiting On" label in my e-mail for the same reason.

An electronic task management tool such as SmartyTask (www.smartytask.com) or Things for Mac (www.culturedcode.com) can filter tasks by context for you. You can jigger any tag-based task list to work this way by creating a tag for each context.

Plotting next actions

When you're at the point of looking at your task list, you need to be in a place of *action*, not a place of mentally re-reviewing each and every item to figure out what to do next. Contexts are an important filter, and so is the concept of a next action.

In a nutshell, a next action is something you can do *right now*. If you need to do another task first, then *that* task is the next action, and all tasks dependent on it are *not* next actions. Your main task list should have *only* next actions on it.

Here's an example. Say you want to throw a party for your team at work. You first need to pick a day. "Pick a date" is your next action. You cannot hire a catering company until you know the date, so you would *not* put "hire Acme Caterers" on your list until *after* you picked the date.

Most electronic task managers do not support dependent tasks like this. As a workaround, tag your next action tasks (or e-mails you can respond to right away!) with "Next." Once it's completed, tag the next task in the series.

Embracing inboxes

It's not practical to have a single inbox. You have your e-mail inbox (or a few e-mail inboxes!), your physical mailbox at home, your paper inbox at work, and potentially even more than that. Any efforts you make to combine these inboxes (especially by writing down every single e-mail-related task you have, which I've seen numerous people do) is simply redundant effort.

Instead, embrace all your inboxes. Just make sure you commit to processing each one on a regular basis during a weekly review (explained next). When you start to trust (that's the key word here!) that you'll check every inbox regularly, you can start to drop sticky notes, memos, tickets, and e-mails-to-yourself into your inboxes, and know that those tasks will get handled.

Performing weekly reviews

Once a week, David Allen suggests going through a weekly review checklist. This includes processing all of your inboxes, reviewing your goals, conducting a brain dump (covered next), and looking at your tickler.

Most people I've worked with find the weekly review too much to do all at once. It can take a few hours, especially in the beginning, and especially if you tend to drop things into your inboxes throughout the week and wait until your review to do most of the processing. If this is the case for you, distribute your weekly review items throughout the week. For example, review your goals on Sunday nights, process your snail mail on Tuesdays, and clean out your personal e-mail inbox on Wednesdays. A separate "Weekly Review" checklist will help establish trust in your system.

Remember inboxes that aren't as obvious, such as cleaning out your wallet and clearing off your refrigerator.

Tickling your memory

A tickler file "tickles" your memory regarding future events and obligations. The analog version is made up of 43 folders: one for each month (Jan – Dec), and one for each day of the month (1–31). Put the numbered folder corresponding to today's date in the front, and the month folder corresponding to *next* month behind the last day of this month. For example, if today is April 14, the front folder would be "14" and the "May" folder would be first among the months.

You then file future reminders — ranging from notes scribbled on a napkin to concert tickets and wedding invitations — in the folder corresponding to the month in which you need to remind yourself. On the first of each month, take that month's folder and distribute the reminders into the corresponding days. For example, if it's currently April and I have concert tickets for November 7, I would put these tickets in the "November" folder. Come November 1, I open the "November" folder and put these tickets in the "7" folder. Each morning (or the evening before), I look in that day's folder for any reminders I need to take care of.

Ticklers are also great for recurring tasks that don't necessarily happen on a regular schedule, like oil changes. Put a reminder in the "1" folder so on the first day of every month, you remind yourself to schedule an oil change *if* you need it.

You can re-create a tickler in an electronic calendar by setting each "tickle" as its own calendar event. You can use recurring events for things like oil change reminders. However, you still need at least *one* folder to hold physical items like tickets and invitations. Simply put a reminder to check this folder on your calendar as the reminder.

Doing brain dumps

At least once a week — and when you start your efficiency journey, perhaps even multiple times a day — you need to do a *brain dump*. This involves grabbing a blank sheet of paper (or blank word processing document) and writing down everything on your mind. Then put the brain dump into your inbox and process it out into new projects and tasks during your next Weekly Review.

Setting areas of responsibility

Individual goal setting is an important part of fostering an empowered and motivated employee. Every employee should have a list of his individual areas of responsibility — for example, "Customer Support" and "Event Planning." This list may be short, but it's important because during regular reviews, he needs to ensure that he always has an active project (if there is one, at least) in each area.

Beyond active projects, what are the *goals* within that area? Articulate them, and read them often.

7 Habits of Highly Effective People: Stephen Covey's rules to live by

Part productivity system, part rules to live by, Stephen Covey's *7 Habits of Highly Effective People* spawned an entire section of tools at your nearest office supply store and millions of fans. You can use it alongside the tactics described in the previous section, or try it first alone.

Habit #1: Be proactive

This habit is one to instill company-wide, and is an important one to keep in mind when your efforts to increase efficiency become challenging or you start to question their worth. If you can take responsibility for some of your own failings, then you empower yourself to be able to *change them*. If you blame rising costs or lost productivity on Roman gods, the weather, or the economy, then you are powerless to improve things. Don't be a victim, and don't let your employees become victims.

Habit #2: Begin with the end in mind

This habit goes hand-in-hand with defining areas of responsibility. It's all too easy to slog through work for months or even years and lose sight of the big picture, especially in positions that are somewhat removed from the end product. For example, an employee on the early stage of a medical device assembly line may give little or no thought to the way they are positively changing (or saving!) another person's entire life. Not only do you have to articulate the big picture, but you have to remind yourself —and everyone around you —of it constantly.

Guy Kawasaki, a venture capitalist and early Apple employee, often rants about meaningless company mission statements when he gives talks and in his books. Does your organization have a mission statement? Is it specific and inspiring, or is it a generic hobbling of feel-good phrases? If the latter — fix it! Your mission should reinvigorate a tired employee at the end of a long day, not look good atop a white paper.

Zig Ziglar once said, "Motivation is like showering: required daily." Remember that.

Habit #3: Put first things first

This is one of those adages that makes perfect sense, yet one that you forget all the time. It's important to prioritize your daily tasks according to your actual priorities (a.k.a. your areas of responsibility). Lean is ruthless about this, encouraging you to flat-out eliminate tasks that are not core to your end result. Although *some* administrative tasks are inevitable, they should not start your day or they snowball into other, equally administrative tasks. Each night, outline the real priorities for the next day, and when you start the day, start with those priorities. Empower your employees to do the same by first modeling this behavior yourself and then encouraging them to follow suit.

Habit #4: Think win-win

All too many organizations accidentally set themselves up for inefficiencies by pitting employees against one another in ways that discourage collaboration and/or encourage cutting corners. This risks team synergy, product/service quality, and ultimately your entire company's success.

For example, a contest to see which department can save the most time is a universally bad idea. People will do the absolute bare minimum, failing to double-check quality control and risking serious mistakes. They will also be secretive about any productivity gains they do come across, benefiting individual employees at the expense of the entire organization's productivity. *Don't do this.* Bring everyone to the table, brainstorm improvements collaboratively, and be inclusive. As each employee moves along in her efficiency-enhancing journey, encouraging sharing of what worked (and what did not) is what leads to a positive ripple effect across the organization.

Habit #5: Seek first to understand, then to be understood

In a nutshell, this habit is all about listening *without* inserting yourself into the communication. When you are constantly giving advice and asking questions from an autobiographical perspective, you miss out on really hearing the other person's point of view. Sometimes, increasing efficiency in your organization requires challenging your own views, and it almost always involves challenging the status quo. Don't push back on others' ideas and experiences with your own ideas — try them out first.

Habit #6: Synergize

More than just a buzz word, *synergy* is about fostering productive team collaboration without sacrificing any individual input. For example, it's rare for one efficiency solution to be effective across multiple organizations in the exact same form, just as it's rare for one solution to be equally effective across every employee in the same organization. Your team needs an overarching goal (say, cutting back the time spent on e-mail) but each team member may arrive there in a different way.

Habit #7: Sharpen the saw

This habit is in perfect alignment with Balanced Scorecard Strategy: An efficient organization is one that measures, honors, and encourages personal growth. This may take the form of learning new skills directly related to one's current position, learning new skills to take on a brand-new position, and also learning new skills that don't relate directly to a particular role but still contribute to that employee feeling empowered, confident, and happy. Employees are more than just their work — they are also spouses, black belts, triathletes, linguists, and everything else under the sun.

This is probably the most actionable habit for an employer, because there are many small and attainable ways you can encourage your employees to improve themselves. This can range from providing budgets or reimbursements for personal growth activities (ranging from yoga class to college courses), flexible time schedules to accommodate outside activities, free workshops and brown bag lunches for employees on a variety of topics (perhaps even led by other employees!), flexible time off (in hourly increments instead of entire days, allowing for the occasional late start or early departure), and/or company holidays designed to give employees time off to tackle specific personal projects.

The Pomodoro Technique: Total focus, frequent breaks

Less of a system and more of a technique, the Pomodoro Technique involves focusing fully on a task for 25 minutes, and then taking a five-minute break. After four 25-minute blocks, you should take a longer break (say, for lunch, or a long walk).

Every 25-minute period is called a "pomodoro" (Italian for *tomato*).

The thinking behind this technique is that it ultimately produces higher-quality work and creates more productive employees. It was developed from a time management study carried out by Francesco Cirillo. Knowing a short break is just around the corner is enough of a motivation to start most *any* task, versus the mental commitment involved in taking the first step in a task you know will take hours (or, perhaps worse, an unknown amount of time).

Discovering Time Management Techniques

Someone could write a book on time management techniques alone (and someone did: *Successful Time Management For Dummies*), but there are a few techniques I find essential to being an efficient individual, including planning for tomorrow today, allowing yourself large segments of time in which to work, and outsourcing where possible.

Planning tomorrow today

Planning more than a single day out is an excellent exercise that you should definitely undertake occasionally, but it's too much work to do on a daily basis. Plus, the farther out you plan, the less accurate the plan, and if each week your daily plan is entirely out of whack by Friday, you aren't going to trust your system, and it's therefore inefficient.

Instead, set aside 5 to 10 minutes at the end of each day to review what you accomplished that day and set priorities for the next day. Don't simply assign yourself a few tasks from your existing list — you can make those choices on your own much more naturally and effectively when tomorrow comes around. What you *do* need to surface, though, are any tasks that *must* be done (either because they are due that day, or a future due date is dependent upon it) and any events, such as meetings, for which you may need to prepare.

I print out index cards listing tasks that recur each day (such as clearing out certain e-mail folders or going for a run), with spaces to list events and MITs (Most Important Tasks) for that day. Even though I maintain a calendar religiously, it helps to write down the events and mentally check whether I feel prepared for each one. If I don't, I do whatever's necessary to *get* prepared that evening, rather than risk showing up unprepared the following day. This creates a much calmer daily routine, and I'm always grateful for the few minutes I spared the night before to allow myself to look ahead.

Time-blocking for ultimate focus

Interruptions kill productivity. Meetings are interruptions, as are five-minute phone calls and quick e-mails. (Even the 'ping' of a new e-mail coming in is a major interruption, but luckily you have the choice to switch it off.) Back-to-back meetings are fine if your main responsibility is to meet with people, but if you're expected to deliver any significant piece of work — whether that be adding a new feature to software, or writing a speech, or researching a topic for a white paper, or frankly planning more than a day ahead — then you need a significant period of time in which to work.

It's essential to block off periods of time solely for working on bigger projects like the ones I just outlined. You must guard these blocks of time carefully, keeping out *any* interruption. I firmly believe that even a single 10-minute coffee meeting in the middle of the afternoon can and will mentally prevent you from getting started on any significant project beforehand. No matter what's on your calendar or what you've committed to yourself, having that stopping point in your head creates resistance to really getting into a flow state.

If you work in a meetings-heavy or highly collaborative environment, try to block off the same period of time each week, so others get used to it. For example, you may declare your Tuesdays as meetings-free, or block off every Wednesday and Friday morning.

Outsourcing and delegating

One common inefficiency I come across, particularly in smaller organizations, is overworked employees taking on tasks outside of their regular responsibilities simply because there is no one else to do them. This can range from the CEO doing his own contact data entry to Roxanne in sales handling new employee paperwork because she enjoys filling out forms (or, more than likely, because she didn't speak up and protest).

Sometimes, particularly for one-off and time-sensitive tasks, this is necessary. We all have drudge work to get through at times. However, tasks that come up regularly (or even occasionally) that take employees away from their core work can often be outsourced, producing faster/cheaper/higher quality results and making that newly freed employee's life a little easier.

Outsourcing or delegating work doesn't have to mean running a call center in another country. Options with far less commitment, and that employees can usually engage with on their own, include:

- ✔ **Zaarly** (www.zaarly.com) is a task marketplace. Post what you need done — ranging from picking up lunch for the office to designing a website — and how much you're willing to pay. Mobile alerts go out to people in the area willing to fulfill your request, and you then assign the task to the first or best person who submits an offer.

- ✔ **Mechanical Turk** (http://aws.amazon.com/mturk/) is a service run by Amazon that farms out repetitive tasks to many individuals. You submit a spreadsheet (or other instructions) of what you need done, and Mechanical Turk then farms those tasks out individually. You pay per completed task — many run in the range of a few cents up to a couple dollars. This is great for repetitive tasks such as finding URLs or e-mail addresses, identifying images, or writing brief product descriptions. You *can* do it yourself, sure, but it's often cheaper and faster (not to mention less boring) to try Turk. You can also ask that each task be assigned multiple times, ensuring quality (because if three separate people give the same answer, there's a good chance it's the correct one).

- ✔ **Elance** (www.elance.com) is an online marketplace for services ranging from website development to social media strategies, article writing, and even legal services. You post your RFP and budget, and service providers bid for the work. This is a nice way to complete projects that do not fall under any particular employee's wheelhouse, such as customizing a blog template, without having to hire an entire new employee or pay a higher rate for a contractor to come into the office.

- ✔ **Temp agencies** can help staff your office for one-off or occasional projects (such as end-of-year filing or archival data entry). If your first thought is to divide a large, off-topic task across multiple team members, a temp may be a better choice, as she frees up your employees to continue doing their real work.

✓ **Employees' teenagers** are also an untapped resource. Not only can they file on the cheap, but they often have serious technical chops and can handle website updates or they can create your Facebook page. Make sure you clear human resources and follow all applicable wage and age laws.

Exploring Task Management Techniques

Task management refers to how you identify, track, and complete individual tasks; time management is how you delegate (and defend!) the actual minutes and hours of your day. Efficient *task* management ultimately saves you significant amounts of *time*.

Assigning context: Knowing what you can do, where

Mentioned earlier as part of the "Getting Things Done" system, contextualizing your tasks also has everything to do with whether you can get into a "flow" state. Remember the last time you were so engrossed in a project that you looked up and four hours had gone by? That's flow. Constantly stopping after you complete a small task and spending time trying to figure out what to do next is *not* flow.

That's where context comes in. It's easier, literally and mentally, to write five successive e-mails on the same topic in a row than it is to send those same five e-mails at various points over two days. Each time you start a new message, you have to remember what you wrote last, to whom you wrote, what the goal was, and so on. If you do them all in a row, however, you can fly through your messages.

Beyond literal contexts relating to place and tools – such as "office" tasks that you absolutely can't do when you're telecommuting, or "scanner" tasks that you can only do at the bulk scanner — you can also use contexts in more creative ways. I have a "brainstorm" context that I use to keep track of tasks related to coming up with ideas or strategies. When I'm in the right kind of mood, I can quickly pull up those sorts of projects and really get my juices flowing. Similarly, a "read" task is good for grouping items that require a bit more concentration than I'm capable of before my first cup of coffee, so I can avoid those first thing in the morning.

You can assign contexts to a task by literally writing them in a column next to each task on a piece of paper (keywords or shorthand helps, but avoid color-coding unless you *always* have access to all the different-colored pens), or tag electronic tasks with context names.

Chunking down projects into manageable tasks

"Write a book."

Many people have this single task on their to-do list (or at least their bucket list). But this is such a monumentally large task (believe me, I know!) that I can guarantee that you'll never look at your list one day and choose *that* to tackle. What you think when you read that task is actually, "What is the first thing I need to do to start writing a book?" Then the task seems so monumental that you move on to another item that you can reasonably check off.

You have to break your projects and tasks down into individual bite-sized pieces. The moment you add a task that you know, deep down, you can't finish in one sitting, you are going to resist it, and that means it will either *never* get done, or it will get done at the last minute and you will resent its very existence.

Many people push back on this idea because it feels laborious to break a project out that much. Don't you already know what to do? Can't you just jot down some keywords and trust that you'll remember when you look at the list? Well . . . no.

My advice: Chunk, chunk, chunk. It's deeply satisfying to mark a task as done. Give yourself that satisfaction as much as possible. This is a great way to build momentum and keep yourself motivated and productive for longer periods of time each day. You will more than make up for the extra minutes it may take to really capture every tiny step, and you'll be seriously more satisfied.

Finding each task's true value: Earned Value Management

Earned Value Management (EVM) is a method of determining — from resource expenditures alone — whether you're over or under budget and whether you're ahead of or behind schedule. On complex projects, EVM is a useful way to identify areas you should investigate for possible current problems or potential future problems.

The key to a meaningful EVM analysis lies in the accuracy of your estimates of EV. To determine EV, you must estimate:

- How much of a task you've completed to date
- How much of the task's total budget you planned to spend for the amount of work you've performed

If you assume that the amount of a task's total budget that should be spent to complete a portion of the task is directly proportional to the amount of the task completed, you should spend 60 percent of the total task budget to complete 60 percent of the task.

For tasks with separate components, like printing brochures or conducting telephone surveys, determining how much of a task you've completed is straightforward. However, if your task entails an integrated work or thought process with no easily divisible parts (such as designing the brochure), the best you can do is make an educated guess.

To estimate the EV in your project, use one of the three following approaches:

- **Percent-complete method:** EV is the product of the fraction representing the amount of an activity that has been completed and the total budget for the activity.

  This method is potentially the most accurate if you correctly determine the fraction of the activity you have completed. However, because that estimate depends on your subjective judgment, this approach is also most vulnerable to errors or purposeful manipulation.

- **Milestone method:** EV is zero until you complete the activity, and it's 100 percent of the total activity budget after you complete it.

  The milestone method is the most conservative and the least accurate. You expect to spend some money while you're working on the task. However, this method doesn't allow you to declare EV greater than $0 until you've completed the entire activity. Therefore, you always appear over budget while you perform the activity.

- **50/50 method:** EV is zero before you start the activity, 50 percent of the total activity budget after you start it, and 100 percent of the activity budget after you finish the activity.

  The 50/50 method is a closer approximation to reality than the milestone method because you can declare an EV greater than $0 while you perform the task. However, this approximation can inadvertently mask overspending.

For example, suppose you've spent $4,000 to complete 30 percent of a task with a $10,000 budget. Arguably, you should've spent about 30 percent of the total task budget, or $3,000, to complete 30 percent of the work on the task, which means you're $1,000 over budget. However, using the 50/50 method, you estimate the EV to be $5,000 (50 percent of the total budget for the task), which makes it appear that you're $1,000 under budget.

As you can see, the milestone method and 50/50 method allow you to approximate EV without estimating the portion of a task that you've completed. Choosing which of the three methods to use for your project requires that you weigh the potential for accuracy against the possibility of subjective data resulting in misleading conclusions.

Contemplating Individual Organization Best Practices

You need to bear a few core concepts in mind when spreading the gospel of individual efficiency across an organization, including the following ideas.

Assigning clear tasks and responsibilities

I would like to clear up a horrible misconception that I come across in nearly every organization I visit: someone "owning" a project has nothing to do with whether multiple people can collaborate on that project. Ownership and collaboration are not mutually exclusive in this context. However, lack of ownership and project failure are pretty tightly coupled.

Whenever there's a new project or task created by a group, make sure someone owns it. That owner is *either* responsible for completing it himself *or* ensuring that someone else completes it. All the team collaboration in the world can coincide with this arrangement, but at the end of the day, the *one* owner is charged with seeing a task or project to fruition. Without this arrangement, it's all too easy for everyone to assume someone else is handling it, often leaving a critical task undone and forgotten.

In the same vein, you need *clear* tasks and responsibilities. "Call Ted" is an unclear task. Why call Ted? Presumably merely dialing Ted's number is not enough to fulfill the task's real intention. The clearer you make a task (or a project mission or a goal), the more easily someone can execute it.

Sending and tracking status updates

I've discussed the positive benefits that the transparency and frequency of regular status updates can provide for your organization, but I really can't say it often enough.

A web-based form service such as Formstack (`www.formstack.com`) or Wufoo (`www.wufoo.com`) makes it easy to generate a basic status update template and distribute its URL to employees. The service can collect the submissions directly, forward them to an external service of your choosing, or simply e-mail them to you and/or the appropriate manager.

A case management system such as ZenDesk (`www.zendesk.com`) or Salesforce (`www.salesforce.com`) can also work for adding regular updates to existing tasks and projects. Although it is traditionally used to track customer support requests, there's nothing stopping your organization from using it for communicating internal updates.

Providing ongoing training resources

Don't make the mistake of assuming that you can offload productivity training to a two-day off-site or brown bag lunch and call it a day. Just like your overall organizational efficiency, you need to stay on top of employee efficiency. People fall back into old habits, pick up new bad habits, change jobs, switch roles, and sometimes just plain forget. On top of this, new software versions and technologies constantly hit the market, every one of which has potential implications for your employees' ability to get things done.

Planning Individual Efficiency Improvements You Can Implement Immediately

Can't wait to start improving individual employee efficiency in your organization? Try these tactics, which you can start sharing with employees (and using yourself!) right away.

Using keyboard shortcuts

Keyboard shortcuts are my favorite efficiency tip, because not only do they save tangible time, but they help preserve a flow state. Jiggling a mouse and moving the cursor seven times — not mention switching between mouse and keyboard — during a single task is subtly jarring. Hitting some additional keys when you're already typing, however, is a smooth experience.

You can pick up some of the more universal keyboard shortcuts, such as the ones for copy and paste, by clicking on the top-most menu of any software program and looking for the shortcut listed to the right of the command you would normally select with your cursor. For example, copying highlighted text is Ctrl+C in Windows or Cmd+C on a Mac.

Learn one or two commands at a time, committing to use the keyboard shortcut each and every time even if it takes you longer that way at first. Soon, you'll be flying through so many shortcuts you won't even realize you're doing it. Shortcuts are exceptionally useful in e-mail programs like Gmail and Outlook, where you can reduce a long string of manual tasks into a two-second set of keystrokes.

Some amazing background software programs such as Activewords (www.activewords.com) for Windows, TextExpander (www.textexpander.com) for Mac, and Quicksilver (www.qsapp.com) for Mac let you launch particular applications or websites, carry out an automated set of actions, or insert a block of text. This last point is a particular time-saver, because you can save literally hundreds of paragraphs, difficult spellings, quotations, or entire form templates and insert them *anywhere* on your computer by just typing the right set of characters. For example, typing "bnk" can insert your standard payment agreement legal text. (The misspelling is intentional — if you made the word "bank" your shortcut, you'd never be able to type the word "bank" without it replacing it with your text!)

Allowing for interruption-free time

Don't assume that employees feel empowered to remove themselves from distracting situations, decline meetings, or politely turn away other employees who walk over to chat. For all the conflicts that arise in the workplace, most people tend to be overtly nice at their own expense.

You can change this by directly and explicitly empowering your employees to protect their own time. If someone needs to be left alone to complete a deliverable, she needs to be able to communicate this clearly and not expect pushback (or have clear authority to push back against the pushback!). In informal workspaces, I've seen funny signs or props used to indicate "please leave me alone right now" without having to explicitly say it out loud. If your floor plan allows, a quiet room (or set of rooms) to which employees can retreat and work in peace is ideal. Although it takes a little while to implement culturally, a shared calendar system across the organization allows individuals to block off periods of interruption-free time in a way that is easily visible to others.

Removing distractions

Stating that distractions detract from productivity may sound obvious, but when is the last time you went on a hunt for possible distractions in your workplace?

This is particularly important if you have an open floor plan. Employees need a place to which they can escape if they need to take a phone call or concentrate.

Distractions to be on the lookout for include boisterous individual employees, phone conversations taking place in an otherwise quiet area, desks near high-activity areas such as the break room, water cooler, or supply closet, or even times when office music gets too loud.

Distractions can also take more subtle forms, such as new e-mail alerts. For employees who do not have time-sensitive e-mail needs (such as on-duty customer support), encourage changing program settings to check (and therefore alert) less frequently, or turn off alerts entirely.

Creating productive workspaces

Every individual employee and department can use the Japanese system of 5S to increase the efficiency of their workspaces. The five basic steps are:

- ✔ **Sort:** Go through everything in the workplace, from office supplies to notes. Remove everything that's not necessary. (Arguably, remove everything that's only peripherally necessary, too — how often do you really need a three-hole punch? It can be put in a common area for the two times a year when you need it.)

- ✔ **Stabilize:** Give each remaining item a dedicated space. Purchase or build the right storage containers for each, such as a workbench for tools or individual containers for loose supplies such as pushpins. Commit to returning each item to its home each time you use it. Sitting among organization encourages efficiency, just as sitting among chaos discourages it.

- ✔ **Shine:** Clean or repair each item as necessary. Every employee should be *proud* of the appearance of his workspace, and this feeling also encourages efficient behavior — the same as how you stand a bit taller when you wear a nice suit versus wearing old jeans and sneakers.

- ✔ **Standardize:** If two workstations are used for the same task or by the same set of employees (particularly if they are shared over multiple shifts), they need to be identical. It causes confusion and introduces many new possibilities for error when there are differences from station to station. Workflows should be documented and each item's "home" location indicated.

- ✔ **Sustain:** Commit to regularly keeping up the productive workspaces you have created. This may mean a dedicated time each day or week for upkeep. Creating a 5S board with before-and-after photos is highly motivational.

Finding Technology Resources

Here are some handy resources and tools to help you and your employees reach higher efficiency.

Productivity systems

- David Allen's Getting Things Done: `www.davidco.com`
- Stephen Covey's 7 Habits of Highly Effective People: `www.stephen covey.com`

Productivity blogs

- Lifehack: `www.lifehack.org`
- Brett Kelly's NerdGap: `www.nerdgap.com`
- Zen Habits: `www.zenhabits.net`

Text expansion and shortcut apps

- ActiveWords: `www.activewords.com`
- TextExpander: `www.textexpander.com`
- Quicksilver: `www.qsapp.com`

Form creation tools

- Formstack: `www.formstack.com`
- Wufoo: `www.wufoo.com`

Time tracking tools

- RescueTime: `www.rescuetime.com`
- David Seah's Emergent Task Timer: `www.davidseah.com`

Chapter 18

Holding Effective Meetings and Events

. . . .

In This Chapter

▶ Understanding what makes a meeting efficient

▶ Thinking about improving meeting efficiency

▶ Measuring meeting efficiency

▶ Identifying when you don't need a meeting — and when you do

▶ Considering alternatives to meetings

▶ Collecting event data

▶ Planning more efficient company events

▶ Applying best meeting practices

. . . .

*W*hen it comes to business efficiency, meetings are polarizing. A meeting of the right length with the right people at the right time trumps pretty much all else. Magic can happen at these moments — new products designed, new slogans written, new directions charted.

Then there's the other 98 percent of meetings. Participants dread them. They start late and end even later. Few agenda items, if any, get resolved — if there even was an agenda. People feel justified in calling a meeting for just about any reason and no one feels like they have the ability to decline. These sorts of meetings beget cranky employees and waste tens of thousands of productive hours, not just in the meetings themselves but in the time required to schedule, reschedule, and often even simply debrief from them.

Making meetings more efficient at your organization has far-reaching positive consequences. Your employees will be happier. Projects will run more smoothly. Teams will reach deadlines more quickly.

The same applies to events — a well-run event, whether it's an internal retreat or a conference for customers in your industry, can inspire and motivate even the most curmudgeonly attendee. Run inefficiently, however, that same event becomes counterproductive to your goals.

Figuring Out What Efficient Meetings and Events Look Like

The keys to efficiency and success are knowing how to convey key information clearly in as little time as possible. It sounds obvious, but companies lose thousands of hours of productivity a year by holding meetings that involve employees who are not involved in the particular issue or in which conversations stray off point so that meetings drag on without clear direction or conclusion. The mere act of holding a meeting can prevent additional hours of collective productivity in travel, preparation, and lost "flow" time as well.

If something is taking longer than it needs to, it is not efficient. Efficient employees know how to get results in less time.

Sound too good to be true? Here's an example of what efficiency looks like in action.

Alan gets to the office at 8 a.m. on Tuesday and heads over to a growing huddle in the corner of the room at 8:15 a.m. for the daily stand-up. In two sentences, he tells his team members that he closed seven bug trouble tickets the day before, and today his plan is to research a new database platform called Node. js. By 8:20 a.m., the group walks back over to their respective desks.

Alan knows that his co-worker Melissa has worked with Node.js before, and he'd like to pick her brain about her experiences with it. He pulls up her Outlook calendar to see when she's available. Their team allows meetings only in the morning so people can work without interruption in the afternoon, and no one ever holds meetings on Wednesdays. He suggests 10 a.m. today or on Thursday. When Melissa gets the request, she chooses which of those times works best for her, and the meeting is then booked on both their calendars.

Today Alan is going to grab burgers with his team for lunch and discuss what features will make it into the next release of their software. The team meets over lunch only once a week, so Alan is free to make lunch plans with his girlfriend any day but Tuesday. The time away from the office is good for his relationship and makes him a more productive programmer for the rest of the afternoon.

Before he heads out to lunch, he logs into the company's event website to check on registrations for the company's upcoming event. He'll be speaking for an hour about the technical hurdles the team overcame in their latest release, and then the product team will give a live demo. Thanks to efficiently getting the word out, registration is almost full, and everyone's excited. Alan is a little nervous to read the audience feedback for his part of the presentation, but he tries to convince himself that he'll funnel any negativity into a better performance next time. Better to know than to not know, right?

A daily stand-up at the start of the day kept everyone abreast of Alan's progress without interrupting the work day. Blocking off meetings to just the mornings leaves his creative juices to flow all afternoon without fear of being bugged, and efficient event management means Alan can grow his expertise and speaking skills without the company having to hire an event planner.

Thinking About Meeting and Event Efficiency

So now you've read an example of efficiency done right. How does your organization match up against this example? Assessing your meeting and event efficiency is the first step to improving it.

This checkup is designed to get your brainstorming juices flowing as to areas in which you can increase efficiency in your organization. There's no right or wrong answer to these questions — they are just intended to get you thinking.

How your organization approaches meetings

Consider your company's current approach to meetings in general:

- Who can call a meeting in your organization? Put another way, can anybody call a meeting?

- How are new meetings announced?

- How are changes in meeting time or location announced?

- How do participants RSVP for meetings?

- How are meeting locations determined? Is there a common tool for planning meeting rooms available?

- Who decides if a meeting will be in-person instead of over the phone or in a chat room?

- Are there any requirements that must be met before someone can call a meeting? In other words, can someone call a meeting for any reason?

- Choose an employee at random. How would you find out if she is free for a meeting on Thursday at 10 a.m.?

- How does a team of two people decide on a time and date for a meeting?

- How does a group of three or more people decide on a time and date for a meeting?

- Does your company hold any regularly scheduled meetings (such as every Friday at 4 p.m.)? If so, how many, and when?

- Do you have a dedicated conference bridge number for phone conferences?

- Does your company have a subscription to a virtual meeting service like GoToMeeting or WebEx?

- Do employees ever hold meetings in a format that is not a group of people physically gathered in the same place, same building, same town, or even same country? To save travel cost and employees being absent, can you organize a meeting using phone or video conferences?

- If an employee is home with a sick child, can he still attend a meeting? How?

- Is there any limit on the number of hours an employee is expected to spend in meetings?

  Bryce needs at least five hours to complete his sales proposal by Friday. If he attends every meeting he is required to attend this week, he will not have five hours available to work on this proposal. What recourse does Bryce have?

- If an employee feels overwhelmed by the number of meetings she is expected to attend, what should she do? Does *she* know this is what she should do?

  Jay called 17 team meetings this week. Nine of them were with no advance notice. What recourse does his team have?

- Nina is asked to participate in a meeting over her lunch break every day this week. How can Nina eat lunch?

- You are in a meeting scheduled for 9 a.m. to 10:30 a.m. It is now 10:35 a.m. and you are still in the meeting. Can you leave?

- Can employees decline meeting requests? On what basis?

- Do the topics get the needed follow-up to make the meetings worthwhile? Were proper action lists created including responsibilities and timelines?

Now think about your last ten scheduled meetings:

- Why was each meeting held?

- Were you well informed beforehand *why* the meeting was called and did you get the necessary details to prepare yourself? Did everyone come prepared or did you have to waste time to talk everyone through the topic (yet) again?

✔ How did you determine why each meeting was held? Is there a record of this information or did you make assumptions about the topic?

✔ What percentage of these meetings had agendas? How closely were these agendas followed?

How your organization approaches events

Think back to your last five events:

✔ How far in advance did you announce the event from when it actually took place?

✔ Did you track registrations?

  • If yes: Could participants self-register online, or did they have to call or e-mail a specific staff member?

  • If no: How did you estimate the number of attendees? How did the actual number of attendees compare to that estimate?

✔ How many different ways did you announce each event?

✔ How many were 100 percent sold out? What percentage of seats did you fill if not 100 percent?

✔ If you served food or provided other resources (e.g., printed handouts), how did you know how much to prepare?

✔ What percentage of registered attendees actually showed up?

✔ Did you provide nametags, and if so, were they preprinted, or did attendees have to write their own names on blank labels?

✔ What sort of check-in process did you have?

✔ Did you have a set schedule of events?

✔ How did you choose which speakers or presentations to feature?

✔ Did you have an icebreaker event or other way to encourage participants to interact?

✔ How did you distribute the schedule of events? How far ahead did you distribute it?

✔ Did you retain any planning notes or resources for future events (e.g., keep a list of vendors)?

✔ Did you have a means of contacting attendees if there was a last-minute venue change?

✔ Did you collect a list of e-mail addresses you could message after the event?

✔ What happened to any leftover event supplies? Food?

If you have loads of food left over from a meeting, find a local shelter that accepts food donations. (Some will not accept catering leftovers, so check.) Designate a person or team of people to deliver any leftovers to the shelter after the event. Remember to also donate extra plates and flatware if you have it—shelters often don't have items we take for granted, like a knife to spread peanut butter or cut a sandwich in half. Don't let good food go to waste!

✔ Did you collect feedback from attendees about the overall event?

- If yes: Did you do anything with that feedback?

- If yes: Did processing that feedback require someone to input handwritten form data into a spreadsheet?

✔ Did you collect feedback from attendees about individual speakers or presentations?

- If yes: Did you do anything with that feedback internally?

- If yes: Did you share that feedback with the presenters?

- If yes: Did processing that feedback require someone to input handwritten form data into a spreadsheet?

✔ Did attendees have a way to see who else was signed up? To interact before the event? To find and connect with one another after the event ended?

Measuring Meeting Efficiency

Measuring your meetings involves tracking the number of hours you and your employees spend sitting around a conference table, on hold on conference calls, and in one-on-ones. It also means measuring employee sentiment about meetings, because the number of minutes spent in meetings is not necessarily inefficient if your employees perceive that as time well spent. A graphic designer may think two hours a week of meetings is too many, but a project manager may be perfectly suited to 30 hours of meetings a week.

Sentiment: How do people feel about meetings?

There's no black and white when it comes to how long or how frequent efficient meetings should be, but a very strong indicator that your company is holding too many (or too few) meetings is your employees' attitudes toward them. Remember, meetings *can* be productive, informative, and even fun. They are not, on the whole, events your employees should dread or take efforts to avoid.

Survey your team with the following questions to get a better understanding of how they currently feel about the state of office meetings:

- ✔ **How many meetings do you think you participated in this past week (no looking!)?** Compare the estimate to the actual number. Feeling like they're in more meetings than they actually are is a sign of meetings fatigue.

- ✔ **How many hours do you think you spent in meetings (without adding it up)?** Compare the estimate to the actual number. Estimating a higher number means they feel meetings take up a disproportionate amount of their time.

- ✔ **How many days has it been since you last had a day with *no* meetings?** If the answer is "I don't remember" or "infinity," your employees may be crying out for meetings-free days or at least afternoons.

  If your company incorporates daily stand-up meetings at the start or end of the day, run this analysis without counting these meetings.

- ✔ **If you needed to have a meeting, do you feel you have the authority to call one?** Whether or not the correct answer here is "yes" depends on your specific company policies regarding who can schedule meetings.

- ✔ **Do you feel you ever have the ability to say "no" when you are invited to a meeting?** If your employees don't feel they have the power to decline meetings, every meeting they are forced to attend is an intrusion, no matter how productive or enjoyable.

- ✔ **Have you ever felt overwhelmed by the number of meetings you needed to attend? How did you address this feeling?** It's not necessarily a red flag if someone says "yes" — we've all felt overwhelmed at times, and when under a tight deadline sometimes a single stand-up meeting can feel like too much time away from our desks. The important part of this question is the second half. "I powered through it" or "I did nothing" are bad responses, indicating this employee doesn't feel they have any recourse or support for defending against intrusions into their schedule.

- ✔ **Do you regularly feel pressured to give up your lunch break over to meetings?** A working lunch here and there is usually unavoidable, but an employee who rarely gets to step outside or take a mental break in the middle of the day is simply not going to perform as well as one who does. If many of your employees feel their lunch breaks are regularly at risk of being co-opted by meetings, you may need to take action to defend them.

- ✔ **Overall, the number of meetings you have each week seems (circle one): just right, too high, too low.** The goal here is for every employee to feel the number of meetings in the company isn't too high or too low.

- ✔ **How do you rate the quality and efficiency of meetings?** Did you get straight to the point and were you able to address and tackle the problem or was it a waste of time, because exactly next Friday at 4 p.m. you will talk about the same stuff again?

✔ (Only for employees with flexible schedules) **Are you able to construct a satisfying schedule given your meeting obligations?** It's meaningless to offer employees the ability to set their own hours and then require everyone to be at an in-person meeting at 8 a.m. and 4:30 p.m. every day.

✔ **Does (Senior) Management lead by example?** Are they on time, come prepared, and finish on time?

Time: How many hours are spent in meetings?

Measuring time spent in or on meetings is a baseline measurement you should track over time. The nature of some organizations may require 1,000 man hours of meetings each week, although a small family-operated retail shop may only need two hours. If that 1,000-hour-a-week figure leaps to 1,200 in three months, however, it can be a signal that meetings are getting out of hand. (It can also mean there's a new project that simply requires more meetings — but if you don't know *why* there's a leap in meeting time, you need to find out.)

The following calculations can help you keep the pulse of meetings in your organization. Remember to take measurements randomly — if everyone knows this is "meetings measurement" week they may artificially alter their behaviors.

✔ What is the average length of a meeting? How does this vary across teams or departments?

✔ What is the average time between when a meeting is first announced and when it is scheduled to occur? What percentage of meetings is announced less than 24 hours before they are scheduled?

✔ What percentage of meetings end by their scheduled end time? On average, how many minutes long do meetings run?

✔ How many meetings are held in an average day?

✔ On average, how many attendees are in each meeting?

✔ What was the total amount of time spent in meetings last week?

Multiply the number of hours each employee spent in a meeting by your company's average hourly wage (or their exact hourly wages, if you have those figures available). How much did you pay in pure wages for people to attend meetings in a given week? (Again, there is no right or wrong answer here — you want to track trends over time.)

✔ How much time elapses, on average, between the scheduled start time of a meeting and the actual start time of a meeting?

✔ What percentage of attendees said at least one word at a given meeting? (Someone will have observed a sampling of meetings to track this metric.)

✔ What is the average amount of time *between* scheduled meetings? If your staff consistently has only small breaks in-between meetings, they won't be able to make effective use of that time.

✔ How much time is spent *scheduling* meetings? You may count this in administrative assistant time or count the number of e-mails in a given scheduling thread.

Knowing When You Need a Meeting (And When You Don't)

The more meetings your organization holds, the less efficient every meeting becomes. Even if every meeting has a clear purpose and sticks perfectly to its timeline, meeting-related burnout is real and pervasive. Little real work actually gets accomplished *in* a meeting, and if employees never have blocks of productive time outside of meetings, productivity becomes a real challenge.

When people feel their time is being respected and that they can trust that a meeting scheduled for 30 minutes will really just take 30 minutes (or less), attitudes improve dramatically and you have energetic attendees ready to don their brainstorming hats and put in their best effort.

How do you find the right meeting balance? You start by understanding when you *actually* need a meeting, and when there's a more efficient alternative to achieve the same end.

Considering the reasons for calling a meeting

Run through the following criteria *before* hitting Send on that calendar invite. This list of questions will not only help you determine whether or not you need a meeting, but also make sure the meetings you do have will be as efficient as possible. You may want to share this list (or a modified version) with your entire team:

✔ **Why do you want this meeting?** It's surprising how many meetings are called simply out of reflex. If you understand *why* you want to have a meeting, you can then make smart decisions regarding all the rest of the criteria in the list. In some organizations, stating an explicit "why" is a requirement for scheduling a meeting.

✔ **What is the expected outcome?** When the meeting ends, how can you objectively measure whether or not it was a success? If the meeting is for status updates, "success" would be hearing an update from each team member. If it's a planning meeting, you'll want to exit with (you guessed it!) a plan, and so on.

✔ **What alternatives are there to holding this meeting?** The answer may honestly be "none," but other possible answers include waiting until the next meeting that's already scheduled, sending an e-mail, taking a stab at the problem on your own, or even holding a different meeting.

✔ **What kind of meeting do you need?** "Meeting" does not have to be synonymous with "a group of people sitting around the same table." You can schedule a phone call, a group video chat, or a time everyone should log in to the same electronic chat room. If your inclination is to have an in-person meeting, ask yourself what advantages being in the same room provides that another type of meeting would not.

✔ **Where will the meeting take place?** Should everyone meet in Conference Room B or at the bar around the corner? Do you need a whiteboard or a speakerphone? If you're holding a phone meeting, who will call whom — or will everyone call into a conference bridge?

✔ **Who needs to be at the meeting?** This question above all others requires the most careful deliberation. Who are the key stakeholders? Who may be offended by *not* being invited? And who doesn't need to be there? As a middle ground, you can always formally invite the people who *need* to be there and then give a more casual "heads-up, you're welcome to come if you're free" e-mail to others.

✔ **How long will this meeting take?** You get better at answering this question correctly the more often you think about it and track the length of previous meetings. When in doubt, book a little extra time for meetings where you absolutely must leave with a decision or deliverable. (Plus people are usually delighted when a meeting finishes ahead of schedule!)

✔ **How soon do you need this meeting?** Just because you had the idea for this meeting today doesn't mean the meeting needs to *be* today. Participants will be less harried and better prepared if you give them ample notice.

Setting a baseline company-wide meetings policy

It's not enough (and in fact, can really backfire) to discourage meetings or provide new communication tools in the absence of clear meetings *policies*. I'm not suggesting a human resources tome, but rather a single page of clear, human-readable guidelines that employees can use to increase their own efficiency or clear up disagreements about whether an action is in line with company goals.

Depending on the size of your organization, you may want some company-wide policies ("no meetings on Tuesdays") and then give each department the flexibility to build on them ("no meetings in the afternoon for the IT department").

You should also think about who should write and distribute the new guidelines. Create them together with various people of various levels of the organization to earn everyone's buy-in.

Some items you may want to address in your company's meeting guidelines:

✔ **Require a "why":** Simply requiring organizers to list a single phrase or sentence describing *why* they are holding a given meeting is the best way to stop unnecessary meetings in their tracks. Have people enter this reason in the description of the calendar event, and send gentle reminders until everyone gets on the same page. Even better: Talk to your IT department about adding a custom field to your internal calendar.

✔ **Meeting rooms:** Ask your IT department to add the meetings rooms as an e-mail address to your e-mail list (e.g., in Outlook), so that you can book them at the same time you send the invitation to your colleagues. This way you can also easily check the availability of the meeting rooms in advance.

✔ **Scheduling:** Trading e-mails back and forth to arrive at the best time and day is one of the most inefficient activities a team can engage in. Use a service like www.tungle.me or internal shared calendars such as Google Calendar or Microsoft Outlook to view participants' busy and free times and arrange one-on-one meetings directly. For group scheduling, use a tool like Doodle, www.doodle.com; When Should We, www.whenshouldwe.com; or GatherGrad, www.gathergrid.com.

✔ **Time limits:** This can get tricky, but some companies set maximum meeting lengths to help keep everyone motivated and on-topic. As a more practical compromise, consider requiring at least a week's notice for meetings over one hour in length. Much more important than limiting the length of a scheduled meeting is empowering employees to *leave* meetings that run past their scheduled end times. Nothing does this better than executives honoring and reminding others of timely end times.

✔ **Frequency limits:** Is there a maximum number of meetings any given employee should be expected to attend in a given week? How about a maximum number of meetings that one person can *call*? The point of this policy is to have something specific to refer back to when addressing an employee who is abusing her meeting privileges or to release an employee from an unreasonable number of meeting obligations so he can tend to the rest of his work.

✔ **When to lay off lunch:** Are lunch meetings acceptable in your organization? How can you protect employees from having their break time perpetually encroached upon? A company policy that limits lunch meetings to once or twice a week gives employees a way to gracefully bow out of excessive lunch meetings if they need to.

✔ **Meeting-free time:** A company-wide block of time in which no one can schedule meetings is a collective *ahh* of productivity. Leaving each department to set its own blocks doesn't work very well, because interdepartmental meetings will invariably conflict. Mondays and Fridays are poor choices; I personally decline all meetings on Wednesdays to ensure I never fall too far behind on work during the week.

✔ **Recourse:** Employees have to have a place to turn when others are not honoring the meeting policies you set. Don't leave it to employees to resolve differences on their own (although they certainly *can* if they so choose). This is usually a job for human resources, but if your company is too small to have dedicated or in-house HR, then you need to explicitly appoint someone else to field and address complaints.

Addressing employees who hold too many meetings

The best, fairest, clearest company meetings policy is essentially worthless if no one enforces it. A company's executive team needs to be ruthless about defending its employees' time, because that time is a nonrenewable resource.

Additionally, employees *know* when someone is not following the guidelines, and if they see one person skirting (or leaping over) the line, they'll grow discouraged and disenchanted quickly. I've been in offices where this feeling is literally *palpable*, and that's not the sort of environment in which anyone wants to work.

Whom to address

Part of an effective company policy is to include specific instructions for reporting problems. There should be instructions on whom to talk to (for example, a manager, or Holly in Human Resources) and what supporting information, if any, is required. A report that Bob calls "lots" of meetings is far less actionable than a calendar screenshot or forwarded e-mails showing 13 meeting requests in the next four days.

With a few exceptions, most people choose to wait until a situation becomes quite dire before raising an issue. Some hope it will resolve itself, that someone else will say something, or that the relevant parties will be able to psychically intuit that there's a problem. Therefore, you may not be able to rely solely on issue reports to know when to get involved.

If someone does raise a complaint, make sure you keep this information totally anonymous. No one will ever speak up again if they fear you will "out" them as a tattletale or troublemaker.

Monitoring the overall number and quality of meetings — something you should be doing — is one way to immediately spot offenders. If you have a calendar color-coded by team and your whole screen is practically orange, then the orange team may be going a little meetings-crazy. Sometimes simply keeping your eyes open can reveal a problem — if Monty is *constantly* in the conference room with someone, you should take a peek at Monty's calendar.

When to address someone

"I've been doing it this way for 12 years" is one of the top change-resistant responses I hear in my line of work. In *every* area of business, you should address issues sooner rather than later. It is infinitely easier to have a casual chat in the elevator questioning whether Kelly may be overdoing it in the meeting request department, than to have to break Kelly of a five-year daily meeting streak.

If for whatever reason your company doesn't have meetings policies and someone's meeting-calling behavior is becoming disruptive, you can still try some of the following suggestions to get them to reduce their meeting numbers; you just have less of a defense if they disagree that their actions are problematic.

How to discuss the problem

No one (at least, I hope no one) holds meetings simply to annoy other people and disrupt their productivity. If someone calls seven meetings a day, there's probably *some* reason. If you're going to effectively redirect this behavior, you need to understand why he feels compelled to call so many meetings, and find some alternatives that still address his needs.

Here are some common reasons I've come across that lead people to organize meetings all day long.

Control issues

Micromanagers *love* meetings. It helps them feel that they have a stronger grasp on what each person is doing if they constantly get to hear updates throughout the day. Unfortunately, no one else loves being micromanaged.

I have also found that micromanagers hold the incorrect belief that constant meetings get people to deliver work faster. This is often true from their perspective — "the squeaky wheel gets the grease" and employees are apt to get the micromanager's tasks done first in hopes of avoiding Yet Another Meeting. However, this causes other work projects to suffer. There are no winners in a squeakiest wheel competition.

To keep micromanagers at bay, you need to offer them alternatives for getting regular status updates that are less intrusive than meetings. Status update forms submitted twice a day help a *lot* here, as does working with a team to set clear and realistic deadlines on a per-task basis. It's important that the person *completing* the task, not the manager, set the deadlines here, and that the manager receives a very clear message from the top that he cannot call meetings regarding deliverables that are not yet due.

More so with this personality type than any other, you also need to be very clear — in numbers, hours, and so on — about the acceptable number of meetings, and assume that they will regularly operate right up to that maximum.

Boredom or loneliness

Don't underestimate the role that *boredom* can play. Someone who schedules a meeting to discuss every minute detail of a plan may simply be masking that they have nothing else to do. This is particularly pervasive with project managers who have light project loads.

To stop this behavior, you can assign additional work or, if company culture allows it, simply make it clear that it's okay to have light workloads sometimes — so she should spend her current free time learning a new skill or on another productive endeavor until things pick back up.

Fear

Ever watched a reality show competition where certain players constantly run their decisions by their teammates, so they can absolve themselves of blame come elimination time? This same dynamic plays out in offices everyday.

If you have a meeting, the logic goes, then other people are equally responsible for the decisions made in that meeting. If a project takes a wrong turn, it's no longer *Teresa's* fault because she can go back and show proof of the 33 separate meetings where no one else suggested an alternative. (The fact that by meeting 33, all everyone wanted to do was get the heck *out* of that meeting notwithstanding.)

There's also a fear of being out of control. This is particularly true with micromanagers.

Confusion

A second fear is the fear of people finding out you are not as competent at a task as they think. In fact, I've met some extremely competent people who *still* have this fear of being "found out." If someone feels unqualified to lead a particular project, they'll be more inclined to line up meeting after meeting to make sure they're on the right track.

Few employees would ever admit to this fear, so it's a tough one to crack. Generally creating a company culture where employees can go to their managers with questions or concerns without fear of retribution is the best way to prevent confusion-induced meeting abuse. If you suspect this to be someone's problem, you can pair her with a more experienced mentor or simply a more confident partner to co-lead the project.

Improving Different Types of Meetings

There are strategies and best practices for enhancing the efficiency of each type of meeting, whether it be a last-minute gathering or a Skype chat. Review these guidelines for ideas to improve your next meeting.

Scheduled, last-minute, and impromptu meetings

If a last-minute meeting is inevitable, the organizer needs to take utmost care that it is one of the most efficient meetings in the history of the company. Table superfluous or non-time-sensitive content for a properly scheduled future meeting.

In-person meetings

Forget chairs and ask all participants (barring any disabilities, of course) to stand during meetings.

When participants are up on their feet, they're less likely to drone on or daydream.

Meetings need to end on-time. This is important for any type of meeting, but particularly when people are gathered together in the same room — there's additional pressure for everyone to stay well past the appointed end time. If the meeting organizer cannot be relied upon to end in a timely manner, someone else needs to be the appointed timekeeper.

Virtual meetings

Remote or freelance team members need to be able to join in on important meetings. To make this possible, subscribe to a virtual meeting service like GoToMeeting (www.gotomeeting.com) or WebEx (www.webex.com) so employees can schedule and spin up virtual meetings on the fly. With these services, you get a telephone conference bridge, video chat, and the ability to share computer screens — use all three or just one for a given meeting.

If employees are going to engage in virtual meetings, they need fast, reliable Internet — so provide it for the office.

Conference calls

Provide a conference bridge number for teams to have group meetings internally or with clients.

A long chain of conferencing in people's personal phone lines is just asking for trouble — no one can ever quite get the process right and invariably the second person on the chain accidentally hangs up on the subsequent five.

Provide a quiet area or room at the office for employees to field conference calls. This may not be necessary if everyone has individual offices but is mission-critical if everyone sits together in one open room. I've even seen offices with actual phone booths inside!

Interactive meetings versus lectures

Some meetings are intended to be brainstorming or knowledge-sharing events in which the participation of everyone is required. These meetings — called interactive meetings — differ from lectures, in which one person has called everyone together to make an announcement, train staff, or deliver a one-sided update.

Interactive meetings can be fantastically informative and productive, but they easily get out of hand if nobody is leading the discussion. Designate a moderator for interactive meetings. It's his job to guide discussions, pick who gets to ask the next question, and wrap things up on time (or earlier, if the situation warrants). Meetings usually do not run themselves.

When calling a meeting, clearly indicate whether a meeting is interactive (where everyone is expected to participate in discussion or idea generation) or more lecture-oriented (where one person or team is presenting to an audience). This helps attendees understand how much to prepare for any given meeting.

Videotape presentations so employees who aren't present can watch later. Watching themselves on video is also a great way for individual employees (or anyone, really!) to improve their public speaking skills. Over time, these videos can form a motivational and/or training library for your entire workforce.

Finally, provide meeting attendees with a mechanism to share feedback on the presenters and/or presentation. You can then share this feedback (perhaps edited and/or anonymized) with the presenters to help them improve in the future.

Lean style: Brief, daily meetings

Try replacing normal status meetings with stand-ups. A "stand-up" meeting is a meeting where participants literally stand up in a group and share very brief (usually under 30 seconds) updates about what they plan to accomplish that day.

Stand-ups are popular in software development teams but can work in just about any environment. Teams usually have stand-ups daily at the start of the day. The casual nature of this meeting means there's no agenda, notes, or waiting for everyone to show up.

Discovering Alternatives to Meetings

Deciding *not* to have a meeting does not mean deciding *not* to communicate. There are a myriad of other options for keeping team members abreast of status updates, soliciting feedback, and building plans for the future without having to gather everyone for a meeting.

Creating ambient awareness with internal messaging tools

Too often, teams hold meetings solely to share updates about what each person has been working on. Although there's some value in this — collecting a team together can spur conversations or discussions that wouldn't otherwise happen — there's also a cost to holding meetings with the sole purpose of *disseminating* information.

You can keep the left hand informed of the right hand's activities without holding a meeting. Meetings are better suited for collaborative activities like brainstorming or planning.

When teams get in the swing of things, using internal communication tools to provide status updates not only frees up a bit more time, but also provides the opportunity to glean a better, more thorough understanding of what everyone else is up to. Instead of waiting for meetings to hear how far along Elisabeth is on her new design, her teammates can be more aware of her activities throughout the day.

I call this "ambient awareness," and you can cultivate it with the right toolset, including the following.

Microblogging

Light like instant messaging or chatting, but without the same expectation of immediacy, microblogs are steadily appearing in an increasing number of organizations.

Each employee can post snippets of text, images (such as design mockups or photographs), and even video to the company microblog; join groups of other users (e.g., a team or area of interest); and subscribe to updates from specific other users or groups. They can then read others' updates as time permits, leaving comments or feedback where appropriate. For example, at the end of the day Nathan can take a peek at Elisabeth's update page to see her latest design mockup. As employees get used to posting tiny snapshots of their day, everyone becomes more aware of what everyone else is doing.

Twitter is a popular microblogging platform for public use, although it doesn't currently offer a private internal version. You can build your own internal network using Status.net (`www.status.net`), Salesforce.com's Chatter (`www.salesforce.com`), or The Hall (`www.hall.com`).

Wikis

A wiki is a living document — a single article that multiple people can edit (sometimes even at the same time, depending on the technology platform). Wikipedia.org is probably the most well-known wiki. When your team employs wikis — especially for tasks of a collaborative nature, such as tracking team to-do lists or product feature lists — team members can not only see the exact current state of things, but can add their own input directly.

See Chapter 16 for more on writing efficient guidelines for these internal communication tools to prevent any of these meeting alternatives from becoming less efficient than holding an actual meeting.

Standardizing cross-department status updates

Another way to avoid meetings that are solely for status updates is to provide a clear, explicit way for each employee to provide regular updates that are accessible to the entire company. Even if no one logs in to look at what Tina in accounting has been up to, they always have the ability to do so if they so choose.

If you don't have an internal system into which you can integrate individual status updates — and most companies do not — then whipping up a simple Web form will do the trick nicely. My favorite easy-to-use form creation services include Formstack (`www.formstack.com`), Wufoo (`www.wufoo.com`), and FormAssembly (`www.formassembly.com`).

Distribute the resulting URL to the form — which doesn't need much more than a field for a person's name and a three-sentence overview of what she did that day — to all your employees, along with clear guidelines on how often updates are expected (such as daily by 5 p.m., or every Thursday by 10 a.m.).

All of the these form creation services give you the option to have the reports routed to a particular email address and/or saved to a database. Depending on your company's technology environment, sharing the status updates company-wide can be as simple as downloading the status updates into an Excel file once a day and posting it to a shared file server.

The downside to ambient communication tools is that you need to trust that your employees will actually read them. The benefit to an organized meeting is that people have no choice but to participate and listen. Make the expectations clear for how often internal status updates, microblogging, and the like should be consumed, and make it clear that meetings will need to resume if employees are perpetually out of step.

Holding Efficient Events and Conferences

Events and conferences hosted by your organization are like meetings on a much larger scale, and with less predictable participants. An event can range from inviting a handful of customers to the office for a demo of the new product line, to a three-day conference with thousands of participants from around the world.

The right time to have an event

The right time to throw an event is when *you have a reason to throw the event.*

Simply thinking it would be fun or interesting to throw an event is not necessarily a good reason to throw one. This is how many companies find themselves with large rooms full of bored attendees (or, worse, large rooms sparsely populated with bored attendees). If your organization is new to events, start small with a single speaker and pizza. You can grow to a giant, internationally renowned conference in time.

Get the word out

Gone are the days when you can issue a press release announcing your event and call it done. Especially in the beginning, you need to publicize your plans in as many places as possible: the local newspaper, industry blogs, your website, local and industry event calendars, your customer mailing list, Twitter, Facebook, and Craigslist, to name a few. Not sure where to start? Search the Internet as though *you* were trying to find an event likes yours to attend — what places come up?

The efficient approach to drumming up attendees for your event lies in tracking where the people who show up came from. This means trying a little of everything in the beginning and closely tracking who signs up, and from where. After you have a clearer picture of where to find the most (or the best) attendees, you'll know where to focus your efforts in the future. Positive events also have a tendency to beget additional future attendees thanks to word of mouth from past participants.

Efficient event registration

Use an electronic event registration service like Eventbrite (www.event brite.com) or Brown Paper Tickets (www.brownpapertickets.com) or simply LinkedIn to create and track signups. Even if the event is free, you still want people to sign up so you have an accurate head count. Listing your event on these sites also provides a marketing boost, as you appear on their overall event calendars. These sites include payment integration, the ability to print nametags and check-in lists on the fly, and even event websites to share additional details.

Keep attendees in the loop

The more information you provide beforehand, the better prepared your attendees will be. Sometimes additional details can also convince people who were on the fence to sign up.

Before the event (as far before as possible), populate the event website with clear directions to the location; related resources regarding the speakers and/or presentation; a schedule; and a list of fellow attendees. If there will be reason for extended interaction or team formation, you may also set up a group mailing list for attendees to chat before and after.

If you used an online registration service, it should have group messaging capability built-in.

Effective icebreakers

One of the key reasons to hold an event instead of simply distributing a newsletter is to get a group of people interacting in the same place. If everyone comes in, sits down, and leaves again without saying a word to one another, you missed a big opportunity. Finding ways to help your attendees connect with one another is a hallmark of an efficient event.

Justin Martenstein, an icebreaker designer and co-organizer of Ignite Seattle, has seen many events off to a great start with the right activity. "The key to an effective icebreaker is giving attendees the chance to work together to create something," shares Martenstein. "Pick two basic building blocks — say, marshmallows and skewers, or paper and tape — and a goal, like constructing the tallest tower or the longest bridge, and let the teams take it from there."

Assign an outgoing employee the task of encouraging groups of three to five people, roping strangers onto teams together. Some participants are shyer than others, so it's important not to make involvement mandatory. However, "even the people who aren't on teams should still have something to watch or strike up a conversation over." Your event will start off on a high note of energy, and now that attendees have had a chance to interact, they'll be livelier during discussions and Q&A sessions.

Follow up after the event

Take advantage of the residual positive energy from your event by sending at least one follow-up message to attendees. If you have an electronic feedback form, include the link. If there are downloadable PDFs and/or if event videos are posted online, include links to those, too. You can also include supplementary information about the presentation and/or speakers.

The purpose of your event should drive the content of your follow-up e-mail. If you're trying to establish authority in your field, be informative. If you're trying to drum up new business, highlight your latest product and share a special coupon just for attendees. Invite attendees to sign up for your organizations' mailing list or subscribe to your blog.

Afterward, write up a resource summary for future company event planners. How much did food cost per person? How close (or off) were your food estimates? How many people showed up versus the number who RSVPed? I know organizations that have their events so nailed down that they know how many slices of pizza to order for a given-size crowd down to the half-slice, and they got there by meticulously tracking (and crunching) data over time.

Collecting Event-Specific Data

There are event metrics that may be readily apparent that your organization can improve upon in the future — perhaps there wasn't enough pizza or you chose a venue without Internet access — but, as the saying goes, you don't know what you don't know. Soliciting feedback from participants (including speakers and presenters themselves) is the most efficient way to make every event you throw even better than the last.

Methods for data collection

Choices for collecting data, such as attendee RSVPs and speaker feedback, include those discussed in the following sections.

Electronic surveys

Build a survey by using a tool like SurveyMonkey (`www.surveymonkey.com`), Formstack (`www.formstack.com`), or Google Forms (`www.google.com/docs`). These services let you create attractive forms with multiple pages and optional advanced features. Mobile versions mean participants can vote right from their seats.

Best of all, they remove any need for manually entering form responses into the computer — you can see real-time graphs of the results ("93 percent of attendees rated Tony five stars") and download all the responses into a spreadsheet.

Using an online survey gives you another chance to capture attendees' e-mail addresses for future follow-up. If you want the maximum number of responses, though, don't *require* an e-mail address to submit the form.

Printed forms

The most common way to solicit feedback is to hand out printed feedback forms and pencils after each event or session. Your team then collects these forms and tallies up the results by hand or in a computer spreadsheet.

The advantage to printed forms is they're easy to hand out and they're right in people's hands. However, they're also easy to throw away or ignore, and processing the forms requires manual effort afterward. If you have to stick with paper, limit your asking to just one or two questions.

Social media

If you have a tech-savvy crowd, you can eschew formal feedback forms and ask people to tweet feedback in real time by using your event's hashtag. A hashtag is a single word prepended with a pound sign (#), such as *#wwdc* for Apple's WorldWide Developer Conference. You can search only for messages that contain this hashtag.

What data to collect

Although the best feedback surveys are brief, the following questions can help you decide on which questions make the final cut:

- How engaging was a given speaker? Funny? Informative? Nervous?
- Name one thing you learned at the event.
- What did you think of the food? (Give a rating of 1 to 5.)
- Did you get lost on your way here?
- Who would you have preferred to hear speak?
- What topic do you wish was covered that was not?
- Describe the icebreaker event in one word.
- How did you hear about this event?
- Would you come again? Would you recommend it to others?

Share feedback about specific presenters *with* those presenters. Just as you can benefit from hearing attendees' complaints and suggestions, so can the event speakers. Don't filter out negative comments unless they are truly abusive or offensive.

Instead of having people write sentences or circle numbers, just have them tear the paper at the appropriate mark to indicate their vote. This avoids having to distribute pencils and is so quick and easy that it encourages greater participation.

When it's time to outsource event management

When an organization first starts hosting events, the responsibility usually falls to an employee with an interest in event planning and/or to the office manager. This is usually fine for the occasional brown bag lunch or evening meet-and-greet — or even for one annual conference or retreat — but at a certain point, the event management responsibilities start encroaching on the rest of that person's job.

The sentiments of the person who's currently in charge of event planning play a large part in dictating when it's time to outsource or pass the torch. You don't want a valuable employee to burn out because she's so harried fielding catering calls in-between her normal daily tasks. On the other hand, some people were just born for event management, and may welcome the temporary pressures as a break from a more monotonous day job.

Don't just assume that Tory will keep on handling event management just because she's been doing it for the last three years. Keep an open line of communication and check in. Make sure she knows exactly who to talk to when she's ready to step back (or step down).

There may also come a time when your company's event management needs exceed Tory's capabilities. Perhaps you're hosting events more frequently, or on a larger scale, and Tory is better suited for handling office birthday parties. Don't let your appreciation for Tory's past efforts hinder your organization's ability to put on events of a higher caliber.

If you need to relieve Tory of event management duties and she resists, look for a compromise — maybe she can continue planning intra-office events (just not external ones), or she can serve as the main point of contact for the new event planner.

Using Best Practices for Meeting Management

Managing meetings and events efficiently involves adopting some best practices, including designating days where no meetings are allowed, using technology to avoid double-booking, and keeping tabs on your organization's use of meetings to recalibrate as necessary.

Have a No Meetings Day

One day each week, don't allow anyone to schedule any meetings.

Whenever possible, No Meetings Day should extend to client and sales meetings, too. The point of this day is to give employees long periods of time to do work, write, research — anything they need or want to do — with the security of knowing that they will not be interrupted. When employees can come to trust that this one day a week, they will be left alone to tackle meaty projects and whittle down their task lists, I've seen seismic shifts in attitude and efficiency. Employees get to catch up and recharge without guilt or defensiveness.

No Meetings Day is an all-or-nothing proposition. The moment one 10 a.m. meeting sneaks in, the premise is ruined. No meetings means *no meetings*. Upper management needs to model this behavior and fully respect the boundary of the day. The potential frustration of having to wait one day for a meeting is far outweighed by the gains in sentiment and output across the office.

You can counter resistance by reminding people that no meetings does not mean no communication. Teams can still e-mail, instant message, microblog, and edit wikis all they want. What they *can't* do is require every team member's attention during a specific period of time during the day. It's up to each individual how available she makes herself by using other communication channels.

This is my personal all-time favorite efficiency practice, and the one I would have the hardest time giving up. Every week, I look forward to the seemingly endless expanse of productive time that is Wednesday. Even if your entire company has the most inefficient meetings possible — constant, impromptu, unstructured meetings that run late — you can benefit from this best practice.

This concept is admittedly less helpful in retail or customer service positions where the very nature of the job involves lots of interactions or meetings, or for roles that almost never have meetings. But for today's increasingly large crop of knowledge workers, a day without meeting interruptions can make a tremendous difference on productivity.

Use electronic scheduling

Before the proliferation of electronic group scheduling services, the most efficient way to get seven people in the same room at the same time was for one person to throw out three different time/date combinations and then tally the resulting e-mail responses to choose the most-favored one. Consider how poorly this scaled when each of those seven people was also trying to arrange seven other meetings.

There is absolutely no reason to schedule meetings like that any longer.

The first step in efficient electronic scheduling is to have each employee use an electronic calendar, like Microsoft Outlook or Google Calendar. These individual calendars are the baseline for sharing availability internally or with clients. Most calendaring systems let the calendar owner decide how much detail to share; for example, she may share an editable version of her calendar with full details with her boss, a read-only version with full details with her immediate team members, and a simple "busy/free" view for clients that lets them see when she is available for meetings but no details about her other appointments.

Electronic calendaring services like Tungle.me (`www.tungle.me`) integrate with calendaring systems like Google Calendar to allow third parties to schedule meetings. Microsoft Outlook calendar gives you the option to add different time zones to your calendar, which is handy for planning intercontinental conference or video calls.

The most efficient systems ask the meeting requestor to suggest at least *two* times, and ultimately leave the final choice to the calendar owner. Until the final meeting time is chosen, all proposed times are shown as "busy" on the meetings calendar to prevent double bookings. When the meeting is booked, it adds the meeting to all parties' calendars. That's what I call efficient!

Stay on top of changes in sentiment

When a team embarks on a new project, there's usually lots of excitement in the air and everyone is gung-ho about going the extra mile. Meetings are full of fresh ideas and big plans. Sometimes, people come early and stay late just to get to work on it, and teams take pride in grabbing a late-night pizza together to power through another deliverable. These sorts of high-energy meetings are generally very productive and minimally intrusive.

Then reality sets in, and things change. Meetings are more of an intrusion than an inspiration. As deadlines loom, people grow increasingly resentful of the now-established pattern of constant meetings because they want to get back to their desks to actually *deliver* something.

This sort of shift in sentiment is common, yet few organizations actively plan ahead for it. Instead, they usually spend some amount of resources *recovering* from it.

Awareness is the best defense in this scenario. After all, actively dissuading those initial excited meetings can derail the momentum needed to get a new project off the ground. However, at the *first* signs of meeting fatigue, someone — usually the project lead — needs to take action and rope back meeting frequency and length to normal levels.

Chapter 19

Painless Project Management

- -

- -

*I*nternal project management is usually rife with inefficiencies. Those inefficiencies are often the hardest to spot because it's easy to believe that if you're planning and managing a project you're being efficient. After all, you're getting work done, delegating tasks, and accomplishing things, right?

Done efficiently, project management has the potential to leave a far-reaching positive influence on every aspect of your business. Morale improves as employees enjoy a sense of accomplishment and come to trust that *announced* projects will one day become *completed* projects. Productivity increases when every team member has clear responsibilities and no time is lost to confusion, miscommunication, or duplication. And the business thrives each time an efficiently organized project meets its objectives.

In this chapter, I go over the architecture of efficient project planning so you can see how much (or little) it resembles your own internal process. I also cover different project management approaches like Six Sigma and Lean so you can find the approach that fits your organization best.

Discovering What Efficient Project Management Looks Like

Halleck has a plan. Today, his company sends out all of its client invoices through the mail. On invoice day, employees try to look extra busy or take sick days because they know they will be roped into helping print, address, and stuff envelopes. Although spreading the manual invoicing labor around helps keep any one person from dying of boredom, ultimately it robs everyone of one productive afternoon a month. Halleck wants to change this.

This project will save time and frustration, but not in a hugely quantifiable way, so Six Sigma is not a good choice for implementation. Instead, Halleck chooses to run this project Lean-style, identifying the wastes present in the current way of doing things and then setting a clear path for how the organization can quickly eliminate those wastes with an electronic alternative.

After mapping out the current invoicing process, Halleck sees some types of Lean waste right away. Overprocessing is a huge waste: Is it really necessary for accounting to manually click "print" on every single client file, walk over to the printer, divide into batches, hand each batch out to a different employee, hand-write addresses on each envelope, stuff and stamp each envelope, and then collect all the mail each and every month? This is too many hours of ongoing work that can be replaced with an electronic solution. All that walking to the printer, envelope stuffing, and handing out envelopes is also unnecessary motion. The days it takes for the customers to receive invoices in the mail, process them, and send back payment is also a significant "waiting" waste.

As a first step, Halleck implements the Plan-Do-Check-Act (PDCA) cycle over a week's time, choosing a sub-group of existing clients with whom he has a personal relationship to try out electronic invoicing. If there are any issues, this group is most likely to be understanding and most likely to give constructive feedback.

Halleck is the project owner, defining the goal ("100 percent of customer invoices will be generated, sent, and tracked electronically within two months"), outlining the steps necessary for reaching the goal, setting due dates for each one, and assembling a project team. Each person will be responsible for his own tasks, but it's up to Halleck to make sure each person has the resources he needs, is on-time, and actually delivers. If a team member falls short, it's up to Halleck to either take that task on himself or reassign it.

Even if you don't read another page of this book, and do nothing else to improve your internal project management efficiency, at least do this: Assign every project or goal an *owner*. If there's no one person in charge of assigning tasks, naming deliverables, clarifying goals, or checking on progress, even the most qualified team in the world, executing each of their roles perfectly, will result in serious confusion and most likely failure.

Performing an Internal Project Management Checkup

Knowing more about how your organization *currently* handles project management often sheds a lot of light on things you can do more efficiently. Consider the following scenarios and questions.

How efficiently are you planning projects?

The following questions can help you understand just how efficiently your organization is setting up your project plans:

- **Does your company have a formal process for defining projects?** Not having a process — even a basic outline — not only leaves room for forgetting key parts of a plan, but means that project plans across departments don't look the same.

- **How do you choose which project to tackle next?** If you don't have selection criteria, you may be ignoring critical projects in favor of less-important ones.

- **Who decides who's in charge of each project? Is there a backup person?** If there's no project owner, there's no one fully responsible for its success. I've found that having a project owner is *the* most important component of successful project management.

- **How will you find out what projects another team is working on?** When the proverbial left hand doesn't know what the right hand is doing, you risk duplication or incompatible results across teams.

- **Does every project have an end date?** An end date is a required part of every project. You need to name a day the project should be complete.

- **Does every project have clearly defined roles?** If every participant is simply "working" on the project, you risk many tasks going undone and unnoticed. Formal roles afford responsibility, and a sense of responsibility often causes people to step up to do better work.

- **Does every project have a goal?** A project without an end goal can never truly complete, and therefore is not a project at all (see the sidebar, "A project by any other name just isn't a project").

- **Does your organization account for risk in its project plans?** Every project contains inherent risks. Assuming that everything will go exactly according to plan is an invitation for fatal project derailment. Planning ahead for risks is the best way to minimize their impact.

- **How do team members know what to do next?** Waiting for someone else to tell you what to do is *waiting*, one of the seven wastes of Lean. Guessing at what to do next is similarly wasteful. Have defined roles and timelines for every member of your project team.

- **Are projects decided and assigned from the top-down, or do departments participate in planning their own projects?** Involving at least some of the people who are responsible for executing a project in its planning phase ensures a more realistic, holistic path.

A project by any other name just isn't a project

People often confuse the following two terms with project:

✔ **Process:** A *process* is a series of routine steps to perform a particular function, such as a procurement process or a budget process. A process isn't a one-time activity that achieves a specific result; instead, it defines *how* a particular function is to be done every time. Processes like the activities that go into buying materials are often parts of projects.

✔ **Program:** This term can describe two different situations. First, a *program* can be a set of goals that gives rise to specific projects, but, unlike a project, a program can never be completely accomplished. For example, a health-awareness program can never completely achieve its goal (the public will never be totally aware of all health issues as a result of a health-awareness program), but one or more projects may accomplish specific results related to the program's goal (such as a workshop on minimizing the risk of heart disease). Second, a program sometimes refers to a group of specified projects that achieve a common goal.

How efficiently are you executing on projects?

Having the greatest project plan in the world isn't much help if you don't see it to fruition. The following questions can help you determine just how successful your organization is at following through:

✔ **What happens when a project milestone is missed?** The sky doesn't have to fall, but missed milestones need to be investigated, their causes addressed, and subsequent milestones reset.

✔ **What happens when a team runs out of resources?** It's not efficient for teams to simply cease to continue, just as it's not efficient for them to casually consume additional resources. Teams need to understand how to adjust the course to make due with the resources they have, or where they can find additional resources — whether that be time, money, man hours, or something else.

✔ **What percent of milestones are met?** It's normal to miss milestones occasionally, but many organizations are horrified to learn they almost never *meet* a deadline.

✔ **How do team members stay abreast of others' progress?** Efficient project teams communicate to share best practices, successes, and unexpected obstacles for the benefit of all other team members.

✔ **What happens on a project's due date?** A project should have a formal checkpoint, whether it's a meeting, an e-mail announcement, or another appropriate process, to verify a project's completion with its audience and plan follow-up. No one should ever assume that a project is done simply because its due date has passed.

✔ **Do your employees consider due dates to be concrete or suggestions?** When an organization reaches the point that few people take deadlines seriously, it's difficult to get *anything* done. This calls for a serious, top-down review of how deadlines are set, and a ruthless pursuit of accurately estimated milestones that teams consistently meet.

How efficiently are you reaching company goals?

Executing every project plan is great — if those project plans ultimately achieve company goals. Find out how efficiently you're using projects to reach milestones with these questions:

✔ **Does your company have goals?** A shocking number do not — or at least, they are not written down or understood by everyone involved. If you don't have a goal, you don't know if you're successful.

✔ **How many company goals have you reached?** More unmet than met goals may indicate inefficient project management, or unrealistic goals.

✔ **How do you track goal progress?** Although some goals are black and white, most involve a steady path to the ultimate end. Tracking progress towards your organization's goals lets everyone see how close you are to succeeding, which can be motivational and informational.

As a measurement exercise to explore how clear your goals are, run your company's current goals by a spouse (or a complete stranger, it doesn't matter). By asking you qualifying questions (such as "How much net profit did you earn this fiscal year?"), can they tell whether or not you've met these goals? If they aren't sure how to figure it out, it may be a sign that your goals are too vague.

A goal is objectively measureable. "Happy employees" is a great idea, but a subpar goal. How happy is happy? Is one unhappy employee too many? A better goal would be 100 percent employee retention after one year, or a 95 percent positive response to anonymous annual evaluations. Heck, "decibels of laughter at the holiday party" is more measureable!

Exploring Project Management Styles

If one specific approach to project management worked for every company in every situation, then there would only be one approach. However, organizations and even specific projects within the same organization frequently have differing needs. There is no *one* most efficient project management style; rather, one style will be most efficient for *your* situation. In the next few pages, I give you the lowdown on the most common types to help you narrow down your search for the best project management fit.

Managing with Six Sigma

Six Sigma project management is meant for big, ambitious, quantitative change. If you need to slash department expenditures by 80 percent or produce the same amount of product at the same level of quality in 20 percent of the time, Six Sigma will give you the toolsets (and the algorithms) to make it happen.

What a Six Sigma project looks like

Every Six Sigma project follows a standardized and systematic method known as *DMAIC (Define-Measure-Analyze-Improve-Control)*, a formalized problem-solving process. The DMAIC process can improve any type of process in any organization and thus improve its efficiency and effectiveness:

- ✔ **Define:** Set the context and objectives for the project.

- ✔ **Measure:** Get the baseline performance and capability of the process or system being improved.

- ✔ **Analyze:** Use data and tools to understand the cause-and-effect relationship in the process or system.

- ✔ **Improve:** Develop the modifications that lead to a validated improvement in the process or system.

- ✔ **Control:** Establish plans and procedures to ensure that the improvements are sustained.

DMAIC is applied by highly trained practitioners who complete improvement projects that are managed to financial targets. In DMAIC, business processes are improved by following a structured method with set steps, or *tollgates*. Only as you start and complete one step are you ready to move on to the next. After moving through all the steps, and only when you can show that the DMAIC project has generated breakthrough benefit, can you then say you've completed a Six Sigma project.

Prior to applying DMAIC, you may need to construct a SIPOC, which stands for Suppliers-Inputs-Process-Outputs-Controls. A SIPOC is a process optimization tool that gives you a big picture of the landscape that you're trying to change.

You build a SIPOC from the inside out, beginning at the center, with the process — of course! It's a six-step approach:

1. Identify the process you want to map and define its scope and boundary points.

   Using action verbs, describe what the process is supposed to do, and in how much time. Define its starting and ending points.

2. Identify the outputs.

   What are the products and the services that will be produced by the process?

3. Define by name, title, or organizational entity the recipients (the customers) of the outputs.

4. Define the customer requirements; what do the customers expect?

   What will they demand? What will they be entitled to in their fair exchange of value?

5. Define the inputs to the process.

   Identify the human, capital, information, materials, and natural resources required by the process to produce the identified outputs.

6. Identify the sources (suppliers) of the inputs.

The Six Sigma approach to project management

Six Sigma projects reach for the stars. If your end goal is not a Six Sigma improvement — defined as a project with an improvement of 70 percent or greater — then it's probably not a good fit for the Six Sigma approach (even though it may be a completely worthwhile project on its own merits).

Everything in a Six Sigma project needs to be measurable *and* measured. You can often stretch certain projects to fit the measuring requirement — such as quantifying employee sentiment via surveys for a project on creating a happier workplace, or organizing a manufacturing floor to use space more efficiently by quantifying feet walked or steps removed. But Six Sigma is better suited for more concrete goals such as expense reduction and product quality improvement.

Six Sigma uses the metric CTX, which stands for *Critical to X* (where X may be quality, cost, delivery time, etc.). This refers to the *cause* of X. Working backward on Critical to Cost, for example, some of the causes may be the cost of raw materials, labor costs (for the amount of time it takes to create a finished product or service), and the prices competitors charge for the same or similar result.

Six Sigma places a particular focus on reducing defects. After all, the term *six sigma* — which now refers to the entire system — originally referred specifically to a process with 3.4 or fewer defects per million opportunities. The Six Sigma equation $y = f(x) + E$ is all about reducing E, the errors, and every opportunity for reducing E should be considered in Six Sigma project planning.

Leading with Lean

Lean projects focus ruthlessly on eliminating the unnecessary, and on the needs of a customer. With Lean, everything is called into question. Why are you keeping inventory? Why is that piece of equipment in its current location? How does Step 14 impact the end customer? Lean project management is a reliable way to literally map out the big picture and identify all the potential efficiency improvements and waste reductions possible along the way.

What a Lean project looks like

A Lean project follows the Plan-Do-Study-Act (PDCA) cycle, as follows:

> ✔ **During the *plan* phase, objectively describe the change you intend to make.** Identify the processes you intend to change, and brainstorm improvement ideas. Define the steps needed to make the change, and form a prediction of the results of the change. Use data quality and analysis tools to support the plan development.
>
> ✔ **Use the *do* phase to implement the plan in a trial or prototype environment — on a small scale and under controlled conditions.** Keep it small enough to conduct the test quickly, but large enough for the results to be statistically valid.
>
> ✔ **In the *check* or *study* phase, examine the results of your trial or prototype.** Quantify the extent to which the changes you made improved the trial process, and extrapolate the results to predict the effects on the larger process.
>
> ✔ **In the *act* phase, implement the changes on the full scale of the process.** Update the value-stream map, standardized work, and specifications, and verify process performance. Report out the results.

The entire PDCA cycle should take place within one week.

Lean is a visual process. Be sure to make drawings, take pictures and video, draw charts, and graph activities throughout the process. Because visuals are so communicative, they speed up the process and document the changes made.

The Lean approach to project management

A Lean approach starts with literally mapping out the process that your project hopes to change or implement. At every step, you keep track of measures such as time taken to execute, wait time, shipping time, and number of defects. As you carefully explore this map, you try to reduce these numbers as much as possible; remove steps entirely; and remove any of the seven types of Lean waste that you see. Basically, every step that your organization takes should *directly* impact the end customer in a positive way, and all other steps should be eliminated or at the very least called into question.

The seven kinds of waste in Lean are waiting, overproduction, the mere existence of inventory, needless motion (for example, reaching behind you for supplies), extra processing, defects, and unnecessary transport.

Discovering extreme project management with Agile

Agile Project Management isn't for every organization — its rapid pace and culture of constant, *face-to-face* communication are a radical shift from how most people conduct business. Used mostly by software companies that have constant deployment cycles, more and more industries are catching on to the Agile way.

To accommodate frequent inspection and adaptation, Agile projects work in iterations (smaller segments of the overall project). On Agile projects, you still have the same type of work that is involved on a traditional waterfall project: You have to create requirements and designs, develop your product, and if necessary, integrate your product with other products. You test the product, fix any problems, and deploy it for use. However, instead of completing these steps for all of your product features at once, you break the project into iterations, also called *sprints*.

What an Agile project looks like

In Stage 1, the product owner identifies product vision. The product vision is your project's destination; it's a definition of what your product is, how it will support your company or organization's strategy, who will use the product, and why people will use the product. On longer projects, revisit the product vision about once a year.

In Stage 2, the product owner creates a product roadmap. The product roadmap is a high-level view of the product requirements, with a loose time frame for when you will develop those requirements. Identifying product requirements and then prioritizing and roughly estimating the effort for those requirements allow you to establish requirement themes and identify requirement gaps. Revise the product roadmap biannually with support from the development team.

In Stage 3, the product owner creates a release plan. The release plan identifies a high-level timetable for the release of working software. The release serves as a mid-term goal that the team can mobilize around. An Agile project will have many releases, with the highest-priority features appearing first. You create a release plan at the beginning of the product vision. The product vision is your project's destination; it's a definition of what your product is, how it will support your company or organization's strategy, who will use the product, and why people will use the product. On longer projects, revisit the product vision about once a year.

In Stage 4, the product owner, the Scrum Master, and the development team plan sprints, also called iterations, and start creating the product within those sprints. Sprint planning sessions take place at the start of each sprint. During sprint planning, the Scrum team determines a sprint goal, with requirements that support the goal and can be completed in the sprint, and outlines how to complete those requirements.

In Stage 5, during each sprint, the development team has daily Scrum meetings to coordinate the day's priorities. In the daily Scrum meeting, you discuss what you completed yesterday, what you will work on today, and any roadblocks you have, so that you can address issues immediately.

In Stage 6, the Scrum team holds a sprint review. In the sprint review, at the end of every sprint, you demonstrate the working product to the product stakeholders.

In Stage 7, the Scrum team holds a sprint retrospective. The sprint retrospective is a meeting where the Scrum team discusses how the sprint went and plans for improvements in the next sprint. Like the sprint review, you have a sprint retrospective at the end of every sprint.

The Agile approach to project management

Agile approaches are based on an empirical control method — a process of making decisions based on the realities observed in the actual project. In the context of software development methodologies, an empirical approach is very effective in both new product development and enhancement and upgrade projects. When you do frequent and firsthand inspections of the work to date, you can make immediate adjustments, if necessary. Empirical control requires:

- ✔ **Transparency:** Everyone involved on an Agile project knows what is going on and how the project is progressing.

- ✔ **Frequent inspection:** The people who are invested in the product and process the most should regularly evaluate the product and process.

- ✔ **Adaptation:** Make adjustments quickly to minimize problems; if inspection shows that you should change, then change immediately.

Agile's four values

Agile is guided by a manifesto outlining four key project management values:

- ✔ **Individuals and interactions over processes and tools:** Agile prescribes in-person communication over e-mails and memos when possible, under the belief that this is the clearest, most efficient way to communicate.

- ✔ **Working software over comprehensive documentation:** In Agile, the term *barely sufficient* is actually a compliment — it means a support is just good enough to enable the end result, which is plenty good enough for Agile. Overly detailed documentation is referred to as *gold-plated* and discouraged.

✔ **Customer collaboration over contract negotiation:** Although traditional companies only interface with customers at two or three points — namely, when the client asks for a product/service and when they accept delivery — an Agile team refers back to the customer again and again for feedback. The "customer" may be an outside person paying for a product, or another internal department requesting a deliverable.

✔ **Responding to change over following a plan:** Agile project management expects change to outpace a team's ability to rework its plans. Team members are empowered and even encouraged to deviate from the set plan and make different (presumably better) decisions in the moment. Then the larger plan can be reworked later.

The 12 principles of Agile

Below is the list of Agile principles, modified slightly to remove specific references to software development (because anyone can be Agile!):

1. Our highest priority is to satisfy the customer through early and continuous delivery of valuable results.

2. Welcome changing requirements, even late in development. Agile processes harness change for the customer's competitive advantage.

3. Deliver working results frequently, from a couple of weeks to a couple of months, with a preference for the shorter timescale.

4. Business people and product creators must work together daily throughout the project.

5. Build projects around motivated individuals. Give them the environment and support they need, and trust them to get the job done.

6. The most efficient and effective method of conveying information to and within a development team is face-to-face conversation.

7. Working end product is the primary measure of progress.

8. Agile processes promote sustainable development. The sponsors, creators, and users should be able to maintain a constant pace indefinitely.

9. Continuous attention to technical excellence and good design enhances agility.

10. Simplicity — the art of maximizing the amount of work not done — is essential.

11. The best architectures, requirements, and designs emerge from self-organizing teams.

12. At regular intervals, the team reflects on how to become more effective, then fine-tunes and adjusts its behavior accordingly.

Balancing between soft and hard management styles

Every manager tends to have their own subtle stylistic differences, but management styles can more broadly be grouped into two categories: hard and soft.

Hard management is inflexible, top-down mandates. You set deadlines and dole out assignments from above, and expect them to be met without question. Tasks will be carried out *your* way. You take advantage of the ability to discipline employees who fall out of line, sometimes doing so publicly. You demand time and attention, even at the expense of other projects and employee responsibilities. This approach is very "my way or the highway."

Soft management is empathetic. You can admit that you are not perfect and do not know everything. You ask questions of and seek out people with greater subject matter expertise than you. Employees can come to you to renegotiate deadlines, responsibilities, or expectations and are given a chance to make their case.

There's a saying that soft management is harder than hard management, and I think that's very true. It's also more efficient. Hard management sees gray areas as black and white, and is not adaptive to different personalities, company cultures, and project types. Top-down demands simply don't work.

However, you don't want to go overboard on the soft and enter "softie" territory. Pushover managers who constantly tolerate subpar performance and don't engender respect among the people they manage ultimately fail when they try to effect change. They are also prime candidates for ladder climbers to walk all over and ultimately supersede. An efficient manager does encourage leadership and growth in his charges, but it shouldn't be at his own personal expense.

Reviewing Efficient Project Management Components

Regardless of the particular school of project management that you choose — or even if you manage projects by the beat of your own drum — efficient projects share a few key characteristics.

Finding the right team members

It may seem obvious, but it's true: The right team members make a world of difference in terms of not just whether your project will succeed, but also how long it will take, what quality the end goal will have, and how long the success will *last*.

When you're forming your next team, consider whether you have the following players in place:

- ✔ **Someone with core skills**: If your project is to develop or revamp custom software, you need someone on the team who can actually develop software. I can't tell you the number of times I've seen *completed* technology project plans that never even consulted a technologist. Ninety-nine times out of a hundred, not having someone with the core relevant skills involved early on means having to redo much of the project planning (and execution) work.

- ✔ **People with diverse skills**: At the same time, you don't want to develop a new software project plan with a team entirely composed of software developers. What about the end users? Who will pipe up with budgetary, human resources, and/or legal considerations that need to be fleshed out earlier rather than later? Even more relevant, it's rare for a single software developer to be able to write code, design an attractive user interface, write persuasive copy, and structure an efficient user experience. Although too many cooks *can* spoil the soup, too few cooks may lead you to believe that the only soup in the store is cabbage soup.

- ✔ **Stakeholders:** Who will be affected by the outcome of the project? If you're changing the way the company does accounting, then the accountants (or an accounting representative) needs to be involved to point out the on-the-ground implications that proposed changes may have.

- ✔ **Outsiders:** Although not always possible, an outside perspective on a project often brings fresh new ideas to the table. At the very least, the right outsider can question the status quo in smart ways. Even if the status quo is ultimately correct, it's dangerous to continue to move forward for too long without making sure the situation hasn't changed.

- ✔ **Decision makers:** Who has the power to approach (or nix) the project? Who can stand in your way? Key decision makers at least need to be invited, even if they ultimately choose not to participate in the team on a deeper level.

The mere fact that you do not include a particular player on your team can be enough to cause an entire project to fail, if that player gets jealous or feels excluded and decides to stand in your way. Always be aware of who the real decision-makers and gate-keepers are, standing between you and your project's success. Then invite them!

Composing a clear plan

No business methodology suggests achieving your organization's goals by crossing your fingers and flying by the seat of your pants. Even Agile Project Management, which largely eschews documentation and detailed project plans, encourages clear plans with goals and milestones on both a macro and micro level. Although the exact components can vary, you need at least the following pieces in your plan:

- ✔ **A clear goal** by which you measure whether or not the project is finished and successful.

- ✔ **A deadline** so team members and external audience members know when to expect the project to end.

- ✔ **A list or summary of required work** that makes the steps necessary to get from the start to the finish clear to all team participants. An efficient project plan is a *map* to the goal, not merely a list of goals.

- ✔ **A good team with assigned responsibilities** that's poised to execute on their individual assignments and not simply wait around for further instruction.

Using Project Management Best Practices

There's more to efficient project management than just having the right team and a clear plan. Learning and mastering certain project management best practices, such as assigning responsibility to others and delegating that responsibility fairly, can take your organization's success to a whole new level.

Assigning responsibility

Nothing causes disillusionment and frustration faster than bringing motivated people together and then giving them no guidance on working with one another. Two or more people may start doing the same activity independently, and other activities may be overlooked entirely. Eventually, these people find tasks that don't require coordination, or they gradually withdraw from the project to work on more rewarding assignments.

To prevent this frustration from becoming a part of your project, work with team members to define the activities that each member works on and the nature of their roles. Possible team member roles include the following:

✔ **Primary responsibility:** Has the overall obligation to ensure the completion of an activity.

✔ **Secondary or supporting responsibility:** Has the obligation to complete part of an activity.

✔ **Approval:** Must approve the results of an activity before work can proceed.

✔ **Consultation resource:** Can provide expert guidance and support if needed.

✔ **Required recipient of project results:** Receives either a physical product from an activity or a report of an activity.

You can visually represent team members' responsibilities on a Responsibility Assignment Matrix, known as a RAM. List responsibilities down the left side of the matrix, and each person or role as a column heading across the top. Within each box, use the letters P (Primary responsibility), S (Secondary responsibility), and A (Approval) to indicate the corresponding level of responsibility. Every row must have at least one letter in it, or it's an immediate sign that no one on the team has any responsibility for that deliverable.

There's a difference between responsibility, authority, and accountability. Someone with responsibility is committed to delivering a given result by a given date. A person with authority has the ability to make binding decisions, such as setting a budget amount or signing a contract. Someone who is accountable for a result faces consequences — positive or negative — for results.

Delegating fairly

Only the smallest of projects can avoid having to delete some degree of responsibility to others. Knowing what to delegate versus what to keep on your own plate, and knowing the six degrees of delegation (see "Understanding the degrees of delegation"), can help you spread responsibility around in a way that contributes to a project's success rather than detracts from it.

Deciding what to delegate

You delegate authority for four reasons:

✔ To free yourself up to do other tasks

✔ To have the most qualified person make decisions

✔ To get another qualified person's perspective on an issue

✔ To develop another person's ability to handle additional assignments prudently and successfully

Although the potential benefits of delegating are significant, not every task can or should be delegated. Consider the following guidelines when deciding which tasks are appropriate candidates for delegation:

- ✔ **Assign yourself to the tasks that you do best.** Suppose you're the best lawyer in town and there's more demand for your services at a fee of $500 per hour than you can meet. Suppose also that you can type twice as fast as the next fastest typist in town, who charges $200 per hour. Should you type all your own legal briefs?

  The answer is no. If you spend an hour typing, you save the $400 you'd have to pay the typist (who'd require two hours at a cost of $200 per hour to do the same work). However, if you spend the same one hour providing legal services, you'd earn $500, which would allow you to pay the typist $400 for the work and still have $100 left over. (This concept is referred to as the *law of comparative advantage*.)

- ✔ **If possible, assign yourself to tasks that aren't on a project's critical path.** A delay on any activity on a project's critical path pushes back the estimated date for project completion. Therefore, when you have to stop working on a task that's on your project's critical path to deal with problems on another task, you immediately delay the entire project.

- ✔ **Don't assign other people to work on a task that you can't clearly describe.** The time you save by not working on the task is more than offset by the time you spend answering questions and continually redirecting the person to whom you've assigned the unclear task.

Understanding the degrees of delegation

Delegation doesn't have to be an all-or-nothing proposition, where you make all decisions yourself or you withdraw from the situation entirely. Consider the following six degrees of delegation, each of which builds on and extends the ones that come before it:

- ✔ **Get in the know.** Get the facts and bring them to me for further action.

- ✔ **Show me the way to go.** Develop alternative actions to take based on the facts you've found.

- ✔ **Go when I say so.** Be prepared to take one or more of the actions you've proposed, but don't do anything until I say so.

- ✔ **Go unless I say *no*.** Tell me what you propose to do and when, and take your recommended actions unless I tell you otherwise.

- ✔ **How'd it go?** Analyze the situation, develop a course of action, take action, and let me know the results.

- ✔ **Just go!** Here's a situation, deal with it.

Each level of delegation entails some degree of independent authority. For example, as your manager, when I ask you to find the facts about a situation, you choose which information sources to consult, which information to share with me, and which to discard. The primary difference between the levels of delegation is the degree of checking with the manager before taking action.

Expecting to change course

No matter how carefully you plan, occurrences you don't anticipate will most likely happen at one point or another during your project. Perhaps an activity turns out to be more involved than you figured, your client's needs and desires change, or new technology evolves. When these types of situations arise, you may need to modify your project plan to respond to them.

Even though change may be necessary and desirable, it always comes at a price. Furthermore, different people may have different opinions about which changes are important and how to implement them.

Responding to change requests

On large projects, formal change-control systems govern how you can receive, assess, and act on requests for changes. But whether you handle change requests formally or informally, always follow these steps:

1. **When you receive a request for change to some aspect of your project, clarify exactly what the request is asking you to do.**

2. **If possible, ask for the request in writing or confirm your understanding of the request by writing it down yourself.**

   In a formal change-control system, people must submit every request for change on a change-request form.

3. **Assess the change's potential effects on all aspects of your project.**

   Also consider what may happen if you don't make the change.

4. **Decide whether you implement the change.**

   If this change affects other people, involve them in the decision, too.

5. **If you decide not to make the change, tell the requestor and explain the reason(s).**

6. **If you decide to make the change, write down the necessary steps to implement the change.**

   In a formal change-control system, all aspects of a change are detailed in a written change order.

7. **Update your project's plan to reflect any adjustments to schedules, outcomes, or resource budgets as a result of the change.**

8. **Tell team members and appropriate audiences about the change and the effect you expect it to have on your project.**

Observe the following guidelines to ensure that you can smoothly incorporate changes into your project:

- ✔ **Don't use the possibility of changes as an excuse for not being thorough in your original planning.** Make your project plan as accurate and complete as possible to reduce the need for future changes.

- ✔ **Remember that change always has a cost.** Don't ignore that cost, figuring you have to make the change anyway. Determining the cost of the change so you can plan for it and, if possible, minimize it.

- ✔ **Assess the effect of change on all aspects of your project.** Maintain a broad perspective — a change early in your project may affect your project from beginning to end.

Understanding your role as an efficient project manager

An efficient project manager has a number of roles and responsibilities. Known by different names, such as project leader or project champion, the person who owns the project is the critical central force to keeping a project moving forward and on target. He or she is the one in charge of clear communication to all stakeholders and the project team members.

The key responsibilities of an efficient project manager include:

- ✔ **Understanding each team member's needs:** This is a skill that every manager can always improve upon, as your knowledge of your team changes when new teams develop and new members come aboard. Some people need lots of hand-holding and reassurance. Others feel stifled by excessive touchpoints and need to be largely left alone. Still others are a bit too rogue for their own good, and need to be roped in a bit despite their desire to be left alone. Efficient project management is about recognizing what every team member needs to perform at their best and providing it to each individual, instead of requiring a universal approach and level of interaction across the team.

- ✔ **Setting clear expectations:** Few things are worse than being told to do something, but not being given a clear picture of what the end product should be or by what day you need to complete it. When possible, provide comparable examples for the deliverables you request of the team.

If there are no such examples, then it's up to you as manager to literally write or draw up a clear picture and share that with the team. The more straight up you are about the style, format, and time of each deliverable, the more likely you are to get it (and the less time your teammates will spend wondering, worrying, or asking for clarification).

✓ **Motivating and inspiring:** Just why is everyone putting time and effort into this project, again? It's all too easy to fail to see the big picture when you're hunkered down in the weeds. Highlight successes. Bring a human face to the end problem. Gently remind the team of their higher purpose and/or the improvement that will result from their efforts.

✓ **Representing:** As manager, you represent the team in company-wide meetings, to upper management, and to other managers and departments. Your team members watch how *you* represent the team and their collective work. You need to be able to clearly articulate your team's mission, how you're getting there, and where you are today. Pinpointing particular successes and good work is also a way to further motivate the team and indirectly signal to members that you appreciate their efforts.

✓ **Delegating effectively:** This responsibility has less to do with *actually* delegating (sometimes, frankly, it *is* more efficient to do things yourself), but rather delegating the right tasks to the right people in the right way. In an ideal project, you dole out assignments that make their recipients stretch (but not far exceed) their current skillsets. In the opposite vein, necessary but boring administrative tasks should be outsourced or spread out fairly to reduce the burden on any one person.

✓ **Being inclusive:** You need to understand the current organizational landscape and make sure that every person who needs to have a voice (or who thinks they should have a voice) actually has one. If you're not sure who you need to bring to the table, go to the people you *know* should be there and ask who else you need to involve.

Finding Technology Resources

Project management tools have evolved beyond paper and pencil (though I still find these tools invaluable — along with some colored markers for drawing Lean value-stream maps!) Check out some of the following technology tools:

Project management tools

There are several project management tools available that can do wonders for your project management efficiency:

✔ **Task Tackler** (www.tasktackler.com): A Web- and mobile-based task and project management application that integrates meta-data about tasks such as completion time, related targets, and required resources.

✔ **Pivotal Tracker** (www.pivotaltracker.com): Particularly useful for Agile project management, with the native capability to write user stories.

✔ **Trello** (www.trello.com): Project management from a single screen for simpler projects and clearer communication.

✔ **LiquidPlanner** (www.liquidplanner.com): LiquidPlanner learns from your team and can start forecasting how long it will take to complete future tasks.

Flow chart tools

Flow charts are particularly useful for constructing Lean value-stream maps electronically (although photographing and e-mailing dry-erase board drawings work, too):

✔ **Omnigraffle** (www.omnigroup.com): for Macs

✔ **Google Drive** (www.google.com/drive): Flow charts in the Cloud that can be worked on collaboratively

✔ **LucidChart** (www.lucidchart.com): A web-based flowchart tool that makes particularly gorgeous drawings and flows

Part V
The Part of Tens

The 5th Wave   By Rich Tennant

"This model comes with a particularly useful function – a simulated static button for breaking out of long winded conversations."

In this part . . .

If you've read a *For Dummies* book before, this section should be like an old friend. These "top ten" efficiency lists are a quick overview of best practices and potential pitfalls. The lists are also a source of ideas for where to start your company's journey toward improving quality, lowering costs, and reaching its goals more efficiently.

Chapter 20

Ten Areas Ripe for Efficiency Improvement

*T*here are literally a million different ways you can try to make your business run more efficiently. If you're looking to jump-start your efforts with a big improvement that will show across your bottom line and your employees' faces, try tackling one of the following ten areas.

Printing Practices

A memo here, a handful of agendas there, and before you know it, your office is printing through reams of paper like there's no tomorrow. Printing is full of hidden costs — calculating the actual life of an ink cartridge requires Nobel-level math, and (although it is healthy to move around a little once in awhile), every time an employee gets up from their desk to grab a printout, the lure of a little water cooler gossip can keep them from their desk for ten minutes or more at a stretch.

Conduct an audit to find out just how many pages your team prints out in a given week and how much you spent over the last year on printers, paper, ink cartridges, and related maintenance. More important than sheer numbers, take a look at *what* is being printed. E-mail agendas and other meeting handouts ahead of time instead of passing them out. Look for ways to electronically distribute memos and customer communications. Sign contracts electronically with Docusign or Echosign instead of printing and signing manually. Bring your whole team on board to brainstorm ways to replace printing on dead trees with more efficient, transferrable, and searchable alternatives.

One misguided printer-related efficiency "improvement" is to ban employees from personal printing. So long as employees aren't printing off entire full-color manuals, it's fine to let them print the occasional life insurance policy or school permission slip.

Your Website

For the majority of businesses, your website is the first thing your potential customers, current clients, vendors, and even competitors see about you. If your site looks like it was built 10 years ago, visitors will assume that the rest of your technology and services are 10 years behind the times, too.

If you're paying an outside web company to make updates every time you want to change a sale listed on the homepage or add a news article, cut it out. Web technology is sufficiently advanced such that you can update basic text on your own without needing to learn any code using a Content Management System (CMS). If you can use a text editor, you can update your site. Popular free platforms include WordPress and Drupal. If you have a custom-built website, require that it include functionality to allow for basic text updates.

Don't overlook the potential for your website to save your business significant money. Instead of paying for direct mail flyers, try posting a full-color PDF on your website and directing your customers to it via e-mail or other advertising. Cut down support costs by posting frequently asked questions and/or solutions so your customers can help themselves, even when your support hot line is closed for the night.

Scheduling System

Few things can eat up hours of your time without your even realizing it like trying to schedule a meeting between three people. Someone throws out a time. A second party suggests a different date. The e-mail thread quickly grows to 17 messages. All the while, each person is also trying to schedule 10 separate meetings with other people in other e-mail threads, everyone hoping that their meetings don't end up colliding.

Make it easy for your employees, business partners, and clients to arrange meetings with you by using a calendar sharing/appointment setting service like www.tungle.me or just use your agenda in Outlook to its full potential. It shows what times you're available and lets others immediately suggest and book times that work for them. And if you are trapped in a scheduling e-mail thread for whatever reason, be assertive and list three dates/times/places that work for you from which the others can choose.

If you're scheduling a group of people, reach consensus with a tool like www. doodle.com that combines multiple scheduling preferences to find a mutually convenient time for large numbers of participants.

Printed Forms

Printed forms are like efficiency consultant bait. When I see one, I'm hooked — on eliminating it. Not only are you committing trees and ink for each printout, but processing the responses (usually by typing them in to a computer) requires human interaction. This is made more difficult by the fact that our increased reliance on electronic communication means our collective handwriting quality has gone down the drain. I recently had to type up a handwritten list of 100 e-mail addresses, and judging by the 80 bounce-back messages I received, I was able to read only about 20 of them correctly.

There are so many free and low-cost form processing services out there that there's no excuse for continuing to lean on paper. You can create forms for customer satisfaction surveys, lead generation forms, and even employee status reports. Check out www.surveymonkey.com, www.formstack.com, or www.wufoo.com for options.

You can also use Adobe Acrobat Professional to create electronic PDF forms that end users can fill out, save, and e-mail to you directly.

Meetings

Meetings are intrusive. Although occasional check-ins are important to ensure that team members are on the same page regarding mutual projects, it's all too easy to find meetings infecting your entire calendar like a virus. Because one meeting all too often begets two more, doing what you can to limit the number of hours you and your employees spend in meetings is necessary for the health of the entire organization.

For internal meetings, encourage a company-wide meetings day, such as Tuesday, during which everyone should aim to schedule all their meetings. If you have a meetings-intensive business, you can encourage meetings-free mornings and suggest employees only schedule afternoon meetings. When your entire day is punctuated by meetings here and there, you can never get into a productive flow to tackle other work.

Keep a "breathing agenda," which means you only plan 60 percent of your day and keep the rest free for the unforeseen, such as phone calls, urgent meetings, or a task that just took longer than expected.

E-mail meeting agendas as far ahead of time as possible so attendees have time to prepare. Remove the chairs from your conference rooms — meetings are magically much shorter when everyone has to stand up. Explore project management software, wikis, and status report e-mails as alternatives to keeping team members up to speed without requiring actual meetings.

Culture is very much at play in terms of meeting length and frequency. If executives constantly call meetings, call them at the last minute, or carry on past allotted meeting times, everyone else will follow suit. You will have meetings about meetings. Getting executives on board to set positive meeting examples will go a long way towards freeing up *thousands* of hours of productive time across your organization.

Finally, make the meetings worth their while by creating a clear action plan including responsibilities and deadlines for matters discussed.

Internal Messaging Use

Within a company, there is usually far too much internal chatter about unimportant details and not enough communication about the bigger picture. Part of this has to do with the flood of information we have to process each day. When you start each day filtering through 250 new e-mails and a stack of interoffice mail, there's no real mechanism for easily determining what's important and what's not. Which e-mails you actually read and which ones you skim may entirely be a matter of chance.

Even a few sentences' worth of company-wide e-mail guidelines, coupled with (this is important) the full cooperation and good example of managers, can go a long way toward improving internal communication efficiency. Move non-work-related conversations like planning office parties to a mailing list marked as "off-topic." Explore a daily digest for news and announcements in lieu of 11 separate e-mails sent throughout the day. Use words like "IMPORTANT" in subject lines judiciously. Install an internal wiki for group collaboration or divvying up tasks, neither of which is well-suited to e-mail threads.

Use internal mailing lists in lieu of e-mailing groups of people. Not only does this help ensure that everyone receives every e-mail, but this makes it much easier for individuals to set up filters in their mail programs. For example, every department can have its own group, which employees from other departments can read at their leisure to catch up on what others in the company are doing.

Turn off the ever-so-enticing "ping" you get to hear when a new e-mail comes in. You not only avoid being tempted to have an immediate look who sent you a message, but you also stay focused on your current task at hand.

Customer Service

The biggest efficiency mistake I see played out again and again in customer service departments is beefing up human-powered resources like support staff and hours before finding ways to help your customers help themselves. The most efficient customer service scenario (aside from one where your customers never experience any problems!) is one in which your customer can quickly and easily resolve their issues in full without ever having to take up a minute of your employees' time.

When employees resolve a particular customer question or complaint, have them commit that solution to a knowledgebase. After you have a modest collection of articles, make them available online for your customers. Services like www.uservoice.com and www.getsatisfaction.com can get you up and running quickly without an IT staff. Ultimately, your support request channel should integrate these solutions, using keywords to suggest the right answer before the customer even submits the final trouble ticket.

If your user base is large enough, a message forum on your website is one way to help your customers help one another. Be sure to monitor the boards closely in the beginning to ensure that questions don't languish unanswered, or new visitors will be less likely to post their own issues.

Be proactive in handing out information you *know* you will be asked for, such as availability dates of products in manufacturing. If you can issue a list and provide it to your customers daily, you avoid getting a great many phone calls for exactly that information.

Data Storage

E-mailing a file back and forth between committee members for revisions or distributing printed handouts for a meeting both seem like fine ideas in the moment, but when you need to find that one great sentence you can't quite remember, searching through your Inboxes may make you regret it. This is particularly true for files in uneditable formats like PDFs — often the person who later needs to make changes doesn't have access to the original. Storing your files in a collaborative, searchable environment alleviates these problems.

Turn printed receipts, order histories, and contracts into fully searchable electronic files with a quality scanner and OCR (Optical Character Recognition) software, which automatically converts scanned words and even handwriting into computer text that you can copy and edit. In a paper-heavy office, it sometimes makes sense for every employee to have a personal scanner at her desk. I am never too far from my ScanSnap.

Most people's desktops and hard drives are completely cluttered with files, and those inefficient behaviors carry over — and multiply tenfold — on a company-wide file server. Cut down on the unruliness with a clear hierarchical folder structure that is "owned" by an individual or team. It's that person's job to police the server in the beginning for files that end up in the wrong place, with the wrong naming convention, and/or that call for additional categorization.

For smaller teams, collaborative document-sharing spaces like Dropbox and Google Drive can work well. If you're large enough to have your own IT team, you may require your own file servers, too. Make sure you have a reliable, secure data backup plan and that there are mechanisms in place for reverting back to earlier versions of a file and for seeing exactly which employees make which changes to collaborative files.

Voicemail

> *Welcome to your voicemail box. To listen to your messages, press 1 now. First message. Sent on January 27, 2015 at 4:51 PM. To skip this message, press 4. To save it, press 7. To delete it, press 9.*
>
> *"Hi, it's me. Call me. Bye."*

Sound familiar? You spend what feels like an eternity listening to the *introduction* to your voicemail and finally reach the actual message only to discover the caller merely hung up. Repeat this even five times a day and not only has every employee wasted half an hour of perfectly good time, but they're probably annoyed — even worse for productivity. Discourage voicemail in your office.

Look into voicemail transcription services that e-mail a written copy of a spoken voicemail.

Time-Off Policies

Switching to flexible hours and a results-oriented workplace may be too much of a shift, at least to start, but there's plenty of gray area to be had here. If you allocate sick time in full days, for example, switch to hours. This way, Sherry can leave a couple of hours early for a 3 p.m. dentist appointment instead of disrupting her team by being gone for an entire day.

You can also streamline the process of requesting time off and raise visibility into which employees will be out of the office at which times by using a shared internal calendar to mark vacation times. Seeing when colleagues are off makes it easier to schedule meetings or for other employees to put in their own time off requests if only a certain number of team members can be gone at a given time.

Chapter 21

Ten Efficiency Best Practices

The path to business efficiency is long and never-ending. Although the rewards are plentiful, remembering a few key points can help keep you on track. Before embarking on your next big efficiency-enhancing project, refresh your mindset by reading through these top ten best practices and making sure your plans are in alignment.

Remember, It's Not All About the Benjamins

There are more metrics to an efficient business than just the bottom line. I repeat: Efficiency is *not* just about saving money. If the goal was simply to profit as much as possible, we'd all be running snake oil pyramid schemes from our parents' basements (no overhead!).

When you're brainstorming new efficiency-enhancing projects or vetting projects to decide which to tackle next, keep non-financial metrics at the front of your mind. Even if this project saves money, does it take more time? Does it reduce unpleasantries or make an employee's job less pleasant? Is the resulting product or service going to be of a lower quality as a result of this change?

It may seem counterintuitive, but sometimes an efficiency-enhancing change will actual cost more in terms of dollars and cents. This can be worth it if there are significant savings in other areas, such as time or quality.

Additionally, many changes, such as equipment upgrades or technology projects, involve an up-front cost that may not lead to cost savings right away, but rather for the long-term.

Look for the Side Effects

It's extremely rare for one change in your organization to *not* have a ripple effect on tens or even hundreds of other areas. You cannot charge ahead with one solution before you consider the cost to other processes, people, or departments. Mind you, the change may be totally worth the resulting costs, but you need to be aware of them.

Simply stepping through the change with the involved team member can uncover hidden consequences or problems.

Make sure to involve people on either end of the change, who can provide particularly valuable feedback. I once had a client discover too late that the printed questionnaires it replaced with electronic surveys also doubled as a "to do" list for the shipping department. No client orders shipped for four days before a shipping employee casually wondered over lunch why customers hadn't placed any orders recently!

The most common side effect I see people overlook is transition time. When you change up a process, you need to train each person on the new procedure. Since most organizations don't have a formal training or documentation system in place, the first few projects take even longer than expected because you need to build a training foundation in the process.

Document Efficiency Projects

Too often I see organizations excitedly implement their first efficiency-enhancing projects, only to neglect to write down why they chose the project, what the goals are, and/or the steps they took to start it. In the throes of a "spring cleaning," no one can imagine *not* remembering the nuances of the project. Except six months later, no one quite remembers — *especially* if the project did not go very well.

So write it down. If in doubt, write more down. For example, maybe you chose a particular equipment upgrade because Joe in Engineering used to work for the company that built that model, or perhaps you chose a less-aggressive Internet marketing strategy because your current sales team doesn't have the requisite computer skills and you didn't want to disrupt the entire company by replacing the whole department.

Imagine you are creating an efficiency time capsule for your business. In five or ten years, what would your company want or need to know about this project? Why did you pick it? What particular motivations are clear to you now but may not be to others when you're gone?

Most importantly, you want to capture what your project delivered in the end!

Involve Everyone

Top-down decisions make perfect sense and even *seem* most efficient — when you're at the top. When you're the person actually on the floor implementing the changes or following a new procedure that now adds two more steps to your routine, it's not so clear.

Never announce a procedure change in a memo. Everyone affected by a policy or procedural change should be involved in some degree beforehand. If your company is too large for this to be practical, then be sure to involve a representative from each shift, group, and/or department and make sure every employee has access to that person.

Including *everyone* may even mean providing an interpreter or having representatives come to work during alternate shifts.

Not only does a degree of ownership, however small, help transform a change from a resented requirement to no big deal, but I promise you'll be surprised at the efficiency insights you can gain from listening to the ears on the ground. In fact, it's often these employees who come up with the first efficiency-improving initiatives on their own, because they have a real incentive to adopt changes that make their jobs easier and/or more enjoyable.

Consider a "train the trainer" program for your changes. The key team member you involved in the efficiency-improving initiative earlier may make a great trainer for the rest of his team.

Keep on Reading

Technology is constantly changing, and that has an impact on your efficiency levels in every area of your business. You always want to be on the lookout for what new equipment upgrades or technology innovations are coming up in your industry, or in the world in general. Reading this book is a great start!

Industry publications, vendor websites, and blogs can all be great resources for learning about new developments as they happen. There are also wealth of specialized books, including many *For Dummies* titles, that can help you learn more about increasing efficiency in specific areas like accounting, customer service, or manufacturing, or with specific methodologies like Six Sigma, Lean, or Balanced Scorecard.

There's also a great deal of benefit to general inspirational and innovation thinking. I try to watch at least one 15-minute TED talk each day at www.ted. org and I recommend that you do the same. The most seemingly unrelated topic may be the one that inspires your next great idea.

But Know When to Stop Reading

At a certain point, you can inform yourself into a tizzy. There's rarely one single correct way to go about something, and if you get too wrapped up in determining the "perfect" way, you'll commit the greatest inefficiency offense of all: never getting started in the first place.

Spending 50 hours researching and evaluating the differences between two nearly identical scanners is the very definition of inefficient, but I've seen it happen. (In fact, I've been guilty of variations on this theme myself.)

Delegate research and recommendations to a trusted assistant or colleague at a certain point if you feel yourself getting lost in the minutiae. After you've decided the general direction and the goals, someone else may be better prepared — and less emotionally invested — to help nail down the details.

Measure Objectively

Don't make your decisions based on gut feelings (at least, not without some supporting data to back them up). Even more importantly, don't decide to do things differently solely because it seems like everyone else is or because you found out your competitor is now doing it this way.

Pretend you're justifying your decisions to your own boss (perhaps you really are!). What are the costs in terms of time, money, quality, and resources? What are the expected gains in those same areas? What are the costs if those gains aren't realized for whatever reason?

Bottom line: Why is this project worth undertaking? Learn more about measuring objectively in Chapter 3.

Know Your Limits

You're probably not going to sign off on a plan for all your employees to move into the basement of your office building and work 16 hours a day for no additional pay — even though that would increase output without increasing costs. However, do you know where your line is in terms of what actions you are and are not willing to entertain in the name of efficiency?

I've had many clients tell me they're willing to do "anything" to save money, but they won't fire any employees. Sometimes they're willing to do "anything" but won't fire one specific employee, even though that person is actually costing the business money. In a different vein, some business owners are not comfortable with new technology and decide that they are unwilling to sign off on projects that they do not know enough about to make an informed decision.

It's fine to have limits — you just have to know what they are. If nothing on this Earth can make you fire Thomas because of how he stood by you when you were struggling to get the business off the ground — even though both you and he know that he's wildly underqualified for his current position — then you have to skip over the "fire Thomas" solution and instead find a way to retain Thomas and increase efficiency in his department.

Know What's Important

Your business has (or should have) certain core values. Perhaps you put happy customers above all else, as reflected by 24/7 phone support and a lifetime satisfaction guarantee. Maybe it's critical that you take good care of your employees, with flexible schedules for working parents and a fund for employees who develop serious illnesses. In these cases, would it save money to cut phone support back to regular business hours and nix the employee medical fund? Sure. But those may be non-negotiable given your organization's greater goals.

Alignment with your corporate culture and goals is a perfectly valid metric by which to measure potential efficiency gains. Although you should know the cost in financial terms of keeping that call center open 24/7 versus just eight hours a day, if providing that degree of customer service is a core tenet of your company, then a suggestion to nix night hours wouldn't pass muster. It's important to identify and document these goals so everyone is on the same page in regard to how ideas are vetted.

Get Outside

Whenever I'm pondering a difficult inefficiency problem, I've found the best thing to do is to work on something else. You never know when inspiration will strike!

If your focus is solely on your business processes day in and day out, you miss the insights you can glean from interacting with other businesses, reading a book, or simply going on a long drive. I've been struck by new efficiency ideas while waiting for dinner at a pho restaurant, disembarking an airplane, and reading *Martha Stewart Living*.

Getting out in the world helps you see how other businesses interact with their customers, integrate technology, communicate their messages, treat staff, and handle other situations that you encounter at your own organization.

Chapter 22

Ten Hidden Hurdles to Overcome in Pursuit of Efficiency

In This Chapter

▶ Understanding why change creates resistance in the workforce

▶ Accepting that sometimes it costs money to save money

▶ Knowing employee support is critical to efficiency

*D*iscussions of efficiency can certainly paint a rosy picture — an efficient organization has happy employees, happy customers, and finances well in the black. However, reality is often slightly less chipper.

Efficiency has real benefits for any organization, but those returns come at a price. Understanding some of the hidden costs involved in the pursuit of efficiency can help prepare you and your team for the ups *and* the downs ahead.

Overcoming Employee Resistance

It's a rare employee I've met who welcomes the changes that come with an efficiency-enhancing plan. You can show — prove, even — how an improvement will make a person's job 500 percent better, and they will likely still resist.

The familiar is comfortable. So it takes 24 steps and a 17-page Excel document to onboard a new client . . . and you can replace all that tedious work with a mail merge document integrated into your CRM software . . . at least you've done those 24 steps and 17 pages before. This new way of doing things may not work, it may generate an incorrect document and leave you responsible for the errors, and so on. People will push back and give every reason under the sun as to why this new way won't work. Overcoming this resistance can be a project in and of itself.

Accepting Monetary Costs

It often costs money to save money. Since you can also measure efficiency gains in terms of time, quality, sentiment, or goal alignment, more often than not it costs money to increase efficiency. If your business is operating in the red and looking to efficiency enhancements to stop hemorrhaging cash, your options will be more limited than if you have at least a modest budget for efficiency improvements with long-term returns.

Maintaining Staff

When people ask exactly what an efficiency consultant does, I half-jokingly respond "fire people and replace them with computers." The unpleasant truth is that to save money and increase operational efficiency, you often have to pay in employees.

Another approach I also find works well is to explain that if the company is doing well because it streamlined its processes and everyone is working more efficiently, the likelihood that people keep their jobs — or the company can even expand — is much higher.

Some positions truly are replaced by machinery or computer programs, although others need to be let go because a particular employee is unable to adapt to new technologies. Further, surveying your company for efficiency improvement often sparks discussions about goals and the future, and sometimes cementing those goals makes it apparent that certain teams or departments are not helping to achieve them.

Not only do efficiency improvements often lead to eliminating one or more positions in your organization, but after things start changing, you may lose more employees than you bargained for. Many people hate change. The mere idea of having to learn a new system or procedure is enough for some people to quit their jobs. Further, when you fire one person, others may fear for their own jobs and resign on the offensive.

Dealing with Frustration

As with all things in life, good things rarely come easily. Change is *hard*. Even if the benefits are huge and far-reaching, odds are that day one (at least) will have its share of hiccups.

The best way to deal with the resulting frustration is to expect it. Day one of a new piece of equipment, software, or procedure is going to be slower and perhaps halt entirely for periods of time. If employees are afraid of getting in trouble, they will try to hide or avoid this frustration, which usually means secretly reverting back to the original way of doing things — entirely defeating the purpose.

If you can create a culture where people can speak up and ask for assistance or make adjustments, and where they are encouraged to take the time they need to learn a new process *right*, you can resolve these frustrations sooner rather than later.

Managing Lots of Change: When It Rains, It Pours

Changes in the name of greater efficiency — or *any* changes, really — can create unintended domino effects. Adopting a new database for storing sales leads can make Joe in sales quit because he'll no longer be able to hide that he plays online poker all day. (But good riddance, Joe.) Switching from a human-powered assembly line to automatic machinery may mean two days of downtime when that hard-to-replace gear breaks. Loading financial history into a new accounting program may reveal you underpaid payroll taxes for the last five years.

Never assume a change will take place in a vacuum. You may not be able to anticipate *what* ripple effect it will have, but you can count on something unexpected happening. The best way to deal with this is simply to expect it. If you stress out or get angry, you jeopardize all future efficiency projects (not to mention upset your team).

Set a strong example by taking the side effects in stride and approaching them with the attitude that you can fix whatever happens. I've seen plenty of companies adapt just fine with this approach, and I've sadly seen a handful implode by resisting change at every step and getting angry when things don't go exactly according to plan.

Finding the Time to be Efficient

Increasing efficiency can be quite time-consuming. In fact, it's important to keep a close eye on the amount of time you and your team devote to thinking about efficiency-related projects, as it's all too easy to lose focus on your original job responsibilities and spend your days brainstorming, vetting, and planning efficiency improvements.

Make sure to put action plans including responsibilities and deadlines in place as soon as possible, which both helps to solidify your thinking and to get you moving on to other tasks.

It's easy to want to start with 100 efficiency-enhancing projects, but that inevitably means that you end up with 100 half-baked endeavors. Instead, commit fully to one or two initial projects. You can build on that momentum to get additional employee buy-in and resources to take up new efficiency projects.

If you can find ways to save key employees time, you can then use that saved time for new efficiency projects.

Staying the Course

When you start a project, you have to stay committed to it. Change takes time and sometimes superhuman amounts of patience. Setting clear goals is an important hedge against the urge to quit or give up, because they remind you why you started in the first place.

Letting your consulting department go so that you can focus resources on building your product is not easy, but it may be absolutely necessary to keep the entire company from facing bankruptcy in two years. Fielding complaints from employees for the three weeks following switching to a new software program may make you want to throw in the towel and go back to the system everyone's used to, but reminding yourself that the new software will ultimately save time and money after everyone gets used to it can help you stick it out.

Setting Limits

So, you've just wrapped up a project that saved your company $1 million, increased product quality, and enabled every employee to work from home one day a week so the entire staff is happier and more productive. Feels great, right? The tendency coming off a big (or even a small) efficiency improvement is to want to do it again and again until your business processes are so clean and devoid of inefficiencies you can eat off them.

Getting to the root of the cause of one inefficiency will invariably surface 20 additional issues you can address. Left unchecked, this process can literally be endless. Although you should always be considering both existing and new projects in light of how they impact your organizations' efficiency goals, you need to accept up front that you can't fix everything. Set limits, whether in number of hours or active projects, on just how far down the path you go. For example, creating an internal IT department to build and maintain custom software to match the absolute most efficient way your team can work is likely overkill if an off-the-shelf solution meets 97 percent of your needs.

Being a Positive Role Model

Listen up, this is crucial! If any change is to be successful within an organization, that change has to be modeled by the higher-ups. Nothing breeds resentment and prevents change from taking hold like a manager who commands his charges to do as he says, not as he does — in other words, who asks everyone to make a change but fails to make that change himself.

The pressure to be a positive role model can be stressful for some executives. It's all too easy for managers to think to themselves that their jobs is too important to bother with attending a training session, learning a new program, or following a new print policy. Further, it's much easier to cut budgets and/or positions from other departments than from one's own. If you cease stocking the employee break room with snacks but everyone sees you raid petty cash to keep goodies in your own office, morale will deteriorate quickly, and it will be that much harder to get cooperation on your next project.

If you're really prepared to eat your own dog food, encourage others to point out when you aren't marching to the efficiency drum. Responding to constructive criticism is yet another feature of a positive role model.

Keeping Everyone Motivated for Change

Beyond reorganizing your desk or choosing new positive behaviors to model, you can't make efficiency changes in your organization by yourself. Not only do you need your employees to learn and adopt new, more efficient processes, but you also need their input to arrive at the most efficient solutions to problems. As a company grows, even its founder has less and less insight into the intricacies of every department. It's impossible to be in all roles at all times, so you need to rely on your employees to give productive, honest feedback (even, and perhaps especially, when it's not what you want to hear).

Therefore, every efficiency project must involve a change management component. If you fail to bring others on board with your ideas, then those ideas will never be implemented fully or correctly.

A proven strategy is to get the most willing persons on board, instead of focusing on turning around the "nonbelievers." After the difficult ones see that everyone gets involved, they are more likely to change their minds.

Solving key employees' pain points first is my preferred way of sustaining motivation. You can then alternate between removing their pain points and removing more systemic ones, building on the goodwill you earn during the former to help gain buy-in for the latter.

Index